DOING
RECONCILIATION

RACISM, RECONCILIATION AND TRANSFORMATION
IN THE CHURCH AND WORLD

Alexander Venter

VINEYARD INTERNATIONAL PUBLISHING
PO Box 53286
Kenilworth 7745
Cape Town, South Africa
Email: vip@vineyardbi.org

Text © Alexander Venter 2004

First published 2004, Vineyard International Publishing, Cape Town, South Africa.

Cover by Mercy Arts Studios, USA
Printed and bound by ABC Press, Cape Town.

ISBN 0-620-32441-4

DEDICATION

To all those who participated in the Johweto reconciliation process in Soweto, from 1984 to 1995, and especially my fellow-leaders: Mokete Mpete, Trevor Ntlhola and James Johnson — you have made this book possible.

To Gilli, your faithful support and full involvement in Johweto while birthing and raising our two children through those years is so much more than I can ever appreciate.

To Virgil Vogt, Reba Place Church (Evanston, Chicago) and the Mennonites; Gordon Cosby and Church of the Savior (Washington, DC.); Jackie Pullinger and St Stephens Society: for your friendship, encouragement and generous support during the Johweto years. This includes other individuals and church groups I have not mentioned that stood by us.

To my two professors:

From David Bosch (Missiology) I learnt that the church is God's suffering servant, driven by compassion to cross any and every barrier in society, to wash feet in the humble name of Jesus.

From Klaus Nürnberger (Theological Ethics) I learnt about the church as the "Impossible Trinitarian Community", in which the suffering love of God, incarnated in Jesus, works for justice and reconciliation in the world by the power of the Spirit.

To the people and leadership at Valley Vineyard Christian Fellowship, thanks for your prayers and support in the writing of this book.

And to the Association of Vineyard Churches in South Africa, may we become a reconciled and reconciling movement of thoroughly indigenised churches.

CONTENTS

A POSITION PAPER

"In the Vineyard we have been strong on mercy, average on development, and weak on justice."

In this statement, Alexander sums up something of the reason why this book is so essential for us as a movement. We want to become a better version of ourselves. What do I mean by this?

We love the things God has done among us, and those into which he has called us. We are, however, aware that we have not lived all the pages of God's story equally well. And yet, his severe mercy ensures that his script does not adapt to our weakness — rather, when we deviate from the script, he exhorts, encourages and lifts us back into it.

Believing that part of his calling on us, and indeed on the whole church, is to be an expression of his reconciling grace, we appointed Alexander to research and write on this subject. *Doing Reconciliation* is the result. It is a moving story, a penetrating examination, and a searing challenge to all of us. We receive it humbly as a position paper which describes a position we aspire to. While it came out of the South African story, I am sure every Christian from every country will read parts of his or her own story in it, and be challenged to become a better version of him or herself.

A position paper in our movement is a mirror that highlights something important, and spells out the Vineyard's position on that aspect of ministry. Reconciliation is the ministry of Jesus with regard to mercy development and justice for the poor and the marginalised in every context. The Vineyard is hereby urged to hear it, grapple with it and find ways to do it.

May God's mercy make us all more merciful.

Agape

Costa Mitchell
National Director, Association of Vineyard Churches
South Africa

FOREWORD

I first met Alexander Venter in the mid-1980s in Soweto, and was immediately impressed by his grasp of the challenges of racism and reconciliation facing South Africa at the time. As a white South African, he is among the few charismatic church leaders who have walked side by side with fellow black believers struggling to make sense of evangelical faith in a troubled and polarised situation. I have enjoyed his friendship ever since, and I respect him as an honest and committed comrade in the faith.

Alexander has done the church in South Africa a good service in taking time to write on a theme that many would rather avoid or wish away. This tendency by some toward denial and retreat in the face of the glaring challenges of transformation and nation building from the ruins of apartheid racism is a sad commentary on the church. It threatens to undermine the witness of the church at a critical time in the history of a nation trying to find its new identity as a non-racial democracy.

Located as he is within the Association of Vineyard Churches (AVC), Alexander is obviously a confirmed charismatic evangelical. He could therefore be expected to fall victim to the inclination of believers in this "stream" toward pragmatic short-cuts, going with what works, without regard to the theological damage caused to the integrity of the church or its prophetic faithfulness. This he has happily avoided.

His treatment of racism, reconciliation and transformation combines sensitivity with theological rigor. In doing this, he has displayed a pastoral and prophetic courage which, in the end, gives the Christian community a powerful tool for a re-discipling in a post-apartheid South Africa that takes full account of the past as it works for a better future. Indeed South Africans have every right to expect that the church, having made heartfelt and tearful confessions regarding their own complicity with apartheid, will somehow demonstrate that there is life beyond confession. Alexander has pointed us in the direction of how we might deliver on that expectation, and hopefully get our racial house in order. We need to do this, if for nothing else but to be good stewards of the miracle that God gave us as a nation in the relatively peaceful transition of 1994.

Alexander has grounded his work on sound biblical foundations as well as, importantly, sociological analysis. Methodologically, this is an important contribution to how evangelicals might go about correcting their hermeneutical blind spots. For while evangelicals tend to swear by the primacy of Scripture in all matters of faith and conduct, this is seldom rooted in social analysis. With practical examples from his own journey of faith, Alexander has indeed helped to shed light on the task at hand if we are to be a faithful witness in a world fraught with divisions of all sorts.

While this book has as its immediate audience the AVC in SA and in other nations, the church more broadly will benefit greatly from this work, both in South Africa and other parts of the world, where the wounds of racism and ethnicity abound.

I fully commend this work to all who hunger and thirst for righteousness in this critical area of the Christian witness.

Moss Ntlha
General Secretary
The Evangelical Alliance of South Africa

PREFACE

This project has been a wonderful yet exacting challenge. It required honesty, self-disclosure and rigorous thinking. However, I must hasten to add that it has been a broad, collaborative project from the start, as I will explain later. I write consciously as a man, as a white man in South Africa (SA), as a middle-class, relatively affluent male, as a husband and father, and a spiritual leader of a Vineyard Christian Fellowship (VCF) in Johannesburg. The importance of this self-awareness, and how it affects my view of things, will become clear as you work through the book.

As you read, you might quickly assume that my unspoken agenda is a mission to my white compatriots about the reality and nature of racism, and our need for reconciliation and transformation. It is much more than that. It is a book about how to reconcile human relationships and overcome conflict, whether it be one-on-one, group or national reconciliation. This book is for everyone, for all races in all countries and places of conflict. I should say right up front that my intention is not to accuse or create guilt in any way for any person or racial group; it is to dismantle racism and foster reconciliation, as honestly, directly and passionately as I know how.

We have a peculiar propensity for abbreviations and acronyms in SA. Directly after this preface, I have included a glossary of abbreviations that you can consult. I put the abbreviation in brackets after the first time I refer to a title or name in the text of the book, and thereafter I use the abbreviation.

Although reconciliation is absolutely crucial and relevant to all people and groups in our global village, this book arises out of a particular context. As the saying goes, "think globally, act locally". This is true, but a qualification is needed. I am convinced that the more our stories are grounded in the reality of our own experiences, in a particular local context, the more relevance and power they have globally. In this way we can make a valid contribution to international thinking. We can adapt the saying in this way: Local knowledge that comes from local action is the foundation for international thinking. We can no longer swallow — let alone digest — abstract, vacuum-packed ideas and concepts. Their real value is determined by the level of contextual reality and life integrity among local people.

It has been said often that South African is a microcosm of the world. The issues and realities we wrestle with are applicable to the world scene, and are common in most nations. We hope that our context and experience is a resource for others. However, let me explain the specific context and motivation of this book, and trust that the reader will enjoy and, more importantly, learn from our story.

THE BOOK'S ORIGIN AND INTENDED AUDIENCE

The book has its recent roots in an incident that took place at the SA National Conference of the Association of Vineyard Churches (AVC) in October 2001. A speaker made reference to colonialism in a way that was offensive to many present. One of our black pastors circulated a paper after the conference raising the issue of racism in the Vineyard and the need for transformation — to indigenise AVC in our South African context. Costa Mitchell, our National Director, acted both at the conference and afterwards to resolve the incident. He said a fuller discussion was needed with a possible Vineyard position paper[1] being written to address the matter. In retrospect, this incident was a powerful "prophetic slip" — of the sanctified Freudian kind! It has confronted us with the need to deal with an issue that has long been there, unheeded or ignored, but threatening to block us at each step of our development.

The national leadership of AVC SA met in February 2002 to discuss, among other things, "the incident" and gave me the mandate to write a Vineyard position paper in dialogue with a working group. The paper would be debated, adapted and finalised as both a theological statement and an actual process for reconciliation and transformation in AVC SA. The purpose would be for all our local congregations to work through the paper and engage in the practical process and programmes that would be proposed (Chapter 9). Further, our hope was that it would guide us in our multicultural relationships, development and involvement in SA, Africa and beyond.

I brainstormed the outline of the paper at a pastors' meeting in Johannesburg in 2002, and then fleshed it out, calling the position paper *The Ephesians 2:15 Process — Racism, Reconciliation and Transformation*. The paper was only partially complete when I presented it at our National Conference in October 2002. Significantly, Trevor Ntlhola (my colleague in Soweto) and I shared our stories rather than lecturing the content of the document. The response was amazing. There was unanimous endorsement from all our pastors and leaders. We all formally committed ourselves as a matter of priority to work it into our congregations so that we could have integrity in our future journey together. Furthermore, the National Conference proposed that all present should give feedback, comment and contributions on the paper, and that I should then expand and complete it in the form of a book, in a style and manner that would be easily accessible to all our people.

With reference to the Vineyard in other countries, we see this position paper as emanating from, and speaking for, the AVC in SA. But our hope is that it will make a significant contribution to our international dialogue and shared life; that it will be of interest and help to other national AVCs — obviously with their own particular contextualisations.

The deeper roots of this book go back to our common but divided history, and the early experience of Vineyard in SA during the 1980s and 1990s. It has to do with our various responses to the apartheid crisis when our nation was polarised between black and white by the racial policies and violent repression of the government. The issue of racism and reconciliation, and our need for transformation, has been with us all along and it will not go away until it receives our undivided attention. *The simple reality is that if we do not deal with the legacy of apartheid **together**, we have no realistic hope of a meaningful future.* It has been said that reality is something you run into when you are wrong. In SA, we are battered at every turn by this unresolved issue. We must address it in order to live, let alone to journey on with any meaningful freedom and unity. However, I am getting ahead of myself.

The primary purpose of this book is not to be a theological statement, but rather to transform lives and to transform Vineyard into an indigenised movement of churches. Every person in our circles of influence needs to read this material and engage in the process of reconciliation. This book is for all our people within the Vineyard in SA. But I need to add quickly that it is also intended for all Christians and churches from various faith traditions. It is our offering to God, praying that he will use our story as a motivation in the wider body of Christ, so that we all work for reconciliation at all levels in society. This is a must for the integrity of our witness as Christians and for the well-being of our nation's future. Furthermore, my hope is that this book will be accessible to people from whatever background — religious or secular. May it challenge your thinking and actions, where you live and work, so that the world may become a better place for all to live in.

INTERNATIONAL APPLICATION

I am also writing with an international audience in mind, especially for the Vineyard in other countries. Racism, reconciliation and transformation are serious issues in every nation on the planet — precisely because we are fallen human beings. Milton poetically and powerfully describes our living in "paradise lost".[2] But worse, our global village is quaking with post-Babel ethnic divisions and conflicts.

Everyone is scattering in a confused scramble for survival. Let me illustrate this with some examples. I will begin at home in SA.

In November 2002 nine bombs exploded in Soweto, the largest black city in SA. A right-wing religious Afrikaner group called Die Boeremag (The Boer Army) claimed responsibility. They said that they had begun their "new freedom struggle"; not from British rule this time, but from "black oppression".[3] After the miracle of the April 1994 elections and the relatively peaceful transition we have been through, this is extremely sad and unnecessary — however, it shows the levels of fear and threat in the Afrikaans community, and the need for genuine reconciliation.

Yet this is tame when compared to the Israeli/Palestinian conflict. The spiral of violence with radical Islamic suicide bombers tearing people apart and the retaliatory West Bank military incursions is unbelievable. And now The Fence is being built, dividing Palestinian from Israeli. All this is a tragic reminder of the desperate need for reconciliation between Jews and Arabs. A Jerusalemite friend of mine sums up the situation as "a terrifying consensus of hatred". The Middle East crisis is extremely emotional and divisive and it will require calm hearts, clear minds and courageous leadership to resolve the issues. It is so serious that I attempted to address the issues at a day seminar for our church. I give some perspective on this issue in Chapter 8.

At the end of September 2002, fourteen members of our congregation returned from a ministry trip to Kosovo. They conducted a conference there specifically motivated by a leader in our congregation having a "Macedonian call" to take the gospel of reconciliation from South Africa to the Albanians in Kosovo. It was their humble contribution to help heal the bloody scars of the ethnic cleansing by the Serbs, in which their men had been murdered and their women systematically raped. Our team came home rejoicing, like the disciples of Jesus in Lk 10:17, telling wonderful stories of what God had done in terms of reconciliation and healing.

My wife and I were invited to address a Vineyard pastors' conference in the Netherlands in October 2002. In the middle of the conference, a siege ensued in Moscow in which 700 Russians were held hostage by 40 Chechen rebels in an opera theatre. There were three Russians at our conference and we prayed publicly with them for a merciful resolution to the crisis. One of the Russians said that Russia was reaping what she had sown — years and years of oppressing these and many other national groups. There were tears of confession and repentance as we prayed for a work of reconciliation to begin, and for a peaceful resolution to the hostage crisis. In the end the 40 rebels were all killed, but over 100 hostages died.

One thinks of all the international bombings — many of them from suicide bombers, a frightening new phenomenon unleashed in our global village. They are motivated by racial and religious convictions of hatred, with rationalisations of a perverted sense of justice and liberation. The Bali bombings on 13 October 2002 killed 202 people, most of them Australians. It shook Australia. Why should there be such racial and religious hatred? Their self-reflection has raised questions as to their own history of racism. Our local city newspaper ran a feature article on racism in Australia.[4] Yet many people think there is no such thing in that part of the world.

The worst of all was 9/11 (11 September 2001), the terrorist horror in the United States. The earth-shattering collapse of the World Trade Centre Twin Towers in New York killed 2 752 people, and the attack on the Pentagon left 189 dead.[5] Our world had indeed been changed forever. The deeper racial and religious divisions were just one outcome. What was our response to 9/11? What have we learnt? Reactive racial hatred and anti-Muslim prejudice? More war on terror, and more killings in more nations? Since 9/11, the wars in Afghanistan and Iraq have killed unknown tens of thousands of people. Is that any better than the hatred that drove the terrorists to perpetrate 9/11 in the first place? The spiral of violence and the legacy of hatred are sure to unleash demons far worse than 9/11. Who wins in all of this? The devil smiles before and after 9/11, on both sides of his face, as he gleefully reaps many more people into eternal damnation. Surely Christians should respond differently. Did any of us humble ourselves, put on sackcloth and ashes — like the survivors who were covered in ash and dust — and cry to God for mercy in the face of such sheer terror and horror? Did we repent from our sins of anger, prejudice and racism? From our sins of materialism, nationalism and militarism? Did any of us enact our prayers by seeking out our "enemies", especially Muslims, in order to love them as Jesus taught, and as he modelled in his life and death? After all, as Christians we are followers of Jesus, are we not?

A Mennonite friend sent me a Special Section article on racism that was published a couple of years ago in a *Christianity Today*.[6] The article reports on the research and findings in a book by two eminent sociologists who argue that the USA, in both church and society, is as racially prejudiced and divided as ever. Especially sad is the statement made that "11 o'clock on Sunday morning is still the most segregated hour in America". The church is supposed to lead society, not lag way behind it. But is it any different in any other Western nation?

I have not even mentioned "The Troubles" in Northern Ireland with its long, bloody history of hatred between Republicans and Unionists, Catholics and Protestants. Earlier I referred to the pain of the Balkans with the unreconciled ethnic and religious tensions that go back for centuries. This unresolved historic ethnic conflict led to the terrible wars in the mid-1990s, resulting in Slobodan Milosevic being held and tried for international war crimes. What about Kashmir with the long battle between Pakistan and India over its disputed territory and people? What about North and South Korea? What rejoicing when that wall of division comes tumbling down — it might eclipse the celebration of the fall of the Berlin Wall in 1989. We must support our Christian brothers and sisters in South Korea, so that they can bring about a peaceful reconciliation and the reunification of Korea (54% of South Korea are Christians — a grave responsibility rests on their shoulders). What about Rwanda trying to rebuild a semblance of nationhood after the horrific orgy of over 800 000 racial killings in the mid-1990s? And Southern Sudan where government-backed Muslim Arabs have over the years systematically enslaved and killed up to 2 million Christians. And so we can go on through Africa and South and Central America, and cite the racial, religious and political struggles that are endemic to various nations.

The point simply is that the story and message of this book is of utmost importance for all people, for all nations. Without exaggeration, it is literally a matter of life and death. "Spaceship Earth"[7] is being torn apart and will be blown to smithereens by the fiery pressure of inter- and intra-national group violence. This will happen if we do not find a way to live together in some measure of meaningful reconciliation, transformation and peace.

THE TITLE AND ITS MEANING

Initially I thought that the title should be taken from the position paper, something like: *One New Humanity* (as in Paul's wonderful vision of God's reconciled people in Eph 2:15). However, in keeping with my first book, *Doing Church*,[8] I decided to call this book *Doing Reconciliation: Racism, Reconciliation and Transformation in the Church and World*. There are two reasons for this decision. Firstly, while still communicating the title of the position paper, it gives continuity in terms of it being a companion volume on church life and issues (with regard to Vineyard at least, although the intended audience is far broader); secondly, it points to the important issue of "being" and "doing". "Doing reconciliation" implies "being reconciled". There is a necessary relationship and tension between the two. This is important and needs further explanation.

Scripture, especially the New Testament (NT), is full of the idea of being and doing. In essence, being and doing has to do with identity and behaviour, with fact and action, reality and response. Paul's particular usage of Greek in his NT writings often results in a framework that is first *indicative* and then *imperative*. The indicative are *statements of being* such as, "you *are* reconciled". They are often followed by the imperative which are *statements of doing* such as, "therefore *be* reconciled" (see 2 Cor 5:18, 20). Indicatives are facts and realities; imperatives are commands and responses. This applies not only to reconciliation, but to all aspects of life in Christ, certainly as Paul sees it. Our *being* gives us our *identity* which, biblically speaking, is found in who God is and what he has done for us in Christ. Our *doing*, that is our *behaviour, actions and work*, are a natural and logical outflow from of our sense of being. Integrity is the consistency between our being and doing, between the inner and outer realities of our lives.

We must be careful not to get it the other way round. Many people find their identity, value and meaning in their doing, in their achievements and performance in life, rather than in being. This can be disastrous, because it leads to a per-formance-based self-image, among other things. I know of people, some of them Christians, who derived their sense of worth and identity from their service ("min-istry"), especially "being relevant and radical" in doing justice and reconciliation work during the apartheid years. And they made sure that they were seen by many to be doing it! When the country went through political change in the early 1990s, they increasingly felt restless and redundant — unless they were "rewarded" with recognition and/or a high profile job or position. Some who were not so fortunate to get such a reward went through an identity crisis: "Is there any meaning after the struggle for justice? What do I do now with my life?" Some Christians even fell away from meaningful faith in Christ as they lost their reason for existence. "The cause" had become the gospel for them, their doing had become their being, and their work for God became their god.

This phenomenon of deriving your identity from your doing, and not your sense of being, is colour-blind — it applies to all races, to all people in all walks of life. It applies to all forms of service, to all positions and titles from the highest to the lowest. It has devastating effects, often breeding patterns of insecurity and control, and resulting in a profound loss of meaning when the "doing" ceases, for what-ever reason. We must be careful since we are so easily seduced from our ultimate source of life, meaning and identity: God's love for us in Jesus of Nazareth. All this becomes very relevant in the work of reconciliation and peace-making.

However, this "being/doing thing" is not neat and tidy and is not a clear-cut either/or reality. Rather, there is a creative tension and reciprocal relationship between the two, but more of this later. In short, this book is about the fact that, in Jesus Christ, we *have been* and *are being* reconciled because of what he has done. Therefore we need to *be* and *get* reconciled, and consequently to *do the work* of reconciliation, as a natural outworking of *who we are*. If there is integrity of being, there will be integrity in doing, and vice versa. Then reconciliation will *not* be an obligation carried out through white-knuckle determination and discipline ("you ought to", "you must", and "you have to"). It will rather be a joyous overflow of love for others, springing from an inner reality of goodness and kindness, which enables you to do routinely what Jesus would do, as if he were you.[9]

Therefore, in choosing this title I deliberately highlight the tension between being and doing. I purposefully imply that our *Doing Reconciliation* should be an overflow of our *being reconciled*.

 ## AN OVERVIEW OF THE CONTENT

Because racism and reconciliation is a sensitive subject for many people, it lends itself to storytelling. We learn in a far less defensive way as we listen to people's stories. There are not many topics that press hot buttons and provoke unprocessed issues like the topic of racism and reconciliation. We all have "stuff" to one degree or another in this regard. Let me appeal to you right up front not to stop reading if your hot buttons are pressed. Do yourself (and me) a favour and commit to reading the whole book before passing judgement!

The book begins with two personal stories (Part One). Storytelling has gained renewed importance in recent years, after the long cold, winter of science and rationalism. This is partly due to the need in our postmodern society for meaning, identity and belonging. Storytelling meets this need by restoring the contextual reality and life integrity mentioned earlier. Many human and social sciences are exploring storytelling as a new "narrative methodology" — as they call it — similar to developments in narrative theology[10] and narrative psychotherapy, for example. The point is that each person's story or experience is unique and important and must be told and listened to. From a biblical viewpoint, these stories find meaning, truth and hope to the extent that they become part of, and are interpreted by, God's greater story in Jesus Christ. In fact, the major part of this book is about interpreting our South African story in the light of God's greater story.

Trevor Ntlhola and I tell our personal stories in the first two chapters. These are just two of many untold individual and group stories that we should listen to. Our ancestors sat night after night around the warm fires of community telling their stories. They were purified and united as they laughed and cried, as they forgave and reconciled, as they were healed and transformed by their stories. This is not quite a community fire, but I pray that something of its warmth will touch you as we share our stories. My story of racism, repentance and reconciliation in apartheid SA led me from Johannesburg into the neighbouring black city of Soweto, from 1983 to 1995. A reconciliation community emerged in which Trevor Ntlhola, my friend and colleague in Soweto, became involved. He shares his journey of racism and the healing that came to him through Johweto (Johweto is the name of our reconciliation community that symbolically joined the names of the white city of *Joh*annesburg and the black city of So*weto*). It is my joy and privilege to have Trevor share his story with you in this book.

Part Two is the position paper that I was commissioned to write. In this section I interpret our stories in the light of God's greater story of reconciliation, which hopefully will lead to new stories which you create around new reconciliation initiatives. In order to make the position paper — this book — accessible to as wide an audience as possible, I have kept the language simple and to the point. Where I use technical terms, theological and otherwise, I explain the meaning. My style is self-disclosing, honest and provocative. I try to challenge and stretch you in your thinking, so hang in there! Although this theological section will inform you, my primary aim is to motivate you to action. Knowledge without local application and action is meaningless.

I have not delved into all the technical theological and political debates involved in reconciliation and justice.[II] I do use references where I give pertinent endnotes, critical comments and pointers for further reading at the end of each chapter. This is particularly for those who want to follow up on various issues. Full details of the references consulted in the endnotes can be found in the References, where the authors are listed alphabetically. You will notice that I use *italics* now and again in the text in order to: a) designate non-English words, b) to emphasise a word or phrase or a point that I am making, and c) to introduce a new thought or semi-subheading at the beginning of a new paragraph.

I begin Part Two by introducing the *proposed vision* of reconciliation and by giving some working definitions for various key words. If you so desire, you can read Chapter 3 before you read the stories in Part One, as it will give you my basic frame of reference and key terms. For example, I use the terms Black, White, Coloured and Indian to describe the primary race groups in our country (from now on I will refer to these race categories in the lower case due to their frequent usage). Knowledge of these groups is important in the big picture: There are about one million Indians from Asian background, now fully South African. The "coloureds" — about three and half million — are from a mix of the indigenous Khoisan tribes, Malay slaves, and black/white intermarriage. The blacks, numbering about 36 million, are from the Nguni and Sotho tribes that migrated into southern Africa many centuries ago. And the whites are the descendents of the European settlers, now about five million Afrikaans and English-speaking Africans. We fully acknowledge that in the kingdom of God there is no black, white, coloured or Indian. These categories and terms, and their usage, should fall away as we are reconciled and grow into the future together. But for functional purposes — and, frankly, to be real and honest about our history in SA — I use them throughout the book.

In Chapter 4 I confront you with our apartheid history, with a view to understanding Vineyard and the broader church's response to the crisis. I consider this to be a very important chapter because I try to show what really happened and where we are currently in SA. Then I explore a biblical theology of racism, reconciliation and transformation in Chapters 5 and 6. I look at the understanding of reconciliation in the broader story of the Bible, and its outworking in Jesus' life and teachings and that of the early church and Paul. These two chapters will give you the biblical foundation and motivation for practicing the ministry of reconciliation — it will also be a good resource for teaching and preaching. This leads to a discussion on three practical models of reconciliation in Chapter 7: the all-important one-on-one reconciliation, how groups and structures can reconcile, and the Johweto model.

Chapter 8 presents the beginning of a broader social theology for the Vineyard, dealing with various related social issues facing the church and the nation of SA. (They are common to most other nations, affecting us all in "Spaceship Earth".) Some of them are direct implications of our discussion on reconciliation, while others are indirectly related. This chapter will give, from a Vineyard perspective, guidance on how we think about, and respond to, these social issues as Christians. We take a position on some sensitive ethical issues. I conclude the position paper in Chapter 9 with practical proposals as to the way forward for our congregations, for all Christians and people in general. This will explain how we can all work towards reconciliation and transformation of both the church and world.

Part Three is an amalgamation of various statements and resources. Chapter 10 is the text of the confession that AVC SA formally identified with, when it was read out at the Truth and Reconciliation Commission (TRC) in 1996. This is a "must read" for all our people and all evangelicals in SA — you need to know what your leaders confessed on your behalf! Chapter 11 includes three resources: a) a programme for mutual storytelling across the social divides; b) a list of suggestions for doing Bible studies, talks and small group discussions on reconciliation, and c) a list of reconciliation organisations and websites from around the world — for those wanting to do research and work in partnership with reconciliation ministries.

It is my privilege to include an Appendix, an important study on the history and understanding of human rights from a Christian perspective by Dr Derek Morphew (originally written in 1991 and now published for the first time). He gives the biblical and historical framework and motivation for Christians to practise human rights. We desperately need a culture of human rights in our nation to reverse the legacy of our history. Human rights needs to be taught and practised in all our churches and in our society — the church being the example and watchdog of our nation. This Appendix is a key resource for all of us.

Finally the References includes the sources that I consulted — both official church documents and statements regarding apartheid, and the authors that I refer to in the book.

SCRIPTURE QUOTATIONS AND ACKNOWLEDGEMENTS

Sometimes when I quote scripture, I use the RAP version. This is the Revised Alexander Paraphrase. I have taken to writing my own version of some passages by doing a comparison of various Bible translations. It is a paraphrase rather than a translation — much like Eugene Peterson's *The Message*. It helps me to take a fresh look at the text, and hopefully it does the same for you. When quoting scriptures directly, I use the New International Version (NIV) without referencing it after the quotation. From time to time I quote the New Revised Standard Version (NRSV) when it is appropriate, because it is a good gender-inclusive translation. Similarly, I am committed to writing in an inclusive language style as far as grammar permits.

I want to thank the many Vineyard leaders and pastors who gave me helpful feedback in the form of corrections and other suggestions on the position paper. Their contributions are included in this book, making it a collaborative work. Special thanks go to the Vineyard International Publishing team (Derek Morhpew, Kim Hough, Rhonda Crouse and Stephan Vosloo); also to Costa Mitchell, Trevor Ntlhola, Moss Ntlha, Michelle Sephton, Jeanie Kriel, Brian Gardner, Mike Mahony,

Muriel Brown, Rodney Jones, Tarrin Webster and Carl Stauffer — all helped with various aspects of the manuscript. Without all of you, this book would not have been possible!

Alexander F Venter
April 2004

NOTES

1. Six position papers have been written during the brief history of the Vineyard addressing various issues of controversy that have arisen, mostly theological and apologetic in nature. The list of papers with a brief discussion can be found in Jackson 1999, pp. 149–171. These position papers are available from Vineyard International Publishing, www.vineyardbi.org.

2. Bush 1966. Milton's long narrative poem "Paradise Lost" begins on p. 201.

3. From an article by Celean Jacobson, "With Their Guns and Their Bibles — The New Right-wing Threat Is Being Fuelled by the Same Old Religious Zealotry and Militant Racism", in the *Sunday Times*, 3 November 2002. She maintains that the "third liberation struggle" has begun for the extreme right-wing Afrikaners. They are being inspired by an old Afrikaner "prophet", Nicholaas (Seers) van Rensburg (1864–1926), who saw a series of visions that are supposedly being fulfilled now, including the third Afrikaner liberation war and its victory. The prophet's life, visions and their meaning is recorded in Snyman 1999.

4. *The Star*, 8 November 2002. The article is a review of a book, *Long Journey to Jigalong*, written by an aboriginal woman telling her and her mother's story of racial pain at the hands of the white government. It has now been made into a film with the same title challenging Australians to reflect on their racist past.

5. The horror is described in Baxter and Downing (eds.) 2001 — they record personal stories of survivors and eye witnesses, and give perspectives from a broad sweep of respected journalists (a British Broadcasting Corporation compilation).

6. The article "Divided by Faith? Color-Blind", *Christianity Today*, 2 October 2000, is a review of the results of sociological research in the evangelical community in the USA, published by Emerson and Smith 2000. The USA Association of Vineyard Churches interviewed Michael Emerson on their book in the church planting magazine *Cutting Edge*, by Bailey (ed.) 2002. They address the topic of reconciliation and multi-ethnic churches in the Vineyard and the broader church.

7. See the haunting illustration of "spaceship earth" in Kubalkova and Cruickshank 1981, p. 220.

8. Venter 2000 is a systematic presentation of the Vineyard (John Wimber's) philosophy of ministry.

9. I owe this, and other such succinct sayings that I use from time to time (especially with regard to discipleship) to Dallas Willard — from his teachings and books (see References).

10. Hauerwas and Jones (eds.) 1989 offer a good introduction to the method and debate on narrative theology.

11. I recommend De Gruchy 2002 as a book written from a SA point of view that dialogues with the more technical issues, both theologically and politically, in the debate on reconciliation.

GLOSSARY OF ABBREVIATIONS AND ACRONYMS

AIDS — Acquired Immune Deficiency Syndrome

ANC — African National Congress

AOG — Assembly of God

AMEC — African Methodist Episcopal Church

APC — Area Pastoral Coordinator (Vineyard)

AU — African Union

AVC — Association of Vineyard Churches

AWB — Afrikaner Weerstandsbeweging (Afrikaner Resistance Movement)

Codesa — Convention for a Democratic South Africa

CSVR — Centre for Study of Violence and Reconciliation

DRC — Dutch Reformed Church (English for NGK)

HIV — Human Immunodeficiency Virus

ICT — Institute for Contextual Theology

IFP — Inkatha Freedom Party

IRO — Internalised Racist Oppression

IRS — Internalised Racist Superiority

MK — Umkhonto We Sizwe (The Spear of the Nation, armed wing of the ANC)

MRM — Men's Repentance Movement

NEPAD — New Partnership for Africa's Development

NGK — Nederduits Gereformeerde Kerk

NGO — Non-governmental Organisation

NIR — National Initiative for Reconciliation

NIV — New International Version

NRSV — New Revised Standard Version

NT — New Testament

OAU — Organisation of African Unity

OT — Old Testament

Pagad — People Against Gangsterism and Drugs

PC — Politically correct

RAP – Revised Alexander Paraphrase

RICC – Rand Initiative for Christian Conciliation

RDP – Reconstruction and Development Programme

RSV – Revised Standard Version

SA – South Africa

SACBC – South African Catholic Bishops Conference

SACC – South African Council of Churches

SACLA – South African Christian Leadership Assembly

SADC – Southern African Development Community

SAR – South African Rand (currency)

SCM – Student Christian Movement

TEASA – The Evangelical Alliance of South Africa

TRC – Truth and Reconciliation Commission

TRC SA R – Truth and Reconciliation Commission of South Africa Report

UN – United Nations

UNISA – University of South Africa

USA – United States of America

VCF – Vineyard Christian Fellowship (local congregation)

WCC – World Council of Churches

WWI – World War I (1914–1918)

WWII – World War II (1939–1945)

PART I

TELLING OUR STORY

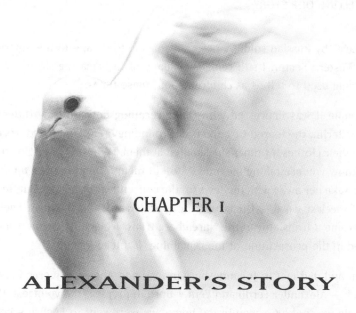

CHAPTER 1

ALEXANDER'S STORY

My father traced the Venter family tree a few years before he died — he passed away in June 1998. Apparently the first Venter immigrants to arrive in the Cape Colony (1813) were from the Flemish part of Belgium, near to the border with the Netherlands. They became pioneer farmers in the Eastern Cape, in close proximity to the Xhosas, one of the black tribes that migrated from central to southern Africa. The Venter immigrants were immediately assimilated into the Afrikaners, who had an emerging sense of identity as indigenised or "Africanised" people. The Dutch, French Huguenot, and some German settlers, became what is now known as the Afrikaans people.[1]

Several Venter families joined many other Afrikaners on the Great Trek inland (1834–1838) after the British took over the government of the Cape Colony. However, my father's family joined a small community of Afrikaners who went to South America in the late 1800s — their way of "escaping" British rule. My dad, like his father, was born in the Argentine, one of nine children raised on a poor pioneer farm on the vast windswept Pampas. His name, Federico Jacobo Venter, reflected his tough Latin American Afrikaner rural upbringing. The Venters, with a few other Afrikaner families, returned to South Africa (SA) at the onset of World War II (WWII).

My mother came to SA a few years after WWII. She was born in Germany and was given the name Helga Thekla Elisabeth Schiele, the only child of an upper-class family. Her paternal grandfather was the Minister of Agriculture in Kaiser Wilhelm II's parliament. She and her mother miraculously survived the war, but they saw unspeakable suffering and endured the final onslaught on Berlin. My mother was subsequently held in the Eastern Sector of Berlin for six months as a so-called "love-slave" by Russian soldiers before managing to escape to the American and British Western Sector. I still remember many of the amazing stories that Ouma and Mummi used to tell us as children about these times.

For example, I was impressed with Ouma recalling how she saw Hitler's secret police in Berlin, the feared Gestapo or SS, rounding up the Jews who wore yellow stars on their clothes. At times she shouted at them, "Why are you doing this? Stop it! We know you are taking them away to kill them." They shut her up by threatening to take her away with the Jews (to the concentration camps). But, in a sense, she had the last word — Ouma was an educated woman, fluent in English, and later became a translator at the Nuremberg trials. Ironically, she personally participated in the prosecution of the remaining Nazi leadership.

My mom and dad met in Johannesburg in 1950 and Angelika, Juergen and I were the result — Alexander Ferdinand Venter born in 1955 was the youngest. When we were little we spoke German in the home, we were sent to English schools, and had my father's Afrikaans-speaking family visiting often. It was turbulent to say the least — especially between my mom and dad. It was certainly a multicultural environment! My dad showed great interest in various cultures and spoke seven different languages fluently, but still, he was a racist. We were sent to English-schools because my mom insisted that we learn English rather than Afrikaans. So for me, the white English South African culture became the predominant influence — mixed, of course, with all of the above!

I want to tell my life journey with regard to racism and reconciliation as honestly and openly as I can. It is not easy to tell your own story — I find it a real test of integrity and character, in many more ways than one. I will rather err on the side of "telling it like it is", so please forgive me if I come across as judgemental or inappropriate in any way.

 ## CHILDHOOD MEMORIES

My earliest awareness of race and racism relates to Durban (where I was born) and my father and mother's attitude toward other people. Thinking about it now makes me realise that we are all products of our particular time and context and very few, if any of us, transcend it. I do not want to misrepresent my parents, as they were generally well-meaning and good people, but the reality is that we absorb who and what our parents are, whether we like it or not.

Some of my earliest memories are of black people coming to our home. Whether coming to work or not, they had to go around to the back door before they would be spoken to. My dad got very angry if any dared to question this expectation. I saw a curious contradiction in my dad. At times he treated them with pity as if they were stupid children (he said as much); at other times he was blatantly abusive to them. He treated the (Asian) Indians who lived in Durban with a mixture of interest and respect, but with caution as they "would always cheat you, no matter what".

That is how stereotypes begin to gain a hold on us. I further learnt from my father that Zulus were hardworking and brave, but rather unintelligent; that Xhosas were lazy, but clever in their scheming and conniving; that the English were not good and were not to be trusted because they were hypocrites, and that Jews were filthy rich and would always get the better of you, given half a chance. The Germans, however, were to be admired — they knew how to handle people and situations in exactly the right way! The Afrikaners who followed suit were to be respected. I remember my Dad telling me how he tried to vote for Eugène Terre' Blanche, the neo-Nazi right-wing leader of the AWB (the Afrikaner Weerstand-beweging — the Afrikaner Resistance Movement). It was in the late 1980s in a city by-election in Cape Town. He was upset when he arrived at the polling station only to find that the AWB were not represented in that ward. Apparently he caused a major scene, arguing vehemently with the only other Afrikaner Conservative Party representative there, eventually storming off without voting.

His racism really came to the fore when he drove his car, especially towards black taxi drivers — to this day not much has changed in this regard for many whites in SA. He kept a supply of old spark plugs next to his seat and when he disapproved of what a driver did to him, he would lean out of his car window and let rip with loud curses and spark plugs, not minding the consequences. Rather traumatic for his wife and children!

I remember my mom asking me to give a jam tin filled with hot tea to the "garden boy" — that was what we called the black man who worked in our garden once a week. My mom complained that "they take too many teaspoons of sugar". From this came the stereotype in my young mind that all black people like heaps and heaps of sugar in their coffee or tea! I went outside and shouted, "Hey Boy, come fetch your tea." I remember seeing, what I now understand to be the smouldering anger of humiliation in his eyes as he glared at me with two outstretched hands saying, "Dankie, my baas." ("Thank you, my master.") He was a "good submissive black man" — SA society had trained him well. He was old enough to be my father or even my grandfather. I did not understand the dynamics involved and it did not register with me; it was normal.

CONVERSION AND TEENAGE YEARS

We moved from Durban to East London where I began high school and there I became a committed Christian (7 June 1968). My conversion was a decisive experience of being born again. Things immediately changed in me. One of them was that a kind of innocent openness and love for all people welled up from within me. I felt an intense desire to tell people about Jesus and to do good. I found a verse that seemed to explain what had happened: "We know we have passed from death to life because we love our brothers and sisters; anyone who does not love remains in death" (1 Jn 3:14 NRSV). I used to stop to tell people about Jesus on my way to school in the mornings. Likewise at school, I tried to win all my friends to Jesus. After school, when I had finished my homework, I often went riding on my bicycle to look for people to talk to and then to pray with them about their problems.

My love and zeal were colour blind. I spoke to all and sundry. But I quickly learnt that my white friends, and whites in general, were more difficult to minister to, whereas I always found black people very receptive. I spoke to black folk everywhere, but mainly on the streets and at the bus stop where they waited after their day's work. I must add that, in retrospect, this love led to a naive transcendence of race and racism. At the time I was not aware of the racially divided socio-political context and the depth of my own conditioning.

However, there was an experience that began to undermine this conditioning. One day, on a street near our home, I had spoken to a large African "mamma" about Jesus. She was sick, so I prayed for her with my hand laid on her head. I heard the cars passing, thinking nothing of it, until I heard a particular familiar sound of a car that came up the road and I knew it was my dad. I did not dare to open my eyes. I prayed furiously because I knew I would be in trouble. Sure enough, my father was very angry when I got home. He shouted at me and gave me a hiding with the leather strap as punishment for the humiliation that he had to endure seeing his son touching a black woman in public, "What will the neighbours think of us if they see you doing that?" My young mind was confused. I knew Jesus loved this woman as he loved all people. Why should my dad be so upset and humiliated about me praying for her? Was it really just because she was black?

Attending a white church and enjoying the black preachers who came once or twice, and then going to a black convention in the black location once a year did not really prick my naive bubble. Sad to say, if anything, my white church reinforced my little white world. After matriculation (graduation from high school) I worked as a messenger in the Houses of Parliament in Cape Town for a few months before I undertook a year of compulsory military training (1973). Fortunately I did not see any military action during my year's service based in South West Africa (now Namibia). Although these experiences made me more aware of apartheid, somehow they did not put me in touch with the racial pain and division in our country.

 ## GROWING AWARENESS

My perceptions began to change when I was sent to Rhodesia (now Zimbabwe) as a full-time trainee pastor in the Assembly of God (AOG). The time of ministry in Rhodesia, from January 1975 to the end of 1977, opened my eyes to the deep hurt caused by white racism and colonialism, and the struggle for African freedom and identity.[2] The bush war — variously called the War of Liberation or the Terrorist War, depending which side (white or black) you were on — had begun in earnest. I was affected by it, causing me to question the generally accepted (white) explanations of reality.

Firstly, I remember the tensions created by some of the black pastors that met with us in our weekly pastors' meetings, when they asked difficult questions about the bush war and whether we could meet in their townships — not just in the white suburbs. These tensions were often seen as a wrongful intrusion of politics. The AOG at the time was divided structurally and functionally (both in Rhodesia and South Africa) into white, black, coloured and Indian, and there were endless tensions and heated conferences about if, and how, these divisions should be resolved.[3] I can remember the painful black/white discussions and divisions at the Witbank National Conference (in SA) that took place in the shadow of the 1976 Soweto uprisings — the government's violent response to the march by black school children who protested the policy to make Afrikaans the language of tuition in all schools. My memory of the conference is of a terrible sense of racial tension and an attitude of dismissal among many of the white pastors — "this is all just politics".

Things became serious for me back in Rhodesia when there was a call to gather every morning from 05.30 to 07.00 in our churches to pray for "our boys in the bush", that "God may give them victory", that "God may protect us from the communists and save our Christian country", and such sentiments. The longer we prayed, the more disillusioned I became and increasingly questioned the motivation and the process. Some men were spending six weeks on patrol call-up having gun fights in the bush with terrorists (or freedom fighters, again depending on which side you were on) and then having four weeks at home and in business, trying to keep a family and job going. For many men this six week/four week cycle continued for a number of years. The pressure was intolerable for some.

I remember a couple having a terrible fight a few apartments above my apartment. The woman screamed for help and I ran upstairs to find the man, who had returned from the bush, holding a gun to her head, threatening to blow her brains out. I managed to defuse the situation but realised that both of them were simply unable to cope because of the six weeks in and four weeks out cycle. I recall how I tried to counsel a desperate young man in our church, my own age, who had returned from the bush and was weeping uncontrollably because he had killed someone. He had been in a fire-fight and had shot some terrorists. And then he had to help put the body of one of his buddies into a body bag — the poor man had been shredded to bits by bullets. I also presided over a funeral of a young man killed while on patrol, and watched the parents weeping. I felt utterly powerless in my feeble attempt to console them. Whatever I said felt empty and meaningless. I thought, "Why? Surely there is something wrong with this? What are we *really* fighting for? To save our Christian nation from the communist hordes or to preserve our nice white colonial lifestyle? Is this worth dying for?"

My perception of reality was shifting and I began to listen to Jeremiah Kainga and Richmond Chuindiza, two of the black AOG pastors who had the courage to speak out about the political situation. They asked about the need for repentance from racism, colonialism and white privilege, and the need for authentic African freedom and identity. As my time in Rhodesia came to an end, I grew increasingly disillusioned with the Ian Smith government explanations and the accepted white Christian view of things that generally supported the ideology of the government.

I was transferred to Cape Town, to pastor the Meadowridge AOG, in 1978. The coloured pastor, Eddie Romans, who lived across the railway line in the coloured township of Retreat, used to invite me to preach there. As we got to know each other, I became aware of the economic and social differences between us, and between our congregations. Our church had relocated to Constantia, one of the wealthiest suburbs in Cape Town, where we had built a wonderful cash-paid-for facility with soft upholstered chairs and wonderful amenities. I was keenly aware of the Retreat church with their stark, long, narrow hall and hard wooden benches, their struggle with poverty, unemployment and many other forms of moral and social brokenness. I really struggled with the differences.

I was particularly affected by the story I heard of a young coloured couple. They had given birth and on registering the baby a week or two later at the relevant government department, were told by the young white clerk that the baby looked like a Bantu (African) and was not coloured. Apparently he held up a written list of ten physical characteristics (of black Africans) and pointed out the flat nose, flared nostrils, big lips, the curly hair and dark complexion, etc. The apartheid Population Registration Act required that all babies be classified as white, black, coloured or Indian, each according to certain criteria. He wanted to register the baby as a Bantu (black) child and have it "sent back" to the Transkei, a thousand kilometres away. The Transkei was the Xhosa "homeland" that most blacks in the Cape Province came from and black babies born in the Cape, at a certain age, had to go back to their families in the Transkei. These were the requirements of a complex system of apartheid control that governed population and people movement through the homelands policy, migratory labour legislation, influx control, pass laws and the Group Areas Act.[4] That was the procedure. No recourse — end of story. The clerk had the power to decide, despite the parents' desperate pleas for understanding. Just imagine the situation! What were they to do?

As it turned out, the baby was eventually registered "coloured" after the intervention of a sympathetic white skin — as shameful as that was. But the damage had been done. The raw reality struck me like a heavy hammer: your racial classification at birth determined your whole life in SA, either on the side of privilege and power, or on the side of oppression, poverty and hopelessness. More frightening was the power given to young white clerks to determine the future of others, often on a very arbitrary and prejudiced basis.[5] What went on in their minds that they could treat human beings in that manner? I used to wonder about white government officials, or even about ordinary whites like me. Was it a matter of naivety, plain indifference, unashamed prejudice, or even outright hatred? I remember seeing the painted signs all over, on park benches, on public toilets, in offices, in shops: "Whites only", and "Non-whites". I saw them from birth. I was so used to it that I was indifferent. Only later, through my friends in Soweto, did I realise the terrible humiliation involved in being called a "non-something". It robbed them of their humanity — they were called non-persons, and were treated accordingly ... often worse than animals.

There were three other key stimuli that awakened me at this time to the need for reconciliation, and which prepared me for the interesting things to come. Firstly, I "discovered", with enormous excitement, the biblical theology of the kingdom of God as taught by George Ladd.[6] This gave me a theological framework for understanding social issues, and replacing the little that my conservative Pentecostal theology had to offer in this regard. Secondly, in 1979 I attended the South African Christian Leadership Assembly (SACLA) together with about 5 000 other Christians representing most denominations in SA. It was a courageous time of wrestling with Christian witness and integrity in the face of the deteriorating apartheid situation. Thirdly, I participated in a progressive ministers' fraternal that worked at reconciliation at grassroots level. It was a challenging and stretching ecumenical process, seeking not only racial, but church reconciliation. I went through these three formative experiences with colleagues Derek Morphew and Costa Mitchell who are now also pastors in the Vineyard.

 # THE VINEYARD AND SOWETO CONNECTION

In 1980 I was called to pastor the Northcliff AOG in Johannesburg, which I led for just over a year. I left the AOG and went to work with John Wimber for eight months in the Yorba Linda Vineyard, in Southern California (1982).[7] I recall a conversation with John in which we were discussing the probable Vineyard church plant back in Johannesburg. I said that, in my opinion, if we planted just another white suburban affluent charismatic church, we would have failed — we would be part of the problem in SA, not part of the solution. We had to respond to our increasingly divided society in some relevant and creative way. I was not sure how, but I felt strongly about this, because my time away from SA had given me a greater sense of clarity and urgency about our situation back home.

We planted the Vineyard in Johannesburg towards the end of 1982, together with two colleagues. A year later I looked around the church one day and saw that we were all the same. We all looked the same, dressed the same, smelt the same and spoke the same way — a nice neat white happy homogenous charismatic church! That was November 1983, just before the referendum in SA on the tricameral parliament.[8] At the same time I was lecturing a module on the kingdom of God to a racially mixed student body at the Christ for Africa Institute. I was recommending a "no" vote due to the blacks being excluded from the political process. This was in the context of heated discussions in the class on the ethics of the kingdom and the political situation.

One young black man, Paul Mpete, challenged me by asking, "Are you not just another white English liberal, a hypocrite trying to patronise blacks by saying nice words to us in front of the whites? You appear to support our struggle for justice, but in reality you want to save your own skin. If you mean what you say, then come into Soweto and meet my friends and see how we live." He was a young black man who had broken through his "inferiority barrier", his fear of whites, and said exactly what he felt and believed — not what whites wanted to hear. Many of the younger blacks had been politicised into asserting their black identity and their human rights, and had been liberated out of the child-parent mode of behaviour. They demanded adult to adult interaction.

I was stung, and immediately responded by taking Paul home late one afternoon to Mapetla, deep in Soweto. I remember driving through these narrow, winding potholed streets, between postage-stamp size houses on matchbox size properties. The streets were full of children of all ages, playing soccer, hopscotch and other games — they had nowhere else to play. They all stopped and stared as we drove past. I was terrified and Paul felt it! He kept giggling and reassuring me, "It'll be okay, they know me." (Paul has the biggest set of strong white teeth you have ever seen — they shine like bright stars on a warm summer's night. His wonderful smile is imprinted on my brain forever!) We came to Mama Marx's house where Paul was renting a room. When I heard her name and how it was spelt, I wondered what I was letting myself in for — was it a communist plot after all? The apartheid government had sold whites the line that the communists had infiltrated the black townships and were to blame for all the "unrest" in the country.

Talking about names, I learnt from Paul that his real name was Mokete (the Sotho word for "a feast"). With his great grin he explained that his father had added Paul as a Western name "so that the white master could have a handle to carry me around, like a suitcase! My dad said the whites could not say the African names, so it would be better for me if I gave them a handle!" Many of our friends in Soweto reverted to their African names over time, a symbolic act of reclaiming their black identity and cultural heritage.

Mama Marx's house was a typical Soweto house with just four rooms: a kitchen, a lounge and two bedrooms with a tiny renovated bathroom and one of those smelly outside toilets (known colloquially as a "long drop"). Mokete's room had a double bed that almost touched the walls on all sides — there was just enough space on either side to wriggle past. He shared the room and bed with John Tsheole, also a student at the Christ for Africa Institute. I was dumbstruck at how small and cramped everything was. Mama Marx was kind and warm, and immediately made tea and brought out biscuits and other eats. Mokete quickly rounded up some of his friends to come and meet his lecturer from Johannesburg. They looked at me as if to ask: Who is this strange white man in Soweto? They were suspicious. Why was I in Soweto? They said I had to be either a communist or ANC sympathiser (the African National Congress, the then banned liberation movement of which Nelson Mandela was a leader), or I was a secret police agent. There was a remote possibility that I could be a priest, as a few white Catholic priests lived in Soweto, but they did not think that possible as I did not look like one. So who was I? What was I doing there? What did I want?

That encounter was difficult and bruising for me, and I remember driving out of Soweto rather bewildered and hurt. I went to bed that night, wrapping my head in my pillow to wipe away my tears as my mind blurred all the images, feelings, tastes, smells and sounds of Soweto into a still small voice. I felt God saying, "Where is your brother?" I thought, "I've seen this movie before! Cain killed Abel and thought he could get away with it." It struck me: My black brother! God was clearly asking me about my oppressed brother, my poor brother, my angry brother, my AOG brothers and sisters who had died in the 1976 Soweto riots (Nicholas Benghu, the leader of the black AOG, had told us at the 1976 Witbank Conference that some of our black youth leaders had been cut down by apartheid bullets as they marched in Soweto).

I answered, "Am I my (black) brother's keeper? God, don't get political on me now! Do you expect me to be accountable for the black blood shed in our country under colonialism and apartheid? I haven't killed anyone, let alone a black man! Are you crazy?" But I knew.

"Yes, you are your brother's keeper. His blood cries out to me from the ground. In fact, his blood is on your hands." God nailed me! I could not say, "I don't know where my brother is" as Cain did (Gen 4:9), because I had just been into Soweto and had seen and heard the raw pain and had touched the blood, as it were, of my Christian brothers and sisters. My heart pounded with the explosive realisation that I had been on the side of power since birth, and that I was part of a system that had caused untold misery and death to people just because they were "non-white". My little Western private individualistic mindset was blown apart; I could not escape the fact that I was tied up in complicit historic group sin and guilt. I knew that I was deeply conditioned by the corporate sins of my fore-fathers, my affluent class, my privileged white status, and I knew I had to do something about it. I had to repent, I had to resolve my part in this deadly divided history, or I feared that I might become like Cain, "a restless wanderer on the earth" (Gen 4:12). This verse has always made me think about what Johnny Clegg, a great South African songwriter, calls "the scatterlings of Africa" — the many white South Africans who are scattered all over the world.

THE BEGINNINGS OF JOHWETO

My resolve to live a life of repentance from my white conditioning quickly took the form of regular visits to Soweto in 1984, which by 1985 had become regular weekly meetings. I brought some of my white friends and Mokete gathered all his radical, angry young comrades (or so it felt), and we began the journey of our lives. Let me first share some impressions, discussions and experiences of Soweto before I explain Johweto — the reconciliation group that emerged out of my friendship with Mokete.

Travelling deep into Soweto was never easy, especially during the state of emergency from 1985 to 1989. We regularly encountered police roadblocks. The tension was tangible, filling the air with uncertainty. It was like a steel cord of military might strangling Soweto; like a thick blanket of oppression, symbolised in the acrid smoke from all the coal stoves and burning tyres which hung over the large orange floodlights that gave Soweto its light. There was a weird, eerie glow at night, especially during winter. At times it burnt our eyes and it was difficult to breathe. Gill (my wife — we married in November 1987) had a full-on asthma attack one night when we stayed over in Soweto for a weekend. We were often aware of a deep sense of desolation and heaviness during our times in Soweto. We used to wonder whether it was us, the suffocating hopelessness of the whole situation, or the oppressive spiritual warfare in which we found ourselves. We felt like David facing Goliath, like a naive little dwarf prodding the enraged giant of apartheid. We got to know life on the other side, a stark contrast to our reality in the plush green suburbs with our fresh, free air.

Our meetings were interesting to say the least. I quickly realised that, before we could worship and pray together meaningfully, we had to clear the air through open and honest dialogue. I came to understand what Jesus meant when he said: "Go and be reconciled before you worship at the altar" (Matt 5:23–24). The questions came thick and fast in the early meetings: Who are you — our brother or our oppressor? Who do you vote for? Do you respond to the apartheid military call-up? Do you come riding around in Soweto in military vehicles shooting up our children? If you do, we'll respond to our government in exile (the ANC) and their military call-up. We'll join MK (Umkhonto we Sizwe, the Spear of the Nation, the military unit of the ANC) and fight you guys in the streets. Do you believe in detention without trial? Do you support the release of Nelson Mandela from prison? How many cars do you have? If you sold just your garden tools, you could buy me a bicycle. Why don't you give me a job?

It was like lancing a boil; the puss squirted out. I felt as if we were a symbol of the white oppression over all the years of colonial presence in southern Africa, and at last some blacks had found some whites on their turf, in their homes, and they could express their suppressed rage, and be "in your face" about it. I kept saying to myself, "Don't take it personally, just absorb their pain," but it was not easy. It also became clear that what was important to me was not important to them; what I understood by the gospel and church was very different for them. They were dealing with bread-and-butter issues, with life and death, with daily political oppression, police raids, anger and pain, hopelessness and crushed dignity, poverty and unemployment, and they had to reconcile that reality with their Christian faith, with their understanding of the gospel of Jesus Christ. My gospel concerned my own spirituality, worship, healing, evangelism, church growth, etc. — but all that now seemed meaningless in the face of their suffering.

It was a radical clash of opposing ideologies, cultures, nationalisms, beliefs, class-consciousness and geographic divides. I was shocked and frightened as I became aware of just how far apart we were, how different our worlds were. Apartheid had been devastatingly effective. Was there any hope? At times I thought I saw the writing on the wall: full-scale civil war and mass bloodshed.[9] As those early meetings exposed my white conditioning, many dark racist thoughts came to the fore. I cannot emphasise enough the fact that one does not know oneself until you are fully exposed to the other side. Only then does prejudice from years of conditioning surface. I really did not think I was a racist — after all, I was a good Christian pastor and I voted for the Progressive Federal Party (the then liberal white opposition political party)! I was mistaken.

In the early days of our meetings, a few of us — blacks and whites — went on a "translocal" ministry trip to Inanda in Natal (now KwaZulu-Natal). We stayed together in a house — a first for many of us. I had a bath in the morning, but there were little black African hairs in the bath. I had a physical reaction; my stomach turned and I felt sick, "Oh no, they didn't clean the bath." The thought of bathing where a black man had bathed was suddenly repulsive to me. I was distressed at my reaction and wondered where it came from. Anyway, I got over it and bathed. Later Mokete came walking out of the same bathroom with a long black hair held between his fingers, complaining rather loudly, "Bushy, next time please clean the bath!" (My nickname was Bushy in those days, partly due to my thick hair.) I was soundly rebuked and realised my racism! We chatted and I told them how I felt. Mokete disclosed his feelings and we all ended up laughing and making fun of it. We became real brothers.

This little incident also taught me that the overwhelming pain of our country and the deep inner racism were not to be seen as fearful, paralysing monsters. I learnt that we could overcome them through meaningful relationships (together with other structural processes). Personal friendship reduces this "big problem" to a person with a history, feelings and thoughts, a name, with a big grin and a lovely face. Then it is easy to love and be loved, to heal and be healed.

This type of exposure brought me to the realisation that I had drunk racism from my mother's white breast, as it were, that I was raised as a nice white boy in a nice white suburban home. That I went to a nice white school and played nice white sports and developed a nice white view of the world. The experiences in Soweto stirred me deeply and made me reflect on my life and ministry: Had it served any real purpose? What had I achieved? At times I felt as if I had been a nice white pastor, preaching nice white sermons to nice white people in nice white churches to maintain nice white lifestyles. I could no longer do that. And when I preached against apartheid and made some of these provocative state-ments to our (white) Vineyard congregation in Johannesburg, it caused much consternation! We had leadership meetings about it and a few families even left the church. My passion was burning white hot – excuse the pun – and I said some unwise things in my preaching, both in SA and overseas.

It was a particularly painful period for me personally — I went through a divorce in 1985; I came into increasing tension with and estrangement from my Vineyard colleagues over Johweto, and I was trying to sort through my (white) guilt. Was I overstating things? Was I taking on false guilt? Was I losing my way? Were we too political? All the whites in our reconciliation group had to face these issues. We made mistakes, and we learnt as we went along. But we knew one thing, we had to walk this road of repentance and reconciliation regardless of the cost — for our own sake, for God's sake, for South Africa's sake.

Some of our discussions in Soweto were so angry and brutal that people walked out while others dissolved into tears. It was a highly politicised context. But more often than not we would end up falling on our knees, crying out to God for mercy — he was our only hope, our only common denominator, nothing else could save or unite us. The divide was so great that, on a few occasions, we wondered if we would come back the next week to meet again. But we did. If we as Christians struggled in this way, what about our nation? Like Joseph's coat, the many different colours would only become one when they were dipped in blood — the blood of Jesus, not the blood of violent revolution. We concluded that only Jesus, through the blood he shed for us, could make us one, and could heal and unite our rainbow nation. We did worship and pray and study the Bible together, but it came out of raw disclosure and a desperate need for God, not from religious ritual or "doing the right thing". I remember how Mokete often used to play his guitar as we sang to God (he and others wrote a number of beautiful Johweto songs), crying out our confusion and pain, and finding the sweet peace of his presence.

During one such session of brokenness and prayer in 1985, after a particularly bruising discussion, I heard Mokete confessing the sins of his people and repenting from worshipping the god of Soweto, the god of black nationalism, revenge and violence. I was cut to the core and began confessing the sins of my people and repenting from worshipping the god of Johannesburg, the god of gold, of white wealth and arrogance, privilege and power. We wept as we spontaneously came up with the name Johweto, the joining of *Joh*annesburg and So*weto*. We heard the call of a new God, the true God, the God of Johweto, the God of justice and reconciliation, the God of repentance and unity, the God of peace and oneness.

And so Johweto was born. We saw our little group, Johweto, as an experiment of the kingdom of God, an alternative kingdom community in our divided society. We wanted to be a place of hope and healing in the struggle for justice and reconciliation in our land.

 ## THE SPIRIT AND PASSION OF JOHWETO

The Johweto journey was driven by a vision of the kingdom. We were carried along by a passion to cross the barriers, to find and love one another as Jesus told us to do. The bottom line was to repent and love one another. Jesus gave this command to love in the context of washing his followers' feet (Jn 13) and this motif that motivated me personally became my life symbol. I taught that the spirit of Johweto, especially for the whites involved, was one of stripping off our power, privileges and pretensions. We had to become naked in our vulnerability and kneel down in humble repentance and service. We had to learn not to presume, but simply to come with the outpoured water of our love and lives, in the hope that it might bring some refreshing and even healing to our brothers and sisters in Soweto.

As whites, we have been locked into superiority. We have an initiating, problem-solving and dominating mindset. Our entire history has been one of whites presuming to know what blacks need and want. Without asking blacks anything, we have prescribed "solutions" which we imposed on them and rammed down their throats. And we wonder why they are so ungrateful and resentful. Often we do this with good, paternalistic "Christian" intentions — as claimed by the English colonialists and the Afrikaners who devised apartheid. In Johweto we tried to repent from this mentality by not assuming to know how the Sowetans felt, how we had hurt them or how we could help them. We wanted to listen and learn, to watch and wait, to weep with those who wept, to learn from them how and when we could wash their feet. For centuries they had knelt daily at our white feet in a servitude that was nothing more than humiliation and inferiority. We had to reverse this. I learnt from David Bosch that the church is the suffering servant in society, crossing any and every barrier with suffering love, simply to wash feet in the name of our Lord.[10]

In spite of these ideals, we stumbled along in our weakness with limited faith. It was not easy and we made many mistakes. There were great difficulties, real sacrifices, painful emotions, and critical choices on both sides. At times, in my lowest moments, I thought that we had opened a can of worms that would consume us, that we had let Leviathan loose from the pit of hell! We had no way of controlling the things that came up from within or that came at us from without. Neither did we have any control over the outcome of what we had let ourselves in for. At times I asked myself what we had started. Where would it lead us? What would become of us? It was a journey of sheer faith.

Mokete and his colleagues continually ran the danger of being seen as sell outs by their community, risking retaliation. In fact, a house of one of our members, whose father was a government councillor, was burnt down one night — he was seen as a collaborator by the young comrades. Fortunately the children escaped with their lives. On the other side, we whites were often seen as "too involved in politics", and even "liberationists and communists" by some in our own community.[11] Despite this, our hearts said that we must repent, we can do no other.

For the whites who came to Johweto, part of the repentance was the regular travelling from Johannesburg to Soweto, a small price to pay as a symbolic reversal of the flow of history (the traffic has been all one way for the benefit of the whites: the blacks came from the location, as it was called, to serve and work in the white city and homes. They learnt our language and culture, etc.). Our travelling included picking up people all around Soweto before the meetings, afterwards dropping them all off again, and then travelling over twenty-five kilometres back to our homes in Johannesburg. Exhausting, but exhilarating! Although there were one or two car accidents late at night deep in Soweto, no one was attacked or badly injured in all the years of Johweto.

On reflection, we lived through a miracle on many levels — the extent to which the Johwetans made sacrifices was amazing, and the protection from violence was supernatural. There were regular roadblocks, outbreaks of violence, criminal elements exploiting the situation, some of us were tear-gassed and baton-charged in marches and "political" meetings.[12] I was interrogated by the secret police and twice they interrupted our Johweto church meetings in Soweto. Another time I was taking Mokete home when we came across a necklace murder[13] a few minutes after it had taken place. We were stopped, questioned and searched by the police. In all these things, God had mercy on us and helped us.

I used to write poetry to process my thoughts and feelings, and to express something of the spirit and emotions of our experiences. I wrote the following poem on 6 October 1986:

uncertainty

driving down narrow streets
soweto is astir
all stand staring
bewildered black eyes
should I exit?
stopping at the room
my friend gets out
hey, this is bad
here comes the mellow yellow
they don't talk
they just shoot
ice blue eyes
long and short guns
they look through me
wat maak jy hier?[14]
all the questions
all the writing
all the searching
feeling the big brother fear
what's happening?
ja-nee two youngsters
now-now by others
necklaced down the narrow street
steel stark terror

i stare straight
my friend has no white teeth
sent to his apartheid room
safe?
follow the mellow yellow out?
as in a nightmare
mesmerised I drive
past the procession
like a cold corpse
in a car coffin
uncertain

When I first went into Soweto, I heard the phrase "the struggle". It referred to the desperate struggle for justice and freedom for the black people. It had a long history of pain and sacrifice. The cost was very high; much blood had been shed. Little did I know that in joining the struggle, my own heart and life would enter a profound inner struggle that I had never experienced before. My baptism into Africa, via Soweto and its seeping sores, caused me to re-examine everything in me, everything that I had built my life on, everything that our nation had been built on. It felt like a searching and searing pain that made me question and probe everything in and around me. It caused tension in my relationships, both near and far, especially with my white friends in Johannesburg. Some really believed I had lost my way. They offered various explanations. I admit that I did not handle it well. The following poem, written on 5 June 1986, expresses some of that pain:

The Struggle

Do you know that feeling?
Yes, I am asking you —
When your heart is
Caught in a vice
So tight
Between divine destiny
(A call that cannot be denied)
And self-imprisonment
That locks you in on every side
To your status-quo lifestyle?

It feels like the agony of death —
Or is it the struggle of new life?

When you sit where "they" sit
And see "their" hopeless plight
And hear "their" hoarse cry
And smell "their" sick poverty
And feel "their" merciless pain
And taste "their" bitter hell.

Then you ask, "What is this life?
What am I doing with my life?"

Do you know that feeling?
Yes, I am telling you —
"This" has a ruthless and dispassionate
Way of staring, of silently questioning
Persistently penetrating and exposing
All the self-righteous junk:
"Shame, we are praying for you"
"Don't be motivated by guilt"
"It's only the calling of some"
"You are not responsible for this mess"
"We cannot all be Mother Teresas"
"And anyway, who was Dietrich Bonhoeffer?"

Do you know what I think?
It all stinks

But what of my own heart?
I die when I think of doing
I die as long as I don't
Jesus, is it really you that I see
In the "distressing disguise of the poor"?
Jesus, is it really you that I hear
Bidding me "come and die"? [15]

SUMMARISING THE JOHWETO JOURNEY

I conclude my story by giving an overview of the main features of Johweto. The full story and all that we learnt will hopefully be the subject of another book. But for the moment, this is how we articulated our journey in 1985:

The Tale of Two Cities

♦ Johannesburg, the pot of white gold sustaining ruling privilege and power, mined on the black backs of cheap migrant labour.

♦ Soweto, the seething cauldron of black nationalism, created by apartheid, with the lid held tightly shut by young white soldiers.

♦ Johannesburg, about 1,5 million people living on 70% of the land area.

♦ Soweto, about 2,5 million people living on 30% of the land area.

♦ The two cities, symbols of South African society, are polarised and divided in every way possible: geographically, ideologically, politically, economically, culturally and religiously.

♦ This sad reality is even worse because we are supposedly a Christian nation with a Christian government[16] — a humiliating shame for all of us!

Enter Johweto, a Modest Proposal for Peace [17]

♦ Johweto is a kingdom community that repents from our social divides by seeking to reconcile Johannesburg and Soweto in an inclusive family of God, prophetically pointing to the future.

♦ It is a non-racial vision of a new emerging South African identity;

♦ An ethical vision of restored human dignity, equality and human rights;

♦ A geographic vision of the renaming of the two cities, making them one;[18]

♦ An economic vision of redistribution, shared resources and development for all;

♦ And a socio-political vision of justice, harmony and peace.

We believe this is possible to the extent that the church leads the way in humility, repentance and reconciliation, seeking the Prince of Peace to give us Johweto in a new SA. We believe that as we do this, God will have mercy on our nation and give us the leaders and the miracles that we need to make this happen.

This was our reason for existence; this was the vision and dream that inflamed our hearts. We sought to be vision and kingdom driven rather than reactionary or struggle driven — although we saw ourselves as part of the struggle for justice.

The Johweto journey, in terms of the formally constituted group, began in early 1985 and ended in late 1995. We grew from a handful of blacks and whites to between 70 and 80 regulars at its peak, roughly half white and half black. Although we did not set out to plant a church, our little reconciliation group became a congregation and was called the Johweto Vineyard. We met on Sunday mornings and on weekday nights in up to five home groups, all in Soweto. I relocated my full-time pastoral involvement from Johannesburg to Johweto in 1987.

As Johweto developed, we spoke of three aspects of our shared life: The family, the farm and the financial base.

The family

The family was the racially mixed congregation that met in Soweto. We went through various phases of growth, activities, seminars, programmes and spiritual formation during our eleven year history. For example, from time to time some of the whites would sleep over in Soweto with their friends and then some blacks would spend nights in Johannesburg with their friends — they were called week-end "encounters". A few of us went overseas together to connect with other Vineyards and reconciliation communities and to share what God was doing with us. Some went on short trips, while others stayed for up to a year with other communities, such as Reba Place Church, Evanston, Chicago. Some individuals and groups came from overseas to spend time with us in Johweto, some on short visits while others spent a year and longer with us.[19]

In 1988 a young man, Trevor Ntlhola, joined us after he had been expelled from his Pentecostal Bible school (see his story in Chapter 2). Trevor proved to be a wonderful learner and faithful brother in all that he gave himself to, and Mokete, James Johnson and I eventually invited him to be part of our core leadership team. James was a longstanding friend of mine and a businessman. He came with me into Soweto to seek reconciliation and justice. Ron and Sandy Gold, who joined Johweto in early 1985, owned a forty-four acre plot (twenty hectares) south of Soweto, near Grassmere, which they offered to us for the work of reconciliation.

The farm

This farm became a focal point for our activities. From 1985 we began meeting there most Saturdays to work together, developing various projects for our Johweto ministry. We saw it as a kind of reconciliation kibbutz, and named it Johweto

Kehillah (Hebrew for "community"). It was an amazing time and place of healing as black and white worked side by side, reversing some of our history where the white bosses watched the blacks doing the physical work. We did everything with our own hands, building a large shade cloth structure, growing vegetables, fencing the entire perimeter, building a community centre with a small hall and a couple of rooms, and then building a cottage. Later we built a factory which one of our men used for a fibreglass manufacturing business.

The Kehillah bordered an informal shack settlement, called the Sweetwaters squatter camp. We got involved with that poor community in various ways. We shared our vegetables and taught them to grow their own vegetables. We helped them with fresh water and employed some of their men and women. A few Johwetans taught at the school in Sweetwaters from time to time — the school council even changed the name to Johweto Preparatory School. We had a weekend "encounter" with the squatters. About twenty-five black and white Johwetans slept over for a weekend with people and families in their shacks in Sweetwaters. It was a real challenge for some of the Soweto members as they realised how affluent they were in contrast to their hosts.

I lived with Ron and Sandy on the Kehillah in the mid-1980s. One Saturday morning I was alone when a woman came from the informal settlement to ask for help. Her uncle Albert had died the day before and they had no money to get help or to call an ambulance. This was a frequent occurrence, people coming from Sweetwaters for help. I called the hospitals and got the perfect run around. Sensing that God was saying to me, "You give him a dignified burial," I offered to make a coffin if she could get some men to dig a grave near their shack. Then our little group would bury him the following day. She agreed. I hastily hammered together a simple coffin out of wooden planks that we had lying around. On the Sunday when we went to bury him, we found a group of family and friends sitting outside the shack waiting and weeping. It was mid-summer, really hot, 14 December 1986 (I have Albert Letsoalo's death certificate before me, which the police later issued). The corpse stank terribly. This was the third day. They had covered the body with newspaper which was swarming with flies. To get the putrefying corpse into the coffin was quite something. Some of our young men bravely helped me. I preached and we prayed for the people and then buried Albert. I will never forget looking at my hands stained with the dark, cold blood that had seeped from the coffin as we carried it to the grave. I felt God saying, "You must get your hands dirty in caring for the poor and dispossessed; their blood is precious to me." Talk about meeting Jesus in the distressing disguise of the poor — a tiny taste of Mother Teresa's life and ministry.

The experiences in the squatter camp, as many called it, had a profound effect on me. As I reflected on the pain and circumstance of these people, I saw what apartheid had done to over 3 million people in all the forced removals. I expressed what I saw, what I felt and understood, in this poem written on 20 November 1988:

The dust bowl camp
where life is bitter drought
in Sweetwaters
where crooked shacks
like old men
lean wearily against the wind
where thin children
queue and carry like ants
where men and women
stare with empty eyes
mesmerised by drunken despair
by poverty and violence

They are like the decimated forest nearby
once rooted and standing tall
in farms and families and all
now laid low by urbanisation
unemployment and dry homelands
they lie there to dry out
waiting for the forced removals
to further fuel
the apartheid bonfire

A little live-in community developed on the Kehillah in the late 1980s, but some time later fell apart due to relational problems and security concerns. We had to work through the pain of the break-up. It was, however, a helpful experience because in 1991 a handful of couples from Johweto bought another smallholding nearer to Soweto and set up a community process. Gill and I helped to pioneer it, and we presently live on the new farm (called The Field) with five other families and two single people. That journey in community has been most interesting and rewarding — another story! The Kehillah is presently being used for an AIDS hospice and empowerment ministry called Emthomjeni, the Zulu word for Fountains of Life. It is being pioneered by the Zone 3 Vineyard from Soweto, which I will refer to later.

The financial base

From my first visit to Soweto, I was faced with financial challenges. The poverty and the need for economic justice, in Soweto and Sweetwaters, pressed itself upon us. James helped to support us financially from his business involvements. He drew a few other business people into a concept and practice of kingdom businesses. The purpose was to restore economic dignity to our Soweto brothers and sisters by starting businesses and creating jobs. It was also a means of generating money for our Johweto family ministry. We decided very early on that we would never ask for money, raise funds or send out appeals — although we graciously received if people gave of their own initiative without strings attached. We committed ourselves to generate money through our own sacrificial giving, an ethic of hard work, kingdom businesses and other entrepreneurial ventures. Most of what we did was financed in this way, and we give God the praise for all his generous provision.

The financial journey was an interesting experiment, resulting in mixed blessings, depending on one's view of things. We invested substantial sums of money in various business initiatives over the years, but most of them were closed down as they became unviable. We could not exercise the financial disciplines or give the business training that was needed. And we had to deal with people's brokenness. We bought two minibuses to empower two of our men in a taxi business, and to generate income for Johweto. After about two years of operating, with minimal returns, both disappeared quietly with their taxis and we have never heard from them again! Some viewed all these experiments as failures; others saw them as economic repentance, as investments in the kingdom of God, growing people and not using them for one's own profit. We considered this an extremely small price to pay for all the years of financial privilege and power that whites had enjoyed.

While we viewed the failed business ventures and empowerment projects as "bread on the waters", our economic repentance had a selfish side too: we were seeking to break the stranglehold that materialism had (and has) over us. And, if we were honest, ultimately to save our own skins! Money was an issue throughout our journey and was the source of much blessing and much pain in relationships. If we have learnt one thing in this regard, it is that we whites did not repent and surrender deeply enough. Simply put, we could have and should have done more. Mammon is still the chief false god — it is clear to me that class division is the deeper issue that undergirds racism. The financial and kingdom business part of our journey is a fascinating story in itself. Gill and I, and a number of others, are now living off the bread that has returned to us after many days, both spiritually and materially (Eccles 11:1–6).

BURYING AND SEEDING JOHWETO

The winds of change blew when FW de Klerk became president of SA. He unbanned various liberation movements in 1990, released political prisoners, including Nelson Mandela, and opened up the whole political process to negotiations. It culminated in 1994 in the first genuinely democratic elections in SA. These changes affected us in Johweto in terms of our planning and development. We realised that the urgency and need to cross the geographic divide into Soweto would shift as people became free to choose where they wanted to live. From 1991 we increasingly saw Johweto as working from the Soweto base into the Kehillah, the new farm, The Field, and into Johannesburg. We acquired a house in Yeoville, near to the Johannesburg city centre, in order to create a small black and white community as a place for ministry in this previously white, but then demographically changing semi-urban area. A number of our people lived and ministered there for a couple of years.

These shifts and other considerations made me realise that I needed to give the overall leadership to either Mokete or Trevor. A Sowetan needed to lead Johweto as it was becoming increasingly untenable for a white man to be team leader, or so I believed. We had begun to talk about some of these things in our leadership team when Mokete's marriage entered a difficult period. He and Nelly went overseas for a year to another reconciliation community to rest, learn and work through their stuff. However, on their return further difficulties arose, and as a leadership team we had to enter into a disciplinary process with Mokete. This was very painful, both for him and for us, and unfortunately it did not go well.

During this time I had a serious car accident (October 1993) which left me in hospital on my back for six weeks, and then at home on my back for another six weeks. I had shattered my right hip, and my left leg was badly broken in two places. While on my back, with lots of time to think and pray, it became clear to me that Trevor was the man, and that I not only had to give him the leadership, but that I should withdraw from Soweto and Johweto. I knew that my involvement was coming to an end. I needed to take the time to groom Trevor and then free him to lead with his own heart and vision, without my ongoing presence. He would need the space to do this as he was quite a bit younger than me. We made a decision in our leadership team to work towards this and, at the end of 1994, we made the announcement and Trevor took over as team leader. I was planning to stay on for 1995 to support him and then take an extended sabbatical to consider my future.

Sadly, at the same time, there was a disaffected faction in Johweto that sought to bring Mokete back into things through the backdoor — from our perspective. This led to a period of mediation and then arbitration in early 1995, with outside leaders who were mutually acceptable to both parties. The worst scenario unfolded and we had to excommunicate Mokete, as well as the little faction that opposed Trevor and the leadership. It was a very dark, painful and evil time for all concerned. I have never before, or since, in my entire ministry as a pastor, experienced a church discipline situation like that. The hurt was especially acute, and was complicated by our black/white reconciliation journey. We had become friends and brothers and sisters. And even more so for Mokete and I. Can you imagine how I felt — and how he must have felt — after all that we had been through together, for it to end like this? I wept. We parted ways and lost contact.

During this time Trevor faithfully led us while I helped him and the church to regroup. It was not long before Trevor felt that Johweto had run its course and that his vision was for a community-based church in Soweto. In September 1995 we had a "thanksgiving funeral" to bury Johweto — a wonderful celebration for a God-given prophetic journey.

The week after the "funeral", Trevor started Zone 3 Vineyard, based in Zone 3, Pimville, Soweto. The congregation has grown strong and healthy. Although it is predominately black, there are a few whites involved. I responded to a call to pastor a Vineyard in Johannesburg, now called Valley Vineyard, and we are working towards a vision of a fully integrated, multicultural church.

Although Johweto was a death in one sense, it has been a resurrection in many others. I see the truth in Jesus' words: "Unless a grain of wheat falls to the ground and dies, it remains only a single seed. But if it dies, it produces many seeds" (and fruit! Jn 12:24). As I journey on in life, I can see more clearly the value and fruit of Johweto in people, both near and far. I can also see fruit in the two congregations, in The Field, the Kehillah and now in the broader Vineyard. Johweto has seeded itself and we give thanks to God for what he has done, and is still doing.

In conclusion, I must share an interesting twist of sheer grace. In the first half of 2002 I began feeling the need to seek contact and reconciliation with Mokete. I realised that six years had passed and I felt that he had apparently made no effort to come back to Trevor, James and I to put things right — that is how I believed it should have been resolved. I figured that as it was now the seventh year, the sabbath year, I needed to "go and find my brother" and seek reconciliation. (I thought I might be seeing the same movie again, "Where is your brother?") I expressed this sentiment to Gill and others around me. I even had a dream about

Mokete in the context of reconciliation. Besides, if I am honest, I was already thinking of the reconciliation paper that I had been commissioned to write for our Vineyard pastors' conference in October, and needed to have all my relationships reconciled! I prayed about meeting Mokete, but did not do anything further.

Then, one morning early in November 2002, Gill met Mokete outside a shopping mall and they spontaneously greeted each other with a warm hug. When she told him that I wanted to meet him, he immediately responded by saying that he had had the same desire for the past couple of months. But most amazingly, early that very morning he had a dream in which he and I had reconciled and were in good relationship! Can you believe it? We immediately followed up. Trevor, James, Mokete and I met and talked things through. We mutually gave and received forgiveness and affirmed each other in a reconciled relationship.

God is so very good! And so the journey of reconciliation continues.

From left: Gill & Alexander Venter; Nelisiwe & Trevor Ntlhola

NOTES

1. Hermann Giliomee gives an important account of the historical formation of the Afrikaner and their sense of identity in Adam and Giliomee 1979, pp. 83–127.

2. Pakenham 1991 on the history of colonialism. If you want to understand Africa correctly, this is a "must read", especially for white people.

3. Recently, the long-standing chairman of the Assembly of God has written a book tracing, for the first time, the history of this denomination in southern Africa, describing some of the outworking of these racial tensions over many years. See Bond 2001.

4. It is not easy, especially for whites, to appreciate the complexity and devastating impact of these apartheid laws. Desmond Tutu gives a personal account of the laws and their impact in Tutu 1999, pp. 10–23. Ernie Regehr also helps us to understand, see Regehr 1979, pp. 15–44. He was authorised and sponsored by the Mennonite Central Committee, as a response to the 1976 Soweto riots, to do a two-year research project on the apartheid laws, their impact and the perceptions involved. His book was banned in SA when it was published and remained banned during the apartheid years. The most comprehensive picture is given in the Truth and Reconciliation Commission of South Africa Report (TRC SA R) volume one, see note 17 of Chapter 4 for details.

5. Tutu confirms such horrifying stories in Tutu 1999, p. 21.

6. Ladd 1959, his basic introduction to the kingdom of God and his detailed study, 1974.

7. I explain this part of my story, the reasons why I left the AOG and joined Vineyard, and the church plant in Johannesburg with the translocal American Vineyard team, in Venter 2000, pp. 14–20.

8. The then President, PW Botha, implemented "reform" by bringing the Indians and coloureds into parliament on a kind of group representative vote, hence the tricameral parliament: one for whites, one for Indians and one for coloureds, but none for the blacks. Only the whites could vote in the referendum, and Botha got his majority "yes" vote for setting up the tricameral system.

9. Similar to the writing on the wall for King Belshazzar: "You have been weighed on the scales and found wanting. Your kingdom is divided and given to the Medes and Persians" (Dan 5:27–28).

10. Bosch 1980 (especially pp. 71–77) and 1991. Oom Dawid, as he was affectionately known, was one of South Africa's most respected theologians and missiologists. I had the privilege of knowing him personally. His life and teaching has impacted me enormously.

11. "When I feed the poor, they call me a Christian or saint. But when I ask why the poor are poor, they call me a communist" — the words of Dom Helder Camara, a Catholic priest who gave his life to the poor in Brazil. "They" were the Brazilian government and the affluent class. See Camara 1969.

12. Almost any meeting that was called to discuss the crisis in Soweto was seen as a banned "political" meeting by the government and was violently broken up by the police.

13. Black youth, "the comrades" (*amaxabane* in Xhosa) used to kill government collaborators and other sellouts (*impimpis*) by identifying and catching the suspect, beating them and putting a car tyre around their neck. They would then fill the inside tube with gasoline, set it alight and dance and sing as the person burned to ashes.

14. Afrikaans for, "What are you doing here?"

15. The words of Dietrich Bonhoffer: "When Christ calls a man, he bids him come and die" in Bonhoffer 1963, p. 7. He was a pastor who stood up against Hitler during WWII. As a result he was imprisoned, tortured and killed by the Gestapo. I also quoted the words of Mother Teresa: "The work we do is only our love for Jesus in action. And that action is our wholehearted and free service — the gift to the poorest of the poor — to Christ in the distressing disguise of the poor." Teresa 1983, p. 22. See Vardey 1995 — a wonderful book on Mother Teresa, her ministry and words.

16. In a census 78% of the population said they were Christian (it was down to 74% in 2000), and the Afrikaner Nationalist government was seen as "the Dutch Reformed Church at prayer" (and politics!).

17. We used a big poster and postcards which we received from the Mennonites in the mid-1980s. It read: A Modest Proposal for Peace — let the Christians of this world agree that they will stop killing each other." Christians literally tortured and killed each other in SA during the apartheid years. See Chikane 1988.

18. We hoped the two cities would be renamed Johweto in a new SA that repents of the apartheid Group Areas Act.

19. I must mention Catherine Wirth from Reba Place Church, Evanston, Chicago; Joanna Haines from St Andrews, Chorelywood, England, and Curtis Chang from Boston, who each stayed with us for between one and four years at a time. A two-week visit to Johweto by ten people is referred to in Noe 2001, pp. 40–41. Killian Noe, leader of Lazarus House — part of the Church of the Saviour in Washington, DC. — brought the group to live and work with us, and she tells of the impact it had on them.

CHAPTER TWO

TREVOR'S STORY

It is a privilege for me to share my journey of reconciliation in SA. On this journey I have found, again and again, that I have had to deal with the meaning of this word "reconciliation". I have realised that the difficulty is not merely with the word itself, but with the attitude of all those around me — and within myself. People understand different things when they hear the word "reconciliation" but, more importantly, people have attitudes that create barriers, and it is these barriers that rear their ugly head and cause problems between people. These problems are commonly called sin, which resides within every one of us. It obscures our motives as we try to practise reconciliation, often making it a "head debate" instead of a "heart experience".

For my part, I think I have a clear understanding of reconciliation, but my struggle is with the actual practice of reconciling with others. Reconciliation is easier said than done. If I am honest, I am sometimes tempted not to enter the reconciliation debate, and to keep my views to myself. Even then, if I have to disclose my views, I am tempted to argue from an intellectual viewpoint. I am tempted not to allow my heart to feel, to experience the process and practice of reconciliation, because it often proves to be painful.

My journey of reconciliation has not been easy — especially as a black man in SA — let alone as a father, husband, friend and pastor. I have learnt that reconciliation happens, or should happen, daily in our relationships, especially in the home and among friends. As an African South African, when I am labeled "black", I put my foot down in resentment, because it is a contemptible caricature of who I really am. I say this because, over the years, I have heard many people, mostly white people, say, "I know the blacks and I love the blacks." I find this painfully insulting and patronising. When I hear this, I feel like saying, Do they really know us blacks? Do they really know me, Trevor Ntlhola? Have they listened to my story and experienced something of my life? What do they mean by "love"? Do they love us like they love their children? Do they love me like they love their pet dog? "Love" is so overused and misused that it has lost its true meaning. I am more than my black skin. I am a person made in God's image. Furthermore, we are not to love "the blacks", "the poor", "the handicapped", "the pygmies", or any other group of people. We are meant to love all people, no matter what their skin colour, their culture or their background.

I want to put up a sign right here, and make you stop and read:

> *CAUTION:*
> *Human Beings Here.*
> *Handle with Care.*

In dealing with reconciliation, we are dealing with people, with very personal experiences and painful memories. This applies to both blacks and whites, to all people from all backgrounds; and also to me as I share my story. We must keep in mind what a wise Jesuit priest said: "Through disclosing my heart and feelings, I am giving you myself, for that is all I have to give, and you can choose to handle me with care, or to break me."[1]

FAMILY BACKGROUND AND CHILDHOOD

I was born on 11 October 1967 in an industrial site which is now known as George Gogh in Johannesburg, SA. Back in 1967, George Gogh was known as the Eastern Native Township, next to an industrial site on the east side of Johannesburg. We lived in a tiny house that literally had two rooms. There were fifteen people in our extended family (including aunts and cousins) who lived with us. We had one tap and one toilet outside the house. I can remember thinking that this was normal, until many years later when I saw how white people lived. Then I understood that it was not normal.

My parents were not married to each other, and I was born out of wedlock. I was the second in a family of three children, the only son. My elder sister, Mantoa Mzaye, is married with three children. My younger sister, Dimakatso Ntlhola, was also married. She died of HIV/AIDS in 2001. My mother told me that when I was born, it rained from 11 am until 4 pm. So they named me Amafu, which means "cloudiness". I do not like my African name, because if it is not pronounced correctly (by leaving out the "A"), it means "death" or "a funeral". I prefer my Western name, Trevor. Apparently my father gave it to me because he was a caddy for a golfer, a Mr Trevor Wilkes from Johannesburg. In African culture rain symbolises something uniquely divine, a blessing to all; maybe my African name does mean something good! According to our culture, my paternal relatives were supposed to come ten days after my birth, to do their ritual cleansing over my mother and me. They only came many days later. My father was very irresponsible and did not play his role as a father in my life. It was my mother who, in the midst of great struggle, had to raise me in those early years.

My father is of the lineage of the Lutyas, from the Hlubi clan in the Xhosa tribe. His name is Nimrod Babalo Lutya. My mother, the beautiful woman who gave birth to me, is Puleng Margaret Ntlhola, from Basotho background. We spoke Sotho at home. Sadly, my father left my mother soon after I was born, and I did not know him until I began to meet with him in my early teens. While I was still very young, my mother met and married Themba Mzaye. She left the home to stay with him, and I remained with my grandmother and aunt, who raised me. Nkgono, my grandmother, helped the family by generating money from making African beer and selling it. I had periodic contact with my mother and stepfather — he tried to play some sort of a fatherly role in my life from a distance. I remember that I used to cry frequently as a child, and I later understood that it was because of the abandonment by my mother. It felt like the emotional umbilical cord had been cut far too early.

In the early 1970s our whole community was forcefully removed and dumped in Soweto. Today Soweto is a city with about 3 million inhabitants. Soweto was entirely reserved for black South Africans, and its name described its usefulness to the apartheid system: the South Western Township. It was the place south of Johannesburg where the whites kept their labour, on the margins of the white society. I still have blurred memories of the SA police pointing their big guns and pushing people into their big trucks for relocation to Soweto. My father told me that they offered them R100 if they would cooperate peacefully. This was my first real introduction to the pain of apartheid.

I remember arriving on the other side, confused and insecure. We were relocated because of the apartheid policy of the Group Areas Act. Apparently we were living in an area that was meant to be lily-white. Our presence devalued the property or hindered their plans for development. We were dumped in a cold little four-roomed house, with no interleading doors, no ceiling or plaster on the walls, no electricity, and only one tap and toilet outside. (I later learnt that the Orlando Power Station, which was in the backyard of Soweto and polluted our air, supplied electricity to the white southern suburbs of Johannesburg, but for years we did not have electricity.) The floor was made of hardened grit that broke into pieces after a few months. We were told we could never own the house; we had to pay rent for as long we lived there.

Most of what I can remember about my upbringing and adulthood unfolded in the township of Soweto. I grew up with my sisters, sister-cousins, grandmother and aunt and, as the only boy surrounded by a league of eight females, I was very spoilt. My grandmother made sure that everything worked for me, her favourite grandson. My cousins and I had a great relationship with each other, but unfortunately it was not the same with my biological parents. I wished that my relationship with my mother had been loving, but it was characterised by coldness and emotional distance. To this very day I long for a healthier and warmer mother-son relationship. I lived with my mother and stepfather for a few years during my mid-teens. My stepfather and I tolerated each other — we did not have the best of relationships.

Later it became crystal clear to me that I had not lived in a normal family, a family with both parents in our home, loving and raising their children together. This realisation was very painful for me, and every day I continue to feel its effects in my life. It adds to the other painful realisation that I have to cope with every day, that I was born black in a nation divided by racist apartheid, a nation that now has to deal with this terrible legacy. I remember the politics and oppression of the country being discussed in our home, but in hushed tones out of fear of the police. We all knew what had happened to the Mandelas and other black activists — some were in prison and some had been killed by the apartheid police.

RELIGIOUS UPBRINGING AND COMING TO FAITH IN JESUS

I still have vague memories of going to church as a young boy with my cousins, to the African Methodist Episcopal Church (AMEC). I hated going to church because my grandmother would rouse me from sleep early on Sunday mornings, and church was boring. However, there were times when I felt as if I could become a priest — I could imagine myself wearing the colourful priestly regalia. When I was twelve, my aunt's friend invited me to her church. Her husband was the pastor, and because I liked the name of the church Ditloholwana tsa Baapostla (The Descendants of the Apostle), it became my church! Everybody had to participate in this church. After the pastor or preacher had read a biblical text and explained its meaning, anyone could preach on that same text or story, giving his or her own interpretation. The preaching was punctuated, every five minutes or so, with hymns and songs from other members who were also keen to preach. The purpose of these interruptions was supposedly to allow the person preaching to catch their breath. Members were required to wear the church uniform. In this way the class consciousness and segregation was transcended but, ironically, we were all totally apolitical and meek recipients of the racist oppression of apartheid. The services were normally from three to six hours on Sundays, and even longer during Easter conventions. On top of that, we would often have night vigils from 10 pm until 6 am the following morning.

Looking back, with my salvation experience and theological training, I realise that this "church" was not really a church. It was one of those syncretistic African indigenous "churches" — strictly speaking, a sect. It had some value, because it instilled a reverence for God in many of us, respect for our elders, and an understanding that church is not an audience, but a community of active participants. But there was one practice that really scared me. We were baptised in a river three times a year: firstly, to be cleansed from sin; secondly, to prepare us for the mid-year school exams; and lastly, to prepare us for the year-end exams. These baptisms were always carried out at four o' clock in the morning, and the immersions were repeated four to seven times in rapid succession. Besides the ordeal itself, imagine being baptised in the middle of winter in freezing water at four in the morning. I had to fight for air to survive the baptism. This is the reason why I have a serious water phobia. To this day I am terrified of swimming. At the age of seven my daughter tried in vain to teach me to swim — I was too scared.

Many of these churches, based on a mix of Old Testament teachings and traditional African beliefs, are mushrooming in Africa. They accommodate themselves to the traditional culture without addressing the socio-political and ethical challenges like racism and reconciliation. In terms of salvation, although some of their leaders are born again, receiving Jesus Christ as Saviour, it is difficult to win them over to Christ. After I was converted to Christ, I went back to visit this "church". To my amazement, the pastor invited me to sit in front with the elders. The pastor preached from Acts 16:30: "Sirs, what must I do to be saved?" When I heard this, I believed that my visit to the church that day was God's leading. After the pastor finished speaking, I took my turn to preach, but I was mildly annoyed by the constant interruption of songs! I kept my composure and took my time to explain the text, emphasising the importance of the salvation that the jailer received. I hope that some of them became genuine Christians after that sermon!

I only became a genuine Christian in 1984, when classmate Agnes Mazibuko led me to the Lord. Agnes was full of zeal for God and his work, and was not ashamed of the gospel of Jesus Christ. I shared a desk with her at school, and in less than a month she had told me all about Jesus Christ. I remember lying to her and saying that I was a born again Christian. She was young and unsophisticated, and she believed my convincing lies.

One Friday morning Agnes told me that the Student Christian Movement (SCM) at our school would meet that afternoon, and she wanted me to *fakaza* (to testify) about what Christ had done in my life. Since I was not a born again Christian, I did not know what she was talking about. Although she explained it to me — she wanted to know when and where and how I became a Christian — I still did not fully understand. I eventually gathered that she wanted me to stand up in front of the SCM and speak about Jesus so that the other students who were not saved would be encouraged to give their lives to Christ. The meeting started. They sang a few songs and waited for me to walk to the front. I was somehow aware that the atmosphere was pregnant with the presence of God, and I felt terribly guilty about my lies. I had no peace and remained convicted and disturbed throughout the service. Immediately after the meeting, I went to her to ask for forgiveness. She challenged me to give my life to Christ and then led me in a prayer of commitment, and the Lord received me into his kingdom.

A few weeks after this happy experience, I attended an evangelistic campaign in our community where I saw the film *Burning Hell*. I once again surrendered my life to the Lord, and later that evening, while I was lying on my bed, beautiful words bubbled out of my mouth. It was wonderful! I kept saying "thank you Jesus" (in English, much to my amazement). There was an indescribable joy bubbling up inside me. It seemed as if I automatically fell in love with the Bible, and within a week I had finished reading the whole New Testament. I was not conscious of any change in my racial or political awareness at that point — I guess it was because of my conditioning as a black person under apartheid.

LEARNING TO WORK WITH GOD — AND DUALISM

After I became a Christian, a friend of mine encouraged and challenged me to share the gospel in my school. I liked the idea of doing evangelism in my school, and the conviction to preach grew in me. I asked the principal to allow me to share the gospel with the entire school in morning assembly. It was 1985, and I was in Grade 10 (Standard 8). The principal responded with enthusiasm and asked me to address the assembly the next morning. He wanted me to do it in English! I had never done it before, especially in English, and I had never seen anyone else doing it in English. That night I could not sleep. I was very anxious to say the least. When I woke up, I decided to ask my teacher to inform the principal that I would no longer be addressing the students that morning. He accepted my withdrawal, but my teacher was very disappointed with me. I could not forgive myself for this failure, for such cowardice at the last minute. I vowed that I would never withdraw again, that I would obey this inner urge to preach, thinking that once I had preached, it would all be over.

The urge to preach pressed within me, so I finally obeyed. I told my teacher I was ready to address the school assembly. The day arrived and I was trembling and shaking. I had not told my friends, and the first they heard of it was when the principal announced that Mr Ntlhola would "now conduct our assembly". I felt as if my knees were knocking with fear, and because I was wearing my short school trousers, I thought everyone was staring at my dancing knees! I preached as best I knew how, in my broken and incomprehensible English. As I was preaching, I became aware that a certain phenomenon had taken place. It was no longer me speaking, but the Holy Sprit was working with me. Before I realised it, my talk was finished. I asked the students to close their eyes and I prayed, and then slipped into the crowd as we sang. The principal thanked me and my fellow students came to congratulate me. It made me feel good inside. I was relieved and thought that it was all over but, to my surprise, the urge to preach came back again, even stronger! I knew it was just the beginning. I knew I would preach and teach the kingdom of God for the rest of my life. My principal asked me to lead the devotional time in our morning assemblies during 1985, and these were interspersed with preaching in other high schools, as invitations came for me to address them.

During that same year, my friends and I decided to preach the gospel in an old-age home in Katlehong, on the eastern edge of Johannesburg. After preaching, I was told by one of our team that we were going to pray for the sick. I struggled with the idea of praying for the sick. In fact, I was very skeptical about divine healing.

My response was, "Go ahead and pray for them, I have done my part in preaching." They went ahead and prayed, but it was not long before I was surprised and embarrassed by a woman who worked at the old-age home. She came to tell me that, seeing I was just standing around, I should come and pray for an old ailing granny whose condition was the worst in the entire home!

When I reached her room, I saw that she was desperately ill, lying in her bed, tucked up in her blanket. She was 88 years old. I remembered what Jesus did when he prayed for some people: he asked bystanders to leave the room while he did the miracle. So I also did that — the lady who brought me there politely left the room. Then I stretched out my hand to touch the granny and I prayed. I had just started praying when she interrupted me with, "Mtanam be ngiga kwazi noku ..." ("My son, I didn't even know how to ..."), and she lifted up her arms. She had not been able to lift any of her limbs, and now she was lifting her arms and legs in the air! She pointed to her sandals, and when I reached for them, I was shaking, because it was the first time I had ever seen such a miracle. She got up from her bed without my help. I was overcome with excitement and shame. Why shame? Because I did not trust Jesus to heal. Before I knew it, she was leading me to the hall where her friends were. They (including my friends) saw her and were shocked into silence for a few seconds, and then they exploded with joy. Almost everyone was expecting her to die soon. Now she was walking by herself. You can imagine how I was feeling, walking tall and thinking, "You see, I am the man of God!" I have not forgotten that day, and never will. This was the first time I ex-perenced working with God in healing — and it happened through my teenage hands!

At this time I had become part of group of young people who were linked to a white Full Gospel church, a Pentecostal denomination. Their pastor, Cedric Coates, preached at our school and invited us to come to their church. Later we became members, but we were not aware of the political implications of a few young black people joining a white church on the edge of town. We were the first blacks to join that church, and apparently some white people left as a result. Our group went around preaching the gospel, trying to do the works of Jesus. We would fast and pray and then use loudhailers to preach on the streets and go from house to house to pray for the sick. This is how we learnt to work with God, but I began to realise that it was dualistic. We just wanted to get souls saved and bodies healed, and we avoided any involvement in what we thought was "politics". We thought that any involvement in "the struggle for justice" was the devil's way of distracting us from God and his work.

I became more aware of this dualism in me when our group met with a few *ama-xabane* at their request (comrades — they were the radical young blacks who were fully involved in the war of liberation). They challenged us as to why we were fraternising with whites. Did we not see what was happening in the country? Did we not see how whites hated the blacks and were killing them? Were we colla-borators (*impimpis*) with the system of apartheid? We all knew what the comrades did to collaborators: they necklaced them by putting an old car tyre around their necks, and filling the tube with petrol. Then they set it alight, and watched and danced as the victim burnt to death. Some of my friends left the meeting because they thought it was too political and they feared for their lives. Somehow I knew that the comrades were right — in principle I agreed with their concerns for our country, although I did not agree with their methods. I found that I could not answer their questions from my Christian standpoint. It became clear to me that I was dualistic in my theology, in my faith and life. Every day in the black town-ships, and in reading the newspapers, I saw the atrocities and brutal oppression of apartheid. Our country was going up in flames and I could not respond to it in terms of my Christian faith, thinking it was "all just politics".

This was late in 1985, after the state of emergency had been declared which remained in force until 1989. SA had effectively become a police state. The black township schools were severely disrupted through protest marches and school boycotts, and this continued for the next three years. The slogan, "Liberation first, education later" was shouted in every township in SA. Thousands of young black people poured out onto the streets and followed the comrades in toyi-toyiing (protest dancing) against the repression of the white regime. They were tear-gassed, beaten up and shot at. Some were killed, many were wounded, and others were detained for lengthy periods without trial. Many disappeared and were never heard of again — some at the hands of the SA police, while others crossed the borders of our country to join the liberation fighters. Those years were very difficult, to say the least. I remember writing my schools exams in 1986, when sud-denly the *amaxabane* came into the hall. They took all the answer sheets from the students and burnt them in front of the principal and his staff. We all ran away. I was so fearful that I thought the last days had come.

I continued to preach at schools when classes resumed. Morris Isaacson High School was one such school. It was well known because it played a primary role in initiating the 1976 protests in Soweto. They had protested against the apartheid regime's policy to impose Afrikaans as the medium of education in the black townships. To take a people's indigenous language from them, by forcing them to learn "die baas se taal" (the master's language), is to emasculate them. The protests began on 16 June 1976, leading to the killing, maiming and imprisonment of many students by the apartheid regime. Soweto became well known because of these protests — a symbol of resistance against apartheid. Subsequently, 16 June has become Youth Day, a national holiday.

With this legacy of political activism and bravery, Morris Isaacson's student body asked me to address the school on the role of religion in the struggle against apartheid in 1987. Such meetings were frequently broken up by the SA police, and the speakers and leaders would be detained and tortured. I gathered enough courage to make this address, despite my many misgivings. I saw that the students were very radical and were divided against their teachers. The tension on the campus was tangible. I felt terribly nervous and fearful and just wanted to preach and leave. God protected us that day from repressive police brutality. I heard later that the students called my preaching "progressive Christianity" (despite my dual-istic beliefs), as opposed to the traditional Christianity in the township churches, which they had largely abandoned as irrelevant to their context and struggle for justice. Despite their praise of my sermon, and although the preparation for my talk made me rethink a number of things, I was still struggling to harmonise my faith and my life context as a black man in SA.

 ## BIBLE COLLEGE AND JUSTICE INVOLVEMENT

Because our schooling became so disrupted, I attended the Full Gospel Bible College in Soweto (1987–1988), and completed my school education by correspon-dence. The Bible College consisted of black students with one white lecturer, who taught us New Testament — the other lecturers were black. The college was poorly equipped: there was no electricity, one communal bathroom, toilets with no doors, and the library could hardly be called a library. In winter we divided into pairs to take turns lighting the fire every morning to heat up the water drum for our morning ablutions. We slept in a shed like cattle, knowing that our white sister college in Pretoria had all the facilities necessary for a good training institution. As young black Bible students, we were content with the humble surroundings and inferior facilities, as we considered it a privilege to learn. On two occasions the white lecturer took photos of each of the students in the class in order to raise funds for us from overseas sponsors. We never heard anything about the donations that were raised, and we felt it confirmed our suspicion of corruption, a stereotype of whites that we already had in our minds. We were often on the receiving end of racist attitudes as well. Because of the dualism in believing that

God and politics did not mix, I did not make an issue of these things. Despite this, I enjoyed the white lecturer's teachings, especially when he taught on the Book of Romans.

This spiritual naivety was shattered towards the end of our studies in September 1988 when our missology lecturer was fired. The students were told that he was expelled because he was teaching us liberation theology. Many of us had heard of liberation theology, but we did not know what it was, and we did not hear it from the expelled lecturer. We sensed that the white Bible College authorities did not want us to know this theology, and took it upon ourselves to read up about it. In fact, during apartheid we learnt that everything the whites did not want us to know was what we really needed to know, and we began to investigate what was banned. I went through a period of a few weeks where I read any political litera-ture — which the government called "subversive"— that I could get hold of.

This is how I came to realise that, up to this point, I had been theologically and politically naive about many things due to the dualistic gospel I had been taught. My church had strongly discouraged political activism, and I went along with it because I had developed a perception that everything had become politicised and worldly. The dichotomy between my faith and my life context had made me into a kind of calm schizophrenic: I was politically aware (or so I believed) and very angry toward whites, but I did not allow myself to feel or express any anger or to get involved in "politics", because I wanted to be a "good" Christian. My faith made me suppress my inner feelings and deny my outer context. A teacher in one of the schools where I conducted morning assembly once said to me, "Why don't you stop this preaching and religion of yours? It does not help one bit — our country is burning." I knew he was telling the truth, and I knew that "Christianity" was making no difference to the crisis in the country. Despite this teacher's comment, I continued to preach my gospel of personal and private salvation, without refer-ence to our polarised and painful context. I was miserable and confused, walking the dusty streets of Soweto with a passionate zeal to serve the Lord, but not knowing how to respond to the intensifying violent repression and suffering all around me. The expulsion of my lecturer was a catalyst that made me pursue more seriously the journey of integrating my faith and life. I became aware that I must "do theology" (as the liberationists called it) by getting involved in the struggle for justice, and not just study theology — especially the kind of dualist theology that I had been fed.

The expulsion of the lecturer, and the consequent questions and protests from the students, led to an official visit from the white Afrikaner president of our denomination. He came to address the student body about two months before our graduation. When he arrived, he and his entourage did not talk to us as a group, but met with each of us alone. We were all told to concentrate on theology and not politics, and were given a document to sign if we wanted to continue studying on that basis. If not, we would be expelled immediately. I could not sign the document in all good conscience, and was expelled together with a number of other students. (My mother, who had bought a new suit for me to wear at my graduation, was bitterly disappointed in me.) The situation became very tense and the authorities called for police protection. We feared the worst. A message was sent to us that a black Christian leader, Moss Ntlha, whom we trusted, was waiting for us outside the gates of the college campus. Some young comrades were also there, and they immediately took us to a safe house in Zone 1, Pimville. I remained in hiding for a month or so, without my parents' knowledge. We played safe as we did not know whether the police would detain us. Despite my mother's worries, I did not go back home because I feared that I would be followed by *impimpis* (police informers), and then the police would know where my family lived, and could harass them. I did not want to put my family in danger.

Shortly before we were expelled from Bible College, Bishop Desmond Tutu issued the highly controversial call for international disinvestment, sanctions and boycotts against the apartheid regime. Tutu said it was the last urgent non-violent intervention that he could think of as a Christian, in order to bring apartheid to an end. He said, "Hit the white man where it hurts most — his pocket — and then he will listen to you!" As students, we understood exactly what Tutu meant, and supported his stance for justice. Our denomination released a press statement opposing Tutu's call. It became clear to us that our white church leaders were right-wing political supporters of the apartheid government. In fact, our denominational president called all our church leaders to a meeting to be addressed by the then Foreign Minister, Mr Pik Botha, to explain the government's anti-sanctions viewpoint. As a student body we rejected this stance and released our own statement disassociating ourselves from the position of our church. We did this at a press conference that was held at the office of the well-known anti-apartheid Afrikaner cleric, Beyers Naudé. In retrospect, we were sure that this action contributed to our expulsion from the college.

CONNECTING WITH VINEYARD
AND JOHWETO

There was another influence that became decisive in bridging the gap between my faith and my context, that helped to bring me to wholeness. It also began my journey of reconciliation. This influence came into my life at the time of the college upheavals, late in 1988. I had been praying that God would lead me to a new spiritual home. A friend invited me to attend a church conference in Johannesburg and, in retrospect, I am convinced that God's answer came through that invitation.

It was fascinating to see how the main speaker was introduced, or not introduced, as was the case. He had come from America with a large team. I was skeptical of American preachers coming to SA and telling us what to do about our situation. I had also become accustomed to the glowing introductions of "the man of God" by local leaders who would recite the endless credentials of such preachers with extravagant praise. This was different. This fat guy got up at the beginning of the meeting and said, "Hi, my name is John Wimber. Let's stand and worship God." He went to the keyboard and led us in worship in a natural and free manner. After that he spoke casually about the goodness of God. I was amazed because I noticed that he had no preacher's voice, and he wore jeans and an ordinary shirt — I thought all real "men of God" wore suits. John was simple, honest, real and warm. I found the whole experience so liberating, from the dress to the style of worship and manner of preaching. As the conference unfolded, I learnt that I was meeting the Vineyard Christian Fellowship.

They announced that after the conference there would mini-conferences around the country, and one of them would be held in Soweto. I was excited and wanted to attend, even more so when I heard that we would get free books! I invited some fellow students from my Bible College to accompany me, and we quickly realised that we were overdressed in our suits. I heard about Johweto, the Vineyard church in Soweto, at these meetings. It so happened that Johweto met not too far from our college. I immediately went along to Johweto and my surprises continued. It was a black and white church in Soweto. I could not believe it! They did the same things that they did at the Vineyard conference, and they dressed the same way too — I eventually surrendered my church uniform (my suit) and dressed in my normal everyday clothes. I enjoyed the songs and intimate worship, the sense of reality and warmth of relationship, and the honest teaching and discussions that followed.

What impressed me most was how relevant this church was to my context in Soweto. They seemed to be taking the crisis in our country seriously — just seeing the whites in the meeting was a shock. I was told that they came every Sunday, and even during the week to small groups that met in various homes in Soweto. I knew how dangerous that was for them, and wondered why they would do that. There was this tall white guy teaching through the Sermon on the Mount. His explanations from the Bible were not dualistic in any way, they addressed my spiritual, emotional and political situation all in one. I thought: What more could I want? Here was a body of Christians that seemed to have the element missing in most of the churches that I had been exposed to. They were simple and straight-forward, and they brought the wholistic[2] reality of the kingdom of God to the people. It was very relevant and liberating for me, a young black man in Soweto, oppressively wrapped in the wings of apartheid. Although I liked the church very much, I was suspicious of the white members. I found it hard to believe that they were in Soweto to seek reconciliation and justice — I was uncertain of their real motives.

That first experience of Johweto came at the time when I knew that I would probably be expelled from the Bible College. Seeking strength and direction for my life, I returned to Johweto the following week. I arrived late during Alexander's teaching — I found out that he was the tall guy — and I saw a white woman sitting on the table. She was wearing a pair of shorts and a T-shirt, and she interupted Alexander while he was teaching. Most African women are very con-servative in their dress, especially when they attend church — they wear their "Sunday best" as I used to. I was amazed at the white women in Johweto, with their sense of freedom to be themselves and to engage boldly in whatever was happening. This woman challenged some explanation from the Sermon on the Mount that Alexander was giving. This dialogue and discussion seemed to happen often, sometimes during the teaching, but mostly after it was over. At some point in the debate they would stop and pray for each other, and for the nation, often with tears and cries to God for help. At times it seemed like chaos, but I would say a "holy chaos". For me this was Johweto Vineyard. I liked it. They were addressing the issues that I, and most black people, were going through every day of our lives in our divided country.

Although I enjoyed the meetings, I was still not sure of the whites. I used to sit near the door so that I could leave straight after the meeting. Alexander and his colleague, Paul Mpete, learnt about my expulsion from Bible College through the local newspaper. They got hold of me before I could slip out and asked if they could help me in any way. I said that I would come back to them with an answer once I had considered it, but I disappeared from the church for a month or two because I was still suspicious. (It was also during the time that I was in hiding after my expulsion from Bible College.) I eventually returned and they sat down with me and listened to my whole story, and then they offered to help sponsor me to do further theological studies. What struck me was the fact that they not only listened to me with compassion, and they not only prayed for me in my fear, anger and rejection from the Bible College, but they did something practical and tangible to help me. They did all this without me being a member of their group! I embarked on my journey of reconciliation with the Johweto Vineyard.

MY JOURNEY WITH JOHWETO

Soon after I began to attend Johweto, two policemen from the Special Branch (National Intelligence) interrupted our meeting and asked what we were doing. There were about forty to fifty of us in the meeting, roughly half white and half black, and we were sitting in discussion groups. Everyone stopped talking and looked up fearfully at these two big white guys at the door. I was intimidated by them, but Alexander immediately stood up and said that if they wanted to speak to us, they should bear in mind that we were having a church meeting, and that they should be polite. Then he offered to speak to the two of them outside so that the meeting could continue uninterrupted. I loved that. I remember the incident clearly because I had just turned twenty-one, and I felt so good that a white man stood up to the white oppressors to protect us. Alexander and the policemen went outside and I was worried that we were going to be arrested, but when Alexander came back in he reassured us that everything would be okay. Later, a similar incident happened with different Special Branch policemen, and it was handled in the same way.

This changed my view of whites. It helped me to trust and to open myself up to reconciliation with them. However, every now and then my deep-seated anger and prejudice would come out. We were engaged in a serious debate on the issues involved in justice and reconciliation when John Gosling, one of the white guys who came with Alexander into Soweto from the beginning, said something that made me explode. I reacted to him angrily saying, "You don't belong here because you are from Europe." John did not become emotional. He calmly and very politely said, "No, I am not from Europe. I was born here, and my parents too. I am a South African." There and then I knew that I was a racist. I felt guilty and kept quiet.

Both Alexander and Paul had said that it is only when you are in a different group or situation that you realise whether you are a racist or not. It made sense, because through Johweto I began to see myself in a new way. The real Trevor was coming out. I had to face all my dark thoughts and angry feelings about white and wealthy people. I know many black people in this country who think that they are not racist, merely because they had nothing to do with the creation of apartheid. They do not realise how deeply apartheid has conditioned all of us — whites and blacks. That day in Johweto made me realise how racist and reactionary I had become. Reactionary racism is as evil as the original racism, the racism of the oppressor. I realised that you eventually become what you hate. For this reason I value a mixed environment, where black and white, rich and poor can expose each other's prejudices and sin, where they can forgive each other and help each other to be healed. That is why I do not want to pastor, if at all possible, a church that only has black people. Currently our Zone 3 Vineyard congregation in Soweto has two white families — they may not realise it, but they make an enormous difference to our fellowship.

As far as I know few people, if any, left Johweto because of the heated discussions between blacks and whites. Johweto helped us to become real and honest with each other and with ourselves. We found our common identity in Jesus who helped us to reconcile. In talking about my journey of reconciliation with my white brothers and sisters from Johannesburg, I am not saying that I am no longer a racist. I see myself as a person who is still recovering from racism and being healed from its wounds. The only place where I think I will be free from racism, both in me and around me, is in heaven. I believe that applies to all of us. Until then, we must pursue the journey of healing from racism, and reconcile with one another as black and white, rich and poor.

There were many other confrontations, and moments of reconciliation and healing, in my relationship with the whites in Johweto. We used to meet on Saturdays at the Johweto Kehillah farm to grow vegetables and build houses and other structures. It was truly liberating for me to see a white person getting his hands dirty, working side by side with blacks. I had never seen this before — all I had seen up to that point was blacks working with spades and tools while the white man stood over them, shouting at them. (I realise now that it is only when I went to Sweden in the 1990s that I saw whites working on the streets, getting their hands dirty.) Through working together on the farm, we were forced to talk, to relate, to make decisions together, to share our experiences about life on opposite sides of the divides in our country. We saw each other tired and irritable, happy and upset, hungry and satisfied. I was conscious that none of us was inferior to the other;

we were all equal. My white friends generally treated me as an adult. They did not talk down to me or parent me. This was reconciliation. There was a sense of justice being restored to me. Slowly I was aware of a confidence that was growing in me; this "white phobia" and "black inferiority" was losing its power over me, and I was becoming free to look the whites in the eye and to challenge them if I felt I had to.

I used to challenge Alexander if I believed he was wrong, both in terms of what he would say, and sometimes in terms of his attitude. This was very good for me because I realised that he had his own problems and was on a journey of healing, just as I was on my journey of healing from inferiority and anger. This growing confidence spilt over into my other interactions with whites who were not in Johweto, and it sometimes led to confrontations. I attended a pastors' meeting in Johannesburg where black and white leaders were to discuss the socio-political issues. The black pastors did not turn up, and I took it upon myself to represent them by presenting the black perspective on things. It became confrontational and I assertively challenged their viewpoints. Costa Mitchell, my fellow Vineyard pastor from Johannesburg, was in the meeting. Afterwards I wondered if he had taken what I had said personally, and if I had offended him. Alexander had not been at the meeting, so I asked him what I should do. He said I should speak to Costa directly and seek reconciliation if there was any offence. I did this, and Costa said he had felt attacked, and we resolved it together. This is how I learnt to reconcile and be healed from my inferiority and my prejudices.

After a car accident in 1993, Alexander was in bed for six weeks. We were forced to have our Johweto leadership meetings in his bedroom. I had to pinch myself because here was this black person, previously called a "Kaffir" in apartheid SA (a derogatory racial description), but now, through the gospel of Jesus Christ, he was called into "die baas se kamer" (the master's bedroom). I went into the bedroom without all my old discomforts and fears as a black man, realising that things were different now. Alexander was my friend, and I saw that church was no longer only a meeting on Sundays in a church building, but it was every day and everywhere, whenever and wherever we needed to meet. On one such occasion we were talking about certain important issues, and I remember Gill, Alexander's wife, coming into the bedroom to say some things to us. I said to Alexander that I was not happy about how his wife walked in and out, and if she wanted to sit in on the meeting, then she should stay and contribute. Then I felt bad about what I had said, but Alexander spoke to Gill when she came back into the room. I felt that he was treating me as an equal, even in front of his wife, and in their own bedroom! Gill joined us and we had a good meeting. I realised that the issue of reconciliation did not only apply to black and white, but also to male and female, and even to husband and wife. Back then I was single, but now that I am married, I fully understand the need for daily forgiveness and reconciliation between spouses!

I was appointed the Senior Pastor of Johweto at the end of 1994. Alexander stepped aside with the agreement of the leadership team, and handed the reins over to me. He was to be my assistant and support me in my leadership role. I found this difficult and humbling, but I knew it was right. What was even more difficult was my first sermon as the Senior Pastor. At the last minute I put aside what I had prepared, because I was struggling with the fact that some of the members were white and much more educated than I was, and most of them were older than me. I decided to talk about myself instead. I disclosed my vulnerability and told them how much I respected them, and that I wanted them to continue to initiate and lead things in Johweto. I continued in this vein and thought that I was saying some profound things. Then one educated white lady raised her hand and interrupted me, and said, "Trevor, please allow us to follow." What I thought was so profound went up in smoke. On the other hand, there were one or two whites who struggled with my leadership and I wondered if it was because I was black or too young. I came to realise that reconciliation is not a one-off experience, but a journey that continues with ever deeper challenges of transformation. On reflection, it was not all rosy and easy, because one or two whites did not treat me properly and we did not reconcile at the deeper levels when it was required.

I had to learn to lead and pastor with confidence, to preach to a mixed group, white and black, educated and uneducated, rich and poor, men and women, old and young, Sunday after Sunday. It was very good for me and I grew. We all worked well together. Towards the end of 1995 we decided that Johweto had run its course and that we needed to bury it. I felt that the shifts in the nation had changed things significantly, and I had a new sense of vision for a community church, to be based in Zone 3, Pimville. I had been challenged by the vision of Bob Lupton, who is working to create community-based churches to uplift poor urban areas through a process of "reneighboring".[3] With the blessing and support of Costa and Alexander, I buried Johweto and started Zone 3 Vineyard. In that same year I fell in love with Nelisiwe, and we were married in the presence of all our Johweto friends.

IN CONCLUSION: SOME REFLECTIONS ON RECONCILIATION IN SOUTH AFRICA

I have become very aware of the fact that reconciliation with God and others does not only apply to blacks and whites, but also to the poor and marginalised, and to the sick and dying. Before my younger sister died of HIV/AIDS in 2001, I had the privilege of helping to care for her, and I conducted her funeral. It is true that sometimes, only when you are personally touched by such suffering and horror, your heart is softened and you become compassionate towards such people. This happened to me. After my sister's death, I motivated our church to a community-based vision of reconciliation and healing for HIV/AIDS sufferers. This has led to a ministry called Emthonjeni (Zulu for Fountains of Life), which operates in Soweto and from the old Johweto Kehillah. We must never forget that reconciliation is a wholistic ministry, not just between God and human beings, and not just between racial groups, but between God and all sorts of people in all kinds of need. Having said that, let me reflect on the great need for reconciliation between black and white and other racial groups in SA.

One Sunday evening in 1999, my daughter Thando and I were sitting side by side, watching a television report on the Truth and Reconciliation Commission presented by Max du Preez. I have great respect for this man because, as an Afrikaner, he is a true African — he has reconciled with blacks and constructively engages the changed context in SA. I saw that Thando was glued to the television screen. Watching what happened to people through the apartheid atrocities stirs up the emotions. It struck me again that night that all this really happened, and we lived through it all. Some of the stories that night were particularly heart-rending, with horrific, repugnant pictures of atrocities. They brought back the old feelings of anger and revenge in me. As black people watching that programme, we knew that we were indeed *be se hlukumezwa* by the previous regime (Zulu for how one feels when one has been wronged — or as the liberation theologians call it, "being sinned against").

I think that was the night when my daughter's racial innocence was lost, when her pristine feelings were trespassed. She was eight years old at that time. As we watched the programme we were quiet and the atmosphere in our lounge was thick with tension. Then, without a hint, she just exploded, "If I had been a child in those days, would those people (the Security Police) have killed me too?" This painful question, filled with raw emotion, took my mind to what Mr JP Opperman (a former apartheid intelligence officer and commander of a hit squad) said, "Depending on the circumstances, I do not have a problem with killing children."[4]

Opperman's comment was certainly not about white kids. My daughter understood, for the first time, the horror of the apartheid system that she had missed by being born the year after Nelson Mandela was released from prison. Thando was really mad and exploded, "We must kill the white people." I allowed her to vent her anger, and then I said, "Imagine killing all your white friends and their parents." She answered, "Of course not those whites, just the bad ones." Then I challenged her, "How will we know good whites from bad whites?" and I tried to explain what had happened and how things had changed in SA. Then she understood — we must forgive all people.

If parents are not genuinely reconciled with their former enemies, their children will be infected with their parents' racist venom. I do not wish my children to hate anyone — and certainly not a particular racial group — because of any unresolved pain and prejudice in me, or in anyone else. On the contrary, I would want my children to grow up loving others, loving people of different races, because of the example of their parents and other people. There is no doubt that we are all shaped by those whom we love and by those whom we hate, by those who love us and by those who refuse to love us. Thando was raised in a racially mixed church and goes to a racially mixed school. She is being shaped and is growing up differently to my generation, and will hopefully be free from racism.

Blacks need to love whites, and whites need to love blacks — this of course includes coloureds and Indians and all other groups in SA. To love means to forgive and to reconcile with each other by finding ways of living peacefully and supportively together. There is a long history, a long legacy to make up for, from the time that whites first arrived at the tip of Africa a few centuries ago to the present day. I believe it can be done because many of us have to reconcile with others on a daily basis: with our loved ones and relatives, our friends, our work colleagues, and even with our neighbours. Surely we can reconcile with each other as various racial groups in SA?

Reconciliation is all about treating people properly. It is never easy. It requires heart and faith. Reconciliation is not an intellectual or academic exercise, it is an exercise in genuine love. It is about emotional and spiritual encounter. Authentic reconciliation is not, and can never be, emotionally neutral and spiritually detached. It often exposes deep hurt and brings about great cathartic release. You can never control reconciliation in a clinical and intellectual manner, because it is a process of people finding each other in the mystery of forgiveness and relationship. Reconciliation logically implies that you allow your heart to be broken and then healed, or you can harden your heart and further multiply (your) hatred and resentment. What applies in daily familial and other relationships, also applies to the apparent complexities and enormity of politics and group reconciliation.

Christians should set the example in this matter of reconciliation, and I am one of them, though I sometimes find that I still harbour unforgiveness and resentment. The incident that took place at our 2001 Vineyard National Conference, which Alexander referred to it in the Preface, revealed once again how sensitive I am to racial comments. I was offended and I wrote a paper of protest, but as the church of Jesus Christ, we were able to forgive and reconcile with each other through dialogue. I realise that there is a perverse satisfaction in me when I get angry and refuse to forgive. Jesus does not allow us that option, because it poisons us. Relationships in Christ make forgiveness and reconciliation easier and more meaningful, and this applies not only between blacks and whites, but between my fellow blacks as well. However, reconciliation does not necessarily depend on relationship, it can be equally genuine if we put our faith in God and seek to reconcile with whoever. To illustrate this, I want to share a hopeful story from an incident that happened in 2003, when I preached at our sister church in Johannesburg, Valley Vineyard. The congregation is about eighty per cent white.

After I had preached, a white woman came up to me and began to cry. She told me that the moment I stood up to preach, the Lord convicted her to share her heart with me. A few weeks before that service, she and her daughter were hijacked at gunpoint and her car was taken from her. She paused and sobbed. I thought it must have been terrible for her. She gathered enough courage to tell me that since that event took place, she was hateful and fearful of black men. She then looked me in the eye and asked, "Would you be happy if I saw you as one of the black guys who hijacked me?" I did not know how to respond and coldly said, "Yes." Then she wept bitterly and eventually said, "Please forgive me for hating you black men." I felt like a bolt of lightning had nailed me to the invisible wall of reconciliation. She waited for my response as if her very next breathe depended on it. I said, "I forgive you." She embraced me for a long time, and then looked at me. This time her face was glowing. I think she deserves a reconciliation award! That experience has challenged and changed me. It gives me hope for our nation. If we do this with each other, we will help each other to forgive and heal the wounds we bear.

Reconciliation is not a game; it is very serious. Our lives depend on it in SA. It can be messy, raw, rough and painful, but it is liberating. Genuine reconciliation is not cheap; it cost God his Son. As we look at Jesus, we see our own sin and mess. We see our guilt and shame, and we own it. We see in our own hearts the hurt and damage that we have caused, both as blacks and whites, or whoever we are. Our hope is in Jesus who forgives us, so that we can forgive one another, and seek forgiveness from one another.

Our reconciliation in SA is still young, fresh and fragile, and failure to maintain and cultivate it will undermine our well-being, personally and nationally. We will begin to falter socially, politically and economically if we do not pursue recon-ciliation. Until blacks genuinely forgive from their hearts, and until whites take on a sorrow that leads to genuine repentance, we can forget about growing an authentic reconciliation, and becoming a blessed and prosperous nation. I am hopeful for our country, and for our churches, because of my own experience in the journey of Johweto. More than a handful of whites reached out to love me across the social and racial barriers. They reached out to love my family and friends, and they have made all the difference.

O se boloke, setjhaba sa heso!

Lord, save our nation!

NOTES

1. This is not a direct quote, but a paraphrase of John Powell's teaching about self-disclosure 1967 and 1969. The "Caution ..." sign is also from John Powell.

2. I (Alexander) spell wholistic with a "w" so as to distinguish it from the New Age usage of "holistic".

3. Lupton 1993.

4. Quoted in Asmal, 1996, p. 74.

PART II

EXPLAINING OUR POSITION

CHAPTER 3

INTRODUCTION
AND DEFINITIONS

For he is our Shalom; in his flesh he has made both groups into one by breaking down the dividing wall, that is, the hostility between us. Thus he destroyed the enmity occasioned by the law with its commandments and ordinances. His purpose was to create in himself **one new humanity** *out of the two, establishing Shalom, reconciling both of them to God in one body through the cross, by which he put to death their hostility.*

Paul's vision statement in Eph 2:14–16 RAP

After this I looked and there was a great multitude that no one could count, **from every nation, from all tribes and peoples and languages,** *standing before the throne and before the Lamb, robed in white, with palm branches in their hands. They cried in a loud voice, saying: "Salvation belongs to our God, who is seated on the throne, and to the Lamb ... because you were slaughtered and by your blood you ransomed for God saints* **from every tribe and language and people and nation;** *you made them to be a kingdom and priests serving our God, and they will reign on earth."*

John's vision statement in Rev 7:9–10; 5:9–10 NRSV

IS RACISM, RECONCILIATION AND TRANSFORMATION AN ISSUE?

It was in Oslo, 10 December 1964, that the youngest person ever received the Nobel Peace Prize. He was thirty-five and his name was Martin Luther King Jr. He received it with dignity and simplicity, in contrast to his great gift of oratory. In 1965 the racial segregation laws in the USA began to be abolished. Blacks received the vote. Martin Luther King Jr., through the civil rights movement, helped to bring about justice for African Americans. He was motivated by strong Christian convictions of non-violent resistance as a means to establishing justice for all. And he paid a heavy price for his faith; he died violently at the hands of a right-wing assassin. The legislation changed and blacks in America were free, "Free at last, thank God, we are free." But what of the whites? Did their hearts change? And to what extent did the discriminatory social structures really change?

In the early morning hours of Sunday, 3 March 1991, the Los Angeles police were chasing a suspected drunken driver. When they stopped him and got him out of his car, history-making events unfolded. An observer caught what happened next on a home video. The police repeatedly beat the man with their batons until he lay sprawled on the ground and then they kicked him viciously. He had to receive extensive treatment in hospital to recover from his injuries. He was a black man and they were white cops. His name was Rodney King. When the story broke and the video was shown on national television, most of the cities in America, let alone Los Angeles, went up in flames. Blacks and Hispanics protested and rioted against the perceived racism of white America. It evidently unleashed a fireball of anger and resentment that had been building for a long time.[1]

It took 26 years and a second King to expose the fact that although the law books had changed, the hearts and minds of Americans had not changed. Racism and anger, hatred and violence were all still there, just below the surface — as Jim Wallis from Sojourners Community in Washington, DC. has said: "Racism is America's original sin."[2] All it took was the right time, the right person and the right place for it to explode. In SA, the racial laws were all abolished in the early to mid-1990s, but have our hearts and minds changed? Are the discriminatory social structures really changing? Will we too have to face the flames of reality? How long will it take before that happens?

This is a challenge and we need to face it

Is racism, reconciliation and transformation an issue? We can say an overwhelming yes! It affects us all, in SA and in almost every other nation on the planet. But whether we realise this, or whether we see it as an issue or not, is debatable. Some would argue that it simply is not an issue, while others would ask why blow it up into something when it is actually a small thing. At worst, let sleeping dogs lie, and at best, there are simply no dogs! However, if it is seen as a challenge, it is often seen as a political concern for the government to take care of. The attitude is, "It will not disrupt my life." The poor and oppressed do not have the luxury or "space" to think and live like this. How can they keep this disruption at bay when they are affected by the legacy of racism in SA every day?

But the space that the privileged and affluent have is often closed down by social reality when tensions and upheavals touch our lives, as with the Rodney King riots. We know this from our common experience in SA. Only then do we begin to think and talk of justice and reconciliation. And sometimes it is too late. Or alternatively, we move to another locality or country where we can have "peace" — if we are fortunate enough to have the means to relocate. One realises that it is all a matter of power and perception, a matter of degrees of manageability, mostly determined by our position in life and the space we have in terms of our comfort zones.

Racism and the need for reconciliation and transformation was "in your face" in SA in the 1980s and 1990s. We had to face it and deal with it because it became a matter of survival, of life and death. While some faced it, others buried their heads in the sands of apathy, and others created places of safety to withdraw into in their homes and among their friends. Others immigrated. No matter how we respond, the challenge remains the same. We simply have to engage in the changed reality around us in SA by seeking a meaningful way forward for the good of all. This has many implications.

Racism has cut deep into the heart of our nation. We cannot afford to "dress the wound lightly."[3] I fear that this superficial attempt at reconciliation has already happened, leading many to believe that "we are now reconciled, so what's the problem?" Reconciliation was emphasised and worked on through the TRC in the mid to late 1990s. It has been the government policy since 1994. Many have felt that "that" is now over — "praise the Lord"! But it is becoming clear that "it" remains a pressing issue requiring our attention. The wound of racism will continue to fester and hurt all of us, in both visible and invisible ways, until we cut deep enough to remove the cancer of hatred and past hurts, and cleanse and heal it with costly reconciliation and ongoing national transformation.

The church must lead the way in this matter. Every one of us must personally take the initiative and play our part. The incident at the Vineyard conference that I referred to in the Preface shows that this is an issue that Vineyard must address. Unless we do, the unresolved racial hurts and perceptions in our Vineyard constituency, and in our country, will continually bedevil and derail us as black and white Africans — let alone as Christians!

We firmly believe that racism, and the need for reconciliation and transformation, is an issue for every person in AVC SA, and for every other Christian in SA and Africa. It will be either a stumbling block or a stepping stone in our growth and development, depending on how we respond to it. History will hold us accountable, as it has with the Americans. All will look back to this time and know whether we rose to the challenge or not — including the international community and the invisible powers, who are witnesses to all that happens. God knows, we need another miracle to follow the one of 1994. We thank God that the pastors and leaders at our AVC National Conference in October 2002 unanimously committed themselves and their congregations to work through this issue of reconciliation. Let me encourage us all to be true to our commitment and work through this book and the suggested process in our congregations.

By way of introduction, we define and approach the issue of racism, reconciliation and transformation in the following manner:

- *Vision and Assumptions:* Do we have a vision for reconciliation? What is it? What are the basic assumptions underlying our approach? What are some of the key concepts and definitions that we are working with? (Chapter 3)

- *History and Legacy:* Do we, and can we, have a "reconciled" understanding of our history and its pain — both SA and AVC SA history? How did we respond to apartheid? What should we take responsibility for? (Chapter 4)

- *Guidance and Theology:* Do we have a biblical theology to guide us in our thinking and acting with regard to racism, reconciliation and transformation? (Chapters 5, 6 and 7)

- *Challenges and Process:* Is there a common understanding of the challenges we now face in AVC SA, and in our nation? What are they? And what is the way forward in terms of a practical process that can bring effective change? (Chapters 8 and 9)

THE VISION BEFORE US

The famous words from the wise old Jewish sage are as relevant as ever, and devastatingly true: "Where there is no vision, the people perish" (Prov 29:18). My RAP version is: "Where there is no clear (God-given) direction and purpose, the people throw off their restraint and discipline, and they indulge themselves".[4] Vision in this verse means a word from God, a revelation of his will for us. Vision gives a sense of direction, meaning, energy and faith. Vision lifts us beyond our lower nature with its corrupt desires. It enables us to transcend our context, to break the log jam and move beyond the status quo. We have to ask ourselves: Why is there such low motivation in our churches, and in the nation, for racial reconciliation? Why is there such evident self-indulgence in our churches and in the general populace? Do things have to get far worse in terms of racial problems and related issues before we turn from our preoccupation with self and are motivated into action? God forbid! There is a better way.

Nelson Mandela, after 27 years in prison, came out smiling with forgiveness and freedom from bitterness, and actively began to seek reconciliation. As President, he embodied and offered an inspiring vision of reconciliation to our nation. The church played a part in the transition to democracy and helped in the TRC process, but the vision seems to have faded. Is there any word from God on this matter? What is the church saying? Should it not take the lead in giving a transforming vision for SA today? It needs to do so first by example and then "if necessary, use words", as Francis of Assisi said.

The nature of vision and its biblical content

We definitely need a vision, and even a model, to motivate and guide us — one that generates passion, commitment and action. While driving into Soweto in the mid-1980s as a white man, I often thought of Martin Luther King Jr. I was inspired by his compelling vision of racial reconciliation and desegregation that impacted and mobilised America. Time and again I called to mind his words: "I have a dream ..." knowing that the whole world had heard of that dream. The power of King's words was such that I often thought of contextualising them for South Africa: "I have a dream that one day ..." and changing the names and places while maintaining the convictions and values.[5] As a Christian, he was inspired by the biblical understanding of vision, which is rooted in the Judeo-Christian heritage of the apocalyptic (the visions that unveil and reveal human history at the end of the world with the coming age of the kingdom of God. Jesus, God's Messiah, will come and sort out the mess, he will rule and reign on planet earth). This basic

Christian or biblical vision of reality, of history, is universal and all encompassing. It inspires authentic faith, hope and action, no matter how bad the prevailing context may be. This kind of hope is desperately needed in our day.[6]

When the going was tough in Soweto, I used to wonder: What am I doing here? Then the vision of God's hope used to enter my mind to reassure and motivate me. My professor said that vision is "an anticipation of the future as it ought to be". But to really fire us up it must become more specific: "The general sense of direction can be translated into particular directives for *personal action* and *public policy*".[7] And we can add *church ministry*. All three applications are crucial. We ought to lead the way as the church, because we are God's community that ought to live out the future kingdom in the present. *Vision is a picture of a preferred future, of God's future for human beings in general, and for us in particular at this time and place in history.* Vision of this nature is beyond our reach, ever pulling us forward, but at the same time it is measurable and achievable — the paradox of the kingdom.[8] As we see the possibilities of God's kingdom clearly, "the powers of the coming age" actually "come upon us" (Heb 6:5 cf. 1 Cor 10:11). It not only anticipates, but motivates and actually creates that preferred future among us. To put it contemporary terms: Vision produces passion, passion produces energy and motivation, and that's what gets the job done.

The million dollar question is: What is the kingdom vision as it affects racism, reconciliation and transformation?

Like Paul in the quotation at the beginning of the chapter, we can use the Hebraic idea of *Shalom*[9] as the key to the biblical vision. *Shalom* is much more than a Hebrew greeting. It means God's peace and prosperity in every aspect of life. Walter Brueggemann defines *Shalom* in this way: "The central vision of world history in the Bible is that all of creation is one, every creature in community with every other, living in harmony and security toward the joy and well-being of every other creature."[10] *Shalom* is essentially about wholeness, which is the blessing of God's presence. It is an all-encompassing relational reality: correct relationship with God (the source relationship), with ourselves as individuals, with each other as neighbours, and with all creation. This results in true peace, harmony, order, security, prosperity and abundance, in all dimensions of our existence on earth. This is *Shalom*. It is Paradise or Eden. Incorrect and broken relationships result in the exact opposite: exile and evil, chaos and disorder.

The biblical vision jumps from the beginning to the end and then back into the past up to the present — if that makes sense! The picture goes like this: From the beginning God made humankind as one united family, the embodiment and instrument of his rule and reign of *Shalom* over all the earth. But sin and exile from Eden (Gen 3–4), and rebellion against God at the tower of Babel (Gen 11), shattered the God-given *Shalom* and scattered people as nations far and wide. This resulted in a reign of evil, enmity, racism and death. However, God restored hope with the promise and picture of the end of the age, the coming of God's kingdom in which people from all nations, tribes and languages will be reconciled and united as his one family again. They will be with him forever and will be the perfect extension of his reign of *Shalom* over all creation through all eternity — John's vision quoted at the beginning of the chapter. Going back into the past two thousand years ago, this future vision was achieved in principle in the life, death and resurrection of Jesus (reversing sin) and in Pentecost (reversing Babel). Through these historical events people of all types are now, in the present, being reconciled into God's family, God's "one new humanity", restoring *Shalom* to the earth — Paul's picture quoted at the beginning of the chapter.

But there is a catch: this reality is not yet fully present. We still wait for the end when it comes in its fullness. The vision pulls us into the future while we try to live it out in the present, struggling against evil in all its forms. The vision calls us to participation and partnership in God's great "Re-*Shaloming*" of the earth. This wonderful enterprise will be consummated when Jesus comes and reigns on earth. Maranatha! Come quickly, Lord Jesus!

Isaiah speaks of the Messiah as the "Prince of *Shalom*" whose government of *Shalom* will "increase" and know "no end" (Is 9:6, 7). *Yeshua ha Notzri*, Jesus the Nazarene is that *Meshiach* who has already re-established the reign of *Shalom* through his life, death and resurrection. As his followers, we are the "one new humanity" through which the reign of *Shalom* increases to the ends of the earth, with no end in sight, into the eternal ages. Isaiah has many pictures of this, including the swords being beaten into ploughshares, spears into pruning hooks, the lion lying down with the lamb and the child playing with the viper (Is 2:4; 11:6–9).

The specific vision before us

But what does this general vision mean for us in particular? Every vision must have a specific and strategic application to a time and place in order for it to be effective. I propose that we hold a threefold vision before us:

 ♦ As individuals — Imagine each of us being so free that we joyfully and
   spontaneously reach out daily in repentance and reconciliation to love

people different from ourselves, especially those who were previously "on the other side". Imagine the healing, joy and harmony we could bring.

♦ As churches — Imagine growing a movement of racially and economically reconciled and integrated small groups and congregations; churches rich with cultural diversity, filled with God's life, love and joy, bubbling over into society with reconciliation and healing. The local church is the hope of the world — we *can* change our nation.[11]

♦ As a nation — Imagine experiencing a shift in the nation's psyche, a change of consciousness away from racial prejudice and practice to genuine mutual acceptance, relational harmony and economic productivity; a nation where human dignity, equal opportunity, sharing of resources and cultural celebration is the norm. We can reverse the trend of Africa and become a model in the community of nations.

The essence and "workability" of this vision comes down to the type of person you and I are becoming. The reality of this vision depends on inner transformation. It is a matter of being and becoming, and then doing, as I mentioned in the Preface. Who are you becoming? Do you want to be transformed into Christ-likeness? Transformed people help to transform their families and groups, who in turn transform society and its structures.[12] The reality is that if racial prejudice is in your heart, it will come out, no matter how politically correct (PC) or socially skilled you may be. You can only suppress your real feelings and beliefs for so long, and then they leak, overflow, or even explode. Who you are communicates louder than what you do or say. On the other hand, if we pursue the above vision with a decisive intention of the will, reinforced by a clear set of disciplines (the means and method of implementation), we will be transformed.[13] More of this later. In short, all it takes is a "critical mass of change agents"[14] for social transformation to happen. A "little leaven leavens the whole lump" as Jesus said (Matt 13:33) — unless God does it through sovereign intervention.

Do you see this vision? Do you see that it is possible? Let us work and pray together toward this end, not only for "then and there", but also for "here and now". As Jesus taught us to pray, "let your reign of love come, let your will of reconciliation be done, here and now on this piece of earth where I am, even as it is done in heaven" (Matt 6:10 RAP).

SOME BASIC ASSUMPTIONS
AND DEFINITIONS

By now you may have picked up some of my basic assumptions. You will also have become aware of key words and how they are being used. Before going into our history and a theology of reconciliation, I need to spell out briefly some of these important assumptions and concepts. You may not agree with some aspects, but the following working definitions will give us a common starting point.

Context

Although we use this word often, I have found that not many people understand its significance. Context is the surrounding reality, the parts that go before and after an event, text of writing, or whatever. Nothing happens in a vacuum. My assumption is that whatever we believe, feel or do, happens in a real life context. This is a big subject, but let me make a few comments.[5]

Some people try to live in a bubble, cut off from their context. But they fool themselves, because all that we do and say affects our context and is affected by our context. During the apartheid years most whites in Johannesburg lived as if Soweto did not exist. But they were affected by Soweto, whether they knew it or not, both in seen and unseen ways. It is always better to acknowledge our context and work with it for the good of all. Neither can we theologise as if we are in an academic or suburban vacuum. While some evangelicals try to produce neat and pure biblical theology — what we can call sterile, vacuum-packed theologies — others produce contextual theologies that at times are nothing more than an ideological mirror of their context (see the definition of ideology below). In short, we need a balanced interaction with our context for a correct perspective on things. It exposes the "lenses" through which we see things and it exposes what we are dealing with.

We need to contextualise what we believe, say and do, so that it is workable in a particular situation — David tried on Saul's armour, but it did not fit. We must be aware of and informed by our context, so that we can do what fits. All the concepts and definitions below must be contextual in order to be effective. A related idea is that we must "indigenise" the Vineyard in SA. That means Vineyard must be less of a white Western phenomenon and become more of a genuine South African movement, representing the full racial and cultural mix of our society.

On the other hand, the kingdom perspective says that there is a transcendent reality or ultimate context that also informs us. It is this kingdom frame of reference that motivates us to engage and transform our immediate context for the better. If we do not have this transcendence, we become passive victims of our social context. We can be seduced and used by a utopian, humanistic cause. Paul says: "Do not allow the system of this world to push you into its mould and way of thinking, but be transformed by the renewing of your mind" (Rom 12:2 RAP). There is a dynamic and reciprocal relationship between us and our context. We live in creative tension with it, but ultimately aim to transform it, because we are kingdom people. The world and its systems is under the control of Satan; we are part of God's kingdom that breaks into this reality to bring *Shalom*.

Church

I assume that the church is the primary, but not the only instrument of God in society. If there is a problem in society, we should see what the church is doing and where it has failed, rather than immediately blaming the government. Peter says that: "The time has come for judgement to begin with the household of God" (1 Pet 4:17 NRSV). It can be argued that, by and large, the church gets the government that it deserves. We will talk about the church-state relationship later, but the basic assumption is that the church needs to repent and get its house in order, for its own sake and for the sake of the nation. We must reconcile and work for reconciliation in society, and thereby lead the way in our country.

By church I mean both the organic reality and the organised expression of God's people. We cannot separate them, only God can. The true "church" is essentially those who are born again with God's eternal kind of life. They are found in any and every formal or informal expression of Christian church denomination and tradition, and only God really knows who is who in the zoo! I also use church to refer to the various organised and institutionalised expressions of "the church" as accepted and understood in "the Christian faith".

Prejudice

Prejudice is a mindset about particular aspects of life that is not based on factual reality. I assume that all of us suffer from prejudice in one form or another, to one extent or another. Often we are not aware of it until we are in a situation where it is exposed. Even then, there is no guarantee that we will see our prejudice. Sometimes psychological denial is so strong that no matter how extreme the exposure, we just do not see our prejudice. But this is rare.

Prejudice says: "Don't confuse me with the facts; my mind is already made up." It is a matter of prejudging or deciding before investigating the facts of the matter. It is a predisposed mentality in the form of unexamined beliefs and/or irrational feelings about an individual, a people group, a position or issue. This often takes the form of generalisations like, "all whites are arrogant pigs", "all blacks are lazy", "you can never trust a man" or "women are fickle". Forgive me for these examples, but it helps to say it and get it out in the open so that it can be dealt with. What prejudice came up in your mind as you read these phrases? Another word for this is "stereotypes" — seeing an individual or group through a mould, category or label. The words "bias" or "favour" are sometimes used: "You are biased about this issue", or "You favour so and so".

Racism

I use racism, the same as racialism, to mean a particular expression and fruit of prejudice with regard to a person or people of another race. Likewise sexism is prejudice with regard to the other gender, most commonly directed against women. When I talk of racism, I include sexism — it is as serious an issue in our society, if not more so. Racism is a set of prejudiced beliefs, feelings and attitudes that is evidenced in racist behaviour. But if racism is defined only as personal prejudice, then it masks the real power of racism, which is structural.

Technically speaking, one can further define racism as prejudice plus power (Racism = Prejudice + Power).[16] In other words, racism is also a phenomenon of power relationships, both organic and institutional. When a person exercises power over another person — whether it is informal and relational or legal and structural — it can either be motivated by prejudice or by fairness and even by love. The former is racism, the latter is justice, and love goes beyond justice to empowering freedom. Prejudice plus power is a lethal combination, and more so when it is incarnated in socio-political structures as we saw in apartheid. This is called "institutionalised racism". Apartheid is the Afrikaans word that describes the policy of racial segregation and "separate development" (as it was later called).[17] Its common usage is synonymous with racism and socio-political oppression.

In summary, racism is both personal prejudice and systemic (power structures and systems in society). The two feed off and reinforce one another, and lead to personal guilt and collective responsibility for racism. People are not born racists, they are made racists. The result is all sorts of internalised and external problems. The reality in SA through the centuries was that all other races were treated like dogs fighting for the crumbs from the white man's table. People who grow up and live in a racist context suffer profoundly with inferiority and superiority.

As stated briefly in the Preface, I use white, black, coloured and Indian to describe the racial groups in our apartheid legacy and mentality. But I acknowledge that in the kingdom of God, and as we mature in AVC and in the nation, these tags should fall away. We must note that "race" is not a biblical word per se and has a recent political history. It came into being through European intellectuals when they developed a new science called anthropology in the mid to late 1800s — the study of humans, in terms of origins, physiological and cultural development. But they did this in the context of European nations, dividing the world into colonies. "Race" was used as a socio-political construct to distinguish Europeans from other "races".[18] In other words, it was discriminatory and, interestingly, it was first used to justify the segregation of Jews in Europe and then to justify European imperialism in the rest of the world.[19]

We can conclude that racism is the vast network of distorted beliefs, attitudes, behaviour and power structures that discriminates against and oppresses other races. Bigotry is a word that summarises all that we have been saying; it means racial and religious pride and prejudice, both personal and systemic. One can even talk of "racist entropy": left to ourselves, we all move to the greatest state of separation, disorder and racism due to our sinful nature. We have to work against this inherent tendency intentionally all the time. Anti-racism or anti-racist is probably the right word to use for persons whose hearts and minds are relatively free from racial prejudice. Anti-racists work for racial healing and reconciliation at both the personal and structural level of transformation, as a realistic and abiding hope in society.

Ideology

Strictly speaking, ideology is the "study or science of ideas", but I will use its more common meaning: Ideology is a set of ideas that explains the position of a particular group and justifies their vital interests. In other words, ideologies are constructs of ideas and meanings in the form of values and norms, mostly in political and economic worldviews and public policies. In reality these "constructs" often serve as a rationalisation and justification of one group's collective interests over against another group's.[20] Just think of the apartheid ideology (Afrikaner interests) or the Marxist ideology (workers' interests). They operate both in the ruling class and in oppressed groups, often causing a clash of ideologies. Ideologies distort the facts of the real situation while justifying the dominant order or status quo. They operate with uncritical ideas, myths and worldviews, but are self-explanatory and convincing. Ideologies tend to become absolutistic and totalitarian, and demand a loyalty that is unacceptable for Christians.

We should always be wary of ideologies because they have a power of their own. They subconsciously condition us into a way of thinking and living, and they even blind us to obvious reality. Biblical theology should critique any and every ideology, but likewise, it is often itself deeply influenced and/or used by ideologies.[21] A number of "contextual theologies" are on offer, all serving a particular group cause or interest like apartheid theology, liberation theology, black theology, feminist theology, gay theology, and so on.

We also need to be aware that there is no such thing as a pure, objective biblical theology ("vacuum-packed"). Mainline theology has been accused of being blind to its own middle-class presuppositions and liberal values.[22] Our subconscious assumptions and presuppositions — whether they be cultural, class or gender — are always part of our interpretation of Scripture and development of theology. Where does that leave us? Is there no such thing as absolute truth and objective theology? We do not have to throw the baby out with the bathwater. We can, by dialogue with church history and public debate with the broader community of faith, have our presuppositions exposed and come to an "almost" ideologically free theology — or at least a fully responsible and self-aware theology.[23]

Reconciliation

By reconciliation I mean the act and/or process of putting things right between two alienated parties in order to restore relationship, justice and harmony. This is done by removing the "enmity" or causes of division, and by restoring a "together-ness" of forgiveness, trust and mutual respect. Some have defined reconciliation as "restoring justice".[24] Because individuals, as well as groups or nations, become alienated, reconciliation has both relational and structural, personal and corporate dimensions.

It could be said that conciliation and not reconciliation is the issue in SA; the latter implies that blacks and whites were once together and then divided. Historically this is not true. Conciliation is the removal of mutual differences in order to build a relationship of togetherness that was not there before. It means working together for the common good. I will use reconciliation but, whenever I do, I include the meaning of conciliation. I use it to refer to both levels of reconciliation, personal and group (or structural). I include the ideas of repentance, forgiveness, restitution, healing of racial wounds and the normalisation of relationships — all associated conditions and connotations of reconciliation.

Transformation

I assume that we all need transformation. It is the process of being changed into what God wants us to be. We can talk of both formation and transformation. Biblically speaking, it takes place through the grace and work of God's Holy Spirit, but not without our willing and obedient responses and cooperation. By this we are continually being changed into God's image and desired purpose.[25] Many, if not most of us, must be "transformed by the renewing of our minds" when it comes to racism (Rom 12:2). This happens at both individual and corporate levels. We are progressively transformed as Christians, as a movement of churches, and as a nation.

Since 1994 the word transformation has acquired two other meanings in SA. It refers to the socio-political transformation that is seeking to "normalise" the situation between black and white. Transformation in this context means the process of redressing the injustices and legacy of the apartheid past, at all levels and structures of our society. This involves things like affirmative action and black empowerment.

The other meaning refers to the Christian process of "City Transformations" that is seeking to bring social renewal through spiritual revival. This is being motivated by George Otis Jr., but I fear it runs the danger of becoming another charismatic escapism from concrete social engagement. We need to take both these meanings into account when we use "transformation". And we need to keep in mind the basic biblical assumption of the Spirit's power and work of transformation. The implication is clear: All reconciliation is aimed at transformation, both personal and social. For AVC SA this means that we are committed to becoming all that God intends for us, reflecting the racial mix and indigenised feel of our country as we contextualise Vineyard and its values at all levels of our church life.

Ethics

Traditionally ethics and morality have been synonymous — to know the difference between right and wrong. It involves the ability to understand moral problems and to make moral judgements. But the more popular usage of ethics has to do with the application of morals, often understood at the level of values and social issues rather than the personal and relational level, which is now commonly associated with morality. I use ethics in this broader social sense. And by "theological ethics" I mean a critical evaluation, from a biblical Christian perspective, of any moral (social) issue before us. People generally think of Christian ethics as the application of the Bible to a problem, whether personal or social. Every day most

Christians seek guidance, to one degree or another, from their faith in God via the Scriptures. A common question is: What must I do in this situation? We will look at a number of such ethical issues in Chapter 8 and give guidance as to how we should respond as Christians.

Theological ethics grounds moral and ethical values in the authority and absolutes of God and his Word. In other words, we base our convictions and judgements on the Bible as the inspired record of God's revelation to humankind. This is in contrast to philosophic or other forms of ethics, that ground their values and judgements in other norms, such as humanistic, logical, cultural, and religious convictions.

In summary, theological ethics can be defined and understood by its three constituent parts. How they operate will become clear as we proceed:[26]

- ♦ What is the issue? (An analysis of the issue and the context.)
- ♦ What ought to be? (The biblical vision, evaluation and critique — what ought to happen in the situation.)
- ♦ How can we be liberated and motivated to bring it about? (The process and power to resolve the issue with the "preferred future" derived from the biblical ethical critique.)

This book, this position paper, is an exercise in biblical theology and Christian ethics.

NOTES

1. On the story of Martin Luther King and the civil rights movement, see Garrow 1986. On the Rodney King episode and the subsequent riots, see Vernon 1993 — he is a Christian and was the Acting Chief Officer of the LAPD on the day the story broke. (I find his treatment overly "spiritual" without an acknowledgement or examination of racism.) A searching black perspective on the race issue followed from West 1993.

2. Wallis 1988.

3. God's complaint — and that of Jeremiah — against the false prophets who say "peace, peace" when there is no peace (because there is no justice), and who try to "dress the wound of my people as though it were not serious" (Jer 6:14; 8:11).

4. The Hebrew word for "perish" is used to describe the sinful actions of the Israelites, casting off their restraint, while Moses was on Mount Sinai (Ex 32:25).

5. His historic speech is recorded in King 1986, pp. 101–106.

6. Moltmann's 1967 well-known *Theology of Hope* expounds this aspect of the biblical vision. Brueggemann, a respected Old Testament scholar, has written three books that

dovetail in a detailed and awesome vision of reality, from the biblical Hebraic view-point. See Brueggemann 1976, 1978, 1986.

7. Nürnberger 1999, p. 277 (italics mine).

8. My discussion on vision and how to "create" it is found in Venter 2000, pp. 83–102.

9. Paul uses the Greek word *eirene* (peace) in Eph 2:14–16, but as a Jew he clearly had the Hebrew reality of *Shalom* in mind.

10. Brueggemann 1976, p. 15. His book is a detailed study of the Hebraic vision of *Shalom*.

11. A key phrase of Bill Hybels, see Hybels 2002.

12. A basic assumption of Dallas Willard's, which I discuss later. He works out this theo-logy of transformation in terms of socio-political policy and structures in Willard 1988, pp. 220–250.

13. Dallas Willard talks about "VIM" (vision, intention, means) as the key human elements in the process of personal and social transformation in God's kingdom. See Willard 2002, pp. 77–92.

14. In scientific terms, the technical definition of "critical mass" is "the smallest mass of fissionable material that will support a self-sustaining chain reaction". The percentage of critical mass required for radical change of the whole differs for various substances.

15. This is not the place to discuss the critical issues related to context, theological method and biblical hermeneutics. The debate goes into contextual theologies and models/methods of "social analysis", and the ideological interaction with context and theological method. For a good guide on biblical interpretation that addresses these contextual and ideological issues, see Thiselton 1980 and McKim 1986. South African theologian, John de Gruchy, has written two books on "doing theology" in terms of context, ideology, hermeneutics and praxis (De Gruchy 1986, 1991). For specific discussions on social analysis and sociological tools in theology, see Bonino 1983 and Noble 1987. A good example of a contextual (liberation) theology, written during the times of great difficulty in SA, is Nolan 1988. Respected British theological ethicist, Ronald Preston, gives a wide-ranging discussion on issues of context, ideology and biblical truth (Preston 1987).

16. This is a common definition of racism in Mennonite and other circles, see Reba Place Church, 8 January 1996, p. 3. See Barndt 1991, pp. 27–50, 75–100, for a study of white racism, power and structures — many people are naive about power and its operation via social structures.

17. For a concise historical socio-political understanding of the development of apartheid, see Müller 1969, pp. 428–431; for the theological origins and understandings of apartheid, see De Gruchy and Villa Vicencio 1983, pp. 10–38, Morphew 1989, pp. 97–117 and Loubser 1987; for a description and critique of how apartheid operated during the

years of oppression, see Adam and Giliomee 1979, pp. 196–257, Nolan 1988, pp. 68–88.

18. Reba Place Church, 8 January 1996, p. 1.

19. Richard Hays rightly places his theological ethical discussion of racism in the context of anti-Semitism. His point of departure is the "Anti-Judaism and Ethnic Conflict" in the New Testament, see Hays 1996, pp. 407–443.

20. For a detailed discussion on the meaning and nature of ideologies, see Leatt, Kneifel and Nürnberger 1988, pp. 273–284 and Loubser 1987, pp. 122–124. See also Ellul 1988 for an incisive view of the role of ideology in Christian theology, especially in liberation and similar contextual theologies that use Marxist assumptions.

21. Leatt, Kneifel and Nürnberger 1988, pp. 285–302, and Ellul 1988. On theology, specifically in the service of apartheid ideology, see Loubser 1987, pp. 124–134.

22. For example, see Balcomb 1993.

23. This is a big issue in academic theology and other disciplines. It has to do with epistemology (how we know things) and hermeneutics (how we interpret things, see note 15). There are generally three approaches: 1. We can have pure, objective truth and universal theology (modern or positivist idealism, called naive realism); 2. We can only have subjective truth and contextual theologies (postmodern or phenomenologist relativism, called reduced realism); 3. We can have relative objective theology that is qualified by publicly debated and verifiable truth (Hebraic or storied realism, called critical realism). This latter approach is the philosophic framework that I follow. A clear and concise treatment of this subject is Wright 1992b, pp. 31–46, applied to literature, history and theology, pp. 47–144. A detailed study of these methodologies in theology, and especially of critical realism, is found in Van Huyssteen 1989.

24. Brown 1978, p. 145 (and pp. 145–176 on Reconciliation). See also the definition of reconciliation in the SA context in the mid-1980s, Nürnberger and Tooke 1988, pp. 84–89. See De Gruchy 2002 on "restoring justice".

25. Transformation is actually transfiguration, a "metamorphosis" into the shining likeness of God (Greek *metamorphoo*, Lk 9:29; 2 Cor 3:18; Rom 12:2). Through computer technology, we can now "morph" people and things, a mere shadow of the Spirit's power that is "morphing" us into God's image.

26. This understanding of theological ethics from Nürnberger 1988, p. 268.

CHAPTER 4

FACING OUR
APARTHEID HISTORY

Those who cannot remember the past are condemned to repeat it

Philosopher George Santayana[1]

*There were two boys living opposite each other. John stole a bicycle from Tom
and then after a year John came to Tom and said, "Tom, I stole your bicycle
and what I need now is reconciliation." Then Tom looked at John and said:
"Where is my bicycle?" He said: "No, I am not talking about your bicycle now,
I am talking about reconciliation."*

*Now we are talking about the survivors of apartheid. Our brothers and
sisters have passed away, and now one will come and say, "I killed your brother.
What I need now is reconciliation." The problem is now it is not a bicycle,
it's a person who died, and it's impossible now that that person will come back.*

Rev. Mxolisi Mpambani[2]

*O Lord, we have sinned and done wrong. We have been wicked and
have rebelled; we have turned away from your commands and laws. O Lord,
we and our kings, our princes and our fathers are covered with shame because
we have sinned against you. We have become an object of scorn to all those
around us. The Lord our God is merciful and forgiving ... O Lord, listen!
O Lord, forgive! Hear our cry for mercy!*

Daniel 9:4–19 RAP

WHY FACE OUR PAST?

In September 2002 Jews gathered at Dachau and Auswitch, and in many other places around the globe, to hold the 50 Year Holocaust Remembrance. Their message was clear and simple: If we do not remember what happened, and teach our children to remember what happened, we will repeat history. I am using Santayana's quote intentionally to link the historical legacy of Nazi Germany with that of apartheid SA. These were the only two nations on earth that legislated racism on the clear assumption of the superiority of one race over others. The results are notorious, and must be remembered.

Not having knowledge of history is like living without a memory — it profoundly affects the choices we make for the present and the future. It is safe to say that there is nothing like a good knowledge of history to give one a correct perspective of human beings, life and the world. However, we are also aware that the history that we have been taught can be deeply prejudiced, built on stereotypes and myths. There is a great need not only to remember, but also to "deconstruct" our history by mutual storytelling from opposite sides of the divide in SA. Then we can rebuild a more accurate view of our common history.

Remembering and retelling: Clearing misconceptions and stumbling blocks.

The holocaust survivors say: "We must forgive, but we must not forget." It does not mean harbouring bitterness — that would not be genuine forgiveness. Nor does it mean using the past as a "kierie" or baseball bat to bludgeon to death every new move towards the future. Remembering and facing our past do not come easily or automatically. In fact, amnesia or "letting bygones be bygones" is the easy way out, especially for those who were on the side of power. The opposite response to amnesia is to become fixated with the past in an unresolved and embittered way, a danger especially for those who were victims or survivors of the power structures. We must not become prisoners of our past.

We need to remember and process our past, in community, in order to gain a more accurate view of things, to cleanse ourselves from misconceptions, to process our pain and to find a common hope for our future. If we do not face our past intentionally, within a safe community of honest dialogue, we will not do it at all. We will either remain arrogantly indifferent to our past pain or we will remain embittered victims. At best we will have an attitude of "every person for themselves, and God have mercy on the rest". At worst, "I'm living for number one, to hell with everyone else." This latter attitude can clearly be seen in the body language of some people, even if they do not say it.

Some say, "It's all over now, why drag up the past? We must move on into the future." But we owe it to our future to deal with our past or we are condemned to repeat it and it will continue to be a source of division among us. We do not have to rehash our whole history; we do need to redress it to the extent that it blocks and/or helps us into the future together. There are many unresolved feelings and perceptions. The reality is that we did experience a radically divided history in SA. It is our choice: We can ignore reality or we can turn stumbling blocks into stepping stones by facing what happened.

Remembering and retelling: Educating the younger generation.

There is another important reason to face our history and to tell it like it is. A whole new generation is growing up in SA that did not have first-hand experience of institutionalised apartheid. They need to know the story, for their sake and for the sake of the nation's future. Our daughter was born in 1990, the year Nelson Mandela was released after 27 years imprisonment. We named her Misha-Joy, a Hebrew derivative for "freedom", reflecting the joy of liberation. She is in a multiracial school — as are many children in SA now — and two of her best friends are black. They interact and integrate naturally, and seem innocent of colour consciousness. It is wonderful to see, but I know that their innocence will be lost as racial prejudice from the "real world' intrudes.

To illustrate my point about this post-apartheid generation, here is a joke that is currently doing the rounds. A little white boy comes home from school and asks his mother, "Can I invite my two friends Mandla and Thabiso to my birthday party?"

She immediately asks, "Are they black?"

He replies, "I don't know. I'll ask them tomorrow."

If this generation can grow up living in a genuinely reconciled and reconciling way of life, SA has a very bright future. But it will not happen automatically. It needs serious intention and intervention. Inevitably, their "racial" innocence will be lost, but it needs to take place through knowing the real story of apartheid, not by the invasion of racist jokes or the racist attitudes and prejudiced actions of others (often their parents). They need to know what really happened in order to counter the racism that is "crouching at the door" waiting to pounce on them, as God warned Cain (see Gen 4:7). Like sex education, do we leave it to the power of peer pressure, stereotypes and prejudicial myths, or do parents proactively engage and tell the real story to their children? Even then, there is no guarantee that it will be without prejudice — sadly we all pass on our "stuff". We owe it to the younger generation and the future of SA to tell our history like it is.

We must remember and our children must be told precisely because our history is not an ordinary history. The extraordinary events that we have lived through have defined us and will determine our common future, for better or worse. It is like the holocaust or, biblically speaking, like the Exodus of Israel or the life, death and resurrection of Jesus of Nazareth. These were no ordinary events. They need to be retold and remembered as a living tradition, so that we can live in the present by the values and power of these historical realities. To prepare the children of Israel to "possess the promised land", Moses (as the parent) told them the story of the exodus and God's covenant with Israel at Sinai, as if they were actually there when it happened. He relived it for them, and with them, because those events defined who they were, and who they were becoming (see Deut 31:12–3; the book of Deuteronomy is Israel's story as a "living past" that empowers the new generation for the future). The death and resurrection of Jesus is the ultimate historical fulfilment of this reality, and we experience it in the present every time we break bread together in his name. Through remembering and retelling, it is present as a living tradition that has an ongoing power for trans-formation. This is drama, re-enactment and impartation at its best. We must find creative and artistic ways of telling our South African story to our children and the nations of the world.

In the Association of Vineyard Churches (AVC), a generation is growing up that does not really know what the church did during the apartheid years. It is evident that there are some wrong assumptions around apartheid and the Vineyard journey in particular. We must set the record straight and take responsibility for the things that we did or did not do, and the things that we need to do.

My intention in this chapter is merely to touch on the key points that affect our view of, and our response to, our common history with the purpose of seeking a reconciled view of things.

THE CONTEXT OF COLONIALISM

The place to start is the broad context of colonialism and its legacy. If we do not have an understanding of colonialism from an African perspective (or Asian or Latin American, i.e. the Third World perspective), we will not be aware of the way it has conditioned us, especially with regard to our world view.

World view can be described as the lenses, or spectacles, through which we see people, life and the world. It is the basic, underlying assumptions that determine our view of reality. For example: Colonialism has conveyed the idea that whites and Westerners are superior, and that blacks and Third World people are inferior. If we do not raise these subconscious assumptions to awareness intentionally and deal with them, we will forever be trying to forget, minimise, or even justify the pain of Africa and her history. Sometimes the assumptions are not subconscious; in some cases they are chosen beliefs that operate intentionally at a conscious level determining attitudes and behaviour.

Pakenham's 3Cs of colonialism

I want to refer to two books that are good examples of material that exposes and challenges our colonial conditioning. The first is Pakenham's *The Scramble for Africa*. It will dispel sentiments such as "colonialism was not that bad". Beginning in the mid to late 1800s, European leaders began the onslaught of conquer, divide and rule. The five main rivals, Germany, Italy, Portugal, France and Britain, sat in Europe and, over a period of a few short years, divided up what is now called the Third World into almost a 100 colonies, arbitrarily creating borders that were determined by a violent balance of greed and power — with Holland and Spain taking some scraps.

In terms of Africa:

> ... the Scramble gave Europe virtually the whole continent: including thirty new colonies and protectorates, 10 million square miles of new territory and 110 million dazed new subjects, acquired by one method or another. Africa was slice like a cake, the pieces swallowed by the European masters.[3]

The 3Cs of commerce, Christianity and civilization, that began with the voyages of discovery in the 17th and 18th centuries, worked hand in hand to penetrate "darkest Africa", leading to the slave trade and a ruthless imperialism that was nothing more than an arrogant paternalism, a kind of "race patriotism".[4] It further led to a radical ongoing exploitation of the colonies and their people for the benefit of the European nations. The growing depth of resentment and resistance in native Africans eventually overflowed into revolution and independence in colony after colony — the scramble out of Africa! And interestingly, South Africa, at the tip of the continent, was the last to gain "independence"[5] after the scramble out had moved all the way down from north to south.

As one of the 3Cs, Christianity's deep entanglement with colonialism has left it carrying a weight of historical baggage. Northern/Western Christianity still has a major credibility problem in the eyes of the Third World.[6] I cannot begin to highlight the excesses of Christian missions such as forced conversions, cultural decimation and commercial exploitation. But, notwithstanding such excesses, thanks be to God that genuine Christianity grew phenomenally. It has produced a huge Third World harvest which is completely overshadowing church growth in North America and Western Europe (which has been in decline in recent decades). This explosive growth may have been due, in part, to Kenyan John Gatu's call in 1971 for a moratorium on Western missionaries to Africa[7] and, more so, due to the indigenisation of Christianity in the Third World.

It would be a big mistake, and a wrong reading of history, to write off all missions during the colonial era as bad. What is clear is that many missionaries who came to Africa made significant contributions and sacrifices, seeding themselves and the gospel, which has led to the amazing harvest that we now see. Despite his (colonial) failures, David Livingstone in his death is a symbol of this sometimes heroic missionary seeding — he was found on his knees beside his bed praying, his head buried in his hands on the pillow.[8] I take it as a picture of the church, in all its weaknesses and failures, humbly moving forward on its knees, serving the world while calling on God. I am not only talking about an evangelistic harvest — some missionaries stood against the colonial powers for the sake of justice in racial and other issues. But again, we have to say that there were many missionaries who were blatant instruments of colonial injustice and imperialism.[9] In the area of education, the missionaries made a major contribution — its impact on Africa is immeasurable. Many of the post-colonial African presidents and leaders were educated in missionary schools, including our Nobel Peace Prize laureates Albert Luthuli and Nelson Mandela.[10]

Fanon's African view of oppressive colonialism

Another "must read", especially for all people of European descent, is Fanon's book, *The Wretched of the Earth*.[11] It shifts the heart and mind towards a compassionate understanding of Africa by giving an African view of colonialism.

Frantz Fanon, an Algerian native who became a psychiatrist, writes very personally and powerfully about colonialism and its legacy, and Africa's fierce resistance and attempt overcome it. The title of his book describes the desperate struggle for survival of oppressed Africans.

Fanon's insightful analysis and sensitive description is profoundly disturbing. Particularly unnerving are his case studies of some of his psychiatric patients who were devastated by the effects of colonialism with its war of repression and subsequent violent revolution in Algeria in the 1960s. The "spiral of violence", as Dom Helder Camara calls it, can continue for decades, and it can only be broken by courageous and sacrificial non-violent intervention and reconciliation.[12]

The more I read Fanon's book, the more my eyes were opened to see not natives writhing in their colonial wounds, but a mirror revealing the true wretched of the earth, the colonialists. As the French philosopher, Jean-Paul Satre, says in his famous preface to the book — speaking on behalf of his fellow Europeans: "Our victims know us by their scars and by their chains, and it is this that makes their evidence irrefutable. It is enough that they show us what we have made of them *for us to realise what we have made of ourselves*" (my italic).[13] In fact, let me conclude these comments on the context and legacy of colonialism by holding up the mirror of Satre's opening words in his preface. Arguably, there is no other summary of colonialism that is as concise and convincing as this:

> Not so very long ago, the earth numbered two thousand million inhabitants: five hundred million men, and one thousand five hundred million natives. The former had the Word; the other had the use of it. Between the two there were hired kinglets, overlords and a bourgeoisie, sham from beginning to end, which served as go-betweens. In the colonies the truth stood naked, but the citizens of the mother country preferred it with clothes on: the native had to love them, something in the way mothers are loved. The European *elite* undertook to manufacture a native *elite*. They picked out promising adolescents; they branded them, as with a red-hot iron, with the principles of western culture; they stuffed their mouths full with high-sounding phrases, grand glutinous words that stuck to the teeth. After a short stay in the mother country they were sent home, whitewashed. These walking lies had nothing left to say to their brothers; they only echoed. From Paris, from London, from Amsterdam we would utter the words "Parthenon! Brotherhood!" and somewhere in Africa or Asia lips would open "... thenon! ... therhood!" It was the golden age.

It came to an end; the mouths opened by themselves; the yellow and black voices still spoke of our humanism but only to reproach us with our inhumanity. We listened (at first) without displeasure to these polite statements of resentment ... "You are making us into monstrosities; your humanism claims we are at one with the rest of humanity but your racist methods set us apart." (Then they spoke further) ... "Let us waste no time in sterile litanies and nauseating mimicry. Leave this Europe where they are never done talking of Man, yet murder men everywhere they find them, at the corner of every one of their own streets, in all the corners of the globe. For centuries they have stifled almost the whole of humanity in the name of so-called spiritual experience." The tone is new. Who dares speak thus? It is an African, a man from the Third World, an ex-"native" (Frantz Fanon). He adds, "Europe now lives at such a mad, reckless pace that she is running headlong into the abyss; we would do well to keep away from it." In other words, she's done for. A truth which is not pleasant to state but of which we are all convinced, are we not, fellow-Europeans, in the marrow of our bones?[14]

And dare we ask the question: To what extent is this true, not only of Europe, but of the Western world in general? It goes further than the West; oppression and racism are endemic in history and part of the DNA of the human race.

THE STORY OF OUR TWO-SIDED SOUTH AFRICAN HISTORY

South Africa is a microcosm of the world divided by the racial reality and legacy of colonialism. Ours is now the all too familiar story of the *black experience of pain and oppression* on the one side, and the *white experience of power and privilege* on the other. In facing this common but divided history, I will focus on a series of snapshots: a broad historical sweep through to the 1980s; the transition and miracle of the early 1990s;[15] the church's response to apartheid — including that of the Vineyard — and finally the Truth and Reconciliation Commission (TRC).

Racism and segregation existed from the earliest days of colonialism, beginning with Jan van Riebeeck's arrival on 6 April 1652 at the Cape of Storms. The name was then changed to the Cape of Good Hope — some would say a prophetic omen! Racial storms due to incompatible attitudes, structures and practices blew across all the years of Dutch and British colonial rule. The conflict was not only between the settlers and natives, but also between the British and Afrikaners, which culminated in the late 1800s in the Anglo-Boer War.[16] (The need for reconciliation and healing between English and Afrikaners is still an unresolved issue for some.) From 1910 the storms gained momentum with the blacks being excluded by the constitution of the Union of SA. In response, the African National Congress (ANC) was born in 1912, uniting blacks against the white government. The racial storm finally grew to its full strength in the form of apartheid — institutionalised segregation. From 1948 to 1990 the Afrikaner nationalist government unleashed the full fury of its racist ideology on the black, Indian and coloured citizens of our country. When its force was fully spent, a new nation was born.[17] A nation of Good Hope? After such a protracted historical storm, we pray that we will be a nation of hope, both locally and internationally.

The coloureds and Indians were publicly associated with the blacks and, in their own minds, they identified themselves as blacks because of the political situation. When others referred to the "blacks", it generally included the coloureds and Indians because they experienced the same racial oppression from the whites. The only difference was in degree. However, it was easier to co-opt them into the apartheid system, as was seen in 1984 when the coloureds and Indians were brought into a tricameral parliamentary system.[18] This and other such attempts at "reform", especially during the 1980s, were meaningless — it merely intensified the resistance in the country. It became increasingly difficult to keep the lid on the African pot boiling with rage and revolution. The nation came close to a bloodbath in the 1976 Soweto riots, and again during the state of emergency from 1985 to 1989. In those years SA was effectively a police state under the repressive and brutal control of the white minority regime. FW de Klerk came to power in 1990 and began normalising the political process. He released Nelson Mandela and unbanned all the liberation movements which led to negotiations in the early 1990s, and the first genuine democratic elections in SA on 27 April 1994.

The key issue to acknowledge in all of this is that we experienced this painful history on both sides of the divide. There are two views of our past (there are many more views — each person's experience is important and must be heard). These two opposing stories must be told courageously and listened to compassionately if we are going to have a reconciled view of things, and if we are going to have a realistic understanding of the legacy of apartheid and the work involved in undoing it. We simply must tell our stories to one another in order to find one another, to establish a common point of departure to redress the wrongs our past, deal with our present and build our future together. This mutual and personal sharing of our divided history assumes a safe and trusting environment with a number of other elements that local churches can provide. There are significant

stories on either side of the divide, especially stories of repentance and reconciliation, that can bring hope and healing to many in our country and beyond. I
encourage you to read stories of people's lives, stories of courage and transformation, that will liberate you from your own prejudices to reach out in love to
others.[19]

This raises the absolute importance *God's story* — of telling and hearing the
stories of the apartheid reality in the light of God's greater story. We are not left
to ourselves with our own subjective experiences, whether personal or corporate.
God's story, climactically told in the life, death and resurrection of Jesus the
Messiah, is a story of merciful and sovereign intervention for our salvation. God
became incarnate in Jesus of Nazareth, suffered our pain, and triumphed over it
for us. God's story and purpose is always to avoid national judgement and personal destruction. But tragically, due to the hardness of our hearts, it sometimes
includes this. The key, however, is that our stories only really find meaning and
purpose when they are seen in the light of what God has done and what he is
doing. From a national perspective, *we need to remind ourselves that we have
lived through an absolute miracle in SA, symbolised forever in the first democratic elections in our nation on 27 April 1994.*[20]

THE MIRACLE OF HISTORICAL CHANGE IN OUR NATION

History has been called "His story" by many Christians, because we believe that
God is sovereign over history, and works in history for the fulfilment of his purposes. There were many factors that led to the miracle of dramatic change in our
nation, but here is a part of God's story.

The South African Council of Churches (SACC) made a controversial call for
prayers to be held for the downfall of the "illegitimate apartheid regime" — as
they called it — at the height of violent repression in 1987–88.[21] President PW
Botha had a stroke in 1989 and FW de Klerk took over the presidency. President
de Klerk rose to the challenge and turned the tide of history by becoming one of
the few leaders internationally ever to have freely negotiated himself out of
power. We must not forget that this took place in the international context of
dramatic political change. The Berlin Wall fell in 1989 due to Gorbachev's glasnost
and perestroika, which represented a brave new thinking and openness that
shook the communist block and swept the globe.[22] This broader context had an

influence on De Klerk as he surrendered white Afrikaner nationalist power to a negotiated democratic process and a new democratic government.

De Klerk secured his place in history for his foresight in releasing Nelson Mandela. Part of the miracle in our country was the man Mandela had become. After 27 years in prison, he came out with no bitterness. He exuded a spirit of forgiveness and reconciliation that challenges all of us, locally and globally. I will never forget Gill and I watching his release on TV with tears streaming down our faces. I recalled the closing sentences of Mandela's lengthy speech on 20 April 1964 during the Rivonia treason trial, after which he resumed his incarceration (he had been captured and imprisoned on 5 August 1962):

> I have cherished the ideal of a democratic and free society in which all persons live together in harmony and with equal opportunities. It is an ideal which I hope to live for and to achieve. But if needs be, it is an ideal for which I am prepared to die.[23]

Thank God he did not die for it, although he faced the death sentence. He has lived to bring it about.

During the transition from 1990 to 1994 there was terrible violence as a result of the jockeying for position. It was well known that the Zulus, mainly represented by the Inkatha Freedom Party (IFP) led by Mangosuthu Buthelezi, were a primary instrument of covert government black-on-black violence. This government-sponsored violence was called the third force. Buthelezi held out on the 1994 elections threatening to turn SA into a civil war bloodbath. Everyone in the nation held their breath. We all knew that this was for real — we had come to the precipice of national disaster, closer than ever before.

This took place in the broader African context of the civil war that broke out in Rwanda. In just 100 days, from 7 April to 17 July 1994, over 800 000 Tutsis and moderate Hutus — including 300 000 Tutsi children — were slaughtered in a genocide perpetrated by the ruling Hutus. They had first dehumanised the Tutsis by calling them cockroaches.[24] It was eventually stopped when the Hutus were defeated by Tutsi rebels, scattering over 2 million starving Hutu refugees into neighbouring countries. We all knew that the stakes were just as high in SA, if not higher. On 18 April 1994, just nine days before the South African elections were to take place, Buthelezi was persuaded by respected Christian leaders to strike a deal with Nelson Mandela and enter the elections. This miracle took place in the rooms of a large football stadium in Durban while 30 000 Christians were praying above them at an all-day Jesus Peace Rally.[25] The elections followed, and the rest is history!

The moral responsibility that comes with such a miracle

What have we done with this miracle? What are we going to do with it? Lose its power in the name of forgetfulness and self-pursuit? Mandela's post-1994 policy of reconciliation and reconstruction, of redressing structural imbalances, has had only relative success. Although he has become an international icon of moral authority, his generous attitude of forgiveness and reconciliation has not transformed our country. Why is this the case?

I personally fear that De Klerk let the whites off the hook too quickly. All the laws have changed, but have our hearts and minds changed? Very few whites have been through a process of reconciliation and transformation of their racial beliefs, attitudes and actions, either during or since apartheid. Only a handful crossed the divides during the years of pain and oppression to experience life on the other side. In doing so, these few were able to face their own demons and repent. It remains the same today. In the main we have still not experienced what history and life was (and is still) like in the black townships and rural areas. We still sit with most of our prejudices intact and growing. The TRC, in the second half of the 1990s, has come and gone. Did that bring about a fundamental change of hearts and attitudes? Are we anywhere nearer genuine reconciliation? I fear that we are presently in danger of losing the higher purpose that God intended with the miracle he gave us in 1994.

We must take responsibility in facing the challenges of our past with its legacy of racism. Most whites now condemn apartheid as having been a bad thing. This has become fashionable. But what are they presently doing in terms of addressing its conditioning and legacy in their own lives, let alone in society? Many whites were relatively inactive and silent during apartheid, and were not neutral as they supposed — by their silence they supported the system.[26] They must now, together with the rest of the nation, take responsibility to redress the apartheid aftermath. Instead we find that many people's racial attitudes are hardening. This is extremely worrying. It has many implications. Political reconciliation and justice has been achieved — the law books have changed — but we still need economic and social reconciliation and justice, which is painfully slow in coming.

Economic and social reconciliation must be pursued at all levels of our society, but the deeper challenge, the heart of the matter, still remains the *spiritual realities*.[27] How do we win the hearts and minds of people? How do we transform the spiritual and mental conditioning of years of racial misbeliefs, attitudes and practices? How do we heal the deep wounds of racial hurt and structural apartheid? Only God's power can do this. Is not the church God's primary instrument in the world?

We have to heal and transform the "inferiority" of the blacks, the "superiority" of the whites, the dislocation of the Indians and the disparate identity of the coloureds. I know these descriptions are generalisations; my meaning is clear.

The issue of cause and change is not an either/or matter. Although the spiritual and personal is the root and primary field of battle, we need *both* private and public change, *both* spiritual and structural transformation. *The serious danger in SA is outward socio-political and economic change without any meaningful inner, personal spiritual transformation.* People experience all the outward societal changes but remain the same in their hearts and minds. The gap between the two is growing rapidly and could end up swallowing us all. Who better to address the spiritual transformation of people and communities than the church? Willard says: "The responsibility for the condition of the world in the years or centuries to come rests upon the leaders and teachers of the Christian church. They alone have at their disposal the means to bring the world effectively under the rule of God."[28]

The need for spiritual transformation raises the issue of the church's response to apartheid.

THE CHURCH'S RESPONSE TO APARTHEID

The historical role of the church in SA with regard to the development of colonial racism and Afrikaner apartheid is well documented.[29] I will comment briefly on the late 1970s and 1980s — the painful years of apartheid repression and crisis.

The mainline or historical churches like the Catholics, Anglicans, Methodists, Congregationalists and Presbyterians were members of the SACC which rejected and opposed apartheid. The rest of the church generally saw them as the liberal ecumenicals[30] who believed that structural change would save the country. Over the years they took a courageous stand and confronted the government time and time again. They wrote many theological and pastoral documents and made pastoral statements to guide their people with regard to thinking, believing and acting against apartheid.[31] But most of their white members in the suburban congregations were reluctant to follow the leaders — they felt that "the church had become too political". They clung to their white views and vested interests, and many left to join the more conservative evangelical, Pentecostal and charismatic churches.

The rest of the church saw the evangelical, Pentecostal and charismatic denominations (and other independent churches) as conservative fundamentalists who believed personal salvation and private prayer would save the country. In practice, these churches were either largely silent and apolitical with regard to the apartheid situation, or they isolated and segregated themselves. In reality, whether they acknowledged it or not, they were part and parcel of the system of white benefit and black oppression. As things worsened in the late 1970s and 1980s, many of the black, coloured and Indian members of these churches experienced a crisis of faith: "How can I reconcile my faith and my church's apolitical stance with my daily reality of government repression and violence?" Many of them entered into solidarity with the struggle for justice and wrote documents to challenge their own denominations.[32] This often resulted in church division along racial lines. This did not really affect the white churches, because most of these denominations had been structurally separate with black, white, coloured and Indian churches. Some are still structurally divided — talk about the church leading the way!

Many of the Afrikaans Reformed churches developed along with racial colonialism in the 1800s and later motivated and justified an apartheid theology and practice from the 1930s to the 1960s.[33] The first signs of a shift took place after the Sharpeville massacre on 21 March 1960 with the subsequent consultation of churches at Cottesloe, Johannesburg.[34] The Dutch Reformed Church (DRC) delegation initially endorsed the Cottesloe statement that basically repudiated racial discrimination in church and society. But President Hendrik Verwoed immediately personally pressured the DRC delegation and the DRC Synod into retracting their support for the statement.[35] As the situation deteriorated in the country, they adjusted their position to distance themselves ideologically from the government, but still did not allow blacks to become members of their congregations.[36] The black, coloured and Indian Afrikaans Reformed churches had always been structurally separate from the white DRC — they had joined the struggle for justice with the SACC churches.[37] At great cost to themselves, and in protest against the DRC church, a few of their white leaders crossed over to join the black sister church.[38] Only at the Rustenburg Consultation of Churches in 1990 was there (apparently) an unequivocal apology to the rest of the church and the nation by the DRC with regard to its participation in apartheid.[39]

In summary

The church's response to racism and apartheid can be summarised by saying that generally it was divided along racial lines. We were clearly divided into racial, economic and ideological camps and congregations. The church was made in the image of apartheid — it was not a model of God's kingdom. The church was a copy of apartheid society with very little credibility as the community of the kingdom. When I preached in Johweto in the 1980s, I used to ask the congregation, "Will there be white churches, black churches, coloured churches, Indian churches, rich churches and poor churches in heaven?" "Noooo ...!" Everyone used to reply loudly. "And yet we are full of them in SA. We even have pro-apartheid churches and anti-apartheid churches. And then there are those who think they are the truly spiritual ones and have nothing to do with politics!" We used to laugh — I was in Soweto where nothing was not political anymore. But then we used to cry too, much more than we laughed, for the same reason. The worst was that SA was seen as a Christian nation (78% of the population claim to be Christians), being ruled by a "Christian government", while genuine Christians were being interrogated, tortured and killed by other genuine (but terribly misguided) Christians.[40] Sadly, this was the fruit of a well-intentioned "Christian" system. The architect of apartheid, Hendrik Verwoed, called it "seeking justice for all groups and not justice for only one group at the cost of the other three".[41]

What a nightmare! How did we, the church, end up allowing this? And doing this?

Ironically, the church received mercy when the new president, FW de Klerk, called on it to put its house in order and "formulate a strategy conducive to negotiation, reconciliation and change".[42] So much for the church leading the nation! As a result, the historic Rustenburg Consultation of Churches took place in November 1990 with the amazing confessions and unity that followed, summarised in the Rustenburg Declaration.[43] This Consultation had a significant impact on both the church and society in terms of the transition and transformation to a new reality in 1994 and beyond.[44]

 ## VINEYARD HISTORY AND RESPONSE TO APARTHEID

I need to give a brief overview of the history of AVC in SA as a context for understanding Vineyard's response to the apartheid crisis.

The first Vineyard congregation was planted in 1982 in Johannesburg by a Californian team led by John Wimber.[45] Throughout the 1980s, as Vineyard developed in SA through church plants and adoptions, the pastors related to a network of ministers called Cape Fellowship Ministries led by Derek Morphew. We did this because we were not strong enough to become an autonomous local AVC — the guideline was that 20 churches were needed to form a national AVC. Obviously our link with John Wimber and the USA Vineyards remained strong and grew during this time. They were our primary oversight.

In 1988 Costa Mitchell was asked by John Wimber to take leadership in beginning to form the AVC in SA. In 1994 the Vineyard pastors and churches became three areas with shadow Area Pastoral Coordinators (the three APCs were Sam Kisten, Derek and I, with Costa as team leader). In April 1997 AVC SA was recognised and released as an autonomous national body. Since then AVC SA has grown in new areas, APCs, task forces and various structures. In terms of the demographics, of the 32 churches at present, about 50% are still predominantly white suburban churches, each with a small percentage racial mix. The rest range from partially to fully racially mixed churches and a few "full on" black, coloured and Indian churches.

Our response to apartheid followed our development in terms of informal and individual responses until we became an Association in 1997. Then we gave an official response in the form of a submission to the TRC in 1998.

We fully acknowledge that through the 1980s and early 1990s, the crisis in the country affected, and was reflected, in the Vineyard. The fact that the movement was started by white Americans among white affluent suburbanites in a highly polarised and politicised SA did not help the situation. A few Vineyard leaders made efforts to inform themselves and their congregations of the apartheid situation. For example, Derek Morphew preached a series of sermons on the conflicting ideologies in SA which was later published as a book.[46]

I was compelled to cross the social divides to protest the repression and seek reconciliation (see Chapter I). This created tensions among leaders and church members in the Johannesburg Vineyard, partly due to my own "prophetic intensity" (a phrase that covers a multitude of unwise words and actions), and partly due to the deep-seated conditioning in the white congregation. I remember the pain of some families leaving the Vineyard in Johannesburg after one of my "apartheid is sinful" sermons and having to process it with my co-pastors, Dave Owen and Costa Mitchell. Although John Wimber endorsed my initiative in the mid-1980s to create a Johweto reconciliation community in Soweto, there were serious reservations about its identity, name, theological stance and other elements. All this clouded our relationships with the Johannesburg and broader Vineyard for a number of years. In retrospect, Johweto was a seed that was planted in the soil of Soweto and has grown up into a fully contextualised African Vineyard, now called Zone 3 Vineyard.[47]

Samuel Kisten from Chatsworth, Durban joined the Vineyard with his Indian congregation in 1982. The fellowship of Indian and white Vineyardites did not seem to be affected much by apartheid, or maybe we politely and mutually did not make it an issue. A Vineyard in Stellenbosch became a mixed congregation with an influx of coloureds as whites reached out into the townships.

Two more happenings are worth mentioning. Because AVC was not formally constituted, it was not officially represented at the historic Rustenburg Consultation of Churches in November 1990. However, Derek Morphew and I had the privilege of attending. Derek was invited in his capacity as a leader in the network of charismatic churches mentioned earlier, and I as an executive member of the National Initiative for Reconciliation (NIR) and leader of the Rand Initiative for Christian Conciliation (RICC). Derek presented a statement at the Consultation on behalf of the group of charismatic churches, the network to which Vineyard in SA was related. He appealed for a new SA with a unity in theology and practice between the mainline "liberal" churches and the evangelical, Pentecostal and charismatic "conservative" churches.[48]

After becoming an AVC in 1997, we formally participated in a submission to the TRC in 1998. Derek Morphew and Moss Ntlha, General Secretary of The Evangelical Alliance of South Africa (TEASA), read a confession at the TRC on behalf of TEASA. As AVC SA, we had formally become a member of TEASA. This confession, with added comments by Derek (Chapter 10), is an important statement and should be carefully read and owned by all Vineyardites, and by all of us who consider ourselves evangelical, charismatic or Pentecostal.

We acknowledge and confess the following:

- That from a white Vineyard viewpoint, we were part of the status quo with its white power, and by and large we were blinded by its ideology, privileges and benefits. We could have, and should have spoken up and done much more to cross the barriers and confront apartheid in those years. We sinned in this regard.

- That from a black viewpoint we acknowledge that it was difficult to integrate into Vineyard due to the political, economic and cultural divides — let alone the different way of doing church. Our white blind spots, apartheid conditioning and Western evangelical/charismatic agenda (with its lack of relevance to the struggle for justice) was a problem to many coloureds, blacks and Indians coming into the Vineyard.

- That we did not, as Vineyard USA or SA, have an adequate social theology to challenge, motivate and guide us into action regarding the apartheid crisis. "Ministry to the poor", which Vineyard is known for, was (and still is) simply not an adequate social theology for our times.

♦ That some of our leaders and the majority of our people did not have, and have not had, direct exposure across the barriers with an experience of healing and transformation from white historical conditioning. Only one or two white leaders had a "Damascus Road conversion" regarding racism and reconciliation, while others have had a slow journey of growing awareness, repentance and transformation. We acknowledge that many Indians, blacks and coloureds in the Vineyard still feel this in the "white body language" in the movement and are seeking a more transformed and indigenous African experience of true Vineyard belonging.

♦ That apartheid conditioning happened on both sides of the apartheid divide, and many of our Indian, coloured and black members still sit with their racial prejudices and past hurt fully in place. They have themselves not been liberated from their ideological perceptions and apartheid baggage by being sufficiently exposed to the other side in a safe community of confrontation and healing.

♦ That we have been slow in implementing a plan to address all the above — a process of reconciliation, transformation and contextualisation. We have not intentionally turned our congregations into safe places for people of different races to find and heal one another intentionally from our past prejudice and pain. This challenge has now been taken up. Hence the reason for this book.

 ## THE TRUTH AND RECONCILIATION COMMISSION

The TRC is so significant that it needs to be discussed. Once again, we have differing perceptions between blacks and whites in this regard. I have found that many whites are ignorant of what actually happened at the TRC, or even what it was all about.

One of the first things the Mandela government did after the 1994 elections was to begin a process of reconciliation by setting up the TRC. In 1976 the United Nations and later The International Court of Justice had declared apartheid a crime against humanity.[49] The debate in the early 1990s was whether to have a Nuremburg type trial or to forget and bury the whole thing. There was a third way

— not criminal prosecution or national amnesia, but *amnesty for those who would tell the truth.*[50] To their eternal credit, a few spiritual leaders like Archbishop Desmond Tutu and Dr Alex Boraine, a Methodist minister and some trusted politicians and judges formulated the TRC with the Christian theology of confession, forgiveness and reconciliation in mind.[51] Although the TRC was a judicial process, Nelson Mandela called the nation as it were to confession in front of the Archbishop, a man of moral and spiritual authority in the struggle against racism. This took place when the Promotion of National Unity and Reconciliation Act No. 34 was signed into law by President Mandela on 19 July 1995. It was then promulgated in the *Government Gazette* on 15 December 1995 to authorise the launch of the TRC.

Tutu and his team met the very next day, 16 December, for their first meeting. This was greatly symbolic as it was the Day of the Covenant (under the apartheid government) commemorating the Battle of Blood River in 1838 when they believed that God delivered the Afrikaner boers from the Zulu warriors. The new government has changed 16 December to Reconciliation Day to bring black and white together in a new SA.[52]

The TRC began its hearings on 15 April 1996 in East London. Will we ever forget the TV image of Desmond Tutu with his head buried in his hands weeping uncontrollably after hearing the first few stories of horror from women who had lost their (male) loved ones to apartheid atrocities? He summed up the first set of hearings as follows:

> We have been shocked and filled with revulsion to hear of the depths to which we are able to sink in our inhumanity to one another: our capacity for sadistic enjoyment of the suffering we have inflicted on one another; the refinement of cruelty in keeping families guessing about the fate and whereabouts of their loved ones, sending them carelessly on a runaround from police station to police station, to hospital and mortuary in a horrendous wild goose chase. That is one side — the ghastly and sombre side of the picture that is emerging thus far.

> But there is another side, a more noble and inspiring one. We have been deeply touched and moved by the resilience of the human spirit. People, who by rights should have had the stuffing knocked our of them, refusing to buckle under the intense suffering and brutality and intimidation; people refusing to give up on the hope of freedom, knowing they were made for something better than the dehumanising awfulness of injustice and oppression; refusing to be intimidated to lower their sights. It is quite

incredible the capacity people have shown to be magnanimous — refusing to be consumed by bitterness and hatred, willing to meet with those who have violated their persons and their rights, willing to meet in a spirit of forgiveness and reconciliation, eager only to know the truth, to know the perpetrator so that they could forgive them.

We have been moved to tears. We have laughed. We have been silent and we have stared the beast of our dark past in the eye. We have survived the ordeal and we are realising that we can indeed transcend the conflicts of the past, we can hold hands as we realise our common humanity ... The generosity of spirit will be full to overflowing when it meets a like generosity. Forgiveness will follow confession and healing will happen, and so contribute to national unity and reconciliation.[53]

So began a profound two years of national heart-searching through storytelling. In fact, we were a nation on the world's operating table having open heart surgery, addressing the pain of gross human rights violations from 1960 to 1994. The Commission received 21 298 statements from victims, over 2 000 of these in public hearings, and 7 127 applications for amnesty from perpetrators. The statements contained 37 672 alleged gross violations of human rights, which included just on 10 000 alleged killings.[54] The process culminated in Desmond Tutu presenting the findings and records of the TRC firstly to President Mandela on 29 October 1998 and then to President Mbeki on 21 March 2003.[55] I must add that one cannot read the reports contained in these seven volumes and not have your heart ripped out by the agony of our common history. What we have lived through in our country, especially for the survivors of apartheid, is unbelievable.

From a theological, historical and international perspective, the TRC was unique and highly significant.[56] Many nations have learnt from the SA experience and are calling on the SA leaders to help settle national and international disputes. But the tragic reality is that, although the TRC was covered on TV and radio, many whites closed their hearts and minds and did not pay too much attention to the proceedings. Few actually attended any hearings. Some openly called it a witch-hunt while others called it an exercise in Afrikaner-bashing.[57] For most blacks it was an unprecedented opportunity to off-load years, decades, and even centuries of pent-up pain. Symbolically, and in reality, it was the first time since 1652 that blacks were able to speak freely without fear and be listened to empathetically. But it was also an opportunity for them to hear the truth and forgive. At one of the hearings, after Lucas Baba Sikwepere had told his sad story, the question was put to him: "How do you feel, Baba, about coming here to tell us your story?" His answer, quoted directly from the transcript of the hearings, echoes the feeling of every black person who told their story: "I feel what ... what has brought my sight back, my eyesight back, is to come back here and tell the story. But I feel what has been making me sick all the time is the fact that I couldn't tell my story. But now I ... it feels like I got my sight back by coming here and telling you the story."[58]

How did the churches respond to the TRC? In June 1997 a handful of ecumenical and evangelical leaders, including a few respected Afrikaners, sent an Open Letter to 12 000 pastors and leaders of Christian organisations in SA. It was a general letter of confession for pastors and churches to acknowledge their failure during the apartheid era. Only 610 signed and returned it, and this was submitted to the TRC on 15 November 1997.[59] This poor response must be put into context. Thirty-four official submissions were made to the TRC by church denominations and Christian organisations, many obviously speaking for thousands of individual pastors and congregations.[60] This must in turn be seen against the backdrop of the 1 800 church denominations in SA, excluding Christian organisations. The church's response was disappointing.

As Moss Ntlha points out: "Denominational confessions, while it is legitimate on its own, for many denominations it was a barrier for progressive action, and gives the individual an alibi to get on with his or her life without working through the issues."[61] This raises the question for all of us: How did I/you respond to the TRC? Four responses, especially among whites, were mentioned at the TRC:[62]

♦ "We are shocked by the revelations of the TRC, had we only known about the atrocities at the time, we would have objected." This is a self-serving myth because it is patently dishonest to claim that any of us were unaware of apartheid, forced removals and pass laws, of police brutality and deaths in detention.

♦ "We knew what was happening and we did everything in our power to object." This is also a myth. The truth is that a tiny minority of whites voiced opposition, mostly in conditions of relative safety and comfort; even fewer engaged directly in action to support the struggle for justice.

♦ "Let bygones be bygones, rehashing the past will only perpetuate divisions and inhibit reconciliation, so let's just build a new future." This response adds insult to injury. It is a monumental deceit because our (white) lives today are largely the product of a grand historical theft ... of land, labour, dignity and, in countless instances, of the lives of black people in our country.

♦ "Faced with our individual and collective guilt, we should be humble and honest, confess our failure and engage in meaningful acts of contrition and restitution." This is obviously the only adequate response in the light of our apartheid history with all its atrocities. Dealing with our (white) guilt, and putting it behind us, is very important for our freedom from imprisonment to internal conditioning and to our common history.[63]

These responses to the TRC raise more issues: Is there really collective guilt? After confession, what next? Has there been any meaningful reconciliation and healing? Has justice been served or subverted through the TRC process? And what about restitution? Have there been any real reparations? *These are serious and disturbing questions — the dilemma is captured in the little parable at the beginning of this chapter.* I remember a similar parable that my friends in Soweto used in the 1980s in order to convey their view of colonialism and apartheid history: "The white man came to us with a Bible in one hand and a gun in the other. And we stood holding our land. Then he said, "Let us pray". We closed our eyes and bowed our heads. When he said, "Amen" we opened our eyes and saw the Bible in our hands and the land in his, while he still held the gun in his other hand."[64]

The only adequate response to this is to put on sackcloth and ashes and cry to God for mercy, confessing our sins and the sins of our forefathers (as Daniel did for Israel — see the quote at the beginning of this chapter — the reality of historical sin and collective guilt). We should have done this in the early 1990s. It is still not too late to do it. If we humble ourselves, confess our sins, and turn form our wicked ways, God will hear us and forgive our sins and heal our land. Surely this does not only apply to Israel (2 Chron 7:14)? After WWII Martin Niemöller, a Lutheran pastor and theologian, was one of the only Germans who travelled around Europe and North America publicly confessing the sins of German Nazism and asking the nations of the world to forgive Germany. At this late stage in SA history, it would still be appropriate, in my opinion, to publicly ask for forgiveness at certain gatherings that lend themselves to such symbolic gestures, and to have a black authoritative representative speak forgiveness, as Tutu did at the Rustenburg Consultation of Churches in 1990. But it goes further and deeper than this. Many people in SA are realising that a cheap reconciliation will simply not do. *We have only now begun the real journey of costly reconciliation through healing, restitution and reconstruction.* And the implications are enormous.

I will address some of the above questions and implications in the next three chapters, but suffice it to say that a number of churches and Christian organisations are currently engaging in their own process to seek a meaningful reconciliation. On 18 September 2002 I was privileged to attend a Reconciliation Summit for Pentecostal, charismatic and evangelical denominational heads. The theme was Beyond Confession. We addressed the basic questions of how we can truly reconcile within our own denominations as blacks, whites, coloureds and Indians, and how we can reconcile with each other as leaders and denominations. The denominational leaders have declared this the *decade of reconciliation*. We need to ask ourselves: How seriously will we, as Vineyard, take up this challenge at local and national level?

 ## THE CURRENT SITUATION IN SOUTH AFRICA

To conclude this discussion on facing our history, I need to comment on the present context in SA with the post-apartheid and post-TRC challenges that we face. Jesus said we must read and interpret the signs of the times (Matt 16:3). Here is a broad-stroke sketch of where we are.

Pre-1994 we sat on opposite sides looking at each other through stereotypes and prejudice. Post-1994 has seen increasing changes at all levels of society. All the old categories and perceptions are being challenged. On the positive side, the dramatic change in our nation with its great leaders like Mandela, Tutu, De Klerk and others is the celebration of the world. Many wonderful achievements can be cited, besides what has already been mentioned. Everyone has the vote in a real democracy. The economy is growing steadily. Major shifts have taken place in the racial mix of city suburbs, schools and businesses — natural integration is a real hope. One can add to this list daily.

Six groups in South Africa

On the negative, side the post-apartheid bubble is bursting and reality is biting. What does it mean to build a new nation? What has changed? Has it been for the good? For the good of whom? Following Balcomb's generalised and functional view,[65] with some of my own adjustments and additions, we can say there are six groups in SA:

Firstly, there is a new political elite in government and civil society, at national and provincial level, all on the gravy train to one extent or another. They have posh salaries, cars and houses, with more than adequate benefits. Many previous church leaders who were in the struggle for justice are now in government positions. For this group, everything is rosy and different.

Secondly, there are those would-be political elites who try hard to get onto the gravy train but cannot — they see change but are not benefiting directly from it.

Their only hope to get "real" money is in the soul-destroying rat race of commerce and big business. But that often depends on who you know.

Thirdly, there are the marginalised, those who realise they will never get on the gravy train and decide to take whatever they can get, including hijacking a coach or two as they pass by. They will continue their crime and violence as long as things don't change — and if change comes, will they themselves be able to change?

Fourthly, many among the poor are simply accepting of their plight. They are the permanent underclass in SA. Life may have changed a little in terms of a new sub-economic house for some but, generally speaking, life remains the same. Although their expectations were raised, they now accept that every day is a slow grind for survival as it has always been and might be forever. This still constitutes by far the majority of our people in the nation.

Fifthly, there are the previously privileged who are deeply dislocated. For many of them, everything has gone wrong, the country is falling apart, standards are dropping on all fronts and crime is increasing. It is a common phenomena for the perpetrator of racism (and other forms of abuse) to blame the victim for the problems.[66] They emigrate either overseas to greener pastures or into suburban enclaves with higher walls, greater security and tighter like-minded friendships. They previously had access to everything by virtue of the colour of their skin, and they now fear the reverse is happening (through affirmative action and reverse racism). Their worst fear is SA going the way of the rest of Africa, the most prominent example currently is the sad situation in Zimbabwe, our neighbour.

But sixthly, there are signs of an emerging group of visionaries and realists, of South Africans of all colours from all walks of life and positions in the social structures, who have hope and faith in the future of SA. They are seeking creative new ways to share, to redress the wrongs of the past, to create jobs and turn the tide towards meaningful upliftment for all. They are turning the tide of negative perceptions by citing the many positive developments that have taken place in our nation since 1994, seeking to stimulate the process of nation building.[67] Among other things, the good news includes growing partnerships between government, business, civic organisations and churches, for the sake of the poor and the general good of society.

The culture in South Africa

These six groups function in, and are somewhat responsible for, the development of a culture of entitlement, self-pity, and corruption and mismanagement. A *culture of entitlement* operates among the previously disadvantaged who believe what was taken (stolen) from them must now be given back by the new government or they will take it — hence the endemic crime and violence with widespread theft in our country. This also operates at a very personal level: The whites had it all, now we blacks can have it all, nice houses, smart cars, high-flying jobs, bigger and better everything.

On the other side there is a *culture of self-pity* among the previously advantaged. They have little or no sense of culpability for what took place under apartheid and believe others want to take away what they legitimately earned and worked hard for. This attitude leads to withdrawal, emigration and, in some cases, white-collar crime.

There is also a *culture of corruption and mismanagement*. Sadly, this also seems to have become endemic in our society, especially in government, at national, provincial and local levels. There is increasing evidence of bribery, nepotism, corruption and misappropriation of funds that hit the newspaper headlines on a weekly, and sometimes daily basis. Where did all this come from? The previous government sowed the seeds of corruption. In all our greedy materialism and naked corruption, we (whites) have been the reference group for the blacks for many decades. All they have seen is what we modelled for them. It is no wonder that materialism and corruption continues after the political changes; it is a matter of character, not colour.

This is not a happy picture, but for those who have eyes to see, it is another *kairos*, an opportunity for the kingdom to break through. The reality is that the church (Christians) is found in most, if not all, of the above groups and cultures in society. The old god of materialism, now being pursued by upwardly mobile blacks, continues to triumph. How are we going to find one another and empower our people to be different and to make a difference? How are we going to create a different society? Is there a theology and process to help us?

Part of the answer is found in the national assembly called by the church in SA in July 2003; the South African Christian Leadership Assembly (SACLA2, the first one was held in 1979, referred to in Chapter 1). All the major denominations were represented as over 4 000 leaders were addressed by prominent church leaders for five days. The slogan was Being Real Christians in the Real South Africa, which assumes and acknowledges that the church should lead the way in society. The basic theme was "entering the promised land". For us to enjoy the full benefits of the miracle of the 1990s — the grapes, the milk and the honey — we need to face the giants that are threatening to destroy us, or at least threaten to keep us from entering fully into the miracle of national transformation. SACLA said that the nation is at another crossroad, threatened by seven giants: HIV and AIDS, crime, violence, racism, poverty and unemployment, sexism, and family in crisis (I will discuss these in Chapter 8). In addressing these giants, the Assembly said that we need to "Turn South Africa around, by crossing the divides, creating hope for the future, as we commit to action."

Four kinds of racists in South Africa

Although post-apartheid SA has seen racial categories overtly replaced by class categories and consciousness, *we still need to face the challenge of racism, including sexism.* I describe this challenge by way of the various types of racists and sexists that I see currently in our nation. I believe that we all — whites, blacks, Indians and coloureds — fall into one of these four categories.[68]

Confirmed racists are those who are still prejudiced and are open about it. They resent or even hate people of other races. This includes the growing phenomenon of xenophobia, where people fear and reject people of other races, for whatever reason. Some believe more than ever that blacks and whites should be apart. For some whites, blacks are still inferior. They say, "Things were better under apartheid." For some blacks, whites are still imperialistic settlers — they should "go back to Europe". Confirmed racists are more upfront and "honest" in their racism, often verbally dumping their offensive opinions and actions on those close at hand. The attitudes of this group are hardening.

Suppressed racists are those who are still prejudiced, but have suppressed it in the name of political correctness, keeping-the-peace, fear of reprisal or self-deception and psychological denial. Many South Africans would protest, "I am not racist, and never have been. Or if I was, I certainly am not one now." It just takes a certain event, issue or person to bring out the prejudice, the racist comments and attitudes. Sometimes it is blatant; at other times they are blind spots. We can only suppress things for so long, then they pop out — what is in the heart comes out sooner or later (as Jesus taught in Matt 12:33–37; 15:18–20). This phenomenon can be called "modern racism" that pays lip service to principles of equality while opposing its implementation with all kinds of rationalisation and maintains negative stereotypes via selective perception, choosing what one wants to see in various groups, e.g. blacks are destroying this country like the rest of Africa.[69]

Recovering racists are those who have acknowledged and faced their racial conditioning — racism is inbred if you were raised in SA — and are taking responsibility for it by consciously working on their thoughts, beliefs, attitudes and actions. They have dealt with their guilt and are free. But freedom is relative; like people recovering from an addiction, they are "in recovery" from racism. They are unlearning old ways and learning new ways of thinking and relating. They are working at inner and outer transformation of their lives (and society).

Preracists or innocents are those who are in the pre-prejudice stage — our children. They are the racially innocent people, unless their parents or others have already infected them with their prejudice. The post-apartheid generation now growing up has a wonderful opportunity to be free from racism in a way other South Africans could never be. We are faced with a serious challenge. When and how will they lose their innocence? As I mentioned at the beginning of this chapter, it will depend on our guidance and modelling, or lack thereof. It will also depend on the choices our children make and how they respond to what happens to them. The extent to which individuals around them change, and how much our society changes, will also affect them. Let us pray that this new generation will enter the new land, taking us with them into the nation of Good Hope.

I trust that this chapter has broken any denial you may have had about our apartheid history and racist reality. In fact, I hope that it has produced in you a humble and contrite heart that God will not despise (Ps 51:17). Like Daniel, may it lead to an honest and prayerful confession of your own need — and that of our nation — with regard to racism, reconciliation and transformation.

NOTES

1. Words over the entrance to the museum at the Dachau holocaust concentration camp, near Nuremberg, Germany (Tutu 1999, p. 32).

2. From a transcript of the TRC public meeting held at the University of Cape Town on 24 January 1997, see Du Toit (ed.) 1998, pp. 119, 121.

3. Pakenham 1991, p. xv.

4. Ibid. p. xvi.

5. I use quotations because 1994 was not a colonial hand over of power as in all the other nations of Africa due to SA becoming a Union in 1910 and then an independent Republic in 1961. In reality 1994 was "freedom at last" from the colonial masters — at least from the black SA experience.

6. Bosch 1991 has an informative discussion on colonialism and Western missions with the problems of racism, culture and historical guilt, pp. 302–312. Brazilian Catholic

Archbishop Dom Helder Camara has written a book that wrestles with the realities of colonialism and the church (Camara 1969).

7. Bosch 1980, pp. 5–6, 1991, p. 518.

8. Pakenham 1991, p. 4.

9. The debate about the missionary's involvement in issues of socio-political justice, or lack thereof, during the colonial era continues (see Bosch 1991, pp. 302–312, Cochrane 1987). See Cuthbertson 1989 for a balanced historical treatment of two well-known London Society missionaries in South Africa in the late 1700s to mid-1800s, Van der Kemp and John Philip — both made a stand against the racist colonialism of their time.

10. Luthuli 1962, pp. 28–32; Mandela 1994, pp. 30–34. These schools were not a guarantee of good leadership, as we see in Robert Mugabe (current President of Zimbabwe) who was also educated at a missionary school.

11. Fanon 1963, and his later book, *Black Skin, White Mask*, 1967, which is equally challenging.

12. Camara 1971. See also Nürnberger, Tooke and Domeris (eds.) 1989 for further discussion on the phenomenon of violence and its downward spiral.

13. Fanon 1963, p. 12.

14. Ibid. pp. 7–8.

15. For an official overview of the historical context, see Truth and Reconciliation Commission of South Africa Report (TRC SA R) vol. two, pp. 1–41. For a concise, helpful chronology of key events regarding our racial history, see TRC SA R vol. three, pp. 12–33.

16. Pakenham 1979, the modern concentration camps, which peaked with Hitler and Stalin, began with the British interning thousands of Afrikaners in squalid concentration camps, leading to the death of over 27 000 women and children.

17. TRC SA R vol. one 1998, pp. 30–35, a list of the key apartheid racial legislation. See pp. 448–477 for a more detailed list of racially based legislation from 1910 to 1995: 18 laws were passed pre-1948; 102 laws were passed between 1948 and 1990, the apartheid era; 25 laws were passed from 1990 to 1995 to dismantle apartheid, to secure negotiations and constitutionally form the new SA.

18. President PW Botha, as an act of "reform", brought the coloureds and Indians into parliament on a proportional representation basis: 178 seats for whites, 85 seats for coloureds and 45 seats for Indians. The blacks were simply left out.

19. Here are a few from my library: Aeschliman 1987 (the authorised biography of John Perkins), Chikane 1988, Miller 1968 (the authorised biography of Martin Luther King Jr.), Mohabir 1988, Luthuli 1962, Malcom X 1964, Mandela 1994, Parks 1992, Price 2002, Ryan 1990 (the authorised biography of Beyers Naudé), Smith 1984, Vos 1998, Wallis 1983, Washington and Kehrein 1993, and Woods 1987 (biography of Steve Biko).

20. The miracle behind the story in Cassidy 1995.

21. This call divided the church along black and white lines (again). It came in the wake of the controversial *Kairos Document* in which certain liberation theologians labelled the apartheid government as evil, and said that it should be directly opposed by all who call themselves Christian, see Institute for Contextual Theology (ICT 1985a).

22. Gorbachev 1987. President de Klerk used the fall of the Berlin Wall as a justification for the unbanning of the liberation movements and the release of political prisoners (February 1990, see TRC SA R vol. three, 1998, p. 28).

23. Mandela 1964, p. 33. This booklet, containing his entire speech, was banned when it was first published to commemorate his 70th birthday on 18 July 1988 (he was still behind bars). I managed to get a copy through my Soweto contacts and read it carefully, remembering his words.

24. Dallaire 2003. General Romeo Dallaire, the United Nations commander on the ground during the genocide, said: "The genocide in Rwanda was a failure of humanity that could easily happen again. I know there is a God because in Rwanda I shook hands with the devil. I have seen him, I have smelled him and I have touched him. I know the devil exists, and therefore I know there is a God ... I think first of all of those who died an agonising death from machete wounds inside the hundreds of sweltering churches, chapels and missions where they'd gone to seek God's protection and ended instead in the arms of Lucifer ... At its heart, the Rwandan story is the story of the failure of humanity to heed a call for help from an endangered people ... The only conclusion I can reach is that we are in desperate need of a transfusion of humanity ... No matter how idealistic the aim sounds, this new century must become the Century of Humanity, when we as human beings rise above race, creed, colour, religion and national self-interest, and put the good of humanity above the good of our own tribe — for the sake of the children and of our future."

25. The roller-coaster "miracle moments" are recorded in Cassidy 1995, pp. 139–214.

26. This is precisely the point made by the *Kairos Document* that stung the white churches into controversy (ICT 1985a).

27. There is still much debate on the issue of how wholistic change takes place, and which level is primary: spiritual or structural, private or political, etc. I believe it must happen on both levels. I basically follow Dallas Willard's analysis and approach of "spirit" being ultimate and primary. It is people (leaders) who make structures and dismantle them. So it comes down to the character and spirituality of individuals (leaders and their teams), whether in churches, civil society or politics, who influence others for better or worse through their policies and structures. Secondly, it is the general public who follow leaders and cooperate with the structures, because of their own character and spirituality — or lack thereof for better or worse, i.e. people either

work with structures or they resist and overthrow them. Therefore, change leaders specifically and people generally at the level of ideas, beliefs, values and practices (character and spirituality) and they will change structures for the common good and transformation of society. The crisis in the world is not unjust structures, it is a crisis of character, of authentic spirituality (Willard 1988, pp. 220–250, 1998, pp. 43–70).

28. Willard 1988, p. 245. I need to qualify this point on Christians and their leaders being responsible for change in society, vis-à-vis other faiths. We can and should work in cooperation with other faiths for societal transformation when it comes to issues of social justice. One can work together on the basis of common values for the good of society without compromising one's integrity of faith and mission. Not to have any thing to do with other religions just because they are non-Christian is short-sighted to say the least.

29. De Gruchy 1979 for a general view and Loubser 1987 for the role of the Afrikaans churches. We must not suppose that the English-speaking churches were not responsible for legitimating racism and apartheid. See Cochrane 1987 for a devastating historical critique in this regard.

30. Ecumenical is from the Greek *oikumene* or *oikonomia*, which means God's household or the whole church under Jesus' headship (Eph 1:10). To be ecumenical is to honour and seek the unity of the whole. Unfortunately it has acquired negative church political connotations.

31. See References. The main documents were from the ICT, SACC and SACBC. The most important and controversial document that stirred up awareness and debate in SA was the liberation theology of the *Kairos Document* (ICT 1985a) and *The Road to Damascus — Kairos and Conversion* (ICT 1989a). For theological debate on Kairos see a key book, Hofmeyer, Du Toit and Froneman (eds.) 1987; also Nolan 1987, Smit 1987, Kritzinger 1988 and Brummer 1994. On the whole idea of confessional statements and official position papers, and subscribing to them, see Nürnberger 1990a and 1991.

32. Concerned Evangelicals 1986 and Pentecostal Forum 1989. They attacked the notion of their fellow conservative church members that one can be apolitical, neutral or transcendent in the apartheid situation. Their analysis was simple (like the "liberal" Kairos theologians): the racist government had become demonised and was killing people; you had to choose, you were either for or against the government. There was no middle ground left to stand on.

33. Loubser 1987 has a detailed account on this development in Part 1 of his book.

34. This was one of the first serious "pass law" marches by a few thousand Africans. It was a peaceful protest, but the police responded with bullets killing 69 people, including eight women and ten children, and wounding 186. This drew international attention

and was a turning point in the country. See De Gruchy 1979, pp. 62–63, Davenport 1977, p. 286. One direct result was the Cottesloe Consultation of Churches, 7–14 Dec 1960 (Cottesloe Consultation 1960).

35. De Gruchy 1979, pp. 65–66, Loubser 1987, p. 87–88.

36. Dutch Reformed Church 1987 and the conservative backlash that caused a split in the DRC and led to the formation of the right-wing Afrikaanse Protestante Kerk (Afrikaans Protestant Church). This backlash is represented in the Continuation Committee of Objecting Members of the DRC (see *Faith and Protest* 1987).

37. Alan Boesak was a leading representative of the theology and stance of the coloured Afrikaans Reformed Church, the Sendingkerk, see Boesak 1977 and 1984.

38. Beyers Naudé was perhaps the most well known, see Ryan 1990. Nico Smith was another white Afrikaner theologian (dominee) who moved into the black township of Mamelodi in 1986 and started a reconciliation ministry called Koinonia, see Koinonia 1987.

39. I say "apparently" because the confession was not given by the DRC's official spokesperson at the consultation, Moderator Johan Heyns (Alberts and Chikane, eds. 1991, pp. 170–176) but by another DRC theologian, Willie Jonker (Ibid. pp. 87–98). It was a very moving experience. Jonker's apology was immediately and graciously accepted by Archbishop Desmond Tutu, which was the cause of significant disturbance and debate among some of the black leaders present (Ibid. pp. 99–102).

40. I have mentioned the Mennonite poster: "A Modest Proposal for Peace: Let the Christians of this world stop killing each other". An example of this: A tongues-speaking Pentecostal pastor from the Apostolic Faith Mission church in the black township, Frank Chikane, was interrogated and tortured by a white tongues-speaking Pentecostal deacon of the same denomination in the neighbouring white city (he was a special branch policeman). See Chikane 1988.

41. Quoted in Cassidy 1989, p. 127. Verwoed further said: "I have earnestly asked myself whether the advocates of total unity of the different races can bring about justice and fairness to everyone. I am absolutely convinced that integration in a country like South Africa cannot possibly succeed ... If meddlesome people keep their hands off us, we shall in a just way, such as behoves a Christian nation, work out solutions in the finest detail and carry them out. We shall provide all our races with happiness and prosperity."

42. Alberts and Chikane (eds.) 1991, p. 14.

43. Ibid. pp. 275–286.

44. As Cottesloe was the turning point in the church's stand against apartheid, so Rustenburg was the turning point in the church regarding repentance, unity and building a new SA. See De Gruchy 1991.

45. I tell the story of the Vineyard plant and involvement in SA in Venter 2000, pp. 16–21.

46. Morphew 1989.

47. Because of my subjective involvement, it would be inappropriate to speak further of the significance of Johweto for AVC SA and beyond, but one aspect should be mentioned. We thoroughly contextualised our Vineyard worship in an African style. Some of our black worship leaders and songwriters are now featured on Vineyard Music CDs, notably *Winds of Worship 14*, *Only You/Fela Jesu* and a totally African Vineyard worship CD *Thula Sizwe*. Some of those songs were written and sung in Johweto in the 1980s.

48. His statement is recorded in Alberts and Chikane (eds.) 1991, pp. 263–264.

49. TRC SA R volume one, 1998, pp. 94–102.

50. Tutu 1999, pp. 10, 45–46. Theologians had been debating issues of national guilt and amnesty during the transition to democracy, for example De Gruchy 1993.

51. The first public document on the legislative and operational framework of the TRC, Justice in Transition 1994. See also Tutu 1999, pp. 25–36, with his concerns about justice, which could be seen to be undermined by an "easy reconciliation" and amnesty, pp. 46–60. See Boraine 2000, and TRC SA R vol. one, pp. 103–134 for a detailed explanation of the concepts and principles of the TRC.

52. Tutu 1999, pp. 61–64.

53. Ibid. pp. 90–91.

54. Krog 2002, p. vii. Antjie Krog was a journalist reporting on the TRC. The official TRC statistics are in TRC SA R vol. one, pp. 165–173, 276, vol. three, pp. 3–11. See the list of categories of violations of human rights and torture methods, vol. five, pp. 1–23.

55. The findings are available from www.gov.za/reports/2003/trc/. The 1998 presentations are in vols one to five, the 2003 presentations in vol. six and seven — see TRC SA R.

56. Boraine 2000, and the debates on theological evaluations and significance of the TRC: Botman and Petersen 1996, Gerloff 1998 (from a German perspective), Krog 1998, Maluleke 1997a and 1997b, Smit 1995.

57. One must be compassionately mindful here of the deep dislocation, guilt and identity crisis that the Afrikaner community has been through, from the 1980s to the present. Only those who have truly faced their past and processed it with confession, forgiveness and reconciliation are free to feel fully Afrikaans with self-respect. Afrikaners like Beyers Naudé (see Ryan 1990), Nico Smith, Willem Verwoed, Piet Meiring and Klippies Kritzinger are examples of this — see their articles in Du Toit (ed.) 1998.

58. Krog 2002, p. 31.

59. Du Toit (ed.) 1998, the Open Letter is on pp. 9–11; the remainder of the book is a

discussion of why we must confess and how we can seek reconciliation and make restitution.

60. Ibid. p. viii. See TRC SA R vol. four, pp. 59–92 for the report on the submissions to the TRC by The Faith Communities (all religions). Of the 41 submissions received, 34 were from the Christian faith.

61. Du Toit (ed.) 1998, p. 27. A van Niekerk says a similar thing on p. 92: "It would be helpful if more personal confessions could be made public ... what he/she actually neglected to do, as an individual ... like racist jokes, a lack of compassion, a refusal to complain against incidents of police violence ..."

62. These four responses come from the Director's submission (Centre for Conflict Resolution) to the TRC on 23 July 1997, see Du Toit (ed.) 1998, pp. 127–129.

63. Barndt 1991, pp. 43–50.

64. Land redistribution is still one of the most emotive and important issues in our nation. "In 1913 The Native's Land Act prescribed that no African person be allowed to own land outside designated reserves (approximately 7% of the land was allocated for African people, subsequently increased in 1936 to 13%)"; a quote from TRC SA R vol. three, p. 12.

65. Balcomb 1998.

66. Ryan 1976, a classic exposé of middle-class ideological defences. See also Barndt 1991, pp. 31–34.

67. Two South Africans got tired of all the destructive talk (especially among the previously advantaged) and published two books detailing many stories and facts of our enormous progress since 1994. See Bowes and Pennington 2002 and 2003.

68. These categories are my own, but informed by Barndt's discussion of white racism in Barndt 1991, pp. 40–50.

69. "Modern Racism and Its Symptoms" from Prof W Jordaan, Head of Psychology at UNISA, in *Towards a Psychology of Reconciliation*, in Du Toit (ed.) 1994, p. 82–84. See also Ryan 1976 on blaming the victim.

CHAPTER 5

A BIBLICAL VIEW OF RACISM, RECONCILIATION AND TRANSFORMATION — THE BACKGROUND STORY

From now on we see no one from a worldly or this-age perspective; and even though we saw Messiah in this way, we do so no longer. If anyone is united with the Messiah, there is a new creation: everything old has passed away, and look, the new has come! And it all comes from God, who has reconciled us to himself through Messiah, and has given us the ministry of reconciliation: that God was in Messiah Jesus reconciling the world to himself, offering forgiveness of sins, and even entrusting to us this message of reconciliation. Therefore we are Messiah's ambassadors going around everywhere with God making his appeal through us. We appeal and persuade you to drop your differences and be reconciled to God and one another. How? Through Jesus the Messiah. He died for our wrongdoing — although he himself never did anything wrong — so that we might be put right with God and share in his rightdoing.

Paul in 2 Cor 5:17–21 RAP

John Wimber used to say that the Bible is a weird book: "Have you read the stories in this book? They are weird." What is even more weird are the many ways in which we interpret the book. And how we use the book. We can make it mean almost anything we want it to say. This has caused major problems in our history. Some Afrikaner Christians used the Bible to justify apartheid and kill black people, while others used the same Bible to overthrow apartheid and kill white people. Our approach in the Vineyard is that we believe the Bible is our final authority for faith and life (the evangelical model). We also learn from what the church has said and done through its history with regard to interpreting the Scriptures (the model of tradition). We ask the Holy Spirit to open our eyes and reveal God's truth, to speak to us and guide us (the Pentecostal model). Ultimately, however, as evangelicals, and for all Christians it comes down to how we interpret and use the Bible. We need to interpret and use it responsibly. The million dollar question is: What is our biblical view on racism, reconciliation and transformation? Answering this question will give us a basis for action.

I begin with a brief historical perspective and an introductory word study on reconciliation, then discuss our basic approach in theological understanding and the background biblical story that gives meaning and definition to reconciliation. I will raise specific issues in Vineyard thinking along the way, relevant to evangelicals, Pentecostals and charismatics. I use certain technical terms, for example, "theology", which is simply the study of God. Or, more accurately, the discipline of reflecting seriously on our faith and understanding of God, primarily via the Scriptures. This chapter and the following is an exercise in biblical theology.

 ## A HISTORICAL-THEOLOGICAL PERSPECTIVE

We need the perspective that only a good knowledge of history can give us. As Vineyard, we need to be aware of, and learn from, our historical and theological roots. They go back to Protestant evangelical faith in the Reformation period in Europe (1500 and 1600s), and the great evangelical awakenings of the 1700s and 1800s in England, North America and places in Europe. The awakenings led to waves of missions into Africa, Asia and South America, alluded to in the previous chapter. Although these awakenings and missions brought about countless evangelical conversions, they also led to large-scale socio-political reforms, especially in England and America. William Wilberforce and Charles Finney were at the forefront of the abolition of slavery. John Wesley campaigned against child labour and other forms of social and structural injustice. Jonathan Edwards modelled the same unity of evangelical belief and practice. More recently, this unity was extraordinarily embodied in Dietrich Bonhoeffer.[1] There was no division between the gospel and social issues in the minds of these men, nor in most of the evangelical church members of those days. They were as passionate about social justice as they were about evangelism, church planting and missions.

With the rise of the social sciences, the mid to late 1800s saw a growing tension between an increasingly liberal interpretation of Scripture with its "social gospel" emphasis, and a reactionary spiritual and "personal gospel" approach.[2] The former developed into a liberal theology that was caricatured in its preoccupation with socio-political issues throughout the 1900s. It further developed with emerging social trends into various contextual theologies, like liberation, feminist and black theologies. These theologies highlighted the evils of structural sin and motivated the many forms of socio-political activism — and even revolution — from the 1950s to the present. Interestingly, apartheid was a typical contextual theology that legitimised Afrikaner nationalist aspirations. The traditional and mainline denominations that associate with the World Council of Churches (WCC) and its affiliate national bodies, are generally, and sometimes unfairly, seen as part of the social gospel grouping. The tag "ecumenicals"[3] has stuck to them.

The reaction to this liberalism was the development of a conservative theology. They clearly saw themselves as the carrier of "orthodoxy" — keeping to the faith and interpretation of the Scriptures that was handed down over the centuries. They accused the liberals of departing from orthodox evangelical Christian faith. Instead of pursuing a holistic gospel approach, they withdrew into a spiritual and private morality. It became an individualised Christianity preoccupied with moral "personal sin management"[4] that was apolitical in stance, or so they claimed and believed. In effect it often meant that they were on the political right wing supporting conservative and even repressive political agendas from the 1950s to the present. They have been tagged as "fundamentalists" because they claim to stick to the fundamentals of Scripture. Their interpretation of Scripture is often "biblicist", which means taking Scriptures out of their historical context and misapplying them to today's context — often too literally. This is often how things are "read into the Scriptures" and how vested interests and other ideological issues are legitimised. We should not interpret Scripture in the light of our experience, but rather understand and evaluate our experience and contemporary society against the whole standard of Scripture.

Conservative evangelical theology has unfortunately fallen into this fundamentalist category, although in its pure orthodox form it was, and is, radical in its social awareness and involvement. We must not confuse conservative evangelicalism with political conservatism. Depending on the particular socio-political issue being addressed, conservative evangelical theology may take a stance that might be seen as left wing, right wing or centrist in political terms. It does not matter how it appears in the public mind or political arena, as long it holds true to biblical values, challenging society and politicians accordingly — it must never find itself in the service of any party political agenda or ideological cause.[5]

The historical-theological separation can be seen as the great betrayal of liberalism and the great reversal of evangelicalism. This late 19th and early 20th century phenomenon entrenched a deeply divided view of things. As a result, throughout the 20th century we have been plagued by a dualistic mindset and approach in theology, church life and general Christianity. Here are some of the damaging dualisms: private vs public, spiritual vs secular, vertical vs horizontal, church vs politics, personal vs social, and evangelical vs ecumenical. As evangelicals, Pentecostals and charismatics we have been profoundly conditioned by these false dichotomies.[6] At worst they reinforce the racial and class divides; at best they make reconciliation and transformation difficult to achieve.

Although our roots are in orthodox evangelicalism with its wholistic gospel, Vineyard has come via the great reversal. We urgently need to recover our heritage in terms of our social theology and activism for the sake of God's kingdom and for the sake of the world. We have experienced the charismatic dimension of Christianity — John Wimber called Vineyard "empowered evangelicals"[7] — but we must learn to use it not only for power evangelism, but also for power justice. How can we do this? Part of the answer is recovering the biblical theology expounded in this book. With this historical perspective in mind, we can focus on reconciliation, including racism and transformation, from a theological viewpoint.

 # AN INTRODUCTORY WORD STUDY

Where does the word reconciliation come from? It came to us from the Latin *reconciliatio*, the word that the Vulgate Bible used to translate Paul's choice of *katallasso*. He used this Greek word to describe God's saving work in Jesus Christ. From the Latin, via the French, we get the English word "reconciliation" which was used in the King James Version of the Bible (1611)[8]. Since words acquire different meanings over years and in various contexts, what did Paul mean when he used *katallasso*? Was there a similar Hebrew concept behind it?

Katallasso comes from the classic Greek world where diplomats and ambassadors used to settle war disputes by making peace treaties. The root word *allasso* means "to change or exchange" as in money (economics) or improving relationships by removing disputes as in exchanging enmity for friendship (political and relational usage). Paul was a master at taking up words in common usage in order to communicate the good news of Jesus — he filled the words with his own meaning.[9] Interestingly, "reconciliation" came from secular political usage into the Christian world, and can be — should be — used once again in the world of politics.[10]

There are 15 occurrences of the noun, verb and derivatives of *katallasso* in the New Testament. The key references are found in Rom 5:10–11, Eph 2:16, Col 1:20–22, and 2 Cor 5:18–19. These will be discussed in more detail later, but reading them one finds that what people would have heard Paul saying was something like this:

> We are all enemies of God and are at war with him due to our sin. But he has had mercy on us and has reconciled us to himself by sending his Son Jesus to die for us, to remove the sin and enmity between us and God. Then Jesus rose again, giving us his Spirit in actual forgiveness, uniting us with God in the gift of righteousness and eternal life. This becomes a reality as we put our trust in Jesus. Those who have done this are his ambassadors, offering this reconciliation to all people who are still foreigners or enemies of God. This reconciliation also means that we who are so different from one another, who are alienated and even enemies of each other, have become one as friends, brothers and sisters in God's family of reconciliation.

At the heart of this idea of reconciliation is a closely-related word and concept that needs comment.[11] It has to do with the basis on which God's anger against our enmity is removed: Jesus' death on the cross satisfied God's justice as a substitute sacrifice for us. In so doing God's wrath against us, and our sin, was put aside and reconciliation has taken place — and takes place as we put our faith in him. In applying *katallasso* to the human dimension, Paul clearly uses it to refer to reconciliation between estranged people. As a result of reconciliation with God, Jews and Gentiles are reconciled to one another in the community of faith (Eph 2:16). Husbands and wives should rather reconcile and not divorce (1 Cor 7:10f). Matthew uses a unique verb derived from *katallasso* in 5:24 to speak of reconciliation between people when sin and disputes affect their relationships.

Is this the whole picture? Paul was a Jew trained in Torah. Was there any Hebraic idea behind his usage of *katallasso*? The answer is yes and no. No, because the word in the Greek translation of the Old Testament (the Septuagint) appears three times and does not help us in finding Paul's source understanding.[12] And yes, because Paul knew that the idea and message of reconciliation was formed and framed by the overarching story of God's dealings with Israel — Israel in exile in her sin, returning to God and to the land; the price of blood sacrifice to remove Israel's sin; the restoration of fellowship and national life, and even *Shalom* with her enemies. Furthermore, the climax of this Jewish frame of reference for Paul was the fulfilment of the new covenant in *Yeshua ha Mashiach* (Jesus the Messiah, Jer 31:31–34; Ezek 36:24–30 cf. Heb 8–10). We can call this Hebraic framework "the grand narrative".[13] This is what Paul was communicating whenever he resorted to certain Greek idioms, like *katallasso*, for the purpose of helping Gentiles understand and believe God's work on earth.

As a point of interest, Rabbinical Judaism (from the Talmud, 300–500AD), used two Hebrew words for the Greek *katallasso*. *Ritstsah* and *piyyes* conveyed the idea of reconciliation with God and with other human beings via the removal of enmity by "making calm" or "becoming pleasant".[14] The Jewish Midrashes (Rabbinical commentaries on the Old Testament) use these words to explain, for example, how Moses reconciled God with Israel by removing God's anger after the golden calf episode at Sinai. The bottom line in Rabbinical Judaism is that God is the object who is reconciled to humans by the removal of his anger by some form of sacrificial intervention. This is in contrast to the Messianic faith of the New Testament where God is the subject — *he* takes the initiative and reconciles humans to *himself* by the sacrifice of his Son, *Yeshua ha Mashiach*. There is a big difference between the two, hence the difference between modern Judaism in all its forms and biblical Messianic Judaism that is commonly called Christianity.

Although there are relatively few usages of the word reconciliation in the Bible, the concept and the process is present everywhere. We can summarise the biblical idea of reconciliation as God reconciling us to himself in Christ, thereby reconciling us to each other in the community of faith. Reconciliation is both an event and a process having the following aspects:

♦ to turn or change (repentance);

♦ to remove enmity, wrath and sin (confession);

♦ to pay the price — the justice of the cross (trusting Jesus in the cost of reconciliation);

♦ to give forgiveness — and receive it if necessary (actually reconciling);

♦ to establish peace (*Shalom*)— restoring fellowship and making restitution if necessary (living out reconciliation by restoring justice).

BIBLICAL THEOLOGY AND
THE KINGDOM OF GOD

To flesh out the picture of reconciliation, this underlying grand narrative must be examined in more detail. This is an exercise in biblical theology which can be defined as the study of God and our faith via the examination of major themes in the Bible, such as covenant or the kingdom of God. Many theologians now agree that Jesus and the kingdom of God is the biblical theology that most comprehensively unlocks the message and meaning of the Bible — the Vineyard has taken it as the foundational framework for its life and ministry.[15]

Keep in mind that as we introduce Jesus and the kingdom and go further into the biblical story, we are dealing with God's overarching story that ultimately defines the meaning of reconciliation.

Understanding the kingdom of God

The core idea of the kingdom is God's reign as king in his Son, Jesus Christ. The kingdom is the dynamic of God's rule that is both present and future at the same time. Jesus is "the Beginning and the End, the First and the Last" — literally "the Last One" (*eschaton* in the Greek, Rev 1:17). *Eschaton* refers to God's original goal and ultimate purpose in creation, the fulfilment of all things, God's first and last word and action that draws all things together under his rule and reign. Jesus is God's *eschaton*. When Jesus came, the end came for Satan and his kingdom, and it was the beginning of deliverance and freedom for people into God's kingdom. Jesus is the "ruler of the kings of the earth ... bringing all things in heaven and earth together under one head ... so that God may be all in all" (Rev 1:5; Eph 1:10; 1 Cor 15:28).

A kingdom perspective embodies the basic framework underlying the biblical revelation. It is a two-age view of reality: This age (kingdom of evil and kingdoms of this world) and the age to come (God's kingdom). This should not be seen as two ages neatly separated serially in time as we know it. The kingdom perspective sees things as God originally intended and as his kingly rule will make it to be in the end. In other words, it is a view from the end back into history and interpreting things accordingly.[16]

This view of God's kingdom refers to the fulfilment of the biblical vision of *Shalom* that I spoke about in Chapter 3. God is the Creator-King who lovingly rules over his creation. Evil entered earth and divided human beings from God, one another and creation itself. *But God* promised he would intervene and restore the reign of *Shalom* at the end of the age (Jesus called it "the kingdom of the heavens"). *But God* has already fulfilled his promise in the coming of Jesus two thousand years ago. Jesus declared war on Satan and his kingdom, and decisively defeated him. However, Jesus did not end this evil age as such, and said he would come back one day when he would consummate the kingdom in all its heavenly fullness. Then heaven will fill the earth and the prayer that Jesus taught us will have become an embodied reality: "Your kingdom has come, your will is now being done here on earth, just as it has always been done in the heavens" (the fulfilled RAP!). In the meantime we, the community of the kingdom, continue the war by enforcing Satan's defeat — we live out the future kingdom in the present because it has already come and is working in and through us into the world.

We are living "between the times", caught in the tension of two ages that overlap, because God's government is both "already" and "not yet".[17] This tension is what Jesus meant when he talked about "the mystery of the kingdom of the heavens" in Matt 13 — these parables illustrate the nature of the kingdom as both "now" and "then". Upholding this tension is crucial for the health, balance and integrity of our beliefs and life practices as followers of Jesus. It will safeguard us from an overemphasis of "kingdom now", which leads to presumption and arrogance, and a naivety about involvement in the world. It will also safeguard us from an overemphasis on "kingdom then", which leads to defeatism and withdrawl, and an overly spiritual view of things, despising this world (so heavenly- minded that we are of no earthly use). Understanding and living in kingdom tension will give us a humble, hopeful, realistic and persevering approach to the gospel and church, and to daily life and society.

Furthermore, a correct understanding of the kingdom of God will dissolve the false dualisms of the previous century. It restores a wholistic approach to life and to the gospel, and is therefore the best framework for teaching reconciliation and social ethics (i.e. the socio-political implications and imperatives of the gospel). It will help us recover our evangelical heritage of the great awakenings of the 18th and 19th centuries that saved multitudes and changed nations. We will share the same motivation to prayerful expectation of the kingdom's breakthrough while living integrated lives of faith, kingdom activism and social witness.

Applying the kingdom of God to reconciliation

As we saw in Chapter 3, the picture of heaven includes no racism, pain, sickness, tears or death, just one happy family made up of every tribe, language and nation.

Note that nations, languages and cultures are not obliterated into a bland uniformity. God's reconciled unity is a rich tapestry of diversity of personalities, colour and culture, although we all have one identity as God's one family in Messiah Jesus (Rev 5:9–10; 7:9; 21:3–4 cf. Gal 3:22–9). This "new age" reality has already broken into history in Jesus and his church.[18] Because the kingdom has come, we continually seek to model heaven on earth as God's reconciled and reconciling community — in all its rich diversity and socio-ethical implications. We work tirelessly against all forms and structures of racism and sexism in church and society, without giving up when the going gets tough. We continually seek to embody heaven on earth in our churches or, more practically, to be the (God's) answers that society is looking for, and so desperately needs.

On the other hand, because the kingdom has not yet finally come, only God can bring it about. Only God can destroy and will destroy evil in terms of racist attitudes and social structures. We remain humbly dependent on him, avoiding any attitude of triumphalism. We cannot force or impose the kingdom, reconciliation or a multicultural expression of church, let alone society. Because the kingdom has not yet come, we self-consciously avoid any manipulative use of it — reconciliation in the kingdom is not an ideology, and must never be used ideologically. Those who make racial reconciliation the cause of the gospel, and of society, create all sorts of problems for themselves and others. Neither do we become ideological or party political about any particular public policy or socio-political issue. We fully engage in all issues, whether personal, church, social or political, but for truth's sake, for justice' sake, for the kingdom's sake. And we engage in the hope of a kingdom breakthrough — either now, or later, or when Jesus comes!

Kingdom people are weird — like the Bible — as I mentioned at the beginning of the chapter. We are a strange mix of hard-nosed realism and irrepressible faith and hope. We are creatures of contradiction. As the Talmudic Rabbinic saying goes: When we pray, we pray as if everything depends on God — because it really does; but when we work, we work as if everything depends on us — because it really does! Both are equally true. We can do no other, because the kingdom is in us and working through us, while at the same time beyond us and independent of us. We are signs of both death and life at the same time. Like Jesus, we are a sign of death to all forms of evil and to those who cling to it in any shape or form — judgement day has come, evil has and will be defeated. At the same time we are signs of life and hope to any who turn and trust Jesus for healing and transformation, because the kingdom has come and is working in and through us (as Paul says in 2 Cor 2:14–17, we are "the aroma of Christ" — through us God "spreads everywhere the fragrance of the knowledge of him").

The church *really is* the instrument of the kingdom in the world. As Jesus said, we *really are* the salt of the earth, the light to the nations and the sheep among wolves (Matt 5:13–16; 10:16). Our presence and activism in society prevents the spread and decay of racism and other forms of evil, while making the world palatable to God by being the earthly sign of God's covenant (salt is the sign of the covenant, Lev 2:13). Our presence and activism in the nations penetrates, exposes and drives back all forms of darkness and evil, while giving hope, sight and direction to those who turn to our light. Our humble vulnerability and readiness to serve and die for the kingdom, has a silencing and redemptive effect on the violence and wildness of this world.[19] But what happens if we lose our saltiness? What happens if we hide our light? What happens if we become wise in our own eyes, proud and self-serving? Jesus says we will be good for nothing. We will be overrun by racism, by violent revolution. We will come under the heel of evil in society, as happened under Nazism and apartheid. We could then fall under the judgements of God and be condemned along with the wicked — WWII is a most horrific reminder to us all. The world suffered terribly partly because the church lost its way in the early 1900s and as a result came under the judgements of history.[20] We learn from this piece of history that the church must always strive to be the community of the kingdom, living God's story of salvation and hope, in the midst of the human story of pain and despair.

This brings me back to the grand narrative. Before I start the biblical story, it will be appropriate at this point to address briefly an aspect of kingdom theology that is relevant to Vineyard — and similar networks and church planting movements — with regard to church growth, culture and reconciliation.

KINGDOM, CHURCH GROWTH AND SOCIAL THEOLOGY

In Vineyard we have been strong in the "power encounter" aspects of the kingdom, in "signs and wonders" and church growth. These are terms and courses that John Wimber popularised in the early 1980s. They had to do with the outworking of Ladd's kingdom theology in terms of church ministry, growth and mission. The church growth movement, to which John contributed significantly,[21] used a kingdom framework for theology, but applied sociological tools in understanding why some churches grow and others do not. In practice this has often resulted in a blurring of the lines between a theological and a sociological view of the church, resulting in some weaknesses.

One of the weaknesses of the church growth paradigm, with its silent pressure to grow churches, is the poor social theology it has produced. The driving force behind much of what happens in many such churches, both in terms of its theologising and programming, is the technology of "how to"[22] — how to grow the church, how to do a seeker-friendly service, how to do this, that and the next thing. This all adds to the goal and motivation of self-propagation by means of a focus on consumer-oriented ministries. "Ministry to the poor", in terms of feeding and clothing the needy, is often the only social concern there is. It becomes an attachment to the real thing, which is growing our church. There is much more to a social theology of the kingdom: What about the inclusive nature of the church as a reconciled and reconciling community? What about a theology of engagement with justice issues, public policy, violence and conflict resolution, economic disparities and wholistic community development?

The main concern that I want to comment on is the "homogeneous unit" principle in the church growth paradigm.[23] This is the idea that the gospel spreads fastest among people of the same or similar (homogeneous) grouping, as in extended families, university students, cultural groups, and so forth. A person becoming a Christian should be helped to reach his or her own family, friends and people group via his or her common language, culture and interests. The gospel spreads quickest among homogeneous people groups and one can see some of this in the way the gospel spread and the church grew in the book of Acts. (But we know that evangelism happens in other ways.)

The confusion comes when the sociological principles identified in church growth are not clearly differentiated from a theological understanding of the nature of the church. The church is first and foremost the community of the kingdom. In church growth thinking, it has become a sociological phenomenon — they work from practice back to theology. The thinking can go like this: A person is born again, which leads to his or her type of people becoming Christians, which in turn can lead to a homogeneous church plant, especially in non-cosmopolitan towns and rural areas. Then the great commission in Matt 28:18–20 is interpreted in those terms: "Go and make disciples of all nations" means plant churches in and through all homogeneous people groups, right down to the very last one. In this way homogeneous churches are justified as the norm, and the implication is that multicultural churches are seen at best as unworkable or, at worst, unbiblical.[24]

The real danger is that homogenous churches and homogeneous church plants can easily be used as a justification for churches being separated on the basis of class, colour or culture, as happened officially in SA, and happens unofficially in most parts of the world. This goes directly against all that Paul taught and fought for in terms of the church's radical unity and its powerful witness in his social context of race, class and gender divisions. Paul's divided social context was just like our current divided context in SA and in our global village. We can say that as a missiological *strategy* of evangelism, the homogeneous unit idea may have some merit, but used as a *theology* of church, it is heresy.[25] This is not a small issue — it has very serious implications, and over the centuries it has cost a lot of blood.

Look at the origins of apartheid in the Afrikaans church in SA.[26] In 1829 a "bastard", a "person of colour", became a believer in Somerset West in the Cape. He was baptised and wanted to take communion. One elder in the local (white) congregation insisted that he be served communion separately because "he (the bastard) was not born a Christian" like the rest of the congregation. This controversy led to the Church Synod ruling that there should be "no discrimination" (1834) against such new "believers of colour". Due to pressure from white church members, the Synod later (1857) passed a ruling that said: No discrimination is "desirable", but due to "the weakness of some" (i.e. white members), coloured churches could be started so that they could "enjoy their Christian privileges separately". The justification was "for mission's sake" so that the gospel could spread easily among the coloured people. This resulted in the "final solution", which was the formation of the NG Sendingkerk in 1881 (the separate coloured Dutch Reformed Mission Church). The end result was that in the 1930s Afrikaans church leaders formally asked the government to legislate racial segregation. Separate racial congregations were no longer justified by the "weakness of some", nor by missions strategy, but by an apartheid theology of church and society. They taught that racial distinctions, cultural identities and linguistic barriers were part of God's will and must be maintained in church and society, and this was part of "the final solution"![27]

The implication is that if we are too pragmatic, if we allow sociological realities and frames of reference to dictate, if we are too driven by church consumerism and the need for success, if we accommodate the weaknesses and discomforts of our people in avoiding the challenges and "unworkability" of multiracial churches, we end up being a copy of secular society and not the community of the kingdom of God. We cease being the salt and light. Our very nature as the church of Jesus Christ is not only compromised and subverted, but lost. And we come under the judgements of the God of history.

I am back to the sober note on which I ended the previous section. Let me resume the grand narrative, looking at the sweeping story of God's reconciling march through history, starting from the beginning of creation, and spelling out the implications for racism, reconciliation and transformation.

LEARNING FROM THE CREATION STORY

In the beginning God made the heavens and the earth. Then he spoke order into his creation and made all things "good" (Gen 1:9, 12, 18, 21, 25); in other words, he thoroughly enjoys his creation! Then the climax, God made humankind in his image and likeness, he made them as male and female to rule over his creation on earth. God looked and this was "very good" (Gen 1:26, 31). In other words, he enjoys us human beings even more; we are the pinnacle of his creation! The picture we have is of Adam and Eve living lives of perfect harmony with God, each other and creation. It was paradise, the Garden of Delight — the Hebrew meaning of Eden. Their wholistic bliss is the picture of God's intention for all of us, for his creation (the idea of *Shalom* described in Chapter 3). The story begins in Genesis with a new earth, with new relational people in a new garden of delight, and ends in Revelation with a heavenly garden city on a new earth filled with God's one renewed and reconciled people. But — there are always "buts" this side of heaven — soon after it begins, the story plunges into tragedy as sin enters and destroys the perfect picture. God immediately steps in and begins to reconcile all things.

This brief summary of the creation story has a number of key implications.

Firstly, we are called to affirm the goodness of creation as wholistic, as relationally interdependent

Creation is good and wholistic, dynamically interrelated and integrated. We are to enjoy creation as he does and not to see it as inherently evil — "the earth is the Lord's and the everything in it" (Ps 24:1). We are called to see all human beings, one another, as the glory of God's creation because we are made in his image and likeness to rule over the earth on his behalf. We are utterly glorious beings, carrying awesome dignity and responsibility, entrusted with God's ongoing work of *Shalom*-creation (Gen 1:26–30; Ps 8:4–8).

This calls us to affirm the sanctity of human life and the dignity of human beings — way above animal or other forms of life. In our day many people are treated worse than animals; some people treat animals much better than they would other human beings. To trample on human dignity and take human life is extremely grave, it is the direct defacing of God's image on earth. No wonder we are in the mess we are in. The wholistic nature of our relational interdependence is destroyed when we do not honour one another, whenever we violate human dignity and take human life.

Secondly, issues of equality and identity are highlighted

As male and female we are created equal in God's image and likeness. We carry God's image both as individuals and as relational beings in our treatment of one another. This affirms the dignity and equality of the sexes in their diversity, and of all persons regardless of colour, class, culture or creed. It challenges any form of discrimination, be it sexism, racism or classism, that destroys human dignity, that murders self-image, that defines some people as inferior and others as superior. There is a great need in our day and generation to teach this doctrine of creation (and of redemption in Jesus Christ) in order to restore people's belief in themselves, to recover the worth, identity and self-image that is so defaced by being downtrodden daily. Many black people have hated themselves, rejected their black skin and angrily asked God, "What did I do wrong that I was born black?" Who made them feel this way and believe this?

This is so important that I need to say more about equality and identity. Equality has to do with essence of being, not with personality or life function per se. Man and woman are created equal (Gen 1:26–27) but are functionally different (Gen 2:7, 15–25; they were made to complement one another in a wholeness of mutual interdependence. The most obvious example is the genital difference and complementarity between male and female). The same applies to all human beings, we are equal in essence but different and complementary in personality and function. Equating equality with function leads to a serious loss of human dignity and identity — how would you feel if you were reduced to your function in life, or if we all had to be equal by doing the same thing all the time? How then is our identity formed? By our relational creation. God made them male and female; in other words, they knew themselves in relationship to God, to one another, and to creation. Personhood is defined by relationships, by community. The power of relationships in identity formation cannot be overstated. We are born by relationship, in relationship and for relationship.[28] We are human becomings more than human beings. We see and know ourselves in the mirror of our treatment of one another.

In this regard, I must mention the phenomenon of "Internalised Racist Oppression" (IRO) and "Internalised Racist Superiority" (IRS). This refers to the identity-shaping power of racism with its two faces: internalised inferiority among victims, and internalised superiority among perpetrators.[29] All of us are profoundly affected by this — whites who think they were not affected by the racism of apartheid are blind. The power of the apartheid signs that we saw every day of our lives, "Whites Only" and "Non-Whites", must not be underestimated. It formed a white identity of superiority, and a non-person identity of inferiority. IRO and IRS runs very deep and has a powerful destructive influence on all race relations and politics in SA. In fact, some whites justify their IRS by still believing the heretical teaching that black people are the descendents of Ham and are cursed, making them inferior by nature, even by biology, to the rest of humanity (Gen 9:18–27).[30]

Thirdly, sin is not trusting God and his arrangements, alienating relationships and destroying God's creation

The devil tempted Adam and Eve by casting doubt on God and his word. (He questioned, "Did God really say ...?" Gen 3:1–6) They sinned by breaking trust. In their pride they wanted to be like God, rupturing their relationship with him. God had said: "Do not eat of that tree ... or you will die." Death in the Hebrew and in the Greek means *separation* (Gen 2:17; Eph 2:1f). It is interesting to note that *apartheid* in Afrikaans basically means separation — its belief and practice brought about death on all fronts. We learn from Gen 3 that Adam and Eve's sin (and ours) resulted in a fourfold death or alienation in relationships:

♦ From God (they hid themselves from God).

♦ Within themselves (they felt guilt and shame, withdrew and covered up).

♦ Between each other (they shifted blame and accused each other — Adam blamed Eve, Eve blamed the serpent, and the serpent did not have a leg to stand on! See Gen 3:11–14. The sobering reality is that they were actually blaming God because he made everything, including one rule — "Do not eat of that one tree" — because he knew what was best for them. They chose not to believe him and then to blame him when what he said would happen actually happened. One of the immediate outworkings of this relational alienation between human beings was violence and murder — Cain killed his own brother Abel, Gen 4. Nothing has changed; we have merely perfected this sinful reality).

♦ And with creation (they were expelled from Eden and would struggle with nature as creation fell under a curse of oppression due to their sin).

Shalom was shattered. But God responded with judgement *and* reconciliation. God judges sin and evil, but seeks to reconcile the sinner.

To summarise this third implication: Without God, our pristine source relationship, we are spiritually dead. This death is passed on in all the dimensions of our personal and corporate lives. We have been plunged from the glory of God's image to the darkness of death in our total depravity. We not only commit sin, we are sinful, i.e. we are born with a sinful nature. Our own inner guilt and shame, with our broken self-image, works its way out in sexism, racism, classism, lying and murder, and all forms of human relational sin. The curse in Gen 3 is basically one of oppression, manipulation and desperate survival all round. We groan under the curse of our own sin. Creation itself does the same, suffering in silent hope, and increasingly groans as in childbirth, awaiting its freedom — which will only come when we are fully and finally free (Rom 8:19–22).

All this tells us that sin is not only private and personal, but profoundly pervasive and real in social, political, creational and cosmic terms. As evangelicals we have to take seriously the more recent understandings of socio-political and structural sin and ecological care to help us come to terms with the depth and spread of evil in our world.[31] These are the "principalities and powers" and "elemental spirits" (Eph 6:12; Col 2:8 NRSV) that incarnate themselves in societal structures, largely through ideology and public policy. When this takes hold, racism and other forms of sin can become systemic and endemic in society, and consequently it becomes oppressively totalitarian in its evil. Prime examples are the communism of Stalin and the Nazism of Hitler. In SA, we ignored the structural sin and evil of apartheid for a long time with great cost to ourselves and our nation. We must name the structural sin, repent from it, and oppose it for the reconciliation and good of society.

Fourthly, God takes the initiative in sheer love and mercy to reconcile all things

Picture Adam and Eve not being at the meeting place for their customary evening walk with God. God searches through the garden, calling out with a lonely, haunting cry, "Adam, Eve, where are you?" This is love. God does not leave us in our hidden withdrawal in the misery of our sin and death. He comes looking behind every bush, every leaf, seeking to save that which is lost. In fact, the story of our lives is that time and again God comes and wins us, even "seduces" us, from our sinful indulgence with his undying love. After confrontation, in his judgement and reconciliation he sheds the innocent blood of animals to make a covering for Adam and Eve (Gen 3:21). For the first time there was the smell of blood, the shedding of blood, in God's creation. It clearly symbolises the sentence of death being carried out *in a substitutionary manner,* to remove the source of enmity between Adam and Eve and God, and symbolically to reconcile them to him. They had to take off their self-made leaf coverings, symbolising the turning away from their own efforts at covering their sin and making themselves acceptable to God. God reconciles in his way, on his terms, and they have to surrender and trust him unconditionally once again. There was a fourfold reconciliation:

♦ with God (substitutionary death and covering with "innocent/sinless" skins);

♦ within themselves (self-acceptance through knowing God's acceptance and forgiveness);

♦ with each other (relationship re-established through mutual forgiveness and acceptance because of God's forgiveness);

♦ with creation (to continue ruling over creation, albeit in an adjusted manner; and there is the promise of creation being released from the curse, Rom 8:18–25).

All this points to God giving up his own Son, Jesus the Messiah, as his sacrificial lamb to take away the sin of the world (Jn 1:29) so that we might be covered in his righteousness and be reconciled to God. Paul specifically says that Jesus is our peace — he breaks the curse and restores *Shalom* as he reconciles us with God and one another (Eph 2:14–17). This involves confession, repentance and faith on our part. Reconciliation with God becomes an experienced reality and progressively leads to reconciliation at all other levels. We must be aware that this is both an event and a process, and it takes place within the "already" and "not yet" framework of the kingdom. More of this later.

Concluding these four implications

It must be noted that no reconciliation was promised or given between: a) God and the serpent, b) the serpent and Adam and Eve, or c) the serpent and creation. The "enmity" between them, caused by the devil, would result in the serpent's head being crushed by the heel of the woman's offspring (as the serpent strikes him, Gen 3:15). In other words, one born of woman (Messiah Jesus) would decisively defeat evil (Satan and his hordes) by suffering in our place as he takes sin and evil upon himself. He would thereby reconcile and free humanity and God's creation into *Shalom* once again.

In the context of his teaching on reconciliation, Paul says: "He who knew no sin became sin for us that we might become the righteousness of God in him" (2 Cor 5:21 RAP). Similarly Jesus alludes to himself symbolically hanging like a snake on the cross so that all who look to him may have the poison of death removed and receive eternal life in reconciliation with God (Jn 3:14–16 cf. Num 21:4–9). The point is that the die is cast from the beginning: *No reconciliation is envisaged with evil or with Satan himself.* There is no universal or ultimate salvation for Satan and his demons. God never reconciles with evil in the way that he reconciles with human beings. Satan and *all* his followers are ultimately left crushed and defeated, separated from God forever. (I say *all*, because it includes human beings who will end up in "the eternal fire prepared for the devil and his angels", Matt 25:41).

BABEL AND THE NATIONS, ISRAEL AND PENTECOST

The grand narrative takes shape with Adam and Eve exiled from the garden. They produce offspring that become increasingly sinful (Gen 4–5), to the point where God destroys humanity, saving Noah and his family in order to start over again (Gen 6–9; note 9:1, 7, 18–19, the renewed commission to "be fruitful and increase in number and fill the earth"). The "nations" listed in Gen 10 come from Noah and his sons. I use inverted commas because they were not nations in the sense of separate identities; they were all one people with one language, one "united nations" as it were.

Babel, the nations and spiritual powers

In their pride, the one "united nations" presumed on God by using their unity to build a tower "into the heavens to make a name for themselves". They wanted to be like God — their sin was the same as the original sin in the garden (Gen 11:1–9 cf. 3:2–6). As with Adam and Eve, God judged them. This time it was not a curse on men and women and creation, but a scattering of humanity. God's judgement was to give them different tongues, scattering them from one another into separate languages, nations and tribes.

Babel, from the Babylonian language, means "gate of the gods". It was the entrance to and from the gods, the world of spiritual power and rule. It is significant that Babylon, is the symbol of the ultimate and final spiritually-inspired socio-political system of evil that will oppose God and his purposes on earth. Jesus will defeat it (Rev 17–18). In the Hebrew, Babel comes from the root *balal*, meaning the "confusion" created by the "mixing" of languages. In English we use "babble" for this sense of tongues-confusion. Apartheid theology used this very point to justify their particular interpretation of Babel. They said that it was not a judgement of God so much as the will of God to keep nations, races and cultures separate from that time on. In essence apartheid theology said: "It is for their own good, because if you mix nations and races you will have confusion, which is not the will of God. God gave each nation an identity and culture. It should not be confused or tampered with by mixing with other races; this is not the will of God."

This way of reasoning is the exact inversion of the traditional interpretation: People were divided into nations and languages *as a judgement of God* on human sinfulness — specifically their arrogant unity and rebellion against God. But as always, God's judgement was tempered with mercy in order to limit the spread of human sinfulness, and to make them seek after God again (Acts 17:26–27). The way he did this was to assign spiritual powers to rule over each of the nations (Deut 4:19; Dan 10:13, 20), instructing them to maintain the set boundaries that he ordained for each of them (Deut 32:8–9; Acts 17:26). The spiritual rulers were also charged with responsibility to ensure social righteousness and political justice, especially for the poor and needy (Ps 82). These spiritual rulers are called by various names in Scripture.[32] They all have their counterpart in the earthly kings and governmental leaders of nations, who are charged with the same responsibility of good governance and social justice, for the good of humanity (Ps 72; Rom 13:1–7; 1 Tim 2:1–8). The heavenly and earthly rulers over the nations are referred to interchangeably, revealing their symbiotic relationship in the sense that what happens in the nation and its leadership is an outworking of what has happened, or is happening, with its unseen powers (e.g. Is 14:4–20; 34:2–4; Ezek 28:1–19).

We have to face the fact that instead of ruling in righteousness, these spiritual and human rulers become corrupt in their power and are judged by the God of history. Lord Acton's saying is proved true again and again: Power tends to corrupt, and absolute power corrupts absolutely. Thus kingdoms rise and fall, God raises up leaders and puts down leaders.

I have given this brief understanding of spiritual reality, nations and history, because it is crucial in the development of the grand narrative.[33] However, there is a greater mercy of God at work, aimed at the eventual salvation of humanity and the nations.

Israel and the covenant

The "united nations" of Gen 10 became the divided and scattered nations of Gen 11; but once again God, in his love, immediately took the initiative and set about "*reshaloming*" the earth, working for reconciliation. Gen 12 begins with God searching the nations of the earth, calling Abram to make of him a new and great nation, *that through his seed all the peoples and nations of the earth would be blessed.* God enters into covenant with Abraham and his offspring Israel (Gen 15), as he did with Adam and Noah (Gen 9). He confirms the covenant with Israel through Moses, revealing himself as YHWH, the God who was, and is, and always will be there for them. He will be their God, and they will be his people. He will give them a new land within boundaries, flowing with milk and honey, a garden of delight. He will rule over them through his Word that he gives them (the Law or Torah, which especially upholds social justice). And he will make them into a kingdom of priests *in order to bring God to the nations and the nations to God* (Ex 19:4–6; Is 42:5–7; 49:6, "that you may bring my salvation to the ends of the earth"). Israel's national purpose is to end the human exile from Eden and the nations' exile from God's rule. Thus Israel became God's chosen nation, with chosen laws, in the chosen land, for a chosen purpose. But identity, nationhood and land depended on faith and obedience in God's Word and purpose, as with Adam and Eve, as with the "united nations". (Did Israel obey and fulfil her purpose? Do not answer before the whole story is told!)

In her pride and rebellion, Israel sinned, and she sinned repeatedly. She broke faith with Yahweh and destroyed their covenant relationship. After many earnest prophetic warnings that went unheeded, Yahweh eventually sent Israel into exile, away from their land and boundaries, to be ruled by other powers, both heavenly and earthly. This was always God's pattern: He called for repentance, he warned of judgement and, as a last resort, he handed them over to foreign gods and powers to oppress his people (the NT equivalent is being handed over to our sinful appetites and demons, e.g. Rom 1:24–32). God judged the people and the land of Israel. He left the land utterly desolate as under a curse (Deut 29:22–28; especially v. 27, cf. Is 5). Israel repeated what had happened with Adam and the earth, with Babel and the nations — the judgements and exile were similar.

But once again, God promised that he would come to them in love to restore them from exile to himself, to their promised land and inheritance. He would make a new covenant with them, giving them a new heart and a new Spirit to obey his word (Jer 31:31–37; Ezek 36:24–32). He would restore them, the land, its boundaries and his rule over them, for the fulfilment of their chosen purpose, the reconciliation of the nations. Their return would be a resurrection from the dead (Ezek 37:1–14).

Isaiah and the prophets show how all the post-exilic promises take on universal and cosmic kingdom overtones that eclipse Israel's land and boundaries, ethnicity and identity, holy temple and Torah. Yahweh will restore *Shalom* in and through a reconciled people (which includes Gentiles from all nations), in a renewed earth (more than Eden and Canaan), with new heavens (God rules directly), with a new temple (God's people and his presence), and a universal Torah written on Spirit-filled hearts and minds.[34] Israel's reconciliation and restoration will lead to the reconciliation and restoration of the nations. Israel's reconciliation to the land is humanity's restoration to Eden, which is but a symbol for inheriting the whole earth (note that Israel inherits *the earth*, not just a piece of real estate in the

Middle East, see Matt 5:5).[35] Israel's restoration of the temple is humanity's re-conciliation with God, which is but a symbol of inheriting the heavens as God's presence, through the headship of Christ and his body, fills all things in every way (Eph 1:20–23)

The key issue is that the fulfilment of these promises is focused on God's Messiah King, in whom God will come and rule, and accomplish all this.

Jesus and the resurrection

Israel returns from exile, but does not experience the fulfilment of these promises until John the Baptiser appears in the wilderness — a symbol of the exile — saying: "Repent for the kingdom of the heavens is at hand." God's Messiah is here. Jesus appears, is baptised and anointed with the Spirit of Yahweh, and as Israel was tested for 40 years in the wilderness, so Jesus is driven into the desert to be tested for 40 days by the devil. In this symbolic exile he proves true to Yahweh, keeping covenant trust on Israel's behalf. Then he enters the physical promised land calling his fellow Israelis to "return" to God and enter into the real pro-mised land, the present kingdom of heaven. He reconciles people to God through forgiving sins, healing sicknesses, delivering people from demons, and defeating death. He proclaims and teaches God's Torah with great authority, radically interpreting it in the light of the Messianic fulfilment of the kingdom of Yahweh.

Jesus sees himself as the embodiment of Israel and her hopes, and he sees his little group of followers as the embodiment of the reconciled Israel that was prophesied. He takes on himself Israel's (and Adam's and the world's) suffering for her sinful pride and rebellion against God. He dies in her place, taking God's judgement upon himself. He dies cut off from God's presence, suffering Israel and humanity's ultimate exile: "My God, my God, why have you forsaken me?" (Matt 27:46). In this way he breaks down the dividing wall of enmity between God and Israel, between God and us, between Israel and the various nations from Babel (Eph 2:14). His bleeding flesh is the tearing of the veil that separated us from God, that separated man from woman, the nations from Israel, the cursed creation from its liberation, and the future age from this present age (Heb 9:3, 8–10; 10:19–22). All the enmity, boundaries, barriers and divisions crumble in the crucifixion of Jesus the Messiah. All the principalities and powers are judged and defeated. Not far from Golgotha where Jesus hung was the great temple. The veil separating the Holy of Holies (God's dwelling) from the nation of Israel and the nations of the world, was literally torn in two, from top to bottom (Lk 23:45). Jesus shouted: "It is finished" (Jn 19:30). The kingdom has come!

But God does not abandon his beloved in the exile of the grave. He physically raises Jesus from the dead on the third day. And significantly, he rose from death to life in a garden full of new blossoms and bright flowers — it was spring — it was Passover in Jerusalem, 30AD. The risen Messiah is more than the gardener in God's new creation (see John 20:10–18);[36] he is the Son of God, the New Adam, the Seed of Abraham, the (re)New(ed) Israel, the Reconciler and Blesser of the Nations, the *Shalom* and *Eschaton* of God (*Eschaton* is the fulfilment of God's goal in creation)! On the evening of his resurrection, Jesus says to his gathered followers: "*Shalom* be upon you. As my Father sent me, even so I am sending you." Then he "breathes into them his Spirit", just as God breathed into Adam the breath of life (Jn 20:21–22).[37] A new creation takes place with the Son of God, the New Adam, kneeling down and breathing a new race into being, in fulfilment of what God said he would do to Israel (Ezek 37:1–14). They, and we, are born "again" (literally "from above", Jn 3:3–8) by God's Spirit, with his eternal kind of life, to rule and reign with him, to increase and multiply, and to re*shalom* the earth. The new age of God's universal kingdom has broken through and has already literally begun in this present evil age. The exile is over, the promises are being fulfilled.

That is why, before he finally ascends into the heavens, the resurrected Christ said to this new humanity, his renewed Israel: "I now have the say over everything in the heavens and on the earth. Therefore you go and make followers of me, reconciling people of all types, from all nations, by plunging them into the reality of the Trinitarian God and teaching them to live out all the implications. I will be with you as you go, at your side, right through to the end of the age, till the job is done" (Matt 28:18–20 RAP, inspired by Dallas Willard's paraphrase). What Jesus is referring to becomes real and complete in his ascension.

The ascension and Pentecost

To complete the story, the Son of God, the New Adam, returns home from his "exile" on earth to the arms of the Father in the heavens, never to be separated again. The ascension of Christ was the mother of all heavenly, cosmic and universal parties! What a reunion! The same person who left heaven returns, but with significant difference. The pre-incarnate Son returns as a resurrected man — a member of the human race is glorified and honoured in the heavens. The ascended Christ is the "first-fruits" of the true and ultimate homecoming of Israel at the end of this age, of all God's born-again one new humanity at the coming of Christ. Imagine the party then. Jesus is our forerunner, preparing the way for all of us by entering the heavens and beginning to rule on our behalf from the Father's right hand, and by daily interceding for us (Heb 7:23–28; 12:1–2).

The party in the heavens included many gifts being given to Jesus: a crown, a title and a throne next to the Father. He was made Lord and Messiah-King. He was given authority over all things in the heavens, on the earth and under the earth, that at the name of Jesus, every knee should bow and every tongue confess that *Yeshua ha Mashiach* is Lord (Acts 2:32–36 cf. Phil 2:6–11).[38] But the greatest gift he received — which he gave to his followers — was what the Father had promised all along, *the gift of the Holy Spirit*. The ascended Christ, with the Father, poured out the *Ruach ha Kodesh*, the Spirit of the Holy One, on his renewed Israel waiting in Jerusalem (in direct fulfilment of Ezek 37 and Joel 2).

I need to describe the empowering "gift of the Spirit" that came at Pentecost (Acts 1:4–5, 8; 2:1–4,38–39). For Jews this Feast of Shavuot was a joyful celebration of the grain harvest but, more importantly, of the promised ingathering of the Gentiles into God's kingdom. Here is the RAP on what happened: Jesus got so excited with the Father and his gifts that he wanted to share it all with his friends. He poured out the party that he was having in the heavens onto the earth. His gathered followers had been quietly waiting in Jerusalem, and praying for just on ten days. Suddenly they were violently invaded and winded with fire! They proceeded to get thoroughly drunk with the Spirit and fell about speaking in different languages that came from surging fountains of inner joy. It made the parties that Matthew had thrown for Jesus look quite tame. It got worse. They overflowed from the upper room, staggering out into the streets and outer courts of the temple area, where thousands of Jews had gathered to celebrate Shavuot. They had come from throughout the Diaspora, where they had been scattered during and after the exile. Without realising it, the renewed Israel was ecstatically and supernaturally speaking in the fifteen different languages of the gathered Jews (Acts 2:5–12). The barriers were crossed as they heard the wonderful works of God being proclaimed in their own tongue. Three thousand came to faith in Jesus as God's Messiah that day and joined the (re)new(ed) Israel.

Pentecost exploded the ethnic, national and cultural confines of Israel. It opened the floodgates for the Jews (Acts 3–6, many priests were reconciled), the half-breeds (Acts 8), the Gentiles and all nations (Acts 10ff) to be reconciled into the kingdom of God. In short, Pentecost effectively reverses the separations and scatterings of Babel. The Spirit's coming empowers the work of the cross, in which the dividing walls are destroyed, gathering and uniting people of all nations, tribes, languages and cultures into one new *koinonia* or shared life.[39] (Messianic) Israel, as God's all-inclusive reconciled and reconciling covenant nation, is at last fulfilling her God-given purpose. Under his rule and reign, such a people are the salt of the earth and the light of the world, bringing salvation to the ends of the earth.

The banishment from Eden is over, the separation of the nations has ended, and Israel is back from exile. The curse on creation has been broken, the dividing barriers have fallen, and the heart of stone has been removed. Messiah has come to establish the new covenant in God's renewed people. The resurrection has begun, Eden has been reborn and is spreading over the earth. Pentecost has empowered one "united nation" with God's ruling Spirit to serve him humbly in the reconciliation and discipling of the nations. In Trinitarian terms, the Father in his love for humanity and Israel, has reconciled us to himself through his Son. Jesus gave himself as our substitutionary sacrifice to remove all sin, enmity and dividing walls. The Father and the Son then sent the Spirit at Pentecost to complete the work of reconciliation in and through the church into the world.

These are the broad strokes of the grand narrative. I will discuss the practical application of the teachings and practice of Jesus, the early church (Acts) and Paul with regard to racism, reconciliation and transformation in the next chapter.

NOTES

1. On Wilberforce, see Cormack 1983; a good discussion on the theology and ethics of Edwards and Wesley is found in White 1981, pp. 256–281, and on Bonhoeffer, pp. 305–311. Bonhoeffer was a Lutheran theologian and pastor who died for his faith due to his opposition to Hitler. He was a great inspiration to South African Christians during the apartheid years, see De Gruchy 1984. Phillips (1967) has made a good study of Bonhoeffer's theology and life. See also Bonhoeffer's books in the References.

2. This process is traced in Lovelace 1979, pp. 27–28; 375–381. Phrases like "social gospel" and other such tags were used by various people as this debate developed, see White 1981, pp. 256–281.

3. Note 30 Chapter 4. This tag is unhelpful because all Christians, evangelicals included, should be ecumenical in their faith and attitude, i.e. loving, honouring and learning from the whole church as John Wimber taught, see Venter 2000, pp. 41–44.

4. A phrase from Dallas Willard (note 6 below).

5. My assumption becomes clear at this point: You can critique socio-political issues from a biblical viewpoint while at the same time accounting for your own philosophic and contextual presuppositions, so that your "biblical view" does not become a guise for your own ideological position. It is really an issue of epistemology — how we know things. This is the subject of great debate in theology, hermeneutics and other disciplines. Balcomb 1993 critiques evangelical theology (in SA under apartheid) as belying a liberal English ideology. For a good discussion on philosophic presuppositions and methodological approaches, see Wright 1992b, pp. 31–46.

6. A devastating critique of these false dichotomies is found in Willard 1998, pp. 43–70. For an attempt at reconciliation between ecumenicals and evangelicals at the theological and missions level, see Glasser 1979.

7. My explanation of the Vineyard identity and its background is found in Venter 2000, pp. 44–45.

8. De Gruchy 2002, p. 24.

9. The key words and concepts used by the apostles to preach Jesus are carefully studied in Morris 1972. For a comprehensive discussion on this reconciliation word study, see Brown 1978, pp. 145–174, Breytenbach in Vorster (ed.) 1986, pp. 1–22, De Gruchy 2002, pp. 24–31 and Morris 1972, pp. 214–250.

10. De Gruchy 2002, p. 46.

11. The word is *hilaskomai* with its derivatives. It means to propitiate or expiate, as in making blood atonement to cover sin, thus removing anger and gaining forgiveness. This relates to an important "technical" debate in theology that goes back to the Hebrew Bible and the cultic practice of blood sacrifice. The debate is whether God's anger is appeased ("propitiated" or placated as in pagan sacrifices. Here the action is directed towards God to get him to change his attitude), or whether God's anger is put aside because justice has been done ("expiated" as in atonement where the action is directed towards the thing that has caused the anger and separation). Some key usages of this word in the New Testament: Rom 3:25; Heb 2:17; 9:28; 1 Jn 2:2. See Brown 1978, pp. 148–166 and Morris 1972, pp. 144–213. For an overview survey of the changing understandings of reconciliation (with its centre in *hilaskomai*, the atoning death of Jesus) throughout the history of the church, from Paul to the present time, see Cilliers Breytenbach in Vorster (ed.) 1986, pp. 6–18 and De Gruchy 2002, pp. 57–76.

12. Jer 31:39; 48:39; Is 9:5; 1 Sam 29:4; see Morris 1972, pp. 215–216. The Greek Septuagint was translated from the Hebrew by 70 Jewish scholars (hence is it often called the LXX) in 2BC.

13. De Gruchy 2002, pp. 47–56 on "the grand narrative". Tom Wright has written extensively and authoritatively on the idea of story — the grand narrative and historical context of Judaism, and the Jewish frame of reference in Paul, see Wright (especially 1997).

14. Morris 1972, pp. 216–225, contains an insightful discussion on Rabbinical Judaism, reconciliation and the New Testament.

15. In technical terms, it is the hermeneutic key, the basic frame of reference to interpret the Bible correctly. See Morphew 1998, p. 8, Venter 2000, pp. 36–38. John Wimber taught and put into practice Ladd's theology of the kingdom: GE Ladd 1959, 1974. I also draw on König 1989 in my discussion on the kingdom.

16. The "this age/future age" and "world's kingdoms/God's kingdom" framework is clear

in Scripture, Dan 2:31–45, Matt 12:32 and Matt 13 (the parables), Mk 10:30; Eph 1:21; 1 Cor 10:11; Heb 6:5; Rev 11:15. The apparent dualism in this framework is not the same as the false dichotomies or dualisms referred to earlier in the chapter (see Ladd 1974, pp. 317–325, and Wright 1992b, pp. 252–259 on eschatological dualism). Strictly speaking, the theology of the kingdom is part of eschatology within the discipline of Systematic Theology (or Dogmatics). Eschatology is the study of the end (times and events), i.e. the second coming of Christ. Adrio König uses the *eschaton* as his point of departure in his remarkable study on Jesus and the kingdom — seeing things from the end (König 1989).

17. The phrase comes from 1 Jn 3:2 NRSV: "We are God's children now (already); what we will be has not yet been revealed."

18. "New Age" was used by Jesus and Christians long before the New Agers arrived on the scene! We have an unprecedented opportunity not to back off from using this term, but rather to use it as a point of discussion and evangelism to explain its real meaning and expose the lies behind the ideas of the postmodern New Age movement.

19. Ellul's revolutionary view of Jesus' teaching on salt, light and sheep (1989, pp. 1–5).

20. Approximately 55 million people died in WWII, 6 million of them Jews that died in the holocaust — what the Nazis called "the final solution". Countless hundreds of thousands of born-again Christians died along with them. See Nürnberger, Tooke and Domeris (eds.) 1989, pp. 165–166 on the cost of WWII. Abraham asked God: "Will you kill the righteous along with the wicked, treating the righteous and the wicked alike? Far be it from you! Will not the Judge of all the earth do right?" (Gen 18:25). Contrary to Sodom and Gomorrah, it seems like the answer in the mid-1900s was a terrifying "yes" from God.

21. The background to John Wimber, Vineyard and the church growth movement in Jackson 1999.

22. Christian Schwarz has done an important critique of this technological paradigm in church growth, see Schwarz 1996.

23. The "homogeneous unit" idea originated with missiologist Donald McGavran (1966 and 1970). It was never intended to be a theology of church or even of missions per se, but it has clouded these issues. Strictly speaking it is a "sociology" of missions and church growth. For a helpful discussion on the theological issues generated by the church growth movement, see Conn (ed.) 1976, and Shenk (ed.) 1983.

24. One of the key debates around the church growth movement is the interpretation of the great commission (the problems of pragmatism vs theology and ecclesiology vs sociology). David Bosch engaged extensively in this debate and convincingly shows that Matthew does not mean what modern church growth thinkers mean by the homogeneous principle — they read back into Scripture modern ideas and categories that

were not in the minds of the NT writers. Matt 28:19 does not mean that the church is commissioned to grow through homogeneous church planting, by discipling every homogeneous group, every ethnia as in national group, subculture and subdialect. Neither does it justify homogeneous churches as the norm of church growth and missions. It is simply a commission to go to all nations, all ethnia as in all types of people everywhere to the ends of the earth (the goyim or unbelievers as in being "a light to the nations", see Is 42:6; 49:6). See Shenk (ed.) 1983, pp. 218–248, Bosch's article, "The Structure of Mission: An Exposition of Matthew 28:16–20", and Bosch 1988, 1991, pp. 56–65.

25. Longenecker 1984, p. 46 expresses similar sentiments regarding the church growth movement. Chris de Wet critiques the church growth paradigm and the homogeneous unit principle in the South African context and finds it wanting in many ways, especially in terms of its inability to be a challenge to a racially divided society. See De Wet 1986.

26. The history that is traced and the following quotes from the official Afrikaans church records, is by Chris Loff (The History of a Heresy) in De Gruchy and Villa-Vicencio (eds.) 1983, pp. 10–23.

27. Loubser 1987 has a detailed study on the historical development of the theology of racial segregation and apartheid, both in church and society. See Morphew 1989, pp. 97–107, for a briefer discussion. We cannot miss the terrifying connotations of "the final solution", see note 20.

28. The Hebrew creation idea of Shalom has a similar meaning in the African idea of community conveyed in the word ubuntu. The notion is enshrined in the Xhosa proverb, umuntu ungumuntu ngabantu, meaning, "a person is a person through persons". The concept is relational and dynamic, "I am a person through you", or "I am a person to the extent that I uphold your personhood". The opposite is, of course, equally true, "I cease to be a person if I neglect to uphold your personhood, let alone intentionally destroy it."

29. These concepts are articulated in Leon-Hartshorn, Shearer and Stoltzfus 2001: "Internalised racist oppression is, at its simplest, people of colour believing the lie that we are less than because we are not white. Racism lies to us, saying we are less intelligent, less beautiful, less capable, and less worthy ... Internalised racist oppression is understanding that basic lie to be true, and then living it out" (p. 20). "It is racism claiming the power to tell people of colour and white people who they are ... Racism attempts to usurp God's authority. It is at the Identity Power level that racism begins to shape us, and tells us what to think and what to feel about ourselves" (p. 46). For a detailed study on the nature and wholistic effects of (white) racism on blacks and other races, see Barndt 1991.

30. Loubser 1987, pp. 7–8. Noah cursed Canaan, Ham's son, to serve Shem, his uncle (i.e. he was not made inferior by nature). The Canaanites were the descendents of Canaan, and it was these tribes that Joshua conquered when he entered "the promised land" — not in Africa (see Gen 9:25–27 cf. 10:15–19).

31. Due to the dualisms mentioned above, evangelicals have had great difficulties with the idea and theology of "structural sin". See Morphew 1989 and the excellent trilogy of biblical studies on this issue by Wink 1984, 1986, 1992.

32. For example: gods (Ps 82:1), sons of the Most High (Ps 82:6), heavenly host (Ps 89:7), spirits (1 Kgs 22:21), stars (Job 38:7), principalities, powers, authorities and rulers in the heavenlies (Dan 10:13; Ps 103:21; Eph 6:12), idols (Amos 5:26), gods, lords, demons (1 Cor 8:4–6; 10:18–20); basic principles of the world or "elementary spirits" (Col 2:8 NRSV).

33. It is not the place to discuss the specifics of the spiritual worldview of the Bible, the "the principalities and powers" in terms of their origins, nature and demise. For a more detailed understanding of nations, rulers, powers and spiritual warfare, see Wink's triology and a more concise understanding in Morphew 1989, pp. 37–44.

34. Morphew 1998, pp. 37–53 for a discussion of these universal/kingdom promises in the prophets.

35. The question of modern Israel and its role in the purposes of God, and the painful Palestinian issue, is centred on the little piece of real estate called the Holy Land. Morphew 1998, pp. 229–246 gives a kingdom perspective on the Israel question. In terms of the land issue, see Brueggemann 1977 and Holwerda 1995, pp. 85–112.

36. For a most astounding study on the resurrection of Jesus Christ with its depth and breadth of meaning, see Wright 2003.

37. John's words in Greek are a direct quote from Gen 2:7 in the Septuagint, the Greek translation of the OT (150BC). In his account of the resurrection in Chapter 20, John intentionally connotes the creation story with the restoration of the Garden of Eden with a new humanity and a new creation. Similarly Luke connotes the resurrection of Jesus with creation and the garden story, in Lk 24. See Wright 2000, pp. 124–128 for his insightful and concise exposition, and 2003, pp. 435–439 and 647–661 for his detailed treatment.

38. The title of Messiah is the Hebrew for King, the same as *Kristos* or Christ in the Greek. For Jews it was blasphemy to apply it to Jesus, the worst crime, and many died for doing so. The title of Lord is *Kyrios* in the Greek, which was the title Caesar took to himself, "The Lord of the Earth". For the Romans it was high treason to attribute it to someone other than Caesar — it was their worst crime, and many died for doing so. When the early Christians (Messianics) went about the Mediterranean world with their slogan "Jesus is Lord", they were being very courageous, radical and politically subversive. However, the Christians did not only mean that Jesus had become the real

ruler of the Roman Empire, but of the whole earth, of under the earth (evil powers) and the heavens (angels). The poor Caesars took it so personally because they were so small-minded — if they saw the bigger picture, their noses might not have been so out of joint (see Acts 17:5–8)!

39. The Greek *koinonia* is translated as fellowship in our English Bible. It essentially means "the sharing of a common life in relational partnership or friendship". See Venter 2000, pp. 163–166 for a detailed explanation.

CHAPTER 6

A BIBLICAL VIEW OF RACISM, RECONCILIATION AND TRANSFORMATION — THE NEW TESTAMENT OUTWORKING

Jesus said, "Come, follow me, and I will form you into fishers of people."

Matt 4:19 RAP

Therefore, there is now no longer Jew nor Gentile, neither slave nor free person, and neither male nor female, because in union with Jesus the Messiah you have all become one.

Paul in Gal 3:28 RAP

As a family, we have had the privilege of going on a number of vacations. The special part for me, especially when the children were younger, was arriving at our destination. I would marvel at their unbridled joy as they would excitedly help us unpack the car, rush around claiming their bedrooms, and then explore their holiday environment. And equally, if not more satisfying, was their excitement at coming home after the long trip back from holiday. They would hug the dogs, get on their bikes and go off to greet friends with stories of discovery and fun — and they would only help us unpack the car under great duress! Can you remember similar excitement at the end of a journey?

I have journeyed through God's great story, the underlying grand narrative of the Bible. Now I will unpack its meaning and practical application from the NT. And probably it is more like homecoming than arriving at a temporal place of rest and enjoyment. Reconciliation and transformation is coming home to our permanent dwelling place in God.

Although homecoming is the ultimate, the journey itself — the grand narrative — is very important because it makes the homecoming all the more meaningful. God's overarching story should be the lens through which we read and interpret our own stories, both individually and corporately, both as church and as a nation. It gives us meaning, understanding and purpose. It defines racism, reconciliation and transformation from God's perspective, and empowers us to live God's reconciling and transforming kingdom here and now.

The next step is to see the fulfilment of this grand narrative in its practical application in the life and teachings of Jesus, the early church, and Paul. This will be followed in the next chapter by a practical theology of reconciliation and transformation by looking at a model of one-on-one reconciliation and then group and structural reconciliation. Let us begin with Jesus.

JESUS ON RACISM, RECONCILIATION AND TRANSFORMATION

Through his death and resurrection, Jesus is God's ultimate means of reconciliation. His life and ministry demonstrates a practical model and method of reconciliation. As a man, Jesus was God's reconciler on earth. This touches on the historical Jesus. Who was Jesus in his historical context? How did he live his life? What was his mission and message — specifically in the socio-political context of his day? I will not enter this debate,[1] but will give a brief picture of how radical Jesus and his community was within his societal context. I will first comment on his model and practice, and then move onto his teachings.

Israel was under the oppression of the Romans. The response of first century Judaism to this pagan oppression was uniform at one level — the Jews and Judaism all resented Rome and its oppression, and expected Messiah to save them. Messianic expectation was high in Israel during the Roman period. At another level, Israel and Judaism was fragmented and divided into various groups and segments of society, each responding to the national crisis with their own differing beliefs and practices.[2] Then John the Baptiser and Jesus entered the situation. Jesus, like John, came as a prophet of Israel announcing the presence and action of God's kingdom, which he embodied in his little mobile community.

The model of Jesus and his inclusive community

Both as Jewish Rabbi and a prophet, *Yeshua* called disciples (*talmudim*) to follow him in a community of students (a *Yeshiva*). Jesus called all sorts of people to follow him, by joining him in a reconciling, inclusive community. He called rough fishermen and even tax collectors to join him. Whereas the former were uneducated, the latter were the most despised group in Israel. The tax collectors exploited their own Jewish brethren in support of the Roman system, besides throwing raucous parties with sinners like drunkards and prostitutes (Matt 9:9–13 cf. 21:31–32; Jesus was invited to such parties — he had a reputation for mixing and partying with "sinners and prostitutes"). Jesus caused not a little stir by eating with Zacchaeus in his home. This symbolised a gracious act of reconciliation. Zacchaeus was a notorious, wealthy tax collector, who had robbed the poor; but as a result of Jesus' visit he repented and made restitution (Lk 19:1–10).

Jesus also called the pure of heart like Nathanael (Jn 1:47), and the passionate nationalist like Simon the Zealot. These two were the religious and ideological opposites of Matthew and the sinners. Simon had associated with the Jewish freedom fighters who were prepared to kill Israeli sell-outs like Matthew, let alone Roman soldiers after carrying their load for one mile. The soldiers used to command Jews to carry their pack (the distance was restricted by law to prevent exploitation). Sometimes at the end of the mile, while they were bending over to pick up their packs, the soldiers were killed by the *Sicarri*, the Jewish freedom fighters. Note how specific and radical Jesus was in his reconciliatory teaching to his followers on this very matter: "Do *not* go one mile, go two miles, turn the other cheek, love your enemies ..." (Matt 5:38–48).

Even Nicodemus, a Pharisee and member of the Sanhedrin, joined up with Jesus (Jn 3:1f cf. 19:38–40). Another prominent member of the Sanhedrin, wealthy Joseph of Arimathea, become a supporter of Jesus and his kingdom movement (Matt 27:57 cf. Mk 15:43–46). On the other side of the socio-political spectrum were the "multitudes", the poor peasants who flocked in their thousands to see and hear Jesus. They were the rural poor, the uneducated, the sinners, the sick and the demonised. His main following came from the impoverished and highly politicised north, Galilee. Among them — peasants and fishermen — were many serious followers of Jesus, 72 of whom he sent out to proclaim and do the works of his reconciling kingdom in every town and village of Israel (Lk 10:1f).

Jesus' community was *not* homogeneous: it was provocatively inclusive of various ideological segments in the context of his society; *therefore* it had something hopeful and challenging to say to his society. He was the reconciler of the opposites of society, creating a reconciling community. He intentionally and purposefully brought the reconciling kingdom of God to them, often by sharing meals with those who responded to him as they realised their need of God. In this way he crossed the spiritual and religious barriers, the clean and unclean boundaries, that were enforced legalistically. Jesus challenged the "Way of Holiness" (in Hebrew, *Halakah*) imposed on the nation by the Jewish leadership, by modelling the kingdom alternative, the "Way of Compassion". Jesus' kingdom way is summarised in his statement: "Be compassionate, just as your Father is compassionate" (Lk 6:36).[3]

Jesus' inclusive community and alternative way is seen especially in his treatment of women and children. Women, some from high society with financial means, and others of questionable character (to say the least), were part of Rabbi *Yeshua's* group (Lk 8:1–3). To have women in his live-in travelling community was revolutionary enough, let alone the type of women they were. Jesus' dignifying treatment of women and children was very radical and prophetic in his context — symbolising the freedom that the kingdom brings from the curse of male domination. Women and children were tantamount to being the property of the husband and father, and they were treated as such. The way he received and responded to children provoked his disciples' prejudice (Mk 10:13–16). In one encounter with a woman at a well Jesus crossed three socio-political and spiritual divides, challenging strongly held stereotypes (Jn 4): as a male he spent time talking to a woman in public; as a Jew he interacted with a Samaritan, a "half-breed"; and as a Rabbi or prophet he talked to a morally-questionable woman (without becoming "unclean"! It was known that prostitutes used to come to the well at noon when the shepherds brought their flocks to drink. See also Jesus' revolutionary and compassionate treatment of another woman who was caught in the act of adultery and about to be stoned — yet without condoning her sin, Jn 8:1–11).

I can cite many more incidences of Jesus' remarkable interaction with women and children, with the sick and demonised, with the poor and broken, with the drunkards and sinners — all the marginalised majority in a society controlled by men. Jesus crossed gender, generation, class, spiritual and ideological boundaries, and reconciled people in his little community. Personal and national identities built on religious and social stereotypes were dismantled and reconstructed by Jesus in his kingdom community. They were God's Israel embodying God's future kingdom in their context. Some scholars maintain that Jesus was proclaiming and embodying Israel's *actual* Year of Jubilee, as in Lk 4:18–19.[4] This verse seems to be the kingdom mandate that Jesus chose for his life mission — in fulfilment from Is 61:1–2. Sins were to be forgiven, all debts cancelled, slaves were to be set free, the playing field was being levelled, everyone had a new and equal chance, because this was "the year of the Lord's favour". True freedom had come, first spiritually and psychologically, then socially, economically and politically.

Jesus reconciles Gentiles into the kingdom

But Jesus went further. He spent lots of time on the northern borders of Israel where Jews and Gentiles lived in close proximity. He deliberately went into Gentile areas, north to Tyre and Sidon, and east of Galilee and the river Jordan, to minister the kingdom.[5] This was in direct fulfilment of Is 9:1–3 where the same geography is mentioned, the area in which the Gentiles, the pagan nations, will see the light of Yahweh when the kingdom comes. Jesus deliberately goes there with his "little flock" of Messianic Israel (to whom he gives the kingdom, Lk 12:32) to bring the light of the kingdom to the Gentiles by healing the sick, casting out demons and teaching God's reign over evil. His body language and geographic movements in Israel and among the Gentiles were clearly strategic and symbolic. Jesus was clever, he knew the Hebrew prophets, and he literally and symbolically sought to fulfil them.

As an example, consider this symbolism: On the west side of the Sea of Galilee Jesus heals Jews and teaches them the kingdom, and great crowds follow him. He feeds 5 000 Jews and they pick up twelve baskets of leftovers. This symbolises that the kingdom of God is first for the Jews — it is more than enough for the twelve tribes of Israel. Then he goes to the east side of Galilee and heals the sick and great crowds (presumably mostly Gentiles) follow him. There he feeds 4 000 Gentiles and takes up seven basketfuls. This symbolises the completion or perfection of God's plan with the Gentiles entering the kingdom — also having more than enough (see Matt 14–15.[6] Paul says "the full number of the Gentiles will come in", Rom 11:25). Eating together is all about sharing in the kingdom through entering the covenant. More significantly, it points to the prophetic fulfilment of the Messianic banquet where all peoples have direct and open fellowship with God. Jesus' meals and feasts were an anticipation and foretaste of the real banquet at the end of the age (Matt 8:11–12).[7]

Jesus clearly loved the Gentile "dogs" — as they were commonly called — his own Jewish people, as well as his diverse "little flock". He told his followers, and other listeners, that he would lay down his life for his "friends" (Jn 15:12–27), and also for the Jewish nation (Jn 10:14–19). When Jesus instructed his kingdom community to "love one another, as I have loved you" (Jn 13:34–35), it really meant something, because of his example. He would not only lay down his life in death, but he laid it down daily in his sacrificial and reconciling love for them in all their differences and diversity. Jesus spoke these words — immediately after the embarrassing foot-washing incident in which he again enacted his outpoured love for them (Jn 13). To press his point home, he added: "By *this love for one another* all people will know that you are my followers." This is the powerful witness of a reconciled and self-sacrificing group in a divided and self-serving society.

Jesus' modelling leads to his teaching on reconciliation

Perhaps the most radical example and teaching of Jesus is to "love your enemies". He modelled it when he ministered to Israel's enemy, a Roman army centurion, in Galilee (the hotbed of Jewish resistance against the oppressive Romans, Matt 8:5–13). Such acts by Jesus were revolutionary — of the non-violent type. As a witness to the kingdom you cannot do anything more powerful than going beyond loving your neighbour, and even your nation, to loving your enemy (Matt 5:43–48).[8] This love of enemy ultimately cost Jesus his life. But even then he was heard saying: "Father, forgive them, for they know not what they are doing" (Lk 23:34). When he said this on the cross, he was referring to both the Jews and the Roman soldiers, who crucified him together. The sheer authority and power of his life of love affected everyone. People, and especially the Israeli leaders, either had to repent and join him, or they had to get rid of him, because he simply left no space for neutrality. Although relatively few joined him, it began a worldwide revolution of love that is on the march to this very day.

Jesus teaches love of neighbour, and even enemies, to be authentic love for God. And he defines it to mean crossing racial and other divides in reconciling acts of love, mercy and healing. Think of the story of the good Samaritan (Lk 10:25–37). This story needs to be contextualised in every country around the world. Jesus' story was very provocative in his context. I will update it a little.[9]

Jesus is asked by a smart Abe what he can do to inherit eternal life. Jesus answers from Torah, to "love God and love your neighbour". Abe tries to be clever and asks Jesus, "Who is my neighbour?" Jesus tells a story: An Israeli Jew is ambushed by a Hamas Palestinian suicide bomber. This horror happens while the Israeli Jew is on his way from Jerusalem to his home in a Jewish settlement in the occupied territories. There he lies, blown apart, on the brink of death, next to the massive new fence that Israel has built in the West Bank. A Rabbi comes by and passes on the other side of the road, too busy and too fearful to get involved. Then a Jewish politician from the Likud party comes past and does the same thing for similar reasons. An Israeli Arab comes by and also passes on the other side. But then a Palestinian peasant comes by — whose brother's farmland has been divided by the

Israeli fence — and he takes pity on the Jew. He helps him, effectively signing his own death warrant as he takes the dying Jewish settler back to his own home in Jenin in order to care for him until he recovers. Then Jesus asks Abe, "Which of these four do you think was a neighbour to the dying man?" Abe replies, "The man who had mercy on him ... the Palestinian."

Mercy is reconciling love in action — totally undeserving and unreasonable, even irrational. I can just hear it: "A Jewish settler? A Palestinian? He would never do that!" Be that as it may, Jesus was not PC. He was thoroughly counterculture and revolutionary, both in Judaism and in general society. He carefully crafted stories that had all the racial, religious and political overtones of his day in order to expose the underlying false assumptions, the prejudices and hateful practices of his society. This is the manner in which Jesus taught the alternative way of reconciling love to his followers and people in general. His teaching method was often to name people and groups provocatively and unashamedly, exposing their false political and social ideas by contrasting and comparing them with his kingdom ideas and practices. He called Herod, the puppet Jewish king, "that fox", because that was exactly who he was — a sly, despicable deceiver of his own people (Lk 13:32). Another example is the Sermon on the Mount (Matt 5–7). Jesus repeatedly says to his followers: "It is said ... but I say ... they do thus and so ... but you must do ... the Pharisees pray and fast this way ... but you must do it my way ..." Messianics (Christians) are different, and we must courageously live out that difference for the sake of the kingdom, for the sake of the world. If we lose our distinctiveness, we and the world are lost. Remember the salt and light?

Jesus' teaching in the Sermon on the Mount is all about the type of people we become. Or, more accurately, it is about the *type of community* we become in the reconciling and transforming power of God's kingdom of love. This is in contrast to the divided, pain-filled and loveless society which the devil rules. Although we are not of this world, we live in this world to challenge, influence and transform it. How do we do this? By losing our life for Christ's sake, not by saving it for our own sake — as in striving for security, status and wealth. Bonhoeffer's famous summary of discipleship and his exposition of the Sermon on the Mount is: When Jesus bids us "Come and follow," he bids us "come and die."[10] We die to self as we follow Jesus in doing his reconciling acts of love across any and every barrier in society.

In conclusion I must mention *Jesus' specific teaching on reconciliation*, from the Sermon on the Mount and from a later teaching on kingdom community (Matt 5:21–26 cf. 18:15–35). In these passages he gives direct instruction on reconciliation and how to accomplish it (a derivative of *katallasso* is used). Jesus insists on the absolute necessity and importance of *one-on-one reconciliation* between people, especially among his followers. After all, he expects us to be leading the world in these matters. The teaching is only prescriptive in the sense that it actually describes what is good for us and society. In other words, by obeying Jesus' teachings we work with reality, not against it. By keeping relationships reconciled, healthy and growing, we "re*shalom*" the earth. Sweeping unresolved stuff under the carpet is to work for the devil — we undermine relationships and enhance disorder. I will spell out Jesus' practical model of one-on-one reconciliation in the next chapter.

THE EARLY CHURCH IN THE BOOK OF ACTS

The coming of the Spirit in Acts 2 was to enable Jesus' followers to live the Sermon on the Mount as the reconciled community of love. As I said earlier, Pentecost was the reversal of Babel (Gen 11) and the empowering of God's one new united nation in fulfilment of Abraham's calling and promise (Gen 12). The acts of the Spirit in and through the church was all about the community of Jesus continuing Jesus' example of crossing the barriers in ever-increasing circles of reconciliation and inclusiveness. It began in Jerusalem (city), spread to Judea (rural poor), to Samaria (half-breeds) and to the ends of the earth (all tongues and nations, Acts 1:8).[11] The promise of the Father was, and still is, that when the Spirit is poured out, he reconciles "all people" from across all barriers. The "sons and daughters will prophesy" (gender barrier), "the young men will see visions and the old men will dream dreams" (generational barriers), and "even the servants, both men and women ..." (class or social barriers, Joel 2:28–32; Acts 1:4–5; 2:16–18).

This inclusiveness and unity takes flesh in Jesus' Jerusalem community as rich and poor share resources in one reconciled fellowship. Sharing the common meal in their homes embodied this reconciliation — it was a celebration of the future kingdom banquet (2:44–46; 4:32–5). A dispute arose between the Greek and Hebrew-speaking Jewish widows over the equitable distribution of food (6:1–7). They resolved the problem, not by forming two separate congregations based on language and culture, but by making practical arrangements.

In Acts 7 we see Stephen before the Jewish leaders in Jerusalem courageously casting a vision of Judaism radically redefined by *Yeshua ha Notzri* (Jesus the Nazarene). He pleads for the centre of Jewish identity and faith to be around

Yeshua as *Meshiach*, and not around ethnicity, temple, Torah or the land. Messianic Judaism transcends these Jewish elements, both for Israel's and the world's sake (the *goyim*, pagan nations). The leaders were so incensed by Stephen's message that they stoned him to death. The blood of this first Messianic martyr was the first seeding of the church; today we are all part of its growing harvest.

The shift from Jewish believers to Gentile converts begins in Acts 8. The Spirit takes Philip across the racial barrier to the Samaritans, where many enter the kingdom through faith in Jesus, and then further on to an important Ethiopian official in charge of the treasury of Candace, Queen of Ethiopia. He too becomes a believer in Jesus and is baptised. Acts 9 sees Rabbi *Shaul* going out to beat up and arrest the Jewish Messianics in Damascus. But God beats him up — or, more accurately, he has a head-on collision with a blinding Light! Jesus arrests him in a calling to take the gospel to "the Gentiles and their kings, *and* to Israel". This leads to Acts 10 where God has to employ a massive movement of angels, trances and visions in order to get Peter beyond his Jewish bigotry, his racial and religious prejudice, to go to the Gentiles and bring them into the one body of Messiah. God made him go to a Roman centurion. Peter had to learn not to call unclean what God had made clean. God told him to make no distinction between Jews and Gentiles (11:12). But even then he was weak in his convictions and prejudices. When other conservative Jewish believers were around, he withdrew from fellowshipping with the Gentile believers in order not to offend Jewish believers. Paul saw this hypocrisy and confronted and rebuked Peter "in front of them all", because Peter "was clearly in the wrong". Even Barnabas was swayed by Peter's prejudicial weakness and did not clearly see the racial implications of the gospel (Gal 2:11–21).

The confrontation between Paul and Peter took place in Antioch which was the first truly racially mixed church (13:1–4). The leadership team in Antioch was made up of Jews and Gentiles (Lucius was a Latin name and he was probably a Gentile); of light and dark-skinned individuals (Niger means black); of poorer and wealthier society (Manaen had been raised with Herod the tetrarch). The church grew to about 30 000 in the context of Antioch's society of about 500 000 citizens made up of Greeks, Romans, Jews, Egyptians, Arabs and Persians. Each of these groups lived largely in their own areas and were in conflict with one another. For example, persecution broke out against the city's Jews during the reign of Caligula (37–41AD).[12] The Antioch church became the base from which the mission to the Roman world took place. It was the model and the seed for all the subsequent church plants, a powerful witness to a segregated and prejudiced society.

The tensions that I mentioned between the conservative Jewish and new Gentile believers eventually overflowed into open dispute and called for a ruling from the early church leaders. This took place at the Jerusalem Council in Acts 15.[13] The issue was simple: The conservative "Judaisers" operated on a "proselyte model" of conversion, that Gentile believers should do Torah observance by keeping the ceremonial and other aspects of the Jewish law in order to be fully incorporated into God's people. For example, Gentiles had to be circumcised and keep Jewish feasts. James, the apostles, the elders and the church representatives all agreed that that would be contrary to the gospel of Jesus and the Spirit's work begun at Pentecost. In other words, they upheld the kingdom or "eschatological model" of conversion, which meant that Gentiles were accepted in the Messiah on an equal basis with Jews, without having to become Jews, take on their ceremonial culture or assume their lifestyle. Paul was in full agreement with this (see Gal 4:9–10; 5:2–12; 6:12–16). The only thing required of Gentile believers was sensitivity in a few matters for the *sake of missions*, because the law of Moses was read in the synagogues throughout the Mediterranean world.[14] Once again, they did not resolve these types of problems by forming separate Jewish and Gentile congregations. They continued in their radical gospel unity, overcoming whatever tensions and differences presented themselves, through the reconciling wisdom and power of the Spirit. The Spirit blew the church across all geographic boundaries and socio-political barriers throughout the known world (Acts 13–28).

JOHN ON JESUS AND "ONENESS"[15]

I cited some stories from John's Gospel in discussing Jesus' model and teachings on reconciliation. I want to comment briefly on how John understood Jesus' teaching on "oneness". It has direct bearing on reconciliation and transformation in the early church, and is applicable to us today. Jesus taught his followers much about YHWH as his Father, and his relationship of oneness with the Father. John builds a theology of *koinonia* (fellowship) out of this oneness between the Father and the Son, between God and us, and with one another: "If we walk in the light as he is in the light, we have fellowship with one another ..." (1 Jn 1:1–7). He depicts it both in Trinitarian terms and in the symbolic language of life, light and love.

In Trinitarian terms, Jesus of Nazareth is the Son of God, sent from the Father to reveal God as Father to Israel and the world, by the indwelling Holy Spirit. Jesus and the Father are one in the Spirit, so much so that Jesus does nothing on his own initiative — he only does what he sees the Father doing (Jn 5:17–21; 10:30;

14:5–11). This does not mean Jesus loses his identity, autonomy and personality. On the contrary, it enhances his personhood. The depth of relational oneness completes Jesus. It brings the Trinitarian reality to earth. We see in Jesus a relational intimacy and coworking with God that gives us hope and faith for something similar. The relationship between the Father and the Son is the original intention, template and goal (*eschaton*) of human creation. All of us instinctively long for this intimacy with God and one another. We all instinctively yearn for this depth of reconciliation, for the ultimate completion and perfection of our humanity in oneness with God and one another. We saw how Adam and Eve experienced this to the full before the fall, and it is now reconciled and restored to us in Jesus Christ. The oneness between husband and wife in the marriage covenant is the closest earthly model of this heavenly reality (Gen 2:23–24 cf. Eph 5:29–32; sexual union is the sacred symbolic consummation of this reconciled reality, that is why it is holy, reserved only for covenant relationship).

Jesus said to his followers: "As the Father has sent me, so I am sending you" (Jn 20:21). Our reconciliation into fellowship with the Father, in the Son and by the Spirit, makes us one with God. We are sent into the world to reveal and model Jesus, as Jesus revealed and modelled the Father. Jesus said: "My Father and I will love you, and we will come and make our home in you," meaning: We will literally incarnate ourselves in you in relational oneness (Jn 14:23). This Father-Jesus model is not only a model for the Jesus-follower relationship, but also applies to believer-believer oneness. Church is a Trinitarian community. The famous high-priestly prayer of Jesus in John 17 is the culmination of this reality. It is the holy of holies of Jesus' teachings on Father-fellowship. Jesus prays not only for his early followers, but for all subsequent generations, including our churches today: "That all of them may be one, Father, just as you are in me and I am in you. May they also be in us so that the world may believe that you have sent me ... may they be brought to complete unity to let the world know that you sent me" (vv. 20–23).

God stakes his personal credibility in a very public way on the unity or disunity of the church. The world will believe in Jesus — as the one sent from God to bring salvation — to the extent that we reconcile and become one with one another, and live out our oneness with God. We literally represent God on earth by the quality (or lack thereof) of our unity in Christ. It is not as if God has great faith in us; it has more to do with the knowledge of his sovereign purpose. He will fulfil what he set out to do. The church worldwide will become one in a dynamic and functional unity, with a mature faith that incarnates the fullness of Christ on earth (Paul's picture in Eph 4:13). The ultimate fulfilment of Jesus' prayer is seen in John's vision of God's throne-room filled with all his people from every nation, tribe and language, worshipping God in a heavenly oneness that consummates the Trinitarian reality (Rev 5:9–10; 7:9–10).

In terms of its earthly incarnation, John's vision and teaching of this same reality is about life, light and love.[16] We share God's eternal kind of life in Christ by his Spirit. Being "born from above" means we live and share God's "common life"[17] with one another in a local fellowship of his followers. The life is the light that came into the world in Jesus, and is now in us, individually as believers and corporately as church. It drives back and overcomes the darkness of evil, sin, hatred and death. How? By the sheer power of love. The light is the reconciling love of God in Christ, and now in us, radiating to the ends of the earth. That is why John makes such a big thing of love. This brings the circle back to Jesus, from whom John learnt these things. Love for one another across any barrier is the ultimate test of whether we have God's life in us: "We know we have passed from death because we love one another. Whoever does not love abides in death" (1 Jn 3:14 NRSV). The context of this verse is the poor person in need, which reminds us of the self-sacrificing and reconciling love that is seen in Jesus. We cannot deceive ourselves with a private and vertical spirituality that says "just God and me". John asks: How can we say we love God whom we cannot see, and yet we do not love people around us whom we see? If this is the case, we are liars, and the truth, let alone God's life, is not in us (1 Jn 4:20–21).

In short, God's intention for us is reconciliation and unity in a true oneness of heart, mind and life. It stems from "sharing the common life" of God. This will manifest itself in practical, reconciling, sacrificial acts of love for one another — and for others across whatever barriers may exist. And indeed, it is the light and the hope of the world.

 # PAUL AND HIS TEACHINGS ON RECONCILIATION

Paul emerged as a formidable leader and formative thinker in the early church. Like Jesus, his life example and teachings are radical and far-reaching. He too died for his faith and work in the ever-advancing and reconciling kingdom of God. As a follow-up to what we looked at in the previous chapter, I will comment on his *katallassso* teachings from personal, to group and cosmic reconciliation.[18] To complete the chapter I will discuss what can be called Paul's "gospel mandate".

Reconciliation with God — principle and personal
2 Cor 5:16—21; Rom 5:6—11; 11:15

Paul took the Greek word for reconciliation from secular usage in the diplomatic world and filled it with Christian meaning. Although he also used other terms such as "redemption" and "justification", the concept of reconciliation became central to his thinking and preaching on God's work of salvation in Jesus Christ.[19] It also became central to his life calling — both the "message" and "ministry" of reconciliation (2 Cor 5:16—21). In the context of his apostleship, he saw himself as Christ's ambassador or envoy, sent out to the nations of the world to offer a peace treaty. In fact, God was "making his appeal through" Paul, "imploring" people to be reconciled to him. On the basis of Jesus' death, where "he became sin for us", God is offering terms of amnesty so that people can be reconciled to him. In Paul's mind "to reconcile" meant "to make peace", to change from a state of hostility and war to harmony and accord with God. It not only makes us personally "new creations" in Christ so that "we might become the righteousness of God", but it also begins in principle "the new creation" for all of cursed creation. Paul says that "the old (age) has gone" and "the new (age of God's kingdom) has come". In other words, all things have already been reconciled to God in Christ. We are just working it out in this age while awaiting its consummation when Jesus returns.

For Paul, the origin and essence of all this is the astonishing outpoured love of God. In Rom 1—3 he shows that we have all sinned, both Jews and Gentiles. The way out of our sin is faith in God's work of salvation through Jesus' death and resurrection (chapters 4—6). The centre point (Rom 5:5—11) of this explanation of salvation is God's amazing love for us: While we were "still sinners", "enemies of God", "Christ died for us". This is the restorative justice of God that "justifies us" before him. In other words, it is "his blood" that fulfils God's just requirements for sin and death, "saves us from God's wrath" and "reconciles us with God". Paul adds to this: "How much more, having been reconciled, shall we be saved through his life!" And therefore, "We rejoice in God through our Lord Jesus Christ, through whom we have now received reconciliation."

What about Rom 11:11—32 and the reconciliation of ethnic or national Israel? Paul speaks of reconciliation (v. 15) at the end of a protracted argument that explains God's salvation in representative terms. Adam represents the human race — in him all die. Jesus represents the New Adam — in Christ all are made alive (those who are reconciled and justified by faith in him); but Jesus is also "the seed of Abraham", fulfilling God's promise of salvation to Israel. Paul's point is that both Jews and Gentiles are sinners, and both are reconciled to God in the same way, by being in Christ. This is Paul's argument from Rom 1–8. What about the nation of Israel? As a nation she rejected her Messiah. Paul answers this in Rom 9–11. By Israel rejecting Jesus, God opened the door to the Gentiles to be reconciled. Does that mean Israel is lost forever? No! "If their rejection is the reconciliation of the world, what will their acceptance be but life from the dead?" (v. 15). Paul clearly says that God has a plan to reconcile Israel, ethnic Jews as a group, to himself (v. 25). Gentile believers have a part in that: By walking in humble integrity with God as a witness to the Jewish people, they will be provoked to jealousy and come to faith in *Yeshua* as the *Meshiach*. They will be "grafted into their own tree again" (v. 24). This is already happening in modern Israel and around the world; many Jews are becoming believers in Messiah Jesus.

Group or cultural reconciliation
Eph 2:11–22; 3:4–11; Col 2:13–23

In Ephesians Paul says that Gentiles were "dead in their sins" (2:1f), "separate" from God and God's people (Israel). But in Messiah they have been "made alive" and are now reconciled to God and his people. Paul's thoughts clearly move from direct reconciliation with God to group reconciliation with one another — in Christ. The key for Paul is, once again, the cross of Jesus. It restores *Shalom* between God and humanity, and between Jews and Gentiles. How does it do this? Firstly, by destroying the dividing wall of hostility between Jew and Gentile. This is the division and enmity brought about by "the Law with its commandments and regulations" (2:15) that separated Jews from Gentiles. These were the boundary markers that kept Jews in and Gentiles out — unless of course they operated on a proselyte model where Gentile converts became full Jews.[20] In terms of salvation, these laws are abolished in Christ's death.

Secondly, the cross of Jesus creates "one new humanity" out of *former* Jews and Gentiles. They are both reconciled "in one body" to God, "thus making peace" (*Shalom*, 2:15). What is this "one body" (2:16) ? It clearly refers to the body of Christ, his one new people, his "holy temple" (2:21) indwelt by his Spirit, which is Paul's central theme in his letter to the Ephesians (it is also the one "olive tree" of Rom 11). The implication is clear: any laws — unjust or otherwise — that divide people and groups are abolished in Jesus' body on the cross, and people and cultures are reconciled in Christ's body on earth.

Paul continues in Eph 3 saying that this reconciliation of Jews and Gentiles as "members of one body" (v. 6) was a mystery kept hidden in God in ages past. Although prophesied in the OT,[21] it has now been revealed and fulfilled through

Jesus and his apostles. God's "intent was that now, *through the church*, the manifold wisdom of God should be made known to the rulers and authorities in the heavenly realms, according to his eternal purpose which he accomplished in Christ Jesus our Lord" (v. 10–11). The spiritual principalities and powers, those assigned to the nations to uphold the boundaries and implement justice, both good and bad rulers, see God's eternal purpose for the nations fulfilled in the one reconciled church. They shake their heads as they see God's wisdom displayed *through us as we ourselves reconcile and unite in peaceful coexistence, and as we do this to people of different races, cultures, groups and tongues, in our local churches*. This reminds me of how our Johweto group used to go out together as blacks and whites in public places to see movies or concerts in the 1980s. We enjoyed the way people from both sides of the racial divide in SA turned their heads and stared at us. Some even showed signs of aggression towards this happy mixed group. We laughed and said to each other, "Look, the powers are confused, they're scratching their heads, they're upset ..."

The laws that "divide and rule", both from spiritual and earthly rulers, are abolished and transcended in the cross of Christ. However, it is only real and meaningful to the extent that it is incarnated in his one new humanity — the local church that daily carries the cross of Jesus. How well do we carry this cross of reconciliation? How well do we embody and manifest God's manifold wisdom? What is the quality of our reconciled relationships in church, marriage, family and in the workplace (Eph 4–6)? Is it such that people and powers, both earthly and heavenly, look at us and see how life should be lived as God intended? The battle is not over. We will continue to "wrestle against principalities and powers" for the sake of the world's reconciliation until Jesus comes (Eph 6:12).

In Col 2:13–23 Paul puts it another way. Jesus "cancelled the written code, with its regulations, that was against us and stood opposed to us; he took it away, nailing it to the cross. And having disarmed the powers and authorities, he made a public spectacle of them, triumphing over them by the cross. Therefore do not let anyone judge you by what you eat or drink, or with regard to a religious festival ... a Sabbath ..." (vv. 14–16). In Paul's mind the church, born of the cross, is the most freeing place on earth. It is the safest place for mutual disclosure of prejudice and pain; for healing from racial and other hurts; for repentance and reconciliation from racial and other sins of divisiveness; and of acceptance of and love for one another, no matter what our differences or background. That is why he gives careful instruction on how to live together. He teaches us how to handle some of the sensitivities around religious and cultural prejudices and scruples about food and holy days. A robust conscience has no scruples with regard to all these things, but for the sake of people with weaker consciences, we should be careful not to cause them to stumble but find ways to love them beyond their scruples (see 1 Cor 8–9; Rom 14–15).

We should read Paul's twenty-one "one another" sayings in his various letters to the churches in this context. He says "accept one another ... bear one another's burdens ... do not judge one another ... forgive one another ..." They all relate directly to the struggles of a shared life in a culturally diverse and mixed congregation. They are clear and specific instructions on reconciled living as a witness to a divided and prejudiced world, both earthly and heavenly. The local church really is the hope of the world.

Cosmic or universal reconciliation
Col 1:20—22

Paul is saying in Col 1 that God not only created the universe through Christ (v. 16), but he also reconciled the universe to himself through Christ (v. 20). The implication is that the universe with its thrones, principalities and rulers, has been disrupted and unbalanced by evil. But it is now reconciled to God through Jesus' death. This does not mean that Satan and his hordes are, or will be, reconciled to God in any ultimate salvation sense. Paul is saying to Christians that they need not fear that the forces of the universe, spiritual or natural, will destroy them and God's creation. God made the universe, and then reconciles and rules it through Christ for our sake. Jesus is our head. He is also the head of all things, the embodiment of God's fullness (vv. 18–19). Therefore the cosmic forces, the weather and the planets, will not only be held in balance until the end, but will be renewed at the coming of Christ, precisely because reconciliation has already taken place. That is why the natural creation itself is waiting in groaning anticipation for that day of liberation at the coming of the Lord (Rom 8:20–22).

Paul's point is that, as believers, we are reconciled out from under the cosmic and earthly domain of enmity and darkness into the rule of Christ. The unstable cosmic powers are no longer a threat to us (vv. 12–13; 21–22). Standing in the realm of light, reconciled to God, we know that through the cross, the powers of the universe are in concord with God and with one another. Peace has been made, *Shalom* has been restored, not only for us, but also for the universe. Paul's conclusion is that we can "continue in our faith ... not moved from the hope held out in the gospel" as we proclaim it "to every creature under heaven" (v. 23).

The implication for us today is that the church has the authority to speak about the reconciliation of powers and structures which threaten the life of individuals and societies. This goes beyond the reconciliation of groups and cultures. It also amplifies the idea of "the manifold wisdom of God being made known through the church". Paul goes so far as to say that we will not only rule over the world in the age to come, we will even sit in judgement over angels (1 Cor 6:1–3). Astonishing! Therefore our present and ongoing work of reconciliation is very important to say. It should be seen as training for reigning in the eternal ages, for ruling over principalities and powers, let alone over church and society in this present age.

PAUL'S GOSPEL MANDATE — GAL 3:26–28 [22]

Paul's understanding of the gospel of reconciliation — discussed above — is best summarised in the early church's baptismal confession quoted at the beginning of this chapter. Paul makes other similar references to baptism and reconciled unity in Christ (1 Cor 12:13; Col 3:11). When people came to faith in Jesus as Messiah, they were publicly baptised with a liturgical confession to their friends and family that they had found a new life and identity in Christ and his one new people. Their former cultural, class and gender labels and identities were buried in the waters of baptism. They were new creations, "sons and daughters of God", "clothed with Christ" in their new life and identity. This was made real in the local fellowship of God's reconciled and united people.[23] We took great delight in Johweto in the 1980s when we baptised new believers because we got them to make a public confession: "I am no longer black nor white, rich nor poor, male nor female. I am now one in Jesus Christ and his people." It had tangible meaning for them in the context of Johweto and SA.

With Richard Longenecker, I call this early church baptismal confession Paul's threefold mandate of the gospel:

♦ the cultural (racial) mandate: "neither Jew nor Gentile";
♦ the social (political/economic) mandate: "neither slave nor free";
♦ the sexual (gender) mandate: "neither male nor female".

Gal 3:28 has also been called "The Magna Carta of the New Humanity". It was a very radical confession in the diverse and divided socio-political context of the day. It not only united people in Christ, but also set out new relationships of oneness (*koinonia*) with one another in the church, as a model to society. In quoting this Good News Mandate or Magna Carta, Paul probably had in mind the reversal of two well-known prayers of thanksgiving. The Jewish men prayed the blessing

(*Berakoth*) every morning: "Blessed be he that he did not make me a Gentile; blessed be he that he did not make me a boor (i.e. an ignorant peasant or slave); and blessed be he that he did not make me a woman." The Greek men also gave thanks "that I was born a human being and not a beast, next, a man and not a woman, thirdly, a Greek and not a barbarian".[24] These chauvinistic "prayers" were directly reversed in the bold claims, liturgy and lifestyle of the early church. (I use quotation marks because these "prayers" are almost blasphemous from Christ's viewpoint.) I have already touched on these three aspects of the gospel mandate in one way or another, so I will simply complete the picture with some pertinent comments.

The cultural mandate

Paul was the apostle who saw most clearly the radical changes that Jesus the Messiah brought: the fulfilment of salvation for Jews first, because salvation is from the Jews; the shift from a proselytising model of conversion for Gentiles, to their full unconditional inclusion in the kingdom of God on the basis of faith in Jesus. This salvation and reconciliation "by grace alone" was made real in the unity of Jesus' local church. Hence the racial or cultural mandate of the Messianic good news: Go and reconcile Jews and Gentiles in the church, which then becomes the model for society. Paul fought for this gospel mandate wherever he went. He fought for the unity of the church, spelling out the implications in all his letters to the churches.

"Neither Jews nor Gentiles" or the teaching of "oneness" in the early church does not mean the denial or renunciation of racial characteristics and ethnic distinctions. It does not mean that Jews cease to be Jews. They continue in their culture, but with the kingdom of God constantly challenging and interacting with it for growth and transformation into the likeness of the Messianic kingdom — the "new age" culture. Neither does it mean that Gentiles lose their national or tribal cultures and cease to be Gentiles — or that they become Jews for that matter. They too are challenged in their cultural ways and racial identities to continue being transformed into a greater kingdom culture and identity of love.[25] *The mystery of the kingdom's transforming work happens precisely in the mutual reconciliation and shared life of the different cultures and races.* Keep them apart and kingdom transformation ceases. Demonic transformation into "divide and rule" takes over once again. Racism and anti-Semitism become the order of the day. Therefore, it is an actual mandate to go and reconcile Jews and Gentiles into one body, for the salvation and transformation of the world.

This is a direct challenge to Gentile congregations in many nations who have no interest in Jews, and would even exclude them, let alone evangelise them. It is also is a direct challenge to the emerging movement of Messianic Judaism that seeks to establish Jewish Messianic congregations in Israel and Western nations (for Diaspora Jews). In the more extreme cases they do it to the exclusion of Gentiles. Their purpose is not only to recover the Jewish roots of Christian faith, but to make it easy for Jews to come to faith in *Yeshua ha Meshiach* in their own culture. This is good and well, but the warnings against this "missions strategy" should be heeded (see my discussion on church growth and apartheid in the Chapter 5). Jews and Gentiles should be together in one congregation. By mentioning the issue of Jewish/Gentile relationships, both in Christ and in the world, past and present, I have touched on a massive subject that raises huge issues with regard to reconciliation. Just think of the complexities of the Middle East, let alone Replacement Theology versus Christian Zionism (I discuss these issues in Chapter 8).[26] In completing this section on Paul's cultural mandate, I need to summarise the historical developments between Jews and Gentiles, with a view to confession and reconciliation.[27]

The spread of the gospel into the Gentile nations increased the strain between sectarian Messianic Judaism — the national Jewish view of early Christianity — and mainline Israeli or Rabbinical Judaism. It eventually led to a split between the synagogue and the church. The fall of Jerusalem in 70AD was the turning point. After the Jewish revolt in 135AD the split became open and acrimonious. Initially the Jews persecuted the (Jewish) church. But with the ever-increasing Gentile membership and political recognition (by Constantine in 311AD), the church began to persecute Jews. They forgot their Jewish roots and became ripe for anti-Semitism, including other forms of racial prejudice and national pride. Paul's warning to Gentile believers about pride, especially with regard to Jews, went unheeded (Rom 11:17–24). The reconciliation between Jews and Gentiles in the early church was a thing of the past.

The sad and bloody history of the church with regard to anti-Semitism is an open secret — *every Christian should read what happened in the crusades, the inquisitions, the pogroms, and the holocaust.*[28] It will leave you utterly shattered, and without excuse. It will make my chapter and confession on apartheid look insignificant — without minimising it. We in the Western church have indeed sinned and done wrong. We and our fathers, and our forefathers, are covered with guilt and shame. As Gentile Christians we take up Daniel's confession and ask God, and all Jews, to forgive us for our 2 000 year "history of contempt", which must now come to an end. May God have mercy on us and speedily bring about the reconciliation that Paul spoke about in which "all Israel will be saved" (Rom 11:25–32).

On the other hand there is a growing reaction from some Jews, whose minds have been deeply conditioned by their historical pain and struggle for survival. This is especially true in post-holocaust theology and debate. For example, if one criticises modern Israel and its governmental policies, one is labelled unpatriotic — if you live in Israel — and anti-Semitic if you live outside Israel. Any serious evangelising of Jews in the name of *Yeshua ha Meshiach* is labelled anti-Semitic. In fact, John's Gospel, because of its frequent references to "the Jews" is seen by some Jewish and Gentile scholars as dangerously anti-Semitic. Besides being anachronistic, this sort of accusation is clearly an overreaction. Part of the problem is that most Jews, from 135AD to the present day, do not distinguish between Christian and Gentile (or Westerner, for that matter); they are synonymous in the Jewish mind. This long protracted error has produced enormous prejudice that covers a multitude of sins. *But have we Christians, at any point in history, given them any good reason to think any differently?* Christians, both Jewish and whatever other nationality, must repent by recovering the integrity of Messiah's name and *our common identity in him and his people.* This is the hope of reconciliation. We must humbly and bravely live out the Messianic identity above and beyond all other identities, whether racial, cultural or national. We must do this precisely in order to heal the prejudice of both Jews *and* Gentiles in an increasingly divided and desperate world.

The social mandate

"Neither slave nor free" is both a principle and a specific mandate. Paul spoke a lot about freedom,[29] although there is no record of him directly addressing the institution of slavery. Jesus announced the Jubilee (Lk 4:18), but we have no account of him directly freeing slaves or overtly challenging its institution as inherently evil. The NT emphasis on freedom is more about personal and spiritual deliverance from slavery to sin and spiritual powers, through the ransom that Christ paid on the cross ("ransom" is the price paid to buy slaves their freedom). The result is that we are so free that we are willing and obedient slaves of Christ. The early Christians used the word "redemption" to explain salvation, similar to the word "reconciliation".[30] However, in this redemption and its message lay the seeds of a radical freedom that the social mandate of the gospel pointed to, which was the eventual downfall of the institution of slavery.[31]

At one level, the mandate meant actual slaves and freepersons finding reconciliation in Christ and the local church. This meant a radical social equality in the local church as a witness to the top-down class structure of society. Slaves were the underclass, the legal property of the owner — they called him master. But in Christ, slaves and masters sat together in real *koinonia*, the fellowship of the common life. This equality was symbolised in the Lord's supper, where their gifts, both natural and spiritual, were shared for the common good. A wonderful example of this is Onesimus, a runaway slave who had stolen from his master and was caught, then led to Christ by Paul in prison. Paul writes to Onesimus's former master, Philemon, and effects forgiveness and reconciliation between the two. Paul even encourages Philemon to receive and support Onesimus's ministry — one tradition says that he later became Bishop of Ephesus.[32] What is important to note is that Paul does *not* engage in a head-on confrontation with slavery, but rather elevates the quality of personal relationships in the church ("brothers"). In other words, Paul works through relationships, not institution. He takes nothing for granted, he even offers to repay Philemon for his loss on Onesimus's behalf.

Paul's "household" teachings about Christian slaves submitting to their masters and Christian masters caring for their slaves (Eph 6:5–9; Col 3:22–4:1) must be seen in this context. Paul is saying that we must not allow our remarkable reconciliation in Christ and his church to bring the gospel into disrepute. For example, we can flaunt our new-found freedom to the detriment of our (working or employment) relationships, and undermine our witness to the world. We must remember that there were more slaves than freepersons in the Roman Empire, and the Greco-Roman economy was largely built on the institution of slavery — its tentacles were buried deep in every fibre of society. The freedom and reconciliation between slaves and freepersons in the local church was radical enough, without even beginning to address slavery per se. But neither should we read Paul's comments on slaves and masters as endorsement, or even reinforcement of the oppressive status quo. Because of his kingdom framework, his statements are in tension with the status quo, as are all his other social teachings.

At another level the mandate meant that slaves would be free and the institution of slavery would come to an end. The seeds of slavery's demise had been sown, because in Christ the future age had broken through — in God's future kingdom there will be no slavery. The church was slow on the uptake, and it actually went backwards from Paul's time. Many church leaders in the second century owned slaves, and some had a reputation for cruelty to the poor and oppressed. Origen (202–254AD) thought of slaves as inferior by birth, fabricating the damnable heresy that slavery resulted from God's curse on the descendants of Ham. This heresy has plagued the church to this day, especially with regard to black slaves and blacks under apartheid. Augustine (354–430AD) helped to formalise the view that, since slavery was a judgement from God, it was ordained by God and therefore part of

God's order and will in society. Calvin (1509–1564) built on this a theology of sub-ordination to the state with its "legitimate" division of orders and structures in society — which included the institution of slavery. All of this was used in the 17th and 18th centuries to legitimise the mass capture and murderous movement of African slaves to the New World. While Luther fuelled the fires of anti-Semitism, Calvin (unwittingly?) fuelled the fires of slavery.[33]

The abolition of slavery in the early 1800s came about only after it had become uneconomical to keep large numbers of slaves — money was a determining factor. What helped to turn the tide, however, was the recovery of Christian conscience. The theological-ethical revision of slavery and the persistent political lobbying by the Finneys and Wilberforces of the 18th and 19th centuries helped to dismantle slavery. Sadly, this great victory won by courageous Christian leaders is being undone before our very eyes. The tragic reality is that currently there are many terrible forms of slave trade. There are sex slaves, forced child labour and child soldiers, and gross exploitation of poor workers, in many nations of the world — all for the benefit of the middle and upper classes. In terms of sex slaves alone, the UN says that more than 1 million people are trafficked every year in the world's most profitable crime. SA has become a key hub for this heinous import and exportation "business".[34]

What can we say of all of this? Are our hands clean? We have to fall to our knees and acknowledge our failure as the church of Jesus Christ. The principle of this mandate, and its implications, has to do with structural reconciliation, socio-political and economic ethics. It is about wholistic freedom for all people, about having mercy on the "disposable" of the earth. In Christ all class consciousness begins to disappear. Rich and poor are reconciled by sharing resources, employer and employee find harmony and synergy, parents and children find God's *Shalom* (Eph 5–6). We have seen this incarnated in Jesus' life and ministry, and in the early church. We have also seen it incarnate in Mother Teresa of Calcutta. Ron Sider and Tom Sine, both radical evangelicals, have challenged Christians to a renewed conscience for the poor of the earth. They call us to learn to live simply so that others can simply live.[35] This calls for a profound repentance from materialism ("Mammon", Matt 6:24), still the chief false god controlling the church of Jesus Christ — at least in the Western church.

We *must* embody this social and economic reconciliation in our local congregations if we are going to have any integrity, let alone authority, as a prophetic challenge to the world. We must address the divide between rich and poor nations and people. We must ethically critique the economic systems of the world — including globalisation. If the church does not work for justice in all aspects of society and public policy, we have betrayed our Lord and Master, and abandoned the world to the devil. *But* I have a dream that one day, because of the church, we will hear the thundering echo of Martin Luther King's famous words: "Freedom ... Freedom ... thank God we are free at last ..." We will hear that reverberate like a massive Mexican wave[36] around the stadium of the earth, from every tribe, language and nation. What an exhilarating and rewarding sight for our Lord and Master!

The sexual mandate

If the cultural mandate goes back to undo Babel and Abraham, and the social mandate goes back to undo the earliest oppression of humans by fellow humans, the sexual mandate definitely goes back to undo the curse in the garden. Redemption in Christ reverses the curse on women — and men for that matter — and reconciles males and females in a new creation, a common life and identity in Christ. It is safe to say that these three mandates were, in principle, immediately embodied in the early church through relational reconciliation and shared life. But it happened in the tension of the "already and not yet" of the kingdom. In other words, the full implications and outworking into social and structural transformation took place along different historical lines. Racism, anti-Semitism and all forms of similar prejudice has been outlawed in most countries — although often still practised. Slavery was abolished almost two centuries ago — although still illegally practised. Other forms of unjust and oppressive economic and political structures have come and gone as Christians have engaged the powers and structures on the basis of theological-ethical truth. The same applies to the outworking of the sexual mandate.

The genuine liberation of women ending the war of the sexes seems to have taken the longest historically, socially and structurally speaking. The Feminist Movement from the 1960s to the present day has been a mixed bag. It has brought about some significant and positive changes for women (and men) in the West. In so doing, it has exposed the church as being slow in working out the implications of the (gender) gospel in society. We have had to play catch-up once again. The Feminist Movement has also unleashed false ideas and spiritual forces that have been destructive. Be that as it may, the gender mandate appears to be the most difficult and lasting challenge regarding the gospel and work of reconciliation. The reason is, among other things, that as male and female we image God. The last thing that Satan wants is the restoration of God's image, let alone his actual presence, on planet earth. Redeemed and reconciled men and women in harmony with God and one another is the worst scenario for Satan. He will do everything in his power to prevent this from happening. He will keep us apart, or at least in a state of cold war with one another. Open warfare is his delight, and he has enjoyed it much of the time in most parts of the world. I am not only referring to divorce and its devastating effects, but to all forms of sexism and abuse — mostly by men against women and children.

Sexism and sexual ethics is a massive and important subject. I will merely comment on the biblical background and historical outworking, and conclude with a story that powerfully embodies all that this mandate is talking about.

The curse and the blessing

The Hebrew and Greek prayers that I quoted earlier bear witness to the low status of women (and children) throughout the ages. Women have always been oppressed in one way or another by men, even when societies worshipped the female form. Patriarchalism and matriarchalism — and all forms of hierarchicalism for that matter — result in sexism, in which both sexes are exploited. I said in Chapter 5 that the essence of the fall and the curse in the garden was control, struggle and oppression: Women will have pain in childbirth, their desire will be for their husband and he will rule over them (Gen 3:16–19). This is not a blessing! It is a curse working its way out at all levels in all societies throughout history, to this present day. Likewise for the man: Nature is cursed and consequently men struggle and sweat to eat and live. In other words, as women are prone to find their identity in mothering and/or marriage and men (now called "love-relationships"), men are prone to find their identity in work and/or success.

Before the fall into sin, Adam and Eve lived in equality, mutuality and complementarity with God and one another. They were a Trinitarian community. This is seen in language like "bone of my bone, flesh of my flesh ... cling together ... become one ... they were both naked and felt no shame" (Gen 2:21–25). This portrays a picture of an equality and unity that was joyful and transparent, fulfilling and interdependent. They did not have to compete with each other, or be ruled over by the other. They did not have to wrestle with nature. They were not ruled by creation. On the contrary, they celebrated and completed one another in mutual love and freedom under God. Nature thrived and yielded its resources and fruit as they mutually and restfully ruled over God's creation, as God intended (Gen 1:26–30).

This is the blessing that Jesus came to restore. He broke the curse through his death, burial and resurrection. The coming age of God's kingdom broke through in Jesus. It frees us from gender issues such as sexism, warped sexuality and gender awareness. We see this in what Jesus says: In the resurrection man and woman will "neither marry nor be given in marriage ... (we) will be like the angels in heaven" (Matt 22:23–30). As with culture, this does not mean males and females lose all distinctions by being dissolved into an androgynous angelic identity. No! It means we find our identity beyond ourselves in God, where our differences and distinctives do not divide, but complement and enrich one another. We will be defined and perfected as males and females in a greater unity and identity of perfected love. In the resurrection sexual loving and bonding, and gender awareness, will be fulfilled and transcended in the perfection of God's heavenly love. This is the love that was lived out on earth in the self-sacrificing and reconciling Jesus of Nazareth. Because of Jesus, we can live this kind of male/female relationship and identity now. In so doing, we will challenge, heal and transform our societies into genuine communities of mature personhood, where equality and dignity, mutuality and love, are the order of the day.[37] We will restore God's image on earth. The local church is, or is supposed to be, the embodiment and instrument of this reality. Put another way, we are not living *in* Eden, but *after* Eden, and therefore we are living *for* Eden.

The NT understanding and practice of this mandate

What did this gender mandate mean in the NT, in the early church? The "oneness" of male and female in Christ is the kingdom principle and mandate of God's new creation, it was understood and worked out in the tension of the already and not yet of the kingdom. In other words, to the extent that "future age" is powerfully present, full equality and mutuality prevails, but to the extent that "this age" is present, hierarchicalism prevails. I cannot examine all the texts and issues in the NT on male/female relationships. I will merely summarise the broad strokes.[38] The arguments and issues in the NT are based on two emphases, one from creation (including the curse), the other from redemption.

There are clearly texts and models in Jesus, Paul and the early church that emphasise the "kingdom now" aspects of redemption. They point to radical equality and mutuality under God's direct headship. In contrast we have texts and examples that highlight the problems between the sexes, gender awareness, cultural and circumstantial sensitivities. These emphasise "kingdom then" with the very real struggles of this present evil age. They also point to creation and the curse, with hierarchical gender headship and contextual issues.

It must be remembered that the early Christians did not live in a kingdom bubble. They operated in a real context of Jewish and Greek cultural beliefs and practices about men, women and children and their roles in society. Because of this, we find the above two emphases mentioned simultaneously and in tension with one another in the same texts. In 1 Cor 11:3–12 Paul addresses contextual and cultural sensitivities in worship — women's public participation and head-coverings. He draws on creation and hierarchical categories for his arguments ("Man is head of the woman ... man was first created"), but qualifies it all by emphasising equality and mutuality in Christ ("In the Lord, man is not independent of woman ... man is born of woman ... everything comes from God").[39] Another example is 1 Tim 2:11–15. Paul addresses a contextual issue by preventing Christian women from teaching like the heretical gnostic women teachers, who wrongly usurped authority over men. They apparently offered sexual favours and/or taught superiority of women over men as in "Eve was first created and then Adam, and Adam was deceived, not Eve".[40] However, Paul ends up referring to the curse being reversed by redemption: "Women will be saved through childbirth." The point is Paul's balanced treatment as he works from context, redemption and creation.

Paul, like Jesus, was a champion of freedom, especially for women. Paul refers to eight women co-workers in Rom 16 (local church leaders, "deaconess", teachers and translocal "apostles"),[41] and to two women co-workers in Philippians 4:2–3. He saw the church as Christ's body functioning via spiritual gifts that were all non-gender specific (including prophecy, teaching and governmental leadership.)[42] As with the social mandate, Paul's "household" teachings about husbands and wives (Eph 5; Col 3), and his other teachings on sexuality and men and women in church (1 Cor 7; 11; 14), should all be read against the backdrop of the radical freedom Christ brought about. His concern was that Christian women should not flaunt their new-found freedom and bring the gospel into disrepute by disregarding the cultural sensitivities of the day. His teachings are always mutual, not only addressed to women: Husbands must love their wives as Christ loved the church, laying down his life for her, caring for her as he cares for his own physical body. This was revolutionary in Paul's day — many men would have had a problem with Paul about this!

In short, Paul's premise and preface was always the kingdom mandate of mutual submission, reconciliation and oneness in Christ (e.g. Eph 5:21f). He worked out the principle within various perceptions and practices, affirming the equality and mutuality of the sexes, while also speaking of female submission and male headship. He worked from creation and redemption, applying them to contextual and cultural issues, not wanting to alienate Jews or Gentiles in this matter.[43]

The outworking of the mandate in the history of the church

The great dignity and mutuality experienced in reconciled male and female relationships in the early church soon lost ground. In broad terms, two extremes emerged. At times women became manipulatively predominant, mainly through prophetic gifts and leadership. This seems to be the case with Maximilla and Prisca, Montanus's two co-leaders. Their Montanist movement was eventually sidelined as a gnostic heresy (160–230AD). More common throughout the church's history was the subordination of women, and even the denigration of women as temptresses. This latter stance was epitomised by Jerome (340–420AD) who was known to have had struggles with his sexual passions. Unfortunately this has often been the case: Men who cannot handle their own sexuality project onto women that dark mystery and oppress them with their own guilt and shame.

At the same time (4th century) there was the unhealthy shift from the classic discipline of chastity to the vow of celibacy for ordained "priests". This was incorrectly presented as Paul's idea in 1 Cor 7, that singleness is preferable to marriage for bishops and priests. Many bishops actually "put their wives away forever" after their ordination. This wrong view of sexuality, and misreading of Paul, has led to enormous problems of sin and abuse through the centuries for most of the men who were not gifted by God as celibates. This is besides the fact that it effectively, and tragically, blocked women from the ordained ministry. Luther and Calvin stood against the priesthood-celibacy issue and sought to lift the dignity and place of women in the church. But they did not address the issue of women and ordination. This has only recently become a public issue (since the Feminist Movement of the 1960/70s), not only for Roman Catholics, but for all churches, from Protestants through to Pentecostals.

The current situation

The aftermath of all this has been devastating — not only in terms of sexism in the church and the current controversy over women in leadership, but also in terms of sexual sin and brokenness. We have recently had the widespread sexual scandal in the Roman Catholic Church. Many priests have been charged with homosexual and heterosexual abuse and paedophilia. Many bishops likewise have simply covered up their own crimes, and swept their priests' crimes under the carpet of internal cover-up.[44] This has probably gone on for centuries. Significantly, as I write this, the first openly practising homosexual bishop, Gene Robinson, has been ordained in the Episcopal Church in the USA. This is totally unprecedented in all of church history. It will have tremendous fallout. We have indeed reached a turning point, perhaps the spiritual equivalent of 9/11.[45] Sadly, Protestants, evangelicals, charismatics and Pentecostals have nothing to say on this matter because there is a regular stream of reports of pastors and ministers who have affairs. What we hear is only the tip of the iceberg. The hidden sophistication and unseen extent of our sexism and sexual sins through internet porn and other structures of oppression and forms of perversion, threatens to sink the church. The *Titanic* did not know it was in danger until it was too late; likewise the church does not seem to see the danger we are in. All this points to the fact that we are profoundly warped, blind and broken in our sexuality and gender relationships.

It seems as if, historically speaking, the fowls have come home to roost. The level of sexual brokenness and sin being poured out in this generation — from the belly of hell — is unprecedented in history. It is suffocating. If God destroyed Sodom and Gomorrah, why should planet earth, let alone its major "sin cities", be spared?[46] Is there any image of God left on earth? Marriage and family has been so broken and changed by divorce, and it has been so radically redefined and reconstituted in every possible postmodern way that we can no longer recognise it. The perversion of male and female relationships has all but destroyed the image of God from the planet. Today we have every contrary permutation of identity, "orientation" and relationship available to the human imagination. And worse, most of them are perfectly acceptable to society, and even protected by law: homosexual, lesbian, bisexual, transsexual, transvestite — not to mention the proliferating forms of so-called heterosexual sin and brokenness. I predict that it is merely a matter of time before paedophilia, bestiality and necrophilia become acceptable. I hope I am proved wrong.

There are many issues that emerge out of this discussion, and that should be on our church agendas, but I want to conclude with what I consider to be the key issue facing us today. That is men taking responsibility for their own sins and broken masculinity, by facing what they have done to women and children (and other men) throughout history.[47] We should begin with Adam's sin of silence when Eve was tempted by Satan — he was standing right beside her (Gen 3:6) — and move on to Cain's murder of his brother; the prosecution and perpetuation of all the wars in history; the systematic oppression and rape of women; the abuse of our children — all of this, right up to the present day. Just stop and think about what men are responsible for throughout history. Because I am a man, I can speak for men, not for women! We men have sinned grievously, (mis)representing God on earth as an arrogant, lustful, abusive male murderer. We urgently need to find forgiveness and healing in reconciliation with God, and with women and children, through Jesus Christ our only Saviour.

Here is a story that sadly encapsulates this issue, as well as all that I have been trying to say with regard to the sexual or gender mandate.

A story of men's repentance

Late one Saturday afternoon, 14 September 2002, a little six-year-old girl was brutally raped by a man named Reuben in the black township of Alexandra in Johannesburg. She was so violently raped that her perineum was ripped open from her vagina to her anus, and her intestines poured out. She was left for dead. At lunchtime the following day, Sunday, some workers discovered her lying in her blood, barely breathing. She was rushed to hospital. The paediatric surgeon who treated her was so horrified that he covered her head and photographed the bloody horror. Then he immediately called a press conference and challenged the journalists to publish the picture on the front pages of our newspapers. His purpose was to hold up to all South Africans the grotesque mirror of our violent sinfulness and demonic shame. In all good conscience they did not publish the picture, but left a big empty square, surrounded by the text telling the tragic story. This was the first I heard about the incident. I was totally horrified.

Later that week an investigative TV programme called *Carte Blanche* had the guts to show the photo. I was watching. I was appalled and overcome, and began to weep and pray. I cried out to God for mercy. "I cannot just sit here and cry and pray. I must do something. God, what can I do?" Suddenly the Lord brought to mind an idea we had talked about in Johweto during apartheid in the 1980s. We spoke about a Repentance March in which we would all put on sackcloth and ashes (literally), and march from the white city of Johannesburg to the black city of Soweto, carrying placards displaying and confessing the sins of apartheid. But we never acted on it as some of us had been on the raw end of police brutality in other marches. Marches were illegal in those days, and sadly we thought twice about this repentance march.

The thought of a Men's Repentance March from Johannesburg to Alexandra came to mind. I promptly preached about it in our church and sent a letter via email and fax to all our men, and to other pastors with whom I had good relationship. I called on them, on all men, to come and march in repentance for the sin against little Lerato,[48] and for the sins of men against women and children in our nation. I quote directly from a section in my letter so that you can feel the conviction and urgency that God put in my heart:

> As the prophets of old did, I want to call on all men to do a REPENTANCE MARCH IN SACKCLOTH AND ASHES (read 2 Sam 3:31; 1 Kings 21:27; Joel 1:13) through Alexandra township out to the spot where little Lerato was raped and left for dead; and there to get on our knees, to humble ourselves, to weep and pray and repent for the sins of men against women and children in our country. I see a movement of repenting men, marching in

silence, some weeping, but all carrying crosses (about 1 metre high and 500 mm across) with cardboard plaques stapled to the cross, each with one male sin written on it — like "rape", "child abuse", "violence", "murder", "wife beating", "adultery", "sodomy", "hijacking", "pornography", "arrogance", "abusive leadership", "drunkenness", "lying", etc. As we walk, I see us telling all who ask "What's this?' about little Lerato, and inviting men to join us and repent with us. Who knows, maybe some actual murderers and rapists will join in and really repent? The man who raped this girl is in prison now, BUT WE CORPORATELY AS MEN are shamed by this and by hundreds of thousands of other rapes that go on every day — *every 28 seconds a woman or child is sexually and/or violently abused by men in this country!* AS MEN, WE ARE PART OF THIS CORPORATE GUILT AND CARRY THE UTTER SHAME OF THIS HORRENDOUS SIN THAT GOES UP AS A STENCH BEFORE GOD. THEREFORE AS MEN, WE MUST CONFESS AND REPENT IN SACKCLOTH AND ASHES (as Daniel did, see Dan 9:3–20).

The Saturday came and between 350 and 400 men turned up — more than half were white men from Johannesburg. We all put on sackcloth and rubbed ash on our heads and faces. Zander, my twelve-year-old son, stood beside me, as did many young boys who joined their fathers in the march of repentance. Robert Kganyago, a pastor-friend from Alexandra, led us. We lifted our cross-placards with the male sins that we were confessing and marched through Alexandra in silence, prayer and repentance. The residents seemed stunned. They just stood and stared. Some women verbally and provocatively dared their men to join the march, while others ululated as they understood what we were doing. They were clearly in agreement, but most of the men just looked on with empty eyes. After about ten kilometres we came to the spot where Lerato was raped. Some women from the township, together with some white women from our church, had gathered there and prayed while we were marching. Lerato's father was also waiting there. He just sat holding his other younger daughter in silence, fixed on the little white cross where Lerato had been left for dead.

I preached from Jonah 3:1–10. Through Jonah God pronounced judgement on Nineveh due to her sin. But the king heard and took off his robes, put on sackcloth and ashes, and sat in the dust. He called on all his subjects to do the same, with fasting and repentance — even the animals had to be covered in sackcloth and ashes! The king said:

> Let everyone call urgently on God. Let them give up their evil ways and their violence. Who knows? God may yet relent and with compassion turn from his fierce anger so that we will not perish.

As a white man, I confessed the devastation that white men had brought on Africa through colonialism, and on South Africa through apartheid. All the rape, greed and pillaging, all the oppressive laws, forced removals, repression and murder. We have sinned terribly before God and our fellow human beings. The seeds we sowed in centuries past have now become a whirlwind harvest of sexual crime and murderous violence unknown in our South African history. Johannesburg is the car-jacking, murder and sexual abuse capital of the world. We are ripe for God's judgement, unless we repent. I told everyone that by tearing our clothes and covering ourselves with sackcloth and ash, we were humbling ourselves and willingly taking on the signs of judgement before judgement actually falls. In my mind I could see the survivors of 9/11 in New York, who emerged from the earth-shattering horror completely bewildered and grey, covered from head to toe in dust and ash. If we humble ourselves in this way, God may "see ... and have compassion ... and not bring the destruction he threatened" (v. 10). I called for our President, Thabo Mbeki, to lead a Million-Man Repentance March in Pretoria, our capital city. If he did, God may well take note!

Then all the men knelt on the ground as we, on behalf of Reuben, asked Lerato's father to forgive us for the horror perpetrated against his little daughter. We did not see what happened, and we did not intervene to stop it. We asked the women and children (some children were also present) to forgive us for men's sins against them. Robert led us in prayer. Many wept, men, women and children. The lonely white cross, stuck in the bloody spot, said it all. A number of men and women came forward and gave their lives to Jesus. Then we piled up all our crosses, bearing all our male sins, and burnt them all. We watched as the flames rose and danced over the fiery grave of our sin and evil. We took an offering for Lerato and gave it to her dad. As the flames died down, we quietly melted away, while some men became flames of fire, dancing home with a new sense of forgiveness and freedom. I also saw a flicker of what could become a national, and even international, Men's Repentance Movement (MRM),[49] where men pour out onto the streets in their thousands to repent openly when and wherever shameful incidents of violent abuse against woman and/or children become public knowledge.

The feedback from the march was overwhelming. Many men (and women) were changed that day. One white man (in his late 40s) in our church, who was homosexually abused as a little boy, wept as he saw his life-long imprisonment of resentment and rage burn up in the flames. After all those years, he was able genuinely to forgive that paedophile monster and find release. I know this man personally — he is free. I also know the middle-aged black woman who was weeping and weeping. She had been badly abused as a child. When I asked her why she was weeping, she said she felt deeply cleansed and empowered that day. Why? How? She saw us as her elder brothers at long last doing something about her abuse. For the first time in her life she saw men taking responsibility for what men did to her personally, and to all women. She was overcome. She felt her womanhood and dignity was being restored. She said that at last men were standing up *for her* by kneeling down before God in humble repentance. She felt that if men were becoming real men through humility and repentance, there may be hope for this sad world.

Restored godly masculinity, in tandem with healed godly femininity, is the greatest force for healing and transformation in our world today. This happens as male and female find themselves reconciled as one in Jesus Christ, our Lord and Master.

Paul's gospel mandate finds us wanting. *Mene Mene Tekel Parsin.* As the church of Jesus Christ, we have seen the writing on the wall, we have been weighed in the balances and found wanting (Dan 5:25—28). Unlike Balshazzar, who reached for royal robes and gold chains, I called on us to fall on our faces in confession of our failings, to strip ourselves of all arrogance and presumption, and to adorn ourselves with humility and repentance. This is the spirit and attitude in which we must approach one another, in which we must seek reconciliation and facilitate reconciliation for others. Then it will have meaning and we will have success.

NOTES

1. The attempt to understand Jesus as a Jew in Israel in first century Judaism has a long history. It raises very important challenges for Christian discipleship, church life and theology. It is a rich and rewarding study and is closely related to the theology of the kingdom by Ladd and Morphew. Much has been written on this subject. My brief guide is as follows: Wright 2000 is a good introduction (an evangelical approach, his full scholarly treatment is Wright 1996). Yoder 1972, a Mennonite, is a classic that guided me through the 1980s in Soweto. Trocme 1973, a French scholar, gives a concise, radical vision of Jesus. A liberal/liberation approach is Nolan 1986, and in between is Borg 1987; both are a helpful contrast to Wright. Wright and Borg debate the key issues chapter by chapter in Borg and Wright 1999. Hays 1996 is an important application of the historical Jesus to NT social ethics.

2. Much is made of these groups and segments of Jewish society. To do justice to this section, one needs to know the broad sweep of society with its socio-political structure: At the top was the Sanhedrin (highest Jewish court and authority), then the temple system with the landowners, then the many Rabbis with their *talmudim* (groups of disciples) and lastly the majority — the poor peasants and sinners. This society and

structure housed the following groups, offering Israel basically four responses to their crisis: 1. withdrawal from society and politics — God will save us (the Essenes or Qumran community in the desert); 2. compromise with the Roman system (the Herodians, and sometimes the Sadducees and Chief Priests); 3. resistance through spirituality — purity of Torah observance and temple worship will save us (the Pharisees, Scribes and the Priests); 4. resistance through violence — pray and fight a holy war and God will deliver us (the Zealots and Sicarri). For a full understanding of this historical context, see Wright 1992b, pp. 167–214. With the entrance of John the Baptiser, and then Jesus (Hebrew *Yeshua*) onto the scene, an alternative option was offered: the way of the kingdom that he understood, embodied and proclaimed — the way of love and sacrifice.

3. The Jewish system of holiness — through Torah observance and temple worship, upheld and enforced by the "religious watchdogs" or "thought police" (mainly scribes and Pharisees) — was most clearly delineated in the purity laws (*halakah*) and the "boundary markers" that differentiated between Jews and Gentiles: circumcision, food (kosher or dietary laws), and keeping the Sabbath. These were the basis of Jewish identity. Jesus was accused of undermining Jewish identity by violating the integrity of this system as he crossed these boundaries (see Wright 1996, pp. 383–398). His alter native way for the nation, embodied in his community, was the way of compassion and mercy (Lk 6:36; Matt 5:48 renders it as: "Be perfect, just as your Father is perfect." Both these versions conclude Jesus' teaching to his followers with "love your enemies"). See Borg 1987, pp. 129–142 for an excellent discussion on Jesus' politics of compassion.

4. Yoder 1972 takes this as his point of departure.

5. One must not get confused by this when contrasted with Jesus' instruction in sending out the twelve and the seventy-two, that they should not go to the Gentiles, but rather to "go only to the lost sheep of the house of Israel" (Matt 10:5–6). In Matt 10 Jesus is intentionally offering Israel the kingdom who, by and large, through their leaders, reject it (Matt 21:42–44).

6. There is debate on this interpretation of these passages, but the fact that the Jews and Gentiles are miraculously fed by Jesus is not in doubt. See Carson's commentary on Matthew in Gaebelein (gen. ed.) 1984, pp. 340–342, 356–359.

7. Morphew 1998, pp. 165–180, discusses the kingdom significance of Jesus' practice of eating and feasting.

8. In this Scripture Jesus is publicly challenging Rabbi Shammai's (a strict school of the Pharisees in Jesus' day) interpretation of Judaism's most basic law of "love your neighbour as yourself" (Lev 19:18; the 613 laws of Moses, the Ten Commandments, and even the *Shema* — love the Lord your God and love your neighbour — are all summarised in "love of neighbour"; see Gal 5:14). Shammai and his Pharisees maintained that once

you had loved your neighbour, you had fulfilled God's law and you were free to hate your enemy. They added that to the commandment, and Jesus refers to their "addition" in Matt 5:43: "You have heard it said, 'Love your neighbour and hate your enemy.' But I tell you, love your enemies ...'"

9. I do not mean any presumption in this contextualisation, but to stick with Jesus I have chosen to keep the modern Israeli context in mind. If I were speaking in East Jerusalem to Palestinians, I would reverse the "labels" in order to challenge them. Over the years I have done this contextualisation and reversal in SA on many occasions, alternatively in white and black groups, in order to teach Jesus' practice of the sacrificial and reconciling love of the kingdom.

10. Bonhoeffer 1963. This and Willard 1998 are the two most challenging expositions of the Sermon on the Mount in my view — they are classics in the true Christian spiritual tradition.

11. As with the historical Jesus, to appreciate the revolutionary nature of the early church, one needs to see it within its Palestinian and Greco-Roman socio-political contexts (as the church expanded). I have found the in-depth 6-volume series *The Book of Acts in Its First Century Setting* very helpful (Winter 1993), especially vols. 2, 4 and 5.

12. Longenecker 1984, p. 30.

13. Longenecker 1981, pp. 439–451 on the Jerusalem Council.

14. They were asked to abstain from food offered to idols, sexual immorality, the meat of strangled animals and blood (Acts 15:28–29). Beyond this, the kingdom frees us totally from being justified before God and accepted into the covenant community through Torah observance, especially the ceremonial aspects. Peter questions the Judaisers: "God made no distinction between us and the Gentiles for he purified their hearts by faith. Now then, why do you try to test God by putting on the necks of the (Gentile) disciples a yoke that neither we nor our fathers have been able to bear? No! We believe that it is through the grace of our Lord Jesus that we are saved, just as they are" (Acts 15:9–11). See Paul's intense battle with the Judaisers (legalists) in Galatians. Col 2:13–23 is also key to this debate.

15. In doing biblical theology one would normally discuss Paul's teachings before John's, because John was chronologically the latest writer in the NT — towards the end of the first century. However, he did have direct contact with the historical Jesus and heard his teachings. Therefore, I deal with John's understanding of Jesus before I discuss Paul. I will not get into the debate of form criticism — the idea that John's Gospel (and other Gospels) was a representation and addressing of the issues the churches were dealing with in his time (which includes the apparent anti-Jewish stance in John's Gospel and how to account for it, see Hays 1996, pp. 424–431).

16. A list of Scriptures at this point would be too long. A study of John's Gospel and his

letters will reveal the clear symbolic development of life, light and love.

17. I love the New English Bible's translation of *koinonia*, "sharing the common life", used for example in Acts 2:42 and following.

18. New Testament and Pauline scholar Cilliers Breytenbach, in a paper "Reconciliation: Shifts in Christian Soteriology", analyses Paul's thinking on reconciliation. He shows God's work of salvation in Jesus moving from the reconciliation of individuals to the reconciliation of cultures, and the reconciliation of the universe. I follow his approach in Vorster (ed.) 1986, pp. 1–25.

19. Reconciliation became central to the theology of salvation (Soteriology) for many theologians throughout the centuries. Since the Reformation, it has been prominent in Protestant theology, and even more so since the two world wars in the previous century. The famous Karl Barth theologised salvation in terms of reconciliation in his *Dogmatics* (see Barth 1961). Likewise, respected Lutheran theologian Wolfhart Pannenburg treats his entire discussion of Soteriology under the heading "The Reconciliation of the World" (in Pannenburg 1991, pp. 397–464). Breytenbach traces the historical usage and development of reconciliation and salvation in Breytenbach 1986. See Morris 1972 for a full study on the key words and concepts that the apostles used to understand and communicate the gospel.

20. The boundary markers referred especially to the ceremonial law like circumcision, food laws, keeping Sabbath and other Jewish feasts. See note 3.

21. Gen 22:18; 26:4; 28:14; Is 49:6; 55:5; Zeph 3:9–10; Zech 8:22.

22. The phrase comes from Longenecker 1984. I follow his excellent exposition of Gal 3:28 in this section. See his commentary on Galatians, 1990, pp. 150–159.

23. Finding a new and common identity is key to the process of reconciliation. Western identity has been built on a humanistic, individual and rational basis that has come through the Enlightenment, but stems from Descarte's "I think, therefore I am". African identity is built on communality (see Chapter 5, note 28), "I belong and participate, therefore I am" (See Setiloane 1986 for a full explanation). This would be similar to the Christian understanding of our new identity in Christ and his people: "I am loved, therefore I am" or, more accurately, "I am accepted and loved in reconciled belonging, therefore I love, and therefore I am."

24. For the composition and background of these two prayers, see Longenecker 1984, p. 33.

25. It is important to note that Isaiah and the prophets "alluded to Gentiles being accepted by God, but continuing to exist as Gentiles in the coming eschatological days, with their salvation not setting aside their national identities" (Longenecker 1984, p. 38, see Is 2:4; 25:6–7, Amos 9:11–12 cf. Acts 15:13–19). The latter Scripture confirms the prophetic picture of God's one people, composed at the core of a restored Israel of Jewish

believers ("David's fallen tent" or God's "cultivated olive tree" in Rom 11), and sur-rounded with a great company of Gentiles (the "remnant of men" or "the wild olive branches grafted in", Rom 11). This was fulfilled in Christ. The Gentiles share in all the Messianic blessings without having to become Jews — although God accepts them as "true Jews" in the heart, as Paul says in Rom 2:28–29. John's vision of heaven confirms this: Gentile nations of all tribes and languages, not lost in an imposed uniformity, but identifiable around God's throne (Rev 5:9; 7:9). The goal for all of us is a uniting king-dom culture and identity of Love.

26. These historical and current theologies are widespread. They determine how we approach Jews, Modern Israel and the Palestinian issue — including how we interpret the prophetic Scriptures. See Morphew 1989, pp. 229–246, for a "kingdom theology" approach to Israel.

27. My summary is almost irresponsible without the backdrop of a careful treatment of the historical developments of Jewish/Gentile relationships, especially with regard to Jews and the (Western) church. For such a treatment see Longenecker 1984, pp. 39–47, Hays 1996, pp. 407–443 and Wilson 1989, pp. 39–106.

28 For a brief summary of the 2 000 year "history of contempt", see Wilson 1989, pp. 87–106 (his phrase). There are two comprehensive and well-documented studies from Christians, see Flannery 1985 and Rausch 1984. For a Jewish view, see Rosenberg 1986. Much is made of Martin Luther's anti-Semitic comments, and the Lutheran and Reformed Replacement Theologies that planted the seeds that ultimately led to the holocaust. This is a hotly debated issue.

29. For a good study on Paul's ethic of freedom, see Richardson 1979.

30. They took the word redemption from secular usage and filled it with their own meaning in order to communicate the gospel, see Morris 1972, pp. 11–64.

31. Longenecker gives a good summary of the issues, developments and challenges regarding slavery in the NT and in church history (1984, pp. 48–69). For a historical survey of slavery and emancipation throughout world history, from ancient times to the twentieth century, see Davis 1984 (Professor of History at Yale University).

32. Ignatius describes Onesimus, in a letter to the Ephesian church, as "a man of inex-pressible love and your Bishop". See Douglas (org. ed.) 1962, p. 910. Read the letter to Philemon in the NT and see Paul's relational sensitivity in handling the situation with Onesimus, which means "useful" (a common name given to slaves in those days).

33. I have drawn these brief comments regarding slavery and church history from Longenecker 1984, pp. 60–66.

34. SA's sex slave trade shame, in *The Sunday Independent*, issue 441, 21 March 2004. There are an estimated 27 million known "modern slaves" of various kinds in our world. The

average cost of a modern slave is US$ 90, compared to US$ 40 000 that it would have cost per slave in 1850 (in today's equivalent value, see www.freetheslaves.net). Kevin Bales (2000) has written a most revealing and disturbing book documenting case studies of modern slavery in five parts of the world.

35. Sider 1978 and Sine 1981.

36. A Mexican wave is common at big football events where the masses of people in the stadium rise to their feet in a massive flowing rhythm like a wave, each person flinging their arms and hands into the air and shouting out loud as the wave hits them — awesome to see!

37. Space does not allow me to go into the transformation of a "society" into a "community". Catholic philosopher John MacMurray has worked out a philosophic base for personhood and community, drawing on the doctrine of the Trinity as the ultimate definition of reality. He says society is contractual role play — if you do this, I will do that — producing individuals with splintered personality and identity. Community is covenantal relationships — mutual love and commitment — producing persons with authentic personhood and transcendent relational identity, i.e. we find our identity as persons in Trinitarian community. The quality of our relationships defines us as persons, beginning with male and female relationships. See note 28 in Chapter 5. See MacMurray 1957, 1961 and Torrance 1996, pp. 37–41.

38. Longenecker (1984, pp. 70–93) offers a concise and balanced discussion. Another balanced and more detailed study is Olsen 1993, especially addressing relatedness in the Triune God and "headship" in Paul's teachings. Bilezikian (1997, pp. 187–202) adopts an equality view of male/female Trinitarian relatedness and headship. Perhaps the latest and most thorough evangelical defence of the equality of women is in Giles 2002. Piper and Grudem (eds.) 1991 present the conservative evangelical hierarchical view. A similar in-depth and multi-disciplinary study from a more liberal woman's viewpoint is Van Leeuwen (proj. ed.) 1993. Torrance (1996, pp. 95–125) has an excellent discussion on gender, sexuality and the Trinity, giving an incisive view of feminism, the church, society and our language about God.

39. I will comment on one "technical" issue — how do we "reconcile" male headship (in this text)? Is it eternal as in Christ's headship, or merely a "this age" phenomenon? If it is the latter, is it transcended in Christ? Is it headship of men over women, or only husbands over wives, i.e. what is the nature of this gender headship in 1 Cor 11? Paul argues from creation before the fall (i.e. headship is not to "rule over her", which is the curse); then he makes it a husband-wife issue, and defines headship in terms of love and service, as modelled in Christ Eph 5:21–33. Notice that he prefaces these words with mutual gender submission to Christ's headship. A redemptive or kingdom model of headship is dynamic: The more the kingdom is present, the more Christ's

loving headship over both man and woman is experienced through a mutuality of submission and shared gifts (the *charismata* are not gender specific, see Rom 12:3–8; Eph 4:7–13; 1 Cor 12:7–28; 14:1f). The creation or "this age" model is one of hierarchical male headship: Christ's rule over the wife (and children) is experienced via the husband's headship — and likewise the local church via exclusive male eldership. And of course, the less the kingdom is present, the more male headship becomes "rule over the woman" — the curse!

40. Longenecker 1984, p. 87.

41. Phoebe the deaconess, Priscilla (she is always mentioned before her husband, showing her prominence in leadership, Acts 18:2, 18–26), Mary, Junias was a feminine name, an apostle, Tryphena, Tryphosa and Persis, Rufus's mother.

42. Scripture references in note 39 above.

43. Peter Richardson says (in relation to 1 Cor 11:2–11 and similar Pauline passages): "In order not to sever all relationships with the Jewish community, Paul advises some concessions, mostly at the level of practices inherited from the oral tradition of Judaism. He wishes to keep himself and the Corinthians sufficiently within Jewish norms to maintain a distinction from the prevailing Greco-Roman behaviour. Confusion with Hellenism might occur if women no longer respected the primacy of their husbands" (Richardson 1979, p. 68).

44. In a fascinating research article entitled "Sex in the Vatican — Sin City", in *Femina* magazine, November 1996, the Catholic church in the USA had paid out just on US$200 million in child molestation lawsuits (this does not take into account other countries). In terms of the vow of "perpetual celibacy", the experts estimate that only 2% of Catholic priests achieve it. At any given time, 20% are involved in sexual affairs with women, around 6% are sexually involved with minors and 15% are actively homosexual. Monsignor Adams, who teaches cannon law and manages moral affairs in the Vatican, is quoted as saying: "I'd say that 30% of local priests have mistresses. Italians don't care. This obsession with sex is an Anglo-Saxon problem!"

45. The world was shaken and changed forever on 11 September 2001 — see my comment in the Preface and its note 5.

46. Sodom and Gomorrah were destroyed not only because of sexual sins (Gen 18–19), but also because of "arrogance, gluttony, and lack of care for the poor and needy" (Ezek 16:49–50). Is this not an accurate description of our postmodern world?

47. As with other issues, I can list reams of books on this topic. I summarise the issues facing men in "A Theological Ethical Perspective on the Crisis in Masculinity and the Men's Movement" (Venter 1993a). Robert Bly is the unofficial founder and "Daddy" of the men's movement that emerged in North America in the 1980s (see Bly 1990). A good book detailing the basic issues facing men, although not overtly Christian, is Keen 1991.

48. The nurses in the hospital gave the little girl the name Lerato to protect her privacy and identity. Lerato is a Sotho name and means love. She has had a series of reconstructive surgery and is adjusting to a new life in another town. Her rapist, Ruben Modiba, was sentenced to life imprisonment.

49. Due to the terrible moral crisis SA is facing, in April 2002 our Deputy President, Jacob Zuma, launched the Moral Regeneration Movement (MRM). He challenged the church to do something about the moral decay in our nation. I maintain the root problem is sin and rotten character, and men must take primary responsibility in this regard. Until the men repent, until we have a Men's Repentance Movement, we will not have a Moral Regeneration Movement in SA; i.e. until we have men repenting, we will not have moral regeneration. We marched in Alexandra under a big banner with the words Men's Repentance Movement emblazoned over an image of a man kneeling with his face to the ground in humility and repentance — the symbol I chose for MRM (for further information contact, office@valleyvcf.org.za).

CHAPTER 7

PRACTICAL BIBLICAL MODELS
OF RECONCILIATION

Therefore, when you are offering your gift at the altar, if you remember
that your brother or sister has something against you, leave your gift
before the altar and go immediately, and first be reconciled to your
brother or sister, and then come and offer your gift ...
If anyone sins against you, go and point out the fault to the person in private.
If the person listens to you, you have won them. But if you are not listened to,
take one or two others along with you, so that every word may be confirmed
by the evidence of two or three witnesses. If the person refuses to listen to
them, tell it to the church; and if the offender refuses to listen even to
the church, let such a person be to you a Gentile and a tax collector.

Jesus in Matt 5:23–24; 18:15–17 RAP

I am not commanding you, but I want to test the sincerity of your love by
comparing it with the earnestness of others. For you know the grace
of our Lord Jesus Christ, that though he was rich, yet for your sakes he
became poor, so that you through his poverty might become rich.

Paul in 2 Cor 8:8–9

The tragic story of little Lerato, and many other far less traumatic stories, play themselves out daily in our lives, in our world. It raises questions about forgiveness and reconciliation, justice and restoration. How will Lerato, and her father and mother, ever forgive Reuben for what he did? Will Reuben ever be able to reconcile with Lerato and her family? If so, how will it happen? Will Lerato ever be able to reconcile herself with what happened to her, and hopefully become a better person through it all?

These painful questions and realities are raised in one way or another daily in our lives. The big traumas come once in while, but often it is the small incidents, the relational hurts, that affect us most. How do we deal with them? How do we forgive and find reconciliation? I want to complete the biblical understanding of reconciliation by discussing practical models of how to reconcile, and how to help others to reconcile. I will discuss a model of one-on-one reconciliation, and a model of group and structural reconciliation. I will conclude this chapter with the practical working model of reconciliation developed in Johweto.[1]

Like Jesus and Paul, I want to begin with one-on-one reconciliation because personal relationship is the foundation of trust for all other forms of reconciliation. Ultimately, all groups and structures come down to the level of relational reality. As with the Trinity, the quality of our personal relationships is the ultimate defining and determining factor in all reality.

A MODEL OF ONE-ON-ONE RECONCILIATION FROM JESUS

Jesus taught specifically on one-on-one reconciliation in Matt 5:21–26 and 18:15–35. I will be working from these texts and their contexts, so you may want to pause and read them carefully. What follows is a practical step-by-step exposition. The heart and context of Jesus' teaching in these passages is about relational reality, about honouring human dignity and upholding God's image by loving one another. That means intentionally resolving relational tensions and differences, conflicts and sins. To avoid conflict resolution and reconciliation is to undermine relationships and human integrity, and to deface further God's image on earth.

Living the life of the kingdom in fulfilment of the intentions of God's law is the context of Matt 5:21–26. It describes living righteously and maturely, just as God lives (vv. 17–20 cf. v. 48).[2] Jesus is talking about life in relationships and community, not about individual living. To illustrate this kind of kingdom life, Jesus firstly uses the example of anger and its effects, and follows with other aspects of personhood and relationships critical to loving community (vv. 27–48). Psychologists would call this first issue anger management. I would venture to say that unresolved anger and contempt is the major cause of relational breakdown. Jesus says it is tantamount to hatred and murder, which is the logical outworking wherever reconciliation does not take place.

The context in Matt 18:15–20 is similar. It is about right living and healthy relationships in the kingdom community of love. Jesus calls in a child and presents the heart of the matter: We must honour the "little ones" among us and not sin against them (the children, the weak, the sick, the needy, etc. vv. 1–9). In fact, we should hold them as models of humility, vulnerability and trust in relationships. We should emulate them if we want to be great in the kingdom. Sinning against any of these "little ones", or any "brother or sister" for that matter, is extremely serious in God's mind. Especially if we cause them to "stumble" (vv. 5–6). He does not want any of these "little ones" to be lost (vv. 10–14). Therefore one should deal drastically with the offence: by cutting off that offending part in you (vv. 7–9) or rehabilitating the offending aspect or person by one-on-one reconciliation and forgiveness, and even community discipline if necessary (vv. 15–32).[3] The latter option is obviously preferable! If we do reconciliation, we will not be maimed. Rather, kingdom community will thrive because we will all grow and be transformed through repentance, humility, love and ongoing forgiveness. Then we will be a witness to the world, not only of reconciliation, but of transformation into God's kind of life and community.

In both these passages Jesus uses going to court with your adversary, and even ending up in prison, as an illustration of the urgent need to reconcile before serious relational, spiritual and psychological consequences set in (5:25–26; 18:30–35). He is not for one minute endorsing, let alone advocating, taking your brother or sister to court. Paul says that among believers, we should never take each other to the courts "before the ungodly for judgement" (1 Cor 6:1–8). We must resolve disputes within, among ourselves, because we will be judging and ruling the world one day. This is so serious for Paul that he says if we cannot resolve the dispute, we should allow ourselves to be wronged or cheated, and just forgive, rather than, "You'll be hearing from my lawyer." It is a crying shame that in the church of Jesus Christ we still take each other to court, whether to resolve business disputes between Christians or fallouts in churches. We simply need to trust Jesus by obeying his teachings on how to resolve conflict in any and every aspect of life, because he is Lord of all, not just of spiritual or church-related issues.

In simple terms, Jesus clearly teaches three basic steps in Matt 5 and 18:

♦ one-on-one *private* reconciliation;

♦ if that fails, inviting two or three people to *mediate* one-on-one reconciliation, and

♦ if that fails, the parties are brought to church *arbitration* and discipline for the purpose of reconciliation.

I have italicised a word in each step which I believe is the essence of what Jesus is teaching: private reconciliation, then mediation and arbitration. The problem is primarily with step one. The church is notorious for its ability to do everything but step one. We are extremely unskilled in maintaining healthy, long-term relationships because we are extremely weak on conflict resolution, and we pay a hefty price for it. The rate of divorce in the church is on a par with that in society. Think of the massive moving population of Christians who easily leave churches because of some dislike or disagreement, and then join up elsewhere until there is another dislike or disagreement. This is not to mention the hundreds of thousands of Christians who have dropped out of church life, too disillusioned even to think about resolving anything with the church.

This is exactly what Paul means when he says many of us are weak and sick, and some die under God's discipline. It is because we do not "discern the body" when we break bread with each other (1 Cor 11:27–32). He is not saying that we must "examine ourselves" in the sense of confessing personal sin to God before we eat, believing that it is a "holy supper" or that the bread and wine is "holy". No! That is a Greek-Latin vertical and private view of the Holy Eucharist. He is saying that we must examine ourselves as to our relationships to see if there is any unresolved stuff; to see if we are caring for the weak, the hungry and the needy in the body. We must not be selfish and finish all the food! We must wait on and serve one another. We must *put things right with each other before we eat and drink*, or we will be eating and drinking God's judgement upon ourselves. This is the biblical-Hebraic horizontal and community view of "breaking bread" with one another in remembrance of Jesus.[4]

If we all practised step one whenever there was any tension or problem with anyone, we would seldom get to step two, and hardly ever have to face step three. I will now spell out the model of reconciliation with some additional steps and psychological insights on the one-on-one process. I must just add that in my estimation much of the extra "how to" detail below is largely a concession to our overly sensitive Western culture. We guard our privacy fiercely, we become quickly defensive and take things far too personally. Having lost robust, healthy

Hebraic community, we have become steeped in the quicksands of a subjective, "insecure sibling society".[5]

The first step of recognition and resolve

The first step in one-on-one reconciliation is recognising or becoming aware of hurt or offence between you and someone else. Anger is a God-given emotion that tells you something is wrong. Many of us do not benefit from anger because we are either controlled by it or we have suppressed it and cannot feel or interpret it. Anger normally tells us we are hurt, then we can go and resolve things before the sun sets: "Do not let the sun go down while you are still angry" (Eph 4:26–27). Seriously – before the sun sets. Paul is right. Jesus is even more demanding: As soon as you are aware, you must immediately leave whatever you are doing (e.g. your worship) and go and be reconciled.

Unresolved anger leads to contempt, which leads to resentment, and then to bitterness, hatred and even murder. As soon as you become aware of a tension or problem, you have to make a decision of recognition: Is this issue such that I must go and talk to the person? Jesus was clear: Any sin, offence or hurt (as in anger and the other five issues mentioned in Matt 5:21–48). I would go further. Any relational tension or misunderstanding needs to be recognised and worked through for the good and growth of both persons. In our farm community where my family lives, we talk about any "shadow" that might come between us, then we go and talk to the person. If we walk in the light with God and one another, we have true fellowship and all darkness is driven out – then shadows become easily visible and can be dealt with in the light of mutual disclosure and forgiveness (1 Jn 1:5–9).

Recognising there is a relational sin, or even a shadow, means deciding to resolve it. Jesus said quite clearly that the onus is on whoever first becomes aware of it to go and put it right, even if the other person is not aware of it. No matter who wronged who, the onus to go is on the first one who becomes aware of the shadow or offence. Once you have become aware, you cannot wait for the other person to come to you – Jesus gives you no room for self-pity or self-righteousness, whether you are the sinner or the one sinned against.

Furthermore, Jesus does not allow you to tell anyone else about it. No, no one else, not even God – he does not listen! And do not tell the devil, he is a notorious gossip! This is partly why Jesus said you must not continue worshipping if you are, or become, aware of any relational problem. You must simply get up and go immediately and talk it through with the person concerned. Gossip is a huge problem in the church, even in counselling relationships. We are party to information we should never hear. We talk about one another instead of talking to one another. It is the biggest destroyer of community. We must "cover each other's backs" by not talking about each other and by refusing to entertain talk about each other. The test is to ask the person who is talking about someone who is not present, "Have you said this to the person?" If not, they should immediately go and talk to the person concerned. If they have said it to the person, the assumption is that it is resolved, and therefore we do not need to hear it. *The point is that recognising there is a problem means you immediately resolve to go and be reconciled.*

The second step of confidential one-on-one confrontation

The second step in personal reconciliation is where you go alone, in private, to disclose to the other person your feelings of alienation and your perceptions as to the causes. The confidential part implies not speaking to anyone else, just to the person concerned. The confrontation part is where we need "anger management"! We need to go in the right spirit. Confrontation is never easy, either for the initiator or the recipient, and most people shy away from it. But Jesus does not allow us this option. Do you see how Jesus calls us to control our emotions and exercise maturity?

He says we must go with the goal of "winning" our brother or sister (18:15). This certainly does not mean winning the argument! It means winning the person over inspite of the issue that separates the two of you. It means winning in the sense of reconciling to one another and thus both of you winning against Satan by quickly closing the door on evil in your relationship. Evil infiltrates and destroys community through relational disruptions. In confronting the person we must keep in mind that we are actually confronting the shadow between us, not the person per se. This influences the spirit in which we come and the manner in which we confront.

The third step of actually reconciling through confession, forgiveness and restoration

The best way to confront is through what the Bible calls confession. Psychologists call it self-disclosure. You have to decide to take control of your emotions and go in the right spirit of humility, vulnerability and confession as Jesus taught. To do this you may need a little "time out" to let your emotions subside — but only until sunset! Emotions are disciplined by a decision to act in a loving, adult manner, by a decision to turn away from the parent or child modes within you. You can handle your emotions in one of three ways:

♦ *Venting* your emotions — *exploding* — damaging those around you, and yourself. This is either the aggressive, intimidating parent mode or the angry, tantrum child mode. Both are selfish acts aimed at controlling the situation.

♦ *Suppressing* your emotions — *imploding* — damaging yourself and those around you. This is the silent, scolding parent mode or the sulking, withdrawn child mode. Likewise, both are loveless attempts at controlling the situation.

♦ *Expressing* your emotions — *disclosing* — reconciling and healing those around you and yourself. This is the adult mode. It is an act of love aimed at vulnerability and relationship, inviting mutual interdependence.

Expressing your feelings is self-disclosure. It is humbling yourself and making yourself vulnerable in an act of reconciling love to the other.[6] We disclose by using "I" language, not "you" language. "You" language is presumptuous and proud, it is accusatory and immediately alienates the other person: "You have done this to me ... you don't care ..." "I" language discloses what you are feeling and owns what you did wrong (if you did anything wrong): "I have a problem that I need to talk to you about. May I? I am feeling angry and upset because I think I might have misunderstood you, or I was hurt by what you said ... can you help me with this please?" "I" language is non-threatening; it is inclusive and inviting. It works through self-disclosure of feelings that reaches out for emotional reconciliation. Often the issue that alienated you in the first place is no longer the issue. It is clouded by the emotions that it stirs, and emotional alienation is now the problem.

Reconciliation happens at *two levels,* those of emotions and perceptions or the facts, what actually happened. Often the best approach to conflict resolution is to clear the emotions and reconcile at the feeling level first. The perceptions about what actually happened can then be addressed together, and more easily reconciled. This helps you to talk with one another and not at one another — each trying to prove their point. Disclosing feelings is just that: "I feel sad ... I feel disappointed ..." It is not: "I feel that you did wrong ... I feel that I was unfairly treated ..." Those are not feelings, they are perceptions as to who did or said what. Once there is a mutual sense of "I am sorry, I did not realise you were feeling that way ..." often forgiveness follows naturally: "Please forgive me for making you feel that way ... forgive me for hurting you." The other person can then easily respond, "I forgive you." It is important to verbalise forgiveness. Whether the perceived cause of this alienation is right or wrong, emotional disclosure almost always unblocks the situation by evoking understanding, forgiveness and reconciliation. On the other hand, emotional explosions or suppression do the opposite; they alienate and destroy.

Once emotional connection has been established, you can deal together with the perceptions or facts of what divided you in the first place. Confession is saying what you feel and perceive, and owning your part in what went wrong. It is identifying and removing the "enmity", the cause of offence (from your perspective) between you. It is not accusing the other person of what they did wrong, but allowing the other person, through your example of self-disclosure, to acknowledge and own their part in what affected the relationship. The most assertive we can become is to point out lovingly the person's wrongdoing, inviting them to own their part in the problem — or to respond well if you are on the receiving end of such assertiveness.

Assertiveness is not easy for people and is often mistaken for aggression, because of our insecurity and defensiveness. Proverbs and Paul's teachings on "admonishing" and "rebuking" one another are desperately needed in our day.[7] Done incorrectly, they can cause more damage than good because of the personal sensitivities involved. However, if done wisely and correctly it is an act of love; it will grow robust adult relationships with healthy and mature people in loving community.

Often at this point in the process perceptions of what actually happened are reconciled and forgiveness naturally follows. The differing perspectives of the problem are reconciled and a common solution is mutually decided on. Justice has been served because wrongdoing is owned and repented of, and forgiveness has been given and received. Reconciliation has taken place fully on the basis of "restorative justice"; the enmity and its cause has been removed and the relationship restored. Justice must be further served if there is any need for reparation or restitution, whether it be material or other.

What happens if the perceptions are not reconciled? What happens if the guilty party does not own up or if justice is not done? Does that mean the two parties should remain unreconciled? Not necessarily. They have a choice. They can go for mediation and do "due diligence" to seek a genuine reconciliation. In fact, if either party at any point in the process asks for mediation (due to not being heard or feeling they are being abused), the next step should be taken. This is costly — in terms of time and emotional energy — but it is the correct next step. Alternatively, the injured party can decide to exercise greater grace by unconditionally forgiving what is not accounted for and on that basis to reconcile with the other person.

Before we go to the next step of mediation, I need to expand on the option to forgive unconditionally, as it raises interesting issues. I will talk in terms of the offending and the injured parties. However, the distinction between the two is often not that clear. In practice one-on-one relational entanglements are often blurred and both parties need to make space for the other in mutual love and forgiveness.

An excursion: Reconciliation, forgiveness and justice

What happens if you decide to forgive and reconcile when the offending party has apparently not done justice by owning their offence, acknowledging their fault? Forgiveness without acknowledgement of wrongdoing can result in letting the person off the hook, a "cheap grace" and thus a "cheap reconciliation", as Bonhoeffer and Bosch call it.[8] However, from the viewpoint of the injured party, this kind of unconditional and generous forgiveness is "costly grace" and "costly reconciliation". They suffer the wrongdoing of the other person and yet release the person unconditionally (see 1 Cor 6:7). Such a gesture will depend on the maturity and quality of the forgiveness that is given. The forgiver must not pretend, only they themselves know how real their forgiveness is. But there is fruit from genuine forgiveness that others can see and measure — though it may take a little time to see. Forgiveness "from the heart", as Jesus calls it (18:35), leads to real freedom in the forgiver and restoration in the relationship. Superficial, convenient or cheap forgiveness — often just to "keep the peace" or "quickly get it over with" — will be seen in the unhappiness of the supposed forgiver and in the nature of their relating. Denial and unforgiveness cannot be hidden for long. Like anger, it leaks and everyone eventually sees it.

The cost of unforgiveness is very high. Jesus says that unforgiveness is actually an unreconciled relationship; it leads to emotional imprisonment and increasing spiritual and psychological torment. Unforgiveness poisons the person and their relationships (5:25–26; 18:32–34). This is part of the reality of unforgiveness that leads to God not forgiving you for your sins, and so you increasingly suffer under evil (Matt 6:12–15; Mk 11:25). Paul says bluntly that unforgiveness opens the door directly for Satan's schemes to enter and take over (2 Cor 2:10–11).

This raises the question: Is forgiveness conditional or unconditional? What is the real basis of forgiveness? What is the relationship between forgiveness and justice? On the one hand, tradition teaches that forgiveness is conditional on confession and repentance (Prov 28:13; 1 Jn 1:9). The TRC in SA said no forgiveness without truth being disclosed and owned — it is amnesty, not amnesia! You have to know what and who you are forgiving before you can really forgive. From the viewpoint of the offender (the one who caused the relational breakdown), costly grace and costly reconciliation is taking full responsibility for their wrongdoing, and being willing to do whatever is necessary to put things right. Paul distinguishes between "godly sorrow" that leads to true repentance and reconciliation, and "worldly sorrow" that leads to false repentance and a cheap reconciliation (2 Cor 7:8–11).[9] We have to encourage the offender to make costly reconciliation for their own sake, let alone for the sake of the forgiver.

On the other hand, the gospel is all about grace, God's unconditional forgiveness. The basis of forgiveness, especially from God, is the "restorative justice" of the cross. God's suffering love suffers our wrongdoing. The sinless Jesus is punished in our place for our sin, and restores or reconciles us to relationship with God. This makes God's forgiveness unconditional, a gift to us at great cost to himself. The justice of the cross, humanly speaking, can be seen as the "injustice" of God's foolishness (1 Cor 1:18–30). The cross is the extravagant grace of his "unjust" mercy, love and forgiveness toward us (18:21–27 cf. Rom 5:6–11). Think of the scandalous way in which the prodigal father forgave the lost son. The elder brother wanted justice before reconciling with his brother (and even with his father). But the father gave unreasonable mercy instead — a prodigal act of sheer grace (Lk 15:11–32). In the cross of Christ, mercy not only satisfies, but actually triumphs over justice. This does not make costly grace cheap, it makes it divine!

Forgiveness and reconciliation between people, especially Christians, should likewise be based on the "unjust" grace of the cross (Eph 4:32: "Forgive one another, just as God, in Christ, forgave you"). That means two things. We look for confession and repentance, and even restitution if necessary, before we forgive and reconcile (Luke's emphasis in 17:3–4). But because God's kind of justice has ultimately been served in the cross, we go beyond requirements and forgive unconditionally in our hearts, and from our hearts as Jesus says (Matthew's emphasis, 18:21–27. Note the extravagant irrationality of this forgiveness: seventy times seven every day if necessary, which might cost a few million dollars in the act of forgiveness). Just how much confession or "payment" do we need to extract from the sinner before we can forgive? Jesus exemplified this grace of forgiveness as they drove the nails through his hands: "Father, forgive them, they know not what they do."

Biblical forgiveness is drawn from the world of economics. Forgiveness means cancelling debts, tearing up the IOUs, releasing the person unconditionally from all payment.[10] It may appear to be cheap grace for the recipient, but it is clearly costly grace for the reconciler. In Israel, every seventh year and in the year of

Jubilee, every fiftieth year, this unconditional cancellation of debts was supposed to happen, literally across the board. Behind the exercising of such grace to forgive is our trust in God and his costly grace to us in Christ Jesus. In other words, *there is no amount of sin, hurt or damage that anyone can do to us that is beyond God's ability to heal, let alone God's grace to forgive. Jesus took all that injustice and indignity upon himself and suffered and died for it in our place. Therefore, we can really trust God and forgive others unconditionally.* We can have faith in the forgiving and healing power of his suffering love and "unjust mercy" displayed in the cross. Consequently, we can forgive others and simply let go, entrusting ourselves and the other person to God.

The fourth step of mediation through two or three witnesses (18:16)

If the confidential one-on-one does not resolve the issue, you ask two or three fellow brothers or sisters to go with you in order to help bring about reconciliation. There is a but here. If you feel that you were not heard, that the matter was not resolved or fully reconciled, *you should first register this with the other person,* and inform him/her that you intend to take the next step of inviting others to help resolve the issue. This gives dignity to the other party in the following ways: It allows a further opportunity to attempt private one-on-one reconciliation before "witnesses" step in; it secures the other person in the knowledge that you are not going to speak behind their back or to get others "on your side", it allows the person to know who your "witnesses" are, and it gives them the opportunity to propose one or two "witnesses" that they have confidence in.

The point of this fourth step (Jesus' step two), is that for the first time in the process, Jesus allows you to speak to someone else about what happened, about how you feel and what the issues are. Even then, strictly speaking, you should only divulge all this in the presence of the other party with "the two or three witnesses" hearing it for the first time, not beforehand or in private with them. The phrase quoted by Jesus here comes from the Hebraic background of God's judicial processes spelt out in the Torah. Two or three people who witness an event or listen to a discussion can verify what happened and what was said. Their word would then be taken as authoritative over against the claims or perceptions of the parties concerned. Embarking on this stage is serious because it puts the issue on a church judicial or discipline footing.

Ideally the two or three should be people agreed to by both parties, but if that is not possible, you take two or three along with you to meet the person. The purpose of drawing in the two or three is not to convince them of your position, nor to gang up on the other person, but to yield to "the witnesses" in their attempt to reconcile the two of you. I view this as the role of *mediation*. The mediators listen carefully to both parties and then feed back what they hear, helping each party to understand and forgive the other. They do this by pointing out to each person where they need to take responsibility. They also help to calm the emotions, to focus on the issue and not to allow any personal abuse. Sometimes it takes two or three mediation meetings to bring about reconciliation. When it comes to facilitating the act of forgiveness and reconciliation, it is advisable to get the two parties to look into each other's eyes and to give and receive forgiveness verbally and specifically.

I will not go into models, methods and skills of mediation — there are many courses available. Business and society in general is becoming more aware of the need for effective conflict resolution, often more so than the church. If this step fails to bring about reconciliation, for whatever reason, formal church discipline must be entered into. Then the word of the two or three mediators on the matter becomes authoritative and even decisive in the church judicial process.

The fifth step of church arbitration and discipline (18:17)

To bring the person or issue "before the church" or to "tell it to the church" does not mean literally to have every church member sit and pass judgement. It may be applicable if the church is small and the issue is big enough, but generally it is brought before the elders who, acting on behalf of the church, address the unresolved crisis. If the unresolved issue reaches this level of formality, it has indeed become a crisis, because it potentially affects the whole church.

I understand this step to be *arbitration*, rather than mediation. Arbitration is like sitting before a magistrate, a judge or a jury. People present their case, the arbitrators listen and ask questions. Then they take all the facts into account, including the "witness" of the mediators, and they make their judgement. The party that is judged to be wrong must now be disciplined with a view to reconciliation with the offended person. If the guilty person responds well to the judgement and whatever discipline is imposed, reconciliation will inevitably take place. If the person responds badly to the judgement and the discipline, there is a final and fearful step that Jesus instructs us to take.

Before I deal with the final step, I want to address the question of whether there is "a court of appeal" in the church. What happens if the person genuinely feels they have been unfairly judged in the matter? Is the arbitration full and final? Arbitration normally means just that. Both parties are required to commit themselves beforehand to the findings and judgements being binding and final, with no further recourse. But sometimes there is reason enough to seek recourse outside. This would then take place through the broader team of pastors in the area. This broader forum for arbitration is most likely needed when a senior leader in a local church remains unreconciled with another leader or with the church itself.[11]

The sixth step of withdrawal of fellowship or expulsion from the church (18:17–20)

Jesus says that if *all* the above steps have been followed, and the person who is judged by the church to be guilty still resists and does not humble him/herself in confession, repentance and reconciliation, there is no other option but expulsion from the fellowship of God's people. We withdraw completely from the person, which actually means "handing the person over to Satan" in the hope that they may come to their senses and turn to God and his people once again, and be reconciled (see 1 Cor 5:1–5 for an example of this extreme measure). It is a fearful and final step that is only taken with great anguish of heart.

All this points to the fact that God gives Christians and churches, through their leaders, remarkable spiritual authority. He recognises and backs up what we decide in terms of church life and discipline. That is precisely what it means when Jesus says: "Whatever you bind on earth will be bound in heaven, and whatever you loose on earth will be loosed in heaven ... if two or three of you on earth agree about anything you ask for, it will be done for you ... For where two or three come together in my name, there I am with them" (18:18–20). When the twos and threes are introduced, there is heightened spiritual presence and authority. Then what happens "on earth" by the agreed initiative and united judgement of the twos and threes is recognised "in heaven" and becomes spiritually binding. We either bind the sin to the person if they do not repent and reconcile with their brother or sister, or we loose the person from their sin if they repent and reconcile. In reality, this is what has already happened in the heavens before God and the spirit world, with all the implications that follow: Either forgiveness and restoration from God, or judgement and discipline from God.[12]

In conclusion, *this is the powerful spiritual reality* behind Jesus' demand that his disciples practise reconciliation as often as is needed. It is also the reality behind Paul's warning in 1 Cor 11:17–34 for us not to be divided in our relationships because it results in weakness, sickness and even death. As I mentioned earlier, we must "discern the body" and reconcile with each other before we break bread or share the Lord's supper together, lest we "eat and drink judgement on ourselves" and "come under the Lord's discipline, so that we are not condemned with the world". The cost of unforgiveness and non-reconciliation is far, far higher than the cost of unconditional forgiveness and genuine reconciliation.

A MODEL OF GROUP AND STRUCTURAL RECONCILIATION FROM KLAUS NÜRNBERGER [13]

In my early days as a Christian, I personally never came across any awareness — let alone teaching — on group and structural reconciliation in evangelical/Pentecostal circles. I first heard about it at SACLA1 in 1979, where some ecumenicals and radical evangelicals addressed the issue. My assumption at that point was simple and clear: If we reconcile with God — are born again — the rest will take care of itself. Just win people to Jesus, then SA, and the world, will get sorted out! We are reconciled and find each other in Christ, so what is all the political fuss about? Why are black and poor Christians complaining? They are unspiritual and too political, they should just trust the Lord and be happy! How naive can you get? Many conservative evangelicals, charismatics and Pentecostals still believe that to be true.[14]

We need to have a workable theology, an ethic or a model of social reconciliation and change for the common good or societal inequalities and conflicts will overrun us. This application of the gospel of reconciliation to our social realities is a profound spiritual responsibility for all Christians and churches. It is as demanding and urgent as one-on-one reconciliation — we do not have a choice. We must diligently pursue both personal and group reconciliation for the common good, for Jesus' sake. He died on the cross for all people, not just for those "born again".

A brief social analysis

It is safe to say that all societies, without exception, have inequalities and discrepancies built around two key realities: group awareness and social structures. They may be ethnic, cultural, class, religious or generational groups — and many more — all with their own hierarchical levels of consciousness. Stated very simply, in any society there are the privileged and the underprivileged — the elite and the underdogs.

When the two basic needs of any society — stability and equality — are threatened, conflict sets in. The powerful want stability and develop all sorts of rationalisations, called ideologies, to justify and secure their group interests. Because they are the powerful, their ideologies are commonly entrenched in social and economic structures that secure their vested interests. The groups that are marginalised and see themselves as less privileged seek equality; they too rationalise their group needs and interests with their own ideologies. This is how selective perception and group interests develop, the source of human conflict. This translates at both personal and group level into false ideas and beliefs, which are lived out via our appetites and corrupt desires, the source and field of all human conflict (2 Cor 10:3–5; Jas 4:1–3).[15]

Although there are some horizontal conflicts between "equal" groups in social structures, most conflicts are about vertical group relationships. When the dissatisfied groups push hard enough, or when the powerful groups secure their interests to the detriment of the underdogs, conflict becomes open and severe. It manifests in many different ways, from common housebreaking, to murder, social unrest and even civil or international war. If left unchecked, conflict quickly becomes systemic, leading to a spiral of violence.[16] *Structural* violence from the powerful leads to violent *resistance* from the marginalised; this in turn leads to *repressive* violence from the top, and *revolutionary* violence from the oppressed, which results in *destructive* violence of a mindless and desperate kind. It takes great leadership and vision to break the spiral and bring about change.

The real battle or enmity is at the ideological and consciousness level, and then the structural level. Convictions and myths or false beliefs come from group perceptions and ideologies that justify group interests and lead to inter-group conflict. We must keep in mind the biblical understanding of three inter-penetrating realities — ideologies, social structures and spiritual powers (discussed in Chapter 5). Here we are dealing with profound spiritual strongholds. These convictions and ideologies — or group consciousness — are powerful and have strong historical roots. We can describe them as a *hierarchy of convictions* that work together to form collective consciousness:

- *Religious or spiritual (metaphysical) convictions* run the deepest and are the most powerful. For example, the Catholic/Protestant conflict in Northern Ireland and the radical Islamic suicide bombers.
- *Cultural or group identity convictions* are equally emotive. For example, tribalism and nationalism as in the disintegration of Yugoslavia in the 1990s — it was a racial conflict with ethnic cleansing between the Serbs, Croats and

Albanians. The roots of this conflict go back centuries in the Balkans.

♦ *Economic and political convictions and class consciousness.* This is an interesting one, because it is a mix of convictions and vested interests. People believe in different economic and political systems, as in capitalism or socialism, but if they can secure their material well-being and power base, almost everything else becomes negotiable. In other words, vested interests subvert and displace convictions — even the most powerful convictions. Class consciousness, materialism and control operates at both individual and group levels. Since the collapse of communism, international capitalism has gained the ascendancy by becoming the global ideology (more of this in Chapter 8).

The point is that these convictions lead to group ideologies, mindsets and consciousness. This leads to group norms and values which create social structures that include some people and exclude others, setting the scene for conflict.

The symbiotic relationship between ideologies and structures needs further comment. Group perceptions and ideologies create and feed off social structures, resulting in group conflict, for example, the creation and maintenance of apartheid by Afrikaner nationalism. The reverse also happens: Structures breed ideologies and create group perceptions that lead to social conflict. For example, those born on the side of privilege are deeply conditioned by the ideology and group interests of the topdogs; those born on the underside create their own counter-ideology for survival and liberation. Change the ideology and the structures change; change the structures and ideologies, and group consciousness will be challenged and shift. We need both types of change, but generally the point of departure is changing mindsets and group interests, for justice' sake. Structural change generally follows.[17] The goal is to find sufficient common perceptions and to reconcile convictions in the various groups, in order to balance and reconcile their respective needs and vested interests for the common good. Then groups and structures are reconciled by a balancing of stability and equity in a just and free society for the good of all. This is more or less the ideal of liberal democracy.[18]

The million dollar question is: How do we do this? How do we transform collective mindsets? How do we reconcile groups and structures in society for the common good? How do we remove the enmity and conflict? One way is to get the powerful to change their prevailing beliefs and ideologies, be willing to renegotiate their vested interests, and change socio-political structures to empower the underdogs for justice and freedom in society. How do you change the mindsets of the powerful and liberate them from their vested interests? Where in history have they ever freely and willingly negotiated away their position of power and privilege?

The other way is for the underdogs to fight so hard that the powerful wake up and change in order to save their own skins, or simply be overthrown by a revolution. Revolutionary violence, together with repressive violence, sows all sorts of other destructive seeds that have to dealt with at a later stage. History shows that most often there is either an ongoing state of (in)tolerance or "cold war" between top and underdog groups, or there is a downward spiral of violence that eventually results in ongoing civil war and revolution. Sometimes the status quo is maintained indefinitely by powerful groups forming horizontal alliances of mutual support with other powerful groups with similar ideologies and/or vested interests. Likewise some underdog groups tolerate the status quo through alliances with other similar groups. There can be no meaningful alliance in vertical relationships unless some radical rearrangements are made for a reasonable reconciliation — and top-down groups remain endemic in all societies. The best one can hope for is some form of reconciled living in a just and fair democracy, and the church has a unique responsibility and role in this regard.

The "impossible Trinitarian community" of Jesus

In principle, Jesus has *already* reconciled groups, powers and structures through his death and resurrection. As his followers, we are not only well placed to make it a reality, but we are commissioned to help bring it about. Jesus said to his followers: "Blessed are the peacemakers, for in making peace between people and groups you are living out your nature as the children of God" (Matt 5:9 RAP). The church is Trinitarian: We are born of the Father, through the peacemaking work of the Son, by the power of the Spirit. As the Trinitarian church, how do we make peace in society? How do we bring about group and structural reconciliation? It begins and ends with the message and ministry of reconciliation, which is the *suffering and redemptive love* of the Father, in Jesus Christ, by the Spirit. This is the "Word of God", God's self-communication to humanity that culminates in Jesus and continues through the church. God's Word of love and reconciliation forms the basis of our convictions and lifestyles as Christians, in contrast to the social mindset and economic context in which we may find ourselves. The Word has a dynamic all of its own in the various processes that bring about group and structural reconciliation.

The missionary dynamic of God's Word leads to syncretisms

As Jesus came from heaven to earth and took on our humanity, so the missionary dynamic of God's Word takes the message of God's reconciling love into every stratum of society, into all the world. In so doing it evangelises people in all walks of life and brings them into the church of Jesus Christ. The church penetrates, and is often found, in all groups and structures of society, from the top to the bottom. In this missionary process, the Word becomes diluted as it were and syncretised into all classes, cultures, traditions and even religions. It takes on the diversity and divisions of people groups and societal structures.

Just as Jesus carried in his flesh our weaknesses, being tempted in all ways as we are, so God's Word incarnates itself in the patterns and perceptions prevalent in society. For better or for worse, it gets mixed up in people's hopes and fears, their interpretations and perceptions of reality. Thus the Word is ideologised in divergent directions, and it stagnates and "dies". In this respect the church is nothing but a replica of the society in which it finds itself. I must emphasise that the suffering and redemptive love of God leads the Word into humanity and into death (as part of his purpose and means of reconciliation).

The ecumenical dynamic of the Word leads to wholesome confrontations

God's Word not only goes out into all the world and dies, it also gathers all God's divergent and disparate people under one head, Jesus Christ, into one body, the church ("ecumenical" dynamic). The Word comes back to life, through the wholesome confrontations in the diversity and differences of God's one people. Through this regathering and wholesome confrontation, the Word is demythologised or de-ideologised, and vested interests are exposed, surrendered and renegotiated. Individuals and groups see things differently and consequently vertical relationships are horizontalised. Reconciliation takes place. This reconciliation is then taken back out into the world as a ministry of reconciliation and peacemaking.

The key to this ecumenical dynamic of the gospel is God's grace — not God's law. The law brings to light our sinful nature, our wrongdoing and shortcomings, and condemns it; the gospel is God's suffering love and unconditional acceptance of us in Christ. God accepts the unacceptable and loves the unlovable, and so must we. Those who love, or are touched by God's love, want to be together. The Word gathers and reconciles us under the umbrella of unconditional love and acceptance of one another as brothers and sisters in Christ (Paul's picture in Eph 2:14–20). The result is an "impossible community" which unites divided groups. We do not gather as private persons. We come as whites and blacks, rich and poor, employers and employees, male and female. We represent and bring our group consciousness, ideologies, cultures and positions in the social structures. Once we have gone beyond the niceties of tea and cake, or enjoying a reconciliation conference, we really begin to find one another in the local church as all the differences surface and the tensions and confrontations begin. Welcome to the family!

This ecumenical encounter happens on the basis of unconditional acceptance in the community of suffering love. We suffer each other's brokenness and differences as we accept each other for who we are. For example, we do not meet each other's norms and values — or those of our group — but we do not pass critical judgement. Acceptance does not mean endorsement; it just facilitates confrontation and transformation.[19] This is resurrection and new birth. The birthing of the reconciled "one new humanity" is painful and traumatic. Our sins, blind spots and distorted perceptions of reality are exposed by each other, by the facts. We see ourselves, our sin and our culture in a new way and we uncover the real causes of societal division and inequality. We deal with our sin and our differences, and we reconcile with God and each other. Our group consciousness and allegiances are challenged as we hear the other side of the story. We discover the real person, beyond the group stereotypes, as we see their need and pain. We are moved by God's love to do something. The employers find or create employment for the unemployed. We lobby for justice in public policy for the sake of the poor and marginalised, because they are our brothers and sisters. We begin to be healed and transformed in our new emerging identity and loyalty to one another as God's family in Jesus' "impossible community".

In this way the monsters of politics, economic structures and social struggles are reduced to relationship — it becomes personal. Love for one another displaces posture and position, and challenges personal comfort and power. It engages, supplants and transcends ideological loyalties and identities. It breaks the power of inferiority and superiority, hatred and revenge. It heals the hurts of racism, sexism and poverty. Most importantly, vertical relationships are horizontalised as the powerful come down to empower the poor and needy — just as Jesus did (see 2 Cor 8:9, quoted at the beginning of this chapter).

In summary, the ecumenical encounter brings about change at the ideological, conviction and group consciousness levels, and also at the needs, vested interests and structural levels. The gospel accepts and confronts us through one another. The gospel not only liberates, heals and transforms us — through one another — but also causes us to transcend our human limitations and group identities. Our faith breaks the power of the hierarchy of convictions over us, and challenges its presence and practice around us. Our faith causes us to transcend time and space, ethnic and social barriers, economic privileges, power relationships and even human rights. We discover that our only right as Christians is to lay down our lives for one another and this world, as our master did. Our radical attachment to Jesus radically frees us from all earthly attachments — not to escape into private spirituality, but to engage the world fully in sacrificial service.

Horizontalising vertical relationships is key

One of the key implications and effects of this reality is the horizontalising of vertical relationships in the name of Jesus. The powerful see the plight of the powerless and come down to help them up. It is God's secret power of love which curbs the abuse of structural power. Horizontalisation becomes a servant-power that changes group consciousness, interests and structures in both church and society. This happens in, and through, the impossible Trinitarian community as:

♦ through God we discover that we were all born equal, having nothing; and we will all die, taking nothing with us. Our faith in the Father-Creator horizontalises our relationships as a matter of principle by virtue of the fact that we were all created equal.

♦ through the Son we discover the grace that, though Jesus was rich, he became poor so that we who are poor can become rich ... in order to help (others who are poor not to enjoy our riches on our own). We follow Jesus by coming down from whatever place we occupy in the social structures in order to empower and uplift those who are lower than us. Our faith in the Reconciler-Redeemer horizontalises our relationships. Paul deliberately applies this paradigm to economic inequalities and discrepancies. The rich must come down, not to give handouts, but hand-ups, genuinely to empower the materially poor. The goal is not a mechanical equality — the ideal of communism — but a dynamic balance of sharing and empowering. The context of 2 Cor 8:9–15 says that those who have should help those who suffer, not to make them dependent on their generosity, but to bring them back onto their feet so that they in turn can share in the joy of giving and empowering others. This paradigm applies to all structural disparities and vertical relationships in church and society.[20]

♦ through the Spirit's conviction we discover that we are all miserable sinners who have lost their right to existence and all status before God and human beings. Yet we have been accepted as sons and daughters of God, the highest possible status for a human being. Our faith in the Holy Spirit, our Sanctifier-Empowerer, horizontalises our relationships by making us all equal.

The effects of ecumenical encounter are both subversive and empowering in society. I have spoken of the reconciling and reviving, the liberating and empowering effect of the ecumenical encounter. The Word drives us out, back to where we came from in the various groups, social structures and places of work; there we bring the transformation we have undergone. We are salt and light as the scattered church. We see things differently, therefore we no longer blindly believe and give loyalty to our group or serve its interests. All our former relationships and group identities are now in tension. We have become subversive in society for the kingdom's sake, for the good of society. In fact, one can understand why some authorities get worried about Christians getting together to talk. The ecumenical encounter is profoundly subversive to any unjust rule, both earthly and spiritual.

The sin of our disunity as the church does not lie in our differences or divides, but in our refusal to have ecumenical encounter. Our sin is that we rather stick to ourselves, to our own churches, and deny society the transforming effect of our unity. We refuse, for whatever reason, to expose ourselves to the highly uncomfortable, challenging and transforming encounter with our "enemy" brothers and sisters, to suffer them as Christ suffered us. We are too busy to meet — "I am doing God's work" — while we deny our very nature and calling as church, by refusing to reconcile with each other and to facilitate reconciliation in society. We are actually refusing to make known the "manifold wisdom of God ... to the rulers and authorities" (Eph 3:10). It is no small wonder that Jesus prayed for us so fervently: "Father, make them one, as we are one" (Jn 17:20–23).

We not only subvert evil in society, but we empower and transform people in society by making peace as we facilitate reconciliation between groups and structures. Our ability through our faith in Christ to transcend the divisive dynamics and group identities in society enables us to reconcile others in Christ. The church is a microcosm of society; if it works for us, it can work for society.[21] We do not come arrogantly, presuming to teach the world. Society has seen enough triumphalism and hypocrisy in the church. We come humbly in the spirit of the Suffering Servant, laying aside our privileges and power, naked in our honesty and vulnerability, kneeling down and simply offering to wash the feet of those who are weary and in need.

The effect of the ecumenical encounter in society, through the church, can be summarised in the following possible ministries (the italicised words are the keys):

♦ Every day we subvert people's convictions and group consciousness. We *expose* ideological positions and *challenge* vested interests with a vision of the kingdom — that which is genuinely good for society. Our corporate church life is *a sign* of hope and healing in society as we *model* the kingdom.

♦ Because we know how to *deal with human sin and brokenness*, we can help society and leaders to face up to wrongdoing and corruption. We can help them to take responsibility and confess, and mediate forgiveness and reconciliation. Think of the TRC in SA facilitated by Archbishop Tutu. This is to be done in the spirit of service, not in the Constantinian model of the church ruling over society (discussed in Chapter 8).

♦ We can *facilitate encounters* between individuals and groups with a programme to address convictions, group consciousness, vested interests and causes of division. Out of an emerging common view of the problems, a common solution can be found for *reconciliation* around mutual interests and structural changes. This happened at the Convention for a Democratic South Africa (Codesa), the highly successful multi-party negotiations in SA in the early 1990s. It led to the new constitution and democracy in 1994. The two key negotiators and many of the facilitators were Christians. We should be the most skilled people in society to facilitate mediation and conflict resolution.

♦ We can *contribute at the level of research and analysis* in terms of group disparities and reconciliation. Because the church is a microcosm of society and we have mutually come to terms with the dynamics that kept us apart, we can offer our experience and expertise in this regard.

♦ The church can make a significant and distinctive contribution in the area of beliefs, values, ethics and justice, by *participating in interdisciplinary teams* for the development of public policy and new social structures. This is a vulnerable service, not an imposition of our values and beliefs on society.

♦ Lastly, if the social context is so polarised by repressive and revolutionary violence, the church can and should make its presence felt by *direct non-violent intervention and resistance.* It should seek to represent the underdog in confronting and negotiating with the oppressor, as was the case in SA — many black Christian leaders, and a handful of whites, engaged the powers in the name of suffering love for the poor and oppressed.

Three models of society using structural power

Where have I come to in this model of group and structural reconciliation? I have said that the church, as a microcosm of society, is the place for group and structural reconciliation in Christ. As the church participates in all spheres of society, it serves the world in influencing and facilitating group reconciliation and structural transformation. I examine the church/state relationship in the next chapter. To complete the picture, I want to show three models of society in terms of the basic motivation and usage of structural power in society, and the church's role in transformation.

Survival as the basic principle and motivation creates a society that operates on competition and ideological justifications. Each person and group for themselves, the survival of the fittest. Israel in Egypt is an example of this, the oppressed and the oppressor, both with legitimating ideologies, each living for their own survival. We see the same thing as Israel conquers Canaan, pursuing her own interests. We see the same principle in the contemporary Western competitive spirit. Structural power and force is used for the survival of your own group and its vested interests. The goal of survival can be achieved in a more just way.

Justice as the motivating principle creates a free and fair society that seeks to balance needs and interests among groups with equal opportunity for all. In this model there is justice for the weak and marginalised. The prophets and kings of Israel sought to build such a society. The belief was that Yahweh himself would execute justice, protect the poor, and judge the rulers if necessary. This is also the ideal of social democracy, in which each group's rights are guaranteed. It overrides the survival motivation and lifts society to a place where structural power is used for equality and justice for all groups. This raises the question of human rights, with its related issues of rule of law and a constitutional democracy. Derek Morphew addresses these issues in detail in Appendix 1.

Concern or care as the motivating principle creates a society built on *agape* (Greek for "love"). This takes society beyond justice and equal rights to a level of mutual concern and even compassion. Caring is the willingness to share one's privileges and rights with other groups that have forfeited their privileges and rights for whatever reason. Israel's journey from survival to justice reached its fulfilment in Messiah Jesus. Jesus and his "impossible community" is the model and motivation of love, concern and compassion. He begins in a position of power, but because he cares, he comes down to empower us. This overrides the principle of justice. As the goal of survival is fulfilled in justice, so the goal of justice is fulfilled in concern. Where concern rules supreme, neither survival nor justice is in danger; they are both secured, fulfilled and transcended. It even affects the Declaration of Human Rights — in which, although aimed at justice, its implementation presupposes concern. Concern as a principle makes more sense in terms of human relationships and politics as a whole than any other principle.[22]

In this third model, structural power is used to serve those that need empowering, as the powerful come down to help others simply because they care. A group geared to concern will sacrifice what is its own by right rather than look on while another group perishes because it has no right to the resources necessary for its survival. Only when care breaks down do people fall back on justice and claim what is theirs by right. Concern (and even trust)[23] is becoming a widely accepted principle in society without any reference to it being a Christian ethic. There are programmes for social security, rehabilitation centres, HIV/AIDS groups, relief for survivors of drought, earthquakes and war. This principle of concern is within the reach of all people for the transformation and common good of our society, politicians included! Christians should be in the forefront of socialising and inter-nalising the norm of concern and compassion in society. We do this by being true followers of Jesus in the structural horizontalising of our own lives and lifestyles.

In conclusion, often the model of the benevolent benefactor or dictator is posed as the best model for society, where the king or autocrat rules in a truly benevo-lent manner. Many believe that Jesus will rule like that on earth when he comes. But this argument is flawed because there is only one Jesus and all other kings or dictators are fallen human beings. All the warnings about having an earthly human king still apply (Deut 17:14–20; 1 Sam 8) — no matter how benevolent they may be. History is littered with the various forms or empty shells of this well-intended idea.[24] The fruit of these systems is clear: The "subjects" remain immature "children", oppressed underdogs, no matter how benevolent the rule may be.

A democracy that secures equality and justice for all has a reasonable chance of growing a free, diverse and adult society. Add the ethic of concern and compas-sion, and the possibilities for a mature and good society increase dramatically. But we can be sure of the fact that the sinfulness of the human heart will crea-tively and constantly militate against any such development. Governments,[25] just like Christians, are locked into a desperate battle against evil in all its forms in society — often most intensely within their own ranks.

Our hope is in God, who ultimately defeats evil by his kind of justice, which is the concern and suffering love of his Word in his people. God's goal is a mature society of godly self-government under the headship of Christ. Jesus' future earthly reign will merely be the visible incarnation of his present invisible government, which is not benevolent dictatorship, but a maturing partnership of godly self-governing followers of Jesus. He rules through delegated authority on the basis and power of sacrificial love. Every time we come down to serve others in his name, Jesus manifests the authority of his kingdom through us. He governs through an ever-increasing and maturing community of co-lovers, of co-servant-leaders. We are indeed in training to reign! The world is desperately looking for a king, for a benevolent dictator who will save them. Let us model God's alternative before they are given what they so desperately want, only to find out too late that it might be the very incarnation of evil itself (see Rev 12–13).

A PRACTICAL THEOLOGY OF RECONCILIATION FROM JOHWETO

I conclude this chapter with a brief explanation of the model of reconciliation that emerged in Johweto. Our "ecumenical encounter and confrontation" in Johweto, to use Nürnberger's language, led to a clear framework of thinking and practice with regard to reconciliation across the divides in SA. This real-life model integrates and summarises the basic elements of the above two models of one-on-one and group/structural reconciliation.

In Johweto we spoke of the five Rs of reconciliation and transformation: repentance, relationship, reconciliation, restitution and restoration.[26] Although they have a developmental order, in practice they were dynamic, interactive and overlapping in terms of their outworking. We even saw them as a circle or spiral of transformation, going around into ever-deepening levels of repentance and restoration. This model and its principles can be applied beyond the race and class issue to the reconciliation challenges you may face in your life, church and society.

Repentance

For us reconciliation began with the recognition of and repentance from racial conditioning and sin. Perkins begins with "relocation"[27] because it is only when you cross the barriers in society that you begin to recognise your own conditioning as you see the plight of others. "Godly sorrow" can then take hold of you, and "true repentance" begins to work (2 Cor 7:10–1). Exposure across the divides in society is absolutely crucial for real repentance. The Marxists and liberationists call it conscientisation: Raising to awareness the real facts of the matter and destroying psychological denial and ideological lies. The Bible calls it repentance (*metanoia*), which means *to turn around* by changing your mind, your ideas and view of things. When we see differently, we are often turned around. Repentance is not passive as in, "There, there, it's a pity." It is active, it makes you get up to go and do something about your sin, about the plight of others.

From the first time I became aware of the divides in SA, and crossed them, I was more and more motivated to go further and further into a life of repentance. Johweto became a journey of repentance as I saw the plight of the oppressed. I realised that my privileged and racist conditioning was so deep that it would only be worked out of me by sustained involvement with the other side.

As whites and blacks, rich and poor, male and female, we learnt that repentance is an attitude and action of self-humbling, the first step towards genuine reconciliation and transformation. Sitting around feeling sorry for ourselves and others is "worldly sorrow" that leads to death. Repentance was turning away from our sin, our racist attitudes, our comforts and securities through concrete action. We did this by turning towards God and those we had sinned against, those on the other side. We kept on doing this for many years, because we learnt that repentance is not a one-off event. It is a lifestyle of turning ever deeper away from, and ever more towards — in this sense repentance is an ongoing spiritual discipline for the sake of health and transformation, both personally and corporately.

Relationship

In Johweto we came to realise that repentance quickly leads to relationship. Repentance disarms people, even your enemies! When people see your attitude and action of repentance, they begin to open up to you. Repentance leads to confession and forgiveness, which leads to openness and, in turn, to trust and relationship. We discovered that the basic value that undergirds reality — who we are and all that we do — is relationship. Both our goal and the means to achieve it became relationship. Whenever we left this base, operating beyond or without relationship, we paid for it dearly. Reaching out for personal friendship through repentance, building trust through honesty and dialogue, was the bread and butter of Johweto. We enjoyed shared meals often — very important in relationship building. It became the context in which confrontation and racial reconciliation could happen.

Friendship "humanises" the problems of society. The issue, whatever it may be, is reduced to a person with a face, feelings, name, history, beliefs, fears and hurts. You realise that you are not dealing with an institution, ideology or structure, you are dealing with a real, living person who has become your friend. Stereotypes fall away, and trust and love grows in the heart. Now you have a problem: You actually care for the other person! Perceptions are changed, and a safety net is built to absorb the emotional fallout from increasingly honest and robust encounters. If we do reconciliation mechanically, ideologically or in a PC way, we can do more harm than good. Raw relational honesty is the seedbed and hothouse of love and trust, which becomes the motivation, means and goal of reconciliation. Relationship turns reconciliation into a kingdom exercise of love — not a guilt trip, religious obligation or a political agenda.

Reconciliation

Repentance leads to relationship which leads to actual reconciliation. Now the parties are ready; they have the good will to accept each other, to put things right, and to build a new future together. This is where actual forgiveness is given and received, where the causes of pain and division are identified and removed. This is where differing perceptions and feelings are reconciled and a common solution and strategy is found — at least between the two parties or within the group. This is where the exchanges of truth and honesty lead to genuine affirmations of mutual love and commitment. The moment of reconciliation is simply amazing, a taste of heaven. Something at the core of our being is fulfilled. We have come home, we have become one. Instinctively we know that the devil is defeated, that God is profoundly pleased and that creation jumps for joy in anticipation of its ultimate liberation (see Rom 8:19–22).

I remember moments in Johweto, and elsewhere, where we wept together as blacks and whites, verbalising forgiveness and hugging each other. It was all the more genuine and meaningful because it came in the context of a long and deepening journey of repentance and relationship. Those sweet moments came every now and then, mostly spontaneously at times of serious relational and political strain, or moments of intense spiritual visitation. Our hearts were raw and open before God and one another. It was not one of those one-off-conference-symbolic-back-slapping-representative-people-group-confessions-and-reconciliation. They have their place, and they can be powerful at the right time, if the right people are present and if it is moved upon by God's Spirit. But there is no substitute for the real thing: Moments of reconciliation in the context of long-term ever deepening relationships.

Restitution

Reconciliation includes restitution. Without reparations or restitution — if it is required — reconciliation is cheap and empty. Repentance, relationship and reconciliation provides the context in which restitution should be naturally and freely forthcoming. If we have to coerce people into restitution, something has gone wrong in their repentance, relationships and reconciliation. Repentance provides the spiritual conviction for restitution: We must bring out fruits for our repentance by our deeds as John the Baptiser and Paul taught (Matt 3:8; Acts 26:20). Relationship provides the social motivation for restitution: We must love our "enemy" brother and sister by putting things right, as Zacchaeus offered to do (Lk 19:8–9). Restitution gives substance and reality to reconciliation, if it is needed.

Only the offended party can let us off the hook of restitution if they decide to do so. On the other hand, forgiveness does not necessarily mean writing off restitution — the offended party can forgive and still require restitution. The offender should have nothing to say about this, except to expect and be willing to make restitution.

In Johweto we became aware of the need for restitution in the process of repentance and relationship. It took the form of "making up" in many small and symbolic ways in the context of personal friendship. It also took the form of group restitution in that we shared spiritual, emotional and material resources as much, and as far as our faith stretched at the time. Trevor and I referred to some of this in the first two chapters, especially the redistribution of finances for kingdom business ventures, education sponsorships, and other forms of life empowerment.

In terms of group and national reconciliation, justice must be seen to be done, or else wounds can fester for generations. Tribal faction fights in various parts of the world often go back to generations of unresolved prejudices and conflicts. Ethnic scores, going back for centuries, were settled in Yugoslavia during the civil war and ethnic cleaning by Serbs on Croats and Albanians in the 1990s. It is highly advisable that the offending group is not let off the hook, and that reparations are made, even if they are more symbolic than the actual amount. How do you quantify historical sin and debt for it to be "repaid"? Read the story at the beginning of Chapter 4: How do you return someone from the dead?

In SA, the TRC served its purpose as a catalyst for confession and a catharsis of forgiveness. But the real question remains: Has reconciliation between black and white really been effected? On the whole, the answer is no. One of the major reasons was the lack of interest in the TRC process, let alone the lack of concrete reparations and restitution for the victims of apartheid from the white community.[28] The reason behind that is the absence of godly sorrow and the lack of repentance among whites — there is still a lot of self-pity and self-preservation. Behind that is the fact that very few whites have ever, to this day, crossed over to the other side and built adult-adult relationships with black people. I fear we have been let off the hook too easily and too quickly by the generosity of the blacks. Let us hope history does not find us wanting. The restitution of land is a big issue that threatens to overrun us — we have seen the tragedy in Zimbabwe in this regard. I discuss this in more detail in Chapter 8.

We joke in SA about "redistribution of wealth" when our houses are broken into and our cars are stolen. But it runs far deeper than that. Big business, wealth tax, capital gains tax, affirmative action, black economic empowerment, land claims and redistribution are all part of the process of restitution and transformation in our country. It is really needed. How otherwise are we going to redress three centuries of privilege and power for whites, and oppression and marginalisation for blacks? The playing field must be levelled, the structures must be changed to open the system to all people. But many whites go through this under duress, with growing resentment, further reinforcing black perceptions of white stereotypes. This is not to minimise the very real struggle going on in the workplace and in other spheres of society during this structural transformation process. Birth is painful. There has been some rank incompetence among affirmative action appointments.[29] There is reverse discrimination and nepotism by some of the new black elite. Corruption is an ongoing problem. However, we need to remember who "they" learnt materialism, job reservation, favouritism and discrimination from. We also need to see all of this in the broader context of structural restitution and transformation, for the good of the whole, and together in a spirit of goodwill *we can, and we will*, win.

Restoration

This five-step process is about restoring the relationship to what it was before the breakdown, and going even further. Often meaningful reconciliation results in deeper trust and friendship. Restoration goes beyond repairing to proactively building and developing. At the personal level, this can mean many different things — empowering the previously disadvantaged person in various ways. Sometimes it even happens in reverse — the sinned against forgives and empowers the offender beyond their former quality of life. An amazing story illustrates this. In 1993 a young American Fulbright scholar, Amy Biehl, was murdered in Gugulethu, Cape Town while helping in preparations for the SA elections. Her parents flew out from the USA and sat through the trial of the three murderers. Motivated by their Christian convictions, they forgave them and set up an Amy Biehl Foundation, in which two of the three murderers are currently employed. Their lives are completely different today and many other previously disadvantaged young South Africans are being empowered through the Foundation.[30] The devil obviously did not know what he was doing; he chose the wrong person to murder that day! As with Jesus; if Satan had known God's hidden wisdom and plan in Christ, he would not have killed the Lord of glory. History is changed because of Jesus' death (see 1 Cor 2:7–8 cf. Jn 12:24).

At the group and structural level of reconciliation, restoration raises the whole issue of redistribution of resources, community develop and nation building to which I have alluded. The last R goes full circle back to the beginning. Repentance across the barriers is "relocation" in Perkins's terms. Relocation is the process of shifting relationships to the other side, of relocating your heart and mind, and then resources, and possibly even your residence. It is a matter of the former top-dog helping the underdog by restoring a quality of life and equality of opportunity, that is comparable with his/her own. It is nothing more than "loving your neighbour as you love yourself". Jesus puts it another way: "Do to others what you would have them do to you." Relationship and reconciliation helps you to see things from the other side, as if you are standing in their shoes. Then efforts towards restoration are a genuine act of love, not a handout or an obligatory PC process.

We can summarise by saying that restitution leads to redistribution of resources, which leads to restoration of community and nation building, for a fair and shared quality of life. At the structural level this would involve relocating business interests and reallocating state resources to places of poverty and marginalisation — as in education, health care and job creation.

We cannot all operate at the macro level — big business and government, provincial and national — but we can all make a contribution at the local level. We did this in Johweto in many practical ways. There is a movement in some local churches and NGOs to reverse the economic and human flow by relocating from the suburbs to the urban ghettos, the black townships and shack settlements. Many blacks get out of the townships as soon they can, leaving a vacuum of leadership and economic muscle. One fears that the townships will become the dustbins of SA society, rundown monuments of our apartheid history, if there is no intentional intervention and restoration. The Perkins Foundation, Bob Lupton and others are working on "return flight" — getting Christians back into places of poverty and pain (often the inner city), in order to redeem and lift the community wholistically.[31] This is part of the ongoing challenge of reconciliation in SA, with the mushrooming of squatter camps around every urban centre — all part of the legacy of apartheid that will be with us for some time to come.

Some Christians and others are aware of the challenges we face, both in SA and in our global village, and are doing something about it.[32] We will look at some related social issues and challenges that emerge out of the study on reconciliation, and how to respond to them as Christians, in the next chapter.

NOTES

1. The story of Johweto is told in the first two chapters. On a technical note, I am moving from doing biblical theology in Chapters 5 and 6 to an exercise in practical theology in this chapter, and then engaging in theological ethics in Chapter 8. Practical theology is learning about God and our faith by reflecting on our practices ("praxis") as Christians and churches. In simple terms, it is learning from what we do, from our working models and methods in church life, by comparing it with Scripture and our context, so that we can do things more effectively under God.

2. Jesus deals with six issues: anger, lust, marriage/divorce, keeping your word, personal injury and enemies. Read Willard's incisive and challenging exposition, 1998, pp. 145–206.

3. There are increasing incidents in SA of communities taking the law into their own hands by punishing criminals without handing them over to the police (or before they hand them over). People are hacked with knives and even killed. This is certainly not what is meant or implied in this Scripture.

4. See Morphew 1998, pp. 293–301 for an exposition of the kingdom-Hebraic view of breaking bread.

5. This is a fascinating study on where we have come to in our postmodern society, the neuroses and complexes of a sibling society. See Bly 1996.

6. John Powell is very insightful on this whole issue: How to handle your emotions, the parent, child and adult modes; the five levels of communication, and the gift of self through disclosure of feelings (the fourth level of communication). Self-disclosure is the gift of love to the other by allowing the other to see and know the real you. Powell explains how all this works in human relationships in terms of conflict resolution and personal growth. See Powell 1967, 1969 (especially pp. 43–102), 1974 (especially pp. 68–93) and 1978.

7. Psalm 141:5; Prov 15:31; 17:10; 19:25; 25:12; **27:5;** Lk17:3; Col 1:28; 3:16; 1 Thess 5:12.

8. Bonhoeffer 1963, pp. 45–60. David Bosch used Bonhoeffer to warn against a cheap reconciliation and called for a costly reconciliation in SA in 1986, in his "Process of Reconciliation and Demands of Obedience — Twelve Theses", in Nürnberger and Tooke (eds.) 1988, pp. 98–112.

9. Note the sevenfold fruit of true repentance and costly reconciliation in verse 11: "See what this godly sorrow has produced in you: what earnestness, what eagerness to clear yourselves, what indignation, what alarm, what longing, what concern, what readiness to see justice done. At every point you have proved yourselves ..."

10. Matt 6:12: "Forgive us our debts, as we also have forgiven our debtors ..." An IOU is "I owe you" — when a person lends money or is in debt to another person, they sometimes

write out a note called an IOU recording the amount owed and the date of repayment.

11. My discussion on the accountability and discipline of leaders is found in Venter 2000, pp. 210–216. I look at the same process of reconciliation in Matthew, but from a leadership angle.

12. The Greek tense is "has been" bound in heaven. The teaching of "binding and loosing" (Matt 16:19; 18:18–20) has been misinterpreted and misapplied by being taken out of its context, especially in charismatic and Pentecostal Christianity. It does not teach a blanket mandate to "legislate in the heavens" through intercession, to bind demons and loose people and God's purposes through "prayer warfare". The words, concept and practice that Jesus is referring to is from Judaism and the Rabbinical judicial discipline of sin — either opening God's kingdom to people who repent or closing the kingdom to those who cling to their sin (see Carson's commentary in Gaebelein 1984, pp. 370–375, 402–404). Peter was given "the keys of the kingdom" in a unique way to open and close the kingdom by preaching the gospel to Jews (at Pentecost, Acts 2) and Gentiles (at Caesarea, Acts 10), and people were bound or loosed depending on their response and Peter's pronouncements over them. The further outworking of "binding and loosing" in the church is seen in Jn 20:23 cf. Acts 5:1–9.

13. In this section I will follow a biblical model taught by Klaus Nürnberger in SA in the 1980s and early 1990s. This is a big subject and I will merely integrate and summarise the material which comes from a few books: Nürnberger 1979, pp. 47–64, Nürnberger and Tooke (eds.) 1988, pp. 113–125, 181–198, Nürnberger 1988, pp. 287–319 and Nürnberger (ed.) 1991, pp. 297–300. Here and there I paraphrase or quote Nürnberger without giving the specific reference.

14. The assumption that enough conversions to Christ will automatically lead to socio-political and structural change is not valid. Likewise, the assumption that conversion to Christ automatically leads to social responsibility is untrue. On both counts history proves us wrong. Only intentional discipleship in the character and teachings of Jesus — lived out in society — coupled with intentional, wise and courageous intervention in societal affairs, brings about social-structural change. Personal piety, an "only evangelism" focus, is often an excuse to withdraw from social involvement and secure one's comfort zones.

15. Paul clearly sees the primary battle at the level of consciousness — ideas and beliefs — and secondly at the level of our lower nature — our corrupted desires (see Rom 1:18–32; 1 Tim 4:1–2; 2 Tim 3:1–5). This is why he talks so much of the "renewing of the mind" which leads to transformation (Rom 12:2).

16. Camara 1971 and Nürnberger, Tooke and Domeris (eds.) 1989.

17. We need to demystify the power of structures by saying that people create structures, and people dismantle structures, i.e. we can bring about radical socio-political change

peacefully through negotiations. We are not victims at the mercy of structures — enough conviction and effort will bring about change in structures. Some Christians give uncritical support and have an almost godly respect for socio-political structures, believing that they are ordained by God — a wrong reading of Rom 13 (discussed in Chapter 8).

18. A biblical and ethical critique of the major international socio-political systems and ideologies is found in Leatt, Kneifel and Nürnberger (eds.) 1988. See Nürnberger (ed.) 1991 for an in-depth theological ethical study on democracy — both liberal and social democracy.

19. This point is important: Accepting people, sinners, homosexuals, drunkards or people of other faiths does not mean we endorse their beliefs, behaviour or lifestyle. It just means we create a safe place where they can be loved, confronted, forgiven, healed and transformed. The reverse is true: If we do not endorse their behaviour or lifestyle, it does not mean we reject them. Churches should be radically open to and accepting of all types of people, sinners and groups — as Jesus was.

20. The 2 Cor 8:9 paradigm summarises the mission and spirit of Jesus in his *kenosis*, his self-humbling and self-giving in suffering love for humanity. It directly challenges structural relationships of all kinds. Jesus' leadership and authority was derived from his self-sacrificing service. He did not cling to power and privilege, but came down, as we see in the washing of the feet, and ultimately in Golgotha. This paradigm is the calling and ethic of every Christian, of every local church (Mk 10:42–45; Jn 13:1–17; Phil 2:1–11).

21. I do not agree with the argument that Christians cannot determine social reality or that what works in the church cannot work in society, because society is filled with unbelievers. This is often an excuse for Christians not to take responsibility for social issues. In fact, many Muslims, humanists, Hindus, etc. put Christians to shame with their level of self-sacrificing social involvement. The biblical teachings, values and social ethics, such as the Ten Commandments, are not for Christians only; they are for the whole world. If faithfully applied in the world, the Ten Commandments will quickly raise to awareness people's need of God. It will lead to evangelism with integrity, because social care and involvement will be for humanity's sake, not as a baited hook for evangelism.

22. Some people have attempted to make love the workable basis for a political approach and system, called "the politics of love" (see well-known ethicist, Reinhold Niebühr, "The Law of Love in Politics and Economics" in Boulton, Kennedy and Verhey (eds.) 1994, pp. 463–467; and also Cassidy 1989, pp. 385–470). The church should be the example of being governed by the politics of love.

23. An interesting study on trust as the new socio-economic ethic is found in Fukuyama 1995. He is a social analyst and continues the theme in his recent study (1999) on

understanding human nature in the reconstruction of the social order since the "end of history" — the end of the ideological era.

24. For example: The best of the brokering system in the ancient world where kings and benefactors cared for peasants, where masters cared for slaves, and the best of the feudal system where lords cared for vassals, and even the best of the colonial system where enlightened imperialists cared for their poor native subjects. In apartheid, Christian Afrikaners genuinely believed God had called them to civilise and care for the heathen blacks as a parent cares for his children. What resulted from the "Christian government" in a "Christian country" implementing its "Christian ideology" of apartheid? And what resulted from all the other systems of patronage?

25. For example, the battle against international crime syndicates and terrorist networks. They are like Satan's spiderweb stretching across the earth, touching almost every nation. This is besides the ongoing battle of corruption within governments — often the very thing that enables international syndicates.

26. It was partly inspired by John Perkins's 3 Rs (relocation, reconciliation and redistribution). His book was a great help in Johweto, see Perkins 1982.

27. Ibid. pp. 59–95.

28. Taking into account the recommendations of the TRC, the SA government has said it can only afford to pay R30 000 (about US$5 000 at the current exchange rate, R6 to $1) as a one-off reparations payment to each person who suffered apartheid atrocities — just on 22 000 apartheid survivors are receiving this grant.

29. As well meaning as affirmative action and other such structural transformation policies may be, if not handled correctly, they can quickly reinforce racial prejudice and division. The American experience and perspective is helpful in this regard, see Bloom 1987, pp. 91–97.

30. The remarkable story seen through the eyes of Sindiwe Magona, the neighbour of one of the killers. She imagines that she was the mother the of the killer and writes to Amy Biehl's mother, exploring the historical context and legacy of apartheid that gave rise to such mindless killing. Mangona 2000.

31. Lupton 1993.

32. I cannot recommend highly enough Nürnberger's (1999) in-depth multi-disciplinary study on the approaching crisis, not only in SA but in our global structures and systems.

CHAPTER 8

GUIDELINES ON SOME RELATED SOCIAL-ETHICAL ISSUES

Are we still of any use?
Dietrich Bonhoeffer[1]

The debate about the future of South Africa is in many ways a debate about the future of our life together in this small earth.
Richard Neuhaus[2]

Therefore, in view of God's amazing mercies, I strongly urge you to offer your bodies to God as living sacrifices — set apart as pleasing to him. This is the most intelligent act of life service and spiritual worship that you can offer God. Do not allow this world to push you into its mould and pattern of thinking, but be transfigured by the renewing of your mind. Then you will be able to prove and approve what God's will is — his good, pleasing and perfect will.
Paul in Rom 12:1–2 RAP

If we let ourselves drift along the stream of history, without knowing it, we shall have chosen the power of suicide, which is at the heart of the world ... in order to preserve the world, it is actually necessary that a genuine revolution should take place.
Jacques Ellul[3]

"ARE WE STILL OF ANY USE?"

It was 9 April 1945, one week after Resurrection Sunday. Dietrich Bonhoeffer conducted a worship service for his fellow inmates in the Nazi prison that morning. After he pronounced the benediction, he was led away to the gallows and hanged until he stopped breathing. He was thirty-nine years old. World War II ended just four weeks later on 8 May 1945. Two years earlier he had been arrested due to his anti-Nazi resistance and his part in a failed plot to assassinate Adolf Hitler. Bonhoeffer asked the above question in a letter from prison, while awaiting his execution: "Are we still of any use?" The confessing church — in contrast to the rest of the church in Germany — had made their stand against Hitler and Nazism, and many of their leaders were in prison. They had done what they could, besides their efforts in continued prayer and their willingness to be martyrs for their faith. What else could they do? Bonhoeffer wondered if the church was still of any use to God and the German society. At the time he asked the question, it seemed there was no hope — the end had come. Part of the answer came only after the war when the German church made a public confession of guilt and began to play an important role in the rebuilding of a very broken society. (The Stuttgart Confession in October 1945, strangely, did not mention the Jewish holocaust.)

By God's grace we have passed through our crisis in SA and have moved to a new place of democratic freedom. As the church, are we still of any use? Bonhoeffer's question is still relevant for us in SA. Do we leave it all up to the government now, or do we still have a role to play in rebuilding our society? If so, what is that role? As I have stated, we must work to dismantle racism, seek reconciliation in society, and be an instrument of healing from racial and other wounds from the past. But there is much more. The church has a vital role to play in all aspects of society and nation building. Vacuums get filled one way or another. The post-apartheid vacuum is being filled, but with what, by whom, for what purpose and for whose benefit? What type of democracy, morality and society is being built? And who is forming it? How can the church help shape our society with values and norms that are for the genuine good of all? How can we translate biblical values into societal norms and help bring about transformation in our nation? These are some of the questions that will guide the discussion as I look at various social issues that arise from the examination of reconciliation and transformation.

In the 1980s Richard Neuhaus rightly said that these issues and their responsible resolution is not just a SA concern, it is applicable to all people and nations in our global village. It is still true today that SA is a microcosm of the world. Do not think that these issues are merely SA challenges. My hope is that the discussion on these social-ethical issues, and the guidance that we offer from a Vineyard perspective, will be helpful and applicable in your context, wherever you may be.

Clear guidance and the renewal of the mind

It is absolutely crucial that clear guidance is given on these social issues so that the church can fulfil its role with diligence and conviction. We are all constantly being pushed, at subconscious, personal and societal levels, into a mould, a pattern of thinking and behaving. If we do not evaluate the mould *consciously and intentionally* and actively work for what we believe in, we will be moulded by evil into its image by default. The default settings of the world are on progressive decay. The law of sinful entropy still rules: Things left to themselves in their natural state will move to the greatest state of disorder because of human depravity — our sinful nature. The Bible teaches this, and history and social reality proves it. What I am saying is illustrated by the old frog experiment that my friends and I did at school. In our science class, when I was a young boy, we put a frog in a beaker and filled it with cold water. Then we set the beaker over a flame. The frog made a few feeble attempts to jump out right at the beginning, but as soon as the water became warm, it became passive and, before it realised what was happening, it was cooked. What naughty little boys do in the name of learning! The point is simple: The slow subconscious (and even conscious) conditioning by the changing environment around us is killing us. This is similar to what Allan Bloom means when he says America has "closed her mind" to its changing reality and is facing death.[4] We need to ask constantly: What is happening and changing in our environment? What are the challenges we now face and what can we do about them?

Paul says we must take decisive action in our bodies as a result of our changed thinking, if we do not want to be slowly conditioned, and eventually cooked, both individually and as a society or nation. Jacques Ellul, a contemporary of Bonhoeffer and part of the French Resistance during WWII, says we need nothing short of a revolution in order to avoid the choice and power of suicide as we drift along the stream of history. And even more so if we are Christians. As God's colony on earth, we have a unique responsibility and calling for society's salvation and transformation. We are called to transform, and even transfigure, not only ourselves (where it begins), but society and creation (where it ends — the *eschaton* or God's goal for creation).

Paul says transformation happens specifically through the renewing of our minds; in other words, seeing and doing things differently from God's perspective. It is not allowing the dominant consciousness and ideology, the prevailing thinking and value system, to push us into its worldview and agenda. We disallow this process of conditioning and eventual death by acquiring God's revolutionary ideas on reality so that we can know and do his will. God's will is that which is genuinely good and perfect for everyone, even if people do not realise it or presently want it. In fact, we know that many presently reject it because they choose darkness and death, the power of suicide rather than light and life. But if we renew our minds in God's reality, and offer our bodies to live out that reality, we choose life, although it may end in physical death or martyrdom. That is why Paul calls it "a living sacrifice". Then we will be transformed and will be God's instruments of transformation. God's government will come to society, and his will be done on earth as it is in heaven — through us, his people. The fullness of this blessed reality will only come when Jesus returns to earth but, until then, we are it, for better or worse!

I am not saying that it is simple to determine God's thinking and will on various matters, or that it is easy to live it out. Imagine the ethical dilemma that Bonhoeffer and the confessing church were in: "Should we as Christians participate in an attempt to kill Hitler before he kills more Jews and Allied troops, and destroys Germany and Europe?" What would you have done? I am sure none of us would like to have been in his shoes. Fortunately, God does not abandon us; he gives us guidance. Paul's appeal is quite clear: In view of God's amazing mercies in saving us into his people and plans on earth, let us put our bodies on the line, in line with God's thinking on matters. In other words, God literally lives in and through our skin to save and transform the world. How this happens, and the degree to which it happens, is determined by our ideas, thoughts and beliefs. Hopefully they represent God's ideas on reality, and are worth dying for. The church, if it is true to God and his Word, is deeply subversive of evil in all its patterns in society, and profoundly transformative of people in all their ways in the world.

Continued sin leads to mental deception and growing unintelligence, and consequent moral decay through corrupt character and sinful desires (Rom 1:18–32 cf. 12:1–2). The result is a downward spiral of ethical confusion with an eventual rationalisation and justification of naked evil. This is borne out by history and current social reality. The opposite is equally true: Reconciliation and obedience to God leads to mental renewal and quickening intelligence, with consequent moral character and emotional refinement, and an increasing ethical clarity and authority on all matters. Paul expects Christians to be intellectually, emotionally and ethically not only the smartest and sharpest, but also the most loving and courageous people on earth. He expects us to be those who bravely and bodily live out God's answers for society, even to the point of death (not suicide, as in the basic death wish of the world, and now incarnated in the terrorist suicide bombers).[5]

Social-ethical theology and social issues

The church must go beyond dismantling racism and ministering reconciliation and healing. The church must be proactive by being clear in its thinking and engagement in the issues that challenge society. As Christians, we need to be involved proactively in the process of nation building and societal transformation. We need to develop a mature social theology. This chapter (this book) is an attempt to plant and water the seeds of such a theology in the Vineyard movement. A comprehensive social theology would undergird and address three of the basic levels of social engagement for the Christian (besides evangelism and church planting):

♦ *Mercy ministry* — caring for the immediate needs of people by alleviating the symptoms of pain and poverty. This would take various forms of relief work like feeding the hungry and clothing the naked.

♦ *Justice ministry* — engaging in the causes of social pain and poverty. This would mean dealing with public policy, working for human rights and conflict resolution.

♦ *Development ministry* — building up a community in various ways by addressing the brokenness in that society. This would mean building infra-structure, education and basic skills training, helping people to start busi-nesses, and general wholistic development work.

We must "not only give people fish to eat, but teach them how to fish" (a Chinese proverb). We need to go further by analysing and helping people to redress the causes of their hunger and poverty. That would raise the question of whether they have the means of production, the tools with which to fish. If they do, we teach them how to use the tools. If not, we would give them fishing rods and hooks, or teach them how to make them out of the raw material available to them. Then they can grow out of poverty and hunger into a sustainable, if not prosperous, life.

In the Vineyard we have been strong on mercy, average on development and weak on justice. These levels of social involvement raise many ethical issues. Conversely, the ethical issues must be addressed in a way that touches on all three levels: symptoms (mercy ministry), causes (justice work) and development (building community).

I will not give a detailed theological-ethical treatment of all the major social issues that we face.[6] Each is weighty in its own right. I will simply state our general position as Vineyard, aimed at giving clear, concise guidance as to how we think about and practically respond to the issues I have chosen to address. I am aware that as I offer these guidelines, I will be making many assumptions, hopefully in a non-ideological manner.

The first ethical issue is "in-house": I start with the church in terms of its unity and multicultural possibilities. Then I look at Islam, Israel and interfaith dialogue, and follow with the church/state relationship and the issue of development and globalisation. These are more universal in their interest. Finally I address the seven SACLA "giants" that I referred to in Chapter 4, which are more specific to the SA context. Seven issues were identified that the church and the nation need to overcome so that our new democracy can fully "inherit the land". They are poverty, land and unemployment; Human Immunodeficiency Virus (HIV) and Acquired Immune Deficiency Syndrome (AIDS); violence; crime; sexism; racism, and the family in crisis.

CHURCH UNITY AND CULTURE

The best form of prophetic witness is embodiment. In the Vineyard, we believe that our presence and impact as servants in society is the most effective means of prophecy or "being prophetic". Our actions speak louder than our words. Who we are is seen in what we do and that gives us authority to speak to society. By being reconciled and united, by caring for AIDS orphans, feeding the hungry, seeking justice for the oppressed, we have an integrity of witness and can influence our world. Mother Teresa and the authority that God gave her in the world, is a case in point. This prophetic, incarnational integrity applies first and foremost to church unity, to reconciliation within the church of Jesus Christ. What do we have to say to the world when we are still divided denominationally, racially, and in other ways? Because of the critical importance of church unity, my comments will be more detailed than the perspectives on the other issues to be discussed.

The unity of the church

In Chapter 6 I mentioned the fact that God has staked his credibility in the eyes of the world on the unity (or disunity) of the church. It comes directly from Jesus' prayer in Jn 17:20—23: "... That they may be one ... so that the world may believe that you have sent me." This prayer specifically includes us today, the contemporary worldwide church (v. 20). Our historical and current disunity is a scandal, a shame on God's name. We have swallowed the camel of division while trying to strain out the gnats of doctrinal purity. No wonder the world does not believe in Jesus, the one sent to reveal the Father. It is Jesus, not the invisible "God in heaven", who is the centre of angry controversy and questioning credibility in the world today. People will believe by the millions in the (God)man Jesus, as the Messiah sent by God to save the world, if the church unites in reconciling love, and operates as one in the world. The church is Jesus to this world, nothing more and nothing less, for better or worse.

We want to be truly ecumenical in the sense of seeking the unity and fellowship of the whole church of Jesus Christ. How God is going to sort out the structural and doctrinal denominational divisions is his doing. Our doing is to foster reconciliation, unity and working together among all churches in our local areas, for the common good. This requires visionary and loving spiritual leadership. Our unity is not based on common vision and values, neither on common philosophies of ministry, methods of working, or compatible personalities. Diversity in these aspects is to be expected, accepted and even celebrated within a deeper unity of "the faith". Authentic unity is based on the few non-negotiables of "the faith that was once entrusted" to us by the apostles of the early church (Jude 3). There are a few core doctrines that define Christianity, and there are many peripheral doctrines on which we can agree to disagree and maintain a genuine unity of faith and fellowship.

Paul lists some of these central beliefs as the basis of our unity: one body, one Spirit, one hope, one Lord, one faith, one baptism, one God and Father of all (Eph 4:4–6, the context of unity/disunity is important: It moves from relational unity to the basis of our unity, diversity of gifting, people and functions for a mature "unity in the faith". Read vv. 1–13). Unity is not uniformity. Paradoxically it is most maturely expressed through diversity. For example, Israel's identity and unity under God was expressed in the diversity of the twelve tribes. The Apostolic Creed summarises the basic non-negotiable doctrines or beliefs that identify us as Christian, that unite us as "one holy catholic and apostolic church" ("catholic" meaning "universal").

We believe that we must give space for all Christian churches and seek reconciliation in a united witness and working together, on the basis of God's love, for this world and the early church creeds. Conversely, we reject all forms of spiritual or theological elitism, and church or denominational withdrawal from broader ecumenical fellowship. We see this as sectarian and anti-Christ — in the sense of continuing to undermine Christ's credibility and literally to work against him. The achieving of our God-given goal of world evangelisation and the return of Christ is directly dependent on our reconciliation and unity in loving service to the world. In other words, as we become one "they will believe" in Jesus. Jesus also said: "The gospel of the kingdom will be preached in the whole world as a testimony to all nations, and then the end will come" (Matt 24:14).

Reconciliation, culture and the kingdom

Church unity includes the issue of cultural-racial reconciliation within the church — we discussed this in Chapter 6 under Paul's gospel mandate. The work of Christ on the cross and the work of the Spirit at Pentecost reconciles and unites all races and cultures in the church. We believe that this multicultural unity in Christ is to be expressed in the local congregation in a non-ideological manner, in a way that is reasonable and possible within the particular context. But what does this mean? What does it look like?

Firstly, it does not mean that racial identities and expressions are obliterated, curtailed or subsumed into a dominant mono-culture, whatever that may be. Often the culture that is politically dominant in a particular context becomes the prevailing mono-culture in the local church. We need to subvert creatively this cultural imperialism. But it goes further, and gets worse. Churches and denominations create their own Christian subcultures which evolve in a number of ways (cultures are never static, they always evolve with changing contexts and values). The success culture of many high-profile influential churches becomes the model or reference for many other churches. Pastors who are desperate for growth quickly adopt these new models and cultures in pursuit of success. We deplore the tragic mess in many African cities and black townships resulting from churches becoming clones of American tele-evangelists and Western prosperity teachings — among other so-called success models. It is all about money, position, prestige and power in the midst of a sea of pain and poverty.[7] It is a deceptive mirage for those in the desert of desperation or, as Marx called it, an opiate for the people. All this is a form of Christian imperialism in a new guise.

Secondly, there is a church or religious tradition, a Christian culture, that has stagnated in religious ritual and institutionalism. Generally speaking, it is irrelevant to, and out of touch with, the changing societal culture. The opposite extreme to church tradition is the end result of an overreaction by some indigenous Christians and churches to colonial missions. It is a rejection of Western Christian or church culture through a process of "enculturation" in the indigenous church. The vision and intention of a native church free from colonial culture, expressing a healthy indigenised Christianity, is correct and laudable. It is the process of indigenising kingdom values in a native culture, or in our own culture. In some cases the overreaction has resulted in syncretism. In our context in SA, it happens when traditional African cultural beliefs and practices are uncritically mixed with Christian beliefs and practices in the church. The result is a steady journey back to paganism. Both this and the above cultural extremes end up in idolatry (paganism in both

Western and African forms). We must distinguish between the kingdom and our own values and culture, and between indigenising kingdom values and taking on cultural elements — whether religious or indigenous cultural elements (which the kingdom of God challenges and in some cases opposes).

The kingdom of God is always in tension with any and every culture. It always evaluates, challenges and transforms (aspects of) culture, while also accepting, celebrating and even enriching (aspects of) culture. The kingdom, if it has any transcendent culture of its own, will only be fully expressed and experienced in the age to come. But it breaks through into the church in this present age to make its presence felt in the world. The breakthrough is a foretaste, a hopeful sign of what is to come. That sign brings all other people and cultures into tension. Some Christians think, and even teach, that the kingdom breakthrough is a restoration of Jewish or Hebraic culture in the church. Jewish culture is no more the kingdom of God than the clothes that a person may wear is the person him or herself. The clothes are an expression of the person, not the person him or herself. God may have expressed himself in history through a particular (Hebraic) culture, but that does not make that culture God. God has, and can, reveal himself through many types of clothing. Biblical Hebraic faith and culture, "the Jewish roots of Christian faith" (not Jewish culture per se) may be his original outfit or his best suit to date,[8] but that does not invalidate or devalue all his other suits. Just wait until he comes — "You ain't seen nothin' yet!" Joseph's coat of many colours is the faintest shadow of that ultimate reality that we see in Revelation — the glorified Christ and his bride — the rainbow glory of God surrounding his throne as "every tongue, every nation, every tribe ..." worship him.

We need a correct understanding and awareness of culture.[9] All cultures are made of the good, the bad and the neutral.

- ◆ All cultures have *good aspects* to them, the "residue reminders" of God's image in the rich diversity of creation, peoples and nations. For example, there are glorious aspects of cultural heritage in many African language-groups. The kingdom of God celebrates and even enhances the beauty and richness of these aspects of culture, and I am sure that we will see their original intention and ultimate fulfilment when the kingdom comes. The church should not impose cultural "stuff" on people, whether it be "church" culture or Western culture, such as forms of dress and social etiquette. We should openly express, and be enriched by, the good that lies in all cultures.

- ◆ All cultures have *bad aspects* because we are all fallen human beings with false beliefs, corrupt desires, oppressive traditions and sinful patterns of behaviour. There are many forms of cultural superstitions and demonic oppressions that, in some cases, are openly worshipped. Although it is defended with "this is my culture", it is idolatry. The kingdom of God challenges these aspects of culture and seeks to liberate people from these sinful expressions and oppressions of evil. The church should sensitively, but courageously, challenge and evangelise these aspects of culture — not with the arrogant assumption that its own culture is superior, but because people are being oppressed or exploited by (evil aspects of) their culture, and they need God's liberation.

♦ The *neutral aspects* are the human elements that are natural and somewhat indifferent in terms of the kingdom of God. For example, whether you wear a hat or not, whether you burp after a meal or not (depending which culture you are in), is hardly a kingdom issue. The kingdom does not necessarily challenge or endorse these aspects of culture. They only become moral issues if we do not make space for one another in these diverse expressions, and if we are insensitive and hurt each other. Paul addresses this issue with regard to people's scruples and conscience in Rom 14: vegetarians or meat eaters, wine drinkers or abstainers, Sabbath keepers or whatever — these are not important. What is important is that we accept each other, make room for each other, and make sure that our freedom and cultural practices are not a source of stumbling or imposition on others.

The bottom line is that all cultures need the kingdom of God. Without the transcendent kingdom breaking in, cultural entropy takes over — things left to themselves move towards disorder and evil, because of the fall of humanity into sin. The interface of cultures and the kingdom is redemptive and rich with instruction, and what better place for this to happen than in the church of Jesus Christ?

Multicultural congregations

Where does all this leave us in terms of how to plant and build multicultural congregations? The debate in the Western church (and in Vineyard circles) has been about mono-cultural or multicultural (homogenous or heterogeneous) churches. The focus of the debate should be shifted to multicultural church — how do we build multicultural environments and congregations? Multicultural churches are the norm in the NT, and it should be the same for us, for all the reasons in this book. Homogeneous churches should be the exception. However, we must not be ideological about this by trying to impose the ideal or wrongfully manipulating it into existence.[10] Mono-cultural churches have NT integrity if it is a matter of functionality within, and a reflection of their homogenous context. But if they are homogeneous by belief, pride, prejudice, convenience or comfort, they are deceived and the kingdom challenges them as to the integrity of their gospel witness.

The debate ought to focus on how we plant and build multicultural churches. After my Johweto experience, I learnt that we must not complicate the issue. At one level it is very simple. There are many ways to build multicultural congregations, there is no one formula, or "do the following things and it will work".[11] Some who have tried and apparently failed have spread the word that "it does not work". Our problem is that our Western values of consumerism, comfort, seeker focus, pragmatism, instant results, growth and success, profile and power all militate against us. If we do what the people want, we will always end up building something that secures their comforts and vested interests. The kingdom, in contrast, simultaneously secures us and takes us beyond our own (in)securities. Multicultural congregations are not natural to fallen human beings, any more than following Jesus is. It goes against everything in our lower nature, but it certainly appeals to our faith or kingdom nature.

In Johweto I learnt that it is not about "how to build multicultural environments"; it is about "why we must build them". Gordon Cosby from Church of the Savior in Washington, DC. counselled me in the 1980s: "It's not about structure, it's about spirit; it's not about form, it's about faith." If you really believe God wants this, you will find a way, with the help of God's Pentecost-Spirit, to build what you believe in. The frightening reality is that you see what you really believe (not what you say you believe) in what you have built around you. To build heterogeneous churches takes strong faith-intention, diligent relational work, much persevering love, and lots of trial and error. We are not naturally endowed with multicultural skills and sensitivities — we learn to love by being in a mixed environment where acceptance, love and forgiveness become the order of the day. The reward in terms of loving across the barriers, and the sheer richness of God's image in the diversity and fullness of life, is unparalleled.

There are many models on how to build multicultural environments. You can have small groups that are homogenous built around, for instance, similar callings, interests or cultural identities with mixed congregational meetings. These larger meetings would have mixed cultural worship and other multicultural expressions and participation to meet the needs of the various people groups. This requires loving acceptance, sensitivity training and giving big space to serve one another in our diversity and differences, for Christ's sake.[12] You can have racially mixed small groups and some congregational meetings that are culture-specific, but then everyone comes together for a regular multicultural church celebration. Some churches have operated on the model of one church (via its pastoral team and offices) with culture or language-specific congregations that meet at different times. Their small groups are both homogenous and heterogeneous.

I preached with an interpreter most Sundays for ten years in Soweto and it was fine. The language barrier was not that big a deal. I believe that the symbolic value of our unity with translators enriches our faith much more than language-specific congregations that exist for the sake of functionality. But again, we cannot be ideological. We can build racially reconciled and multicultural environments in many creative ways, as long as we have integrity with our unity in the gospel, and we serve and honour one another in our dignity and diversity as God's people.

We are called to love one another in our different needs and expressions. Jesus repeatedly said to his followers (Lk 6:27–36; Matt 5:45–48) that to greet your friends, to love those who are like you — or those who love you in return — means very little because that is exactly what society does. We are not to be like that, as convenient as that may be. We are to love those who are different to us, even our enemies, because in this way people see and know that we are his followers. "By your love ... will all people know that you are my disciples" (Jn 13:35). The test is not only to love others across the barriers in mission (when we go and do things at our convenience to others who are different to us), but to love the same diverse and needy people in the family, integrating them into our daily lives in congregational or home group belonging. The ultimate test of love is not mission and ministry; it is being family.

INTERFAITH DIALOGUE, ISLAM AND ISRAEL

Similar to our view of culture, and in accordance with Paul in Rom 1–3, we ought not to see other faiths or religions as either all good or all bad. They are a mix. Other faiths should be viewed as human attempts at knowing and understanding the God of the Bible in light of his *general revelation* in creation and in human (moral) conscience. All such expressions of religious faith are caught in the web of the fall of humanity in sin and depravity. This is besides the effect of the fall of the spiritual powers over nations and peoples: They seek power and worship by incarnating themselves in society and structures through wrong ideas, false beliefs, corrupt desires and vested interests. Besides the general revelation of God, the Bible also teaches the *specific revelation* of God in Christ. God has revealed himself in history specifically through *biblical* Judaism, which culminated in the historical person of Jesus Christ, God's Messiah. Jesus is God's ultimate and specific revelation of himself to humanity. The followers of Jesus — call it Messianic Judaism or the Christian faith — are the custodians and messengers of the faith of the (G)god of the Bible, the one and only true God.[13] The message and ministry entrusted to Christians is reconciliation with God and other human beings through Jesus Christ.

In view of God's special revelation in Christ, Christians should not fear interfaith dialogue. We can humbly "compare notes" and debate ideas and beliefs in a sensitive and non-judgemental manner. However, in the final analysis the (God)man Jesus of Nazareth — and his uniqueness as God's only Son — will be the controversial point of debate, and we might have to agree to disagree. No form of dialogue or working together should remove any person's right to evangelise people of other faiths in Jesus' name sensitively and lovingly. If we surrender the uniqueness of Jesus and our world mission in his name, we surrender our identity as his followers. Jesus is the rock of offence and the stone of stumbling; we should not be ashamed of him. The key factor in all of this is our attitude: Christian arrogance is infamous throughout history and has caused enormous problems. We need to (re)learn the suffering love and courageous humility of our Master and his early followers as we engage unbelief and other systems of faith in society. At the same time we have to realise that we can never reconcile in any ultimate sense with any of these religions — even with our "sister" monotheistic faiths of modern Judaism and Islam — because of the uniqueness of Christ. We genuinely believe that Jesus, and real faith in him, is God's means of saving and reconciling people, and this world, from both immediate and ultimate destruction. We believe that this is a matter of objective reality, a universal fact, which will stand or fall as history unfolds. We do not have to be defensive or apologetic about it, neither should we be arrogant or militant about it.

If this is the case, the question naturally presents itself: What then is our relationship with other faiths — can we reconcile with them in any way at all? We can "reconcile" with them in the sense of a dialogue and partnership for the common good of society. We can learn from and work with other religions to the extent that they propagate something of God's truth and values as seen in creation and basic morality. For example, on the basis of universal human rights we can and should work together for the common good, for reconciliation in racially and economically divided societies. During the 1980s our Johweto group cooperated with some multifaith marches and initiatives in resisting apartheid — and we did not lose our integrity as Christians! If anything, it enhanced our witness. A more current example is that we all need to cooperate on the basis of compassion to fight the AIDS pandemic, arguably the greatest weapon of mass destruction to date. We do not have to fear truth, no matter where it comes from (I am talking about self-evident truth, not speculation, half-truths or misbeliefs). Jesus' teachings on God and life can be tested and applied in life experience, and shown to be true to reality. If we believe that Jesus is the way, the truth and the life (Jn 14:6–7), as Christians we have nothing to fear by engaging other faiths in open dialogue and non-binding partnerships for societal reconciliation and nation building. In fact, we should take the initiative and lead the way in creating such partnerships, because many of our current social problems will only be resolved by large-scale cooperative effort.

Islam and Christianity

The need for large-scale cooperative effort can be seen in the international crisis that 9/11 has precipitated.[14] It has polarised the world into the "international alliance of free and just nations" and "international terrorism" or "the Christian West" and "Islamic fundamentalism". Public perceptions are very emotive and powerful and, ironically, even more so if they are based on half-truths and mis-beliefs. The perception that Christianity is part of the West's increasingly militaristic approach to international affairs is very real, especially in the Arab world. The deep resentment and rage among Muslims against the perceived "terrorist" Western nations has contributed to the horrific phenomenon of suicide bombers (a complex phenomenon with multiple motivating factors). Our witness and integrity as the church of Jesus Christ is once again before the world jury, and George Bush and Tony Blair's military responses to 9/11 have not necessarily helped the Christian cause. "Just war" can quickly become a guise for "holy war"[15] on both sides of the divide, the perpetrators and the retaliators. We easily and quickly believe we are killing for righteousness' sake, for God's sake. But which god? In whose name are we killing people? Because of the complexities of how the changed international context affects just war theology, my personal view — not a Vineyard position — is that Christians and the organised church should publicly distance themselves from such Western (and Eastern) militaristic attitudes and actions for the sake of their integrity and witness. I believe that nationalism and patriotism have no place in a Christian response to 9/11, or to any war. The church will have to do something daring and symbolic, similar to what Jesus did in Israel two thousand years ago, to change the international perceptions concerning Christianity, especially in the eyes of Muslims.

To reverse the view, how do Christians see Muslims? Arguably, our prejudice is equal to their prejudice against us. We must distinguish between the main body of Islam which deplores social injustice and acts of terrorism, such as suicide bombers, and those radical Muslims who believe in and perpetrate such deeds. The latter are blinded by hatred, driven by perverted "revenge-Jihad" (holy war) theologies, and deeply deceived by promises of paradise. The evil behind this will not stop until children are used as suicide bombers — which has already begun. Sacrificing children is the ultimate worship for Molech, the Ammonite god, who is Satan in one of his many disguises (Lev 18:21; 20:2–5; Deut 12:31). Fortunately, not all Muslims agree with such fanaticism. Even if the Koran teaches Jihad against "the infidel" until all the world has submitted to Allah and Islam, that does not make Islamic faith demonic, nor all Muslims terrorists, as many conservative Christians are tempted to believe. While we must not be naive about Islam, we must not demonise it. We need to inform ourselves first-hand by reading and study, by openly engaging with Muslims in dialogue and works of suffering love — and with all people and groups for that matter — in the name of Jesus.

Jesus of Nazareth, through his life and teachings, through his death and resurrection, has forever abolished holy war theology, whether it be Christian, Muslim or Jewish. In fact, Jesus moves us — as his followers — beyond all war theologies, even "just war", to his own example of laying down his life. We can call it true martyrdom. Christians should follow Jesus by doing the exact opposite to the suicide bombers: We should go to people, especially our enemies, with our bodies wrapped in God's unconditional love, and blow ourselves apart (metaphorically of course) in sacrificial service to the world, and in the process take as many people to heaven as we possibly can. Jesus said to his followers: "Love your enemies ... deny yourself, take up your cross and follow me." This is radical, non-violent love-intervention, which is daily, godly martyrdom, the exact opposite of the demonic "theology" and practice of the one-off suicide bombers.[16] Mother Teresa did this; for most of her adult life she laid down her life daily for the poor and dying. I am sure that she has taken many to heaven with her.

The Middle East crisis, Israel and our response as Christians

The growing international polarisation, with its West-East and Christian-Islamic tremors, has its epicentre in the Middle East — the Israeli/Palestinian conflict. How should Christians respond to this current crisis? Is reconciliation between Jew and Arab possible? I commented briefly on this issue in Chapter 6 under Paul's cultural mandate of the gospel. I pointed out that one's view of the situation is determined by one's interpretation of the Scriptures.

The essence of the issue is about a territorial view of God. The Jewish/Israeli view, as they interpret their Scriptures, is about a territorial faith and God: The holy land, the holy city, the holy temple mount, and Torah. The Islamic view (the decisive influence in the Palestinians and Arab world) is also about a territorial religion: The land's submission to Allah, Mohammed's ascension from Jerusalem, the Mosque of Omar, and the Koran. These two opposing "theologies" are actually political-territorial ideologies that will fight to the death unless there is an alternative. Christianity is that alternative: It is a post-territorial faith. The NT fulfils the prophetic stream in the OT by reinterpreting Judaism in Messiah Jesus as a post-territorial faith. From Moses (Deuteronomy) to David (Psalms) and to the prophets (Isaiah, Jeremiah, Ezekiel, Daniel, Zechariah, etc.) there is a promised prophetic or Messianic Judaism that transcends all the territorial boundaries, concepts and realities. This is fulfilled in Christ and Christianity — all territorial promises are fulfilled and universalised: The people of God are all who believe, God's kingdom is proclaimed to the ends of the earth ("the land"), the city is the coming heavenly New Jerusalem, and the temple is God's living people indwelt by his Spirit — both heavenly and earthly. This Christian interpretation of the Scriptures is the Vineyard understanding of it (a kingdom of God interpretation).

There are other frameworks of interpretation held among Christians. In broad terms, one can cite three general approaches to a theology of Israel, the Middle East crisis and our Christian response:

♦ *Dispensational theology* (popularly taught as Christian Zionism) is similar to the Jewish territorial interpretation. Dispensationalism says that God deals with humanity in dispensations: God dealt with Israel up to Jesus' death and resurrection, then with the church for the past two thousand years, and now with Israel once again, since the rebirth of the State of Israel in 1948. It is a "two covenant/two people of God" theology: There is one covenant for Israel, earthly and national, and there is another (new) covenant for the church, heavenly and universal. The two people of God have different identities and destinies. God's spiritual promises and salvation are fulfilled in Christ for the church, and God's national promises and salvation are fulfilled in the physical restoration of Israel to their land, given by divine right (the restoration of the holy city and temple follows). Any "land for peace" deal with Palestinians is against God's will and plays into the hands of the anti-Christ. Christians must support Zionist aspirations of full restoration, including Gaza and the West Bank. This approach translates into support of right-wing politics and Israeli nationalism.

♦ *Replacement theology* says that the church has replaced Israel in totality.

There is no present or future role or significance for Jews or Israel in God's plan. The Middle East crisis can only be settled by negotiation and principles of justice. This approach has been accused of anti-Semitism and a Palestinian bias.

♦ *A kingdom of God* interpretation says that through Messiah Jesus, the kingdom has broken into history creating a community of Messianic believers that transcends territory and ethnicity. There is only one people of God, the believers or church of Jesus Christ in Israel and the Palestinian areas, and internationally. This church should unite and prophesy to both sides of the power structures, which are "this evil age" phenomena. They say to Israelis and Palestinians that the kingdom of God has come, the dividing fence of hostility has come down in the torn body of *Yeshua ha Meshiach*. Reconciliation is possible, relationally and politically, because *Yeshua* has created one new nation that leads the way in a post-territorial freedom, identity and generosity. Holy territory, national destiny, prophetic restoration and such concepts are no longer valid and cannot be used to judge Christian support, or lack thereof, for Israel. Because of the transcendent kingdom, God has a plan to bring the Jews, as a people group, to faith in *Yeshua* when "the veil is lifted" (Rom 11:25–26, Jews in the Diaspora or in Israel).

The kingdom or Messianic ethic that we hold to has certain implications. It would say that the Israeli wall is not the answer, it will breed more hatred and more suicide bombers. The violence from either side, whether it be the Palestinian militias and suicide bombers, or the pre-emptive and retaliatory strikes of the Israeli authorities, has been paid for and absorbed in the body of Jesus on the cross; and it should be absorbed in the body of Messiah in the Middle East as the believers on either side of the divide "make up that which is lacking in the sufferings of Christ" through their ministry of reconciliation (Col 1:24 RAP). Reconciliation and peace is really possible. The believers must embody it in their peacemaking ministry as they establish *Shalom* between Jews and Arabs. In terms of political ethics, the kingdom would say that human rights, justice and negotiations should be the basis of land settlement and statehood, not divine right, prophetic promises, or violent intimidation. Jews (and Palestinians) need not fear and fight. *They can trust God because he sovereignly works out his purposes for Israel (and for the Arab nations) through human agency.* The Jews, of all people on earth, have learned through history that God is sovereign over all human rulers and uses even the worst of them to achieve his purposes for his people, as painful as that has been. God assures us that "all Israel will be saved" (Rom 11:26) and "justice (will) roll on like a river" (Amos 5:24) throughout the Middle East, and to the ends of the earth.

We do not take sides and support a political party, a particular government or nation. We pray for the visionary and courageous leadership that will be required to overcome the crisis. We support a negotiated, just settlement where both sides compromise for the common good. We oppose injustice and killing on either side of the divide. We oppose the notion that any criticism of Israel's government policies and actions, and/or agreement with the Palestinian cause for an independent state, is being anti-Semitic (anti-Semitism is hatred of Jews because they are Jews; in other words, for racial and religious reasons. This we utterly deplore. Sometimes opposition to unjust policies is the most patriotic action one can take, as some courageous elite Israeli soldiers and pilots have done).[17] We pray that the eyes that have been blinded will be opened to see the true Messiah, because this is a spiritual battle.[18] We support and pray for the Messianic body in Israel and the Palestinian areas, that like the prophets of old they will stand up, unite, and be counted — for justice' sake, for the sake of the poor and the dying, for the sake of making peace in Messiah's name.

THE RELATIONSHIP BETWEEN CHURCH AND STATE

We celebrate ten years of democracy in SA in 2004, including the miracle of negotiations and the elections in April 1994. Under apartheid we were a church in reaction to government and society, but since the "normalisation" of our political process, *how should the church relate to the government of the day?* What would a proactive relationship between church and state in a democratic and pluralistic context look like? What guidance does Scripture give us?[19]

In history there have been three general approaches to the church/state relationship:

♦ *Kingdom of God approach:* With the coming of the kingdom in the NT, there was a separation of church and state, which led to a kind of critical partnership with government and society. That meant a constructive engagement on matters of common good for society, and a critical resistance on matters harmful to society, especially when kingdom values and ethics were violated. I will elaborate on this approach below.

♦ *Constantinian approach:* The union of church and state, which produced an activist involvement either for the state, as in the "state church", or against the state, when the church actively supported the overthrow of the government at certain times in certain contexts. Israel and pagan societies practised this union of faith and politics, and it is seen today in certain Islamic states, especially those under *Shari'ah* law. In terms of Christianity, it became dominant from Constantine (311AD) on through the Middle Ages and is still the frame of reference for church/state relationships in many mainline churches today. The Anabaptists (1500s) were the first "Free Church" to break away from state/church control.

♦ *Pietistic approach:* After the Reformation there was an increasing tendency among some Reformed and evangelical revivalist church groups to withdraw from any engagement with the state and social issues. The pietistic approach is a withdrawal into an apolitical stance: "We do not meddle with politics, our work is spiritual." It amounts to nothing more than an escape from social responsibility and by its disengagement and silence it actually supports the status quo. I described in Chapter 4 how this silent approach was present in many evangelical, Pentecostal and charismatic churches during apartheid. It is still the frame of reference for some.

The kingdom approach in the church/state relationship

In the Vineyard, we reject the latter two approaches and seek to practise the kingdom approach. In Jesus, the kingdom of God entered into this age, redeeming and uniting people from all races and nations, forming "one new humanity" (Eph 2:14–16), a transnational people living under God's government. Jesus taught that the kingdom breaking through brought a separation of state and church. "Give to Caesar what is Caesar's" (recognise the state's realm of authority, e.g. pay taxes), but "give to God what is God's" (recognise the kingdom's authority of worship and allegiance to God, Matt 22:15–22).

Because the kingdom is "already" and "not yet", Christians are citizens both of the kingdom and of their national governments at the same time, but our kingdom citizenship takes precedence. It is our primary commitment and identity, meaning that in matters of belief, morality and conscience "we must obey God rather than man" (Acts 4:19). Only God is to be worshipped, and only he can give us ultimate identity and belonging. We should be weary of patriotism and nationalism. It is so easily exploited by government and various groups for their own purposes. For example, the age-old ploy of condemning people who criticise government policies for being unpatriotic or racist is damaging, as it stokes the fires of real racism. While Christians are witnesses to the coming kingdom, we should seek to be good citizens of the nation. We serve the state and society for the common good, in the humble and sacrificial tradition of the suffering Servant, not in the arrogant triumphalism of "let's take over the government and society in God's name", which is the spirit of the Crusades, the Inquisition, the pogroms and apartheid; all fruits of a Constantinian frame of reference.

In summary, there is a creative tension between state and church. We see government as a God-created structure with a realm of authority to uphold justice for the good of society, especially for the poor and oppressed (Ps 72; 82). In upholding justice and defeating evil, they are to use the "the sword" if necessary (Rom 13:1–7, this raises the debate on capital punishment or no death penalty, on "just war" or pacifism). The church is called to submit to the state for the common good, and to pray for them because we use different "weapons" to fight evil in society (1 Pet 2:13–17; 1 Tim 2:1–8; 2 Cor 10:3–6; Eph 6:12f).

The exception to the above is when government requires the church specifically, or the citizens in general, to adhere to policies that are unjust, that violate basic human rights and kingdom allegiance. Samuel warned the people and the king about the corrupting nature of power, especially when exercised apart from God (1 Sam 8:10–17). In that case, we must choose civil disobedience and submit to the consequences. If the state becomes draconian and evil (Rev 13), we are called upon to intervene non-violently and resist, even to martyrdom, for the sake of justice, the poor and oppressed. The creative tension between church and state plays itself out in many different ways, depending on what government does and how socially engaged and healthy the church is. We should be the "prophetic conscience" of the state and society.

Some implications for a "critical partnership" with the state

Many practical implications emerge from this critical partnership or kingdom approach to the church/state relationship. I will mention four. The first three assume a multiparty democratic context, the last implication is more universal in its application:

Firstly, the "secular state" is good for the church: The church in SA was "protected" by the state under apartheid; now it is not. This is good. It will cause us to have greater integrity and conviction in our life and witness as we "compete" in the open "marketplace" with all other options and belief systems. The church must go further by making its distinctive contribution in the formation of a "public theology" to guide "political policy" for the good of society.[20] The state is a "this age" phenomenon and in that sense it is "secular". We do not believe in "Christian government" in a "Christian nation" — only Jesus will bring that about when he comes. Until then we must live the kingdom. We cannot buy into the Constantinian premise that justifies the existence of Christian political parties. Any failure by them reflects directly on the church, as was the case under apartheid.

Secondly, the church should not be party-political: Distinguishing between the government of the day and the political party that it represents is important in our dealings with the state. As a church we should never identify with any one political party. Neither should pastors or prominent church leaders publicly identify themselves with any one party. As citizens they should vote privately for a party according to their conscience, but as church leaders they should teach their people the criteria of evaluating the parties, freeing the people to vote according to their own conscience. Only in an unjust situation when things are morally polarised should the church say who to vote for. Pastors, ministers and bishops who become politicians should relinquish their church positions and titles. Once again, any failure by them is an embarrassment to the church and Christianity. However, we should pray for and support individual Christians who become politicians — on an individual basis, not a party basis — because they are witnesses to the kingdom in politics, as other Christians are in other spheres of life.

Thirdly, government programmes and political parties should be carefully evaluated, especially when national elections take place: Identifying too closely with a particular government programme or party political policy can be costly for the church. Even more so if the church receives money or benefits directly from it — it compromises the ability of the church to be prophetic. A critical distance, with constructive engagement, is the rule to go by. How do we evaluate parties, policies and programmes, especially when it comes to deciding who to vote for? The criteria for evaluation are clear, but applying them in a "morally mixed" political context is not that straightforward. Begin by informing yourself about each party's leadership, policies, programmes and track record. Then apply the following criteria (as in 2 Sam 23:3–4; Ps 72; 82; Rom 13):

- ◆ Is there respect or fear for God? This does not necessarily mean they must be Christian.
- ◆ Do their leaders have godly character — what is their character content?
- ◆ What is their level of competence for the job and discipline in their work?
- ◆ What are their beliefs, policies and practices in terms of ethical values, e.g. their treatment of people, especially the poor; valuing the sanctity of life; honouring the rule of law; upholding human rights.
- ◆ What is their track record? What fruit have they produced in society?

The answers to these questions should guide you to a vote of conviction, and will help you determine levels of participation in any party political process or government programme that you may want to be involved in.

Fourthly, the church's greatest and distinctive contribution to state and society is ongoing "spiritual warfare". What do I mean by this? I do not mean a disengagement from the state and social issues into a private spiritual battle with invisible forces.[21] The "principalities and powers" (Eph 3:10; 6:12) are invisible spiritual forces that seek to control nations via false beliefs and ideologies, corrupt desires and socio-political structures. They incarnate themselves in the state and societal structures through people, just as God's invisible kingdom indwells and makes itself visible through (God's) people. Hence the clash of two kingdoms, at both spiritual and social (or tactile) levels. These levels are dynamically integrated, not separate spheres of operation. When the kingdom is in ascendancy — through the church's inner health and societal engagement — "righteousness exalts a nation"; in contrast, when sin abounds, "a nation is disgraced" (Prov 14:34). I referred earlier to the distinctive "weapons" that the church uses in this spiritual warfare against the fallen powers. In summary, they are:

♦ *Prayer* (1 Tim 2:1f). We pray to the One who has all the power to discipline all the powers. We do not pray to or verbally attack the "heavenly" or spiritual powers (Jude 8–10) — this is different to rebuking and driving out "embodied" spirits in order to free people, as Jesus modelled for us (Mk 1:21–27 cf. Acts 10:38). We must also confess and repent of the church and nation's sins. Historical and corporate sin, complicit and associative guilt, are realities we need to deal with. We must identify with church and societal failure by "standing in the gap" in order to avert God's judgements (Dan 9; Ezek 22:30–31). We can do this in prayer before God, and in public action before the nation — as in the Men's Repentance March (Chapter 6).

♦ *Presence* (Matt 5:13–16). In being true to our nature as church, we are present in society as the salt that makes the nation palatable to God. Our presence prevents the spread of decay. By doing "good works" in society, we make our presence felt; we shine God's light, driving back the powers of darkness and showing the way for the nation.

♦ *Proclamation or prophecy* (Ezek 3:18–21; Heb 4:12; Eph 6:12–18). In teaching God's ideas, values and beliefs, and by evangelising society with the gospel of Christ, we destroy Satan's kingdom. By warning people, politicians and the nation of the consequences of their sinful choices, we demolish strongholds and defeat evil in society — besides not ending up with their blood on our hands! Our sword, in contrast to the state (Rom 13:4), is not aggression or violence in any form, but the power and persuasion of the Truth, both proclaimed and embodied — the "sword of the Spirit, which is the Word of God" (Eph 6:17).

Application to the African context

Africa — and parts of Central and South America — is in desperate need of political stability and economic development. The church needs to cooperate with the stronger democratic governments in finding ways to intervene assertively in situations of injustice, dictatorship and devastation. We have a truly tragic political and economic history, and it cannot be blamed on colonialism or the Western nations. The potential for a fundamental turn around is very real, especially if the church makes its presence felt (over the past two decades there has been an unparalleled explosion of church growth in Africa).

The church must be strong and clear in its prophetic witness, and challenge African politicians to integrity, servanthood and genuine democratic values. Where are the prophets of Africa? We need more people like Desmond Tutu who have the courage and moral authority to confront national and international leaders without bias. The culture of abuse of power and disregard for human rights urgently needs to be reversed, and it should start in the African church. If Christian leaders set the example by renouncing positions, titles, power pursuit and financial enrichment, and lead from integrity and self-sacrificial service, politicians will be challenged either to follow suit or persecute the Christian leaders to keep them quiet. The worst is when Christian priests and ministers become politicians and presidents, and become corrupt autocrats. *We face an overwhelming crisis in character and leadership on our continent — in both church and civil society.* At one level, solving the problems of Africa is complex and requires a multi-strategic approach, but at another level it is fairly simple: Appoint people of character, people who are disciplined and hardworking, honest and principled, to positions of responsibility. Things will change! Skill and competence come second to character. Our challenge is to grow righteous leadership across the board, because "when the righteous thrive, the people rejoice; when the wicked rule, the people groan" (Prov 29:2).[22]

We encourage and support initiatives like the African Renaissance — also called the New Partnership for Africa's Development (NEPAD). It is envisioned and led by President Thabo Mbeki and other key African leaders. If these leaders commit to serious mutual accountability in terms of governance and a code of ethics, and active partnership for economic development, the people of Africa will have reason to hope for a better future. This process has culminated in the African Union (AU) launching a Pan African parliament (March 2004) for the political growth and economic development of the continent.[23] The Southern African Development Community (SADC) is a regional expression of this African Renaissance, where SA, together with its neighbours, is working together in growing cooperation for the common good. We pray for the success of Nepad, and should do all we can to support it. It would be a disaster if it turns out to be a paper tiger, as the OAU was, instead of reaching its wonderful potential. The vision and process must not be left to the politicians. The church needs to pursue a critical partnership in supporting NEPAD and SADC, cooperating with governmental and non-governmental organisations for the healing, restoration and development of Africa.

In concluding the application to the African context, I want to raise some broader ethical questions. We have examined much that is corrupt in the West, including the legacy of colonialism. We have seen the evil of apartheid, and racism in general. Can we examine the African worldview? What is the right context in which this could take place? Who is qualified to do this, and what would that analysis include? Perhaps no white person has the right to make this examination. I am sure it has been tackled in some ways, but as Africans, we must explore our worldview on all these matters, on politics and economics, male sexuality and the rights of women and children. What about the extended family and its outworking in the modern economy? It seems so exploitative to young people who cannot save because whatever they earn goes to support the extended family. What about labola (bridal payment) and its relevance in today's economy? There are many ethical questions that one could raise under their relevant themes below. I mention them as a unique African challenge with regard to our African worldview.

DEVELOPMENT AND GLOBALISATION

The north-south economic divide has been an issue of ethical debate and concern for many decades. It describes the rich North Americans and Europeans versus the poor Central and South American, African and (some) Asian nations. The categories of First and Third World have all but fallen away. Likewise, since the collapse of communism in the late 1980s and early 1990s, the capitalist/communist divide has disappeared and capitalism has been internationalised. The current terminology is the industrialised nations (including Australia, Japan and other Pacific rim countries) versus the developing and underdeveloped nations (mostly in Africa, South America, Eastern Europe and Asia). The ethical concerns and the tensions between the groups are increasing. And this is taking place within the context of growing globalisation. What does this mean? What are some of the issues involved? And how should we respond as Christians?

The meaning of globalisation, economics and capitalism

Globalisation is essentially the dynamic process of formal and informal trade with a growing global consciousness. Globalisation is about the economic and political relationships, and the communication and technological systems, that are straddling the earth like an all-encompassing invisible octopus. Its tentacles reach into every corner of the globe, forming and manipulating people and communities in both overt and hidden ways. Globalisation is shrinking the globe into a world consciousness, a common culture, a technological network and economic system that is embodied in phrases like the "global village" and "spaceship earth". Although the emergence of globalisation is largely due to the spread of information technology across all sectors of society, the power behind it, and the face that it presents, is capitalism, or "the new capitalism" as Peter Heslam calls it.[24]

This new capitalism has become the dominant global ideology, making national and other boundaries invisible, and raising many challenging issues, especially for politicians, legal experts and ethicists. And not least, for Christians. The ideology or god of materialism ("Mammon" as Jesus calls it, Matt 6:24) is still the greatest challenge to the church.[25] Sadly, for most Christians and even church leaders, economics and its related ethical challenges is unknown territory. It is too important to leave to the economists. We need to apply biblical theology not only to personal materialism, but also to the emerging global economy so that we can sustain and affirm life, protect the earth and build authentic human community.

Economics is basically the process of matching and managing material resources and human needs. The key elements in the economic process include *extracting* what we need from the base resources in nature, *processing* and *producing*, *distributing* and *consuming*. The result is that human needs are met, and waste is produced — which also has to be managed. The management of this economic process leads to various economic and political systems and structures: from "free for all" liberal democratic capitalism, to medium government intervention and control such as democratic socialism (a mix of socialism and capitalism), to full ideological and economic state control such as communism (pure Marxist socialism).[26] Capitalism has become the order of the day.

Information technology has globalised capitalism into a boundary-less system.

Capitalism in its globalised form means that the economic process of extraction, processing, production, distribution and consumption is being driven by the "invisible forces" of local and worldwide supply and demand. People have certain needs which create a demand, which becomes a market supplied by entrepreneurs. This is called the market-driven economy of liberal democratic capitalism. The ideal of capitalism is that incentives, profits and the entrepreneurial spirit of people will lead to the production of more than is needed. The surplus creates wealth and prosperity, which will "trickle down" to the less entrepreneurial, the less fortunate in society. Capitalism purports to increase the size of the pie so that all can have a piece, with more left over. However, we have to ask: Is this really the case? Is there equal opportunity for all to get into the system and to benefit? Who really benefits, and at what cost?

The ethical challenge

The ethical challenge lies in the economic process being fair and just for the good of all. This includes evaluating all economic systems and political structures from an ethical viewpoint. The ethical ideal is equity, prosperity and harmony for all (as it will be in heaven, God's *Shalom*), not allowing some people to have most of the resources and benefits while most people have little or nothing — largely the case in our global village. Furthermore, the ethical challenge is to disallow the radical depletion of natural resources in the economic process, as well as their contamination through waste, pollution and over-population. This too is the tragic truth: The world is facing a serious crisis with regard to resources, pollution and population growth. Many respected scientists are warning of a global catastrophe if we do not reverse the current trends.[27] The greater the gap between the haves and the have-nots, the greater the potential for conflict and war over much needed resources. The poor have led violent revolutions over the price of bread, and wars are being fought over oil reserves, and will be fought over fresh water supplies. (The reasons that politicians give for wars often mask the underlying economic interests. In this sense Karl Marx was right: Money makes the world go round!)

We cannot live in good conscience when over 50% of the world's population lives on US$2,00 a day or less. We simply have to find ways in our economic systems and structures for a just sharing of resources if we are going to survive, let alone thrive, on planet earth. It is directly within the interests of the industrialised nations to genuinely "step down" — in the spirit of what I discussed in Chapter 7 in terms of group and structural reconciliation — in order to help developing and underdeveloped nations to "step up" without any stings attached. What will it take for this to happen? Will global capitalism allow for this?

Capitalism may be the most proficient economic system to date. It has produced the greatest amount of wealth and opportunities for the greatest number of people — compared to all other systems. It has brought liberty and freedom in many nations. There are other positives, but this does not make it a God-given system (as some may suppose).[28] Capitalism — the free flow of ideas, production and trade according to supply and demand — requires a strong moral context or else it can lead to all sorts of greed and exploitation. The fruit has clearly not been all good and the statistics reveal another side to the balance sheet. In many areas where capitalism has been allowed greatest freedom of expression, it has come at great cost: Increasing discrepancies between rich and poor; growing poverty with social dislocation and exclusion; overpopulation of marginalised groups; crime and violence; family breakdown; financial instability and indebtedness; human exploitation and overwork; abuse of power, and the depletion of natural resources, pollution and environmental damage.

All these pose grave threats to social and human well-being. The scale of these threats is so great that a complacent or naively optimistic attitude towards globalisation and the "trickle-down effect" is seriously misplaced. The rich and super-rich, who are increasingly trans- or multinational in location and global in citizenship and consciousness, are profoundly affected by these challenges, whether they face them or not. One can only secure oneself for so long, then reality bites and all suffer, including the rich. The spirit of Jesus says: If you lose your life in caring for others, you find your (God's) real life, both here and in eternity (Matt 10:39 cf. Jn 12:25). We are facing a worldwide crisis. The discrepancies between rich and poor, and the fallout from the emerging global economic system, is a classic set-up for conflict and war. States have failed, there is vast illegal immigration, and cultures that have been sidelined by global progress are vulnerable to extremist ideologies that promote violence. The potential triumph of evil is far greater than humanity has ever seen or imagined. Justice and care, and even compassion, has to intervene for the good of those who suffer and are marginalised by the system.

How do we respond to globalisation?

As Christians, how should we respond to globalisation? We do not need to over-react by writing it off as demonic, the plan of conspiratorial powers to take over the world — be it the Illuminati, the one world government or the New World

Order.[29] We need to evaluate globalisation on sound theological and ethical grounds, not on prophetic paranoia. We need to move beyond mere expressions of compassion towards victims and moral indignation towards the perpetrators. We can do this by addressing the underlying ideas and causes, inspiring people with vision and a work ethic, while bringing relief and empowerment to the poor, thereby seeking to narrow the gap between rich and poor.

This means engaging with the substance and structures of globalised capitalism, while simultaneously committing to wholistic development work in underdeveloped nations.[30] We must work at the level of public policy formation, entering the ethical debate, making representations, lobbying and even protesting if necessary. But we must also encourage the process of wealth creation — and not always criminalise the wealth-makers — while seeking moral responsibility in how it is created and how it can be used to empower the poor effectively. This would include working for the protection and development of minority groups and marginalised nations. For example, in SA we support in principle policies such as affirmative action; they level the economic playing field so that historical imbalances can be redressed and there can be equal opportunity for all. However, if the policies are applied in a way that leads to nepotism and curbs entrepreneurial initiative, it becomes destructive. Internationally, for example, industrialised nations could give developing nations a real "step up" by cancelling their national loans and World Bank debts. Just imagine what would happen if we took God's idea of Jubilee seriously (Lev 25) and had a global jubilee where all national and international debts were cancelled. It would lead to true liberty, human care and compassion and, in all likelihood, a more fair and empowering international economic system would emerge.[31]

 POVERTY, LAND AND UNEMPLOYMENT

If we have to ask what is the most pressing challenge to our society in SA, I would say it is poverty, land and unemployment. Some would say it is the AIDS pandemic, while others maintain that crime and violence, or even the family in crisis is our greatest challenge. The following seven SACLA giants are not in any order of priority — they were presented at the conference as equally challenging, requiring equal attention. The statistics that I quote, including some of my explanations with regard to these giants, are drawn from SACLA reports (especially from a research brief drawn up by Dr Hannah Britton and Paul Graham on the seven giants) and from government and non-government sources.[32]

The words of Jesus: "The poor you will always have with you" (Matt 26:11), are often (mis)used in defence of not doing more for the poor. Little do people realise that it was actually Moses' phrase that Jesus was quoting. It is found in the context of Moses' comprehensive instructions on generous and sacrificial care for the poor (Deut 15:1–18, especially v. 11). Moses says that precisely because we will always have the poor with us, we must help them generously. The context in which Jesus used the words is itself revealing (Matt 26:6–16): The disciples complained that the expensive perfume the woman "wasted" on Jesus — equal to a year's salary — could have been better spent on the poor. But ironically it was being lavished on the poor, and they did not see it. Judas, who protested "the waste", was conspiring to betray Jesus for thirty pieces of silver (Matt 26:14–16). That was the price of a wounded slave (Ex 21:32). This twist ironically put Jesus in the place of the poor — he is not only identified with all wounded slaves, he is also the poor man of Ps 41 who is betrayed by his close friend who eats his bread (Ps 41:9 cf. Mk 14:18).

All this is simply to say that generous care for the poor is true devotion to Jesus, and lavish devotion to Jesus should lead to generous care for the poor. As Mother Teresa says, when we care for the poor and dying we actually "minister to Christ in the distressing disguise of the poor".[33] It is our privilege to do this as part of our worship to God. The church must not leave the problem of poverty, land struggle and unemployment to the government. If the church did something sacrificial and symbolic, like the woman in Matt 26, it would bring about enormous hope in a nation where the discrepancies between the rich and poor have been scandalous to say the least. We need to fully embrace the priority or option for the poor.[34]

Twenty-two million people in SA — half of our population — live below the poverty line, which is based on a household income of less than SAR401 a month.[35] As inflation and cost of living increase daily, the ability of households to survive is threatened. Detailed studies have been done on the nature and extent of poverty in SA, and what can be done about it.[36]

The challenge of unemployment

Two key dimensions of the nature and challenge of poverty are unemployment and the land issue. The unemployment figures continue to rise in SA. It is not easy to get an accurate figure, but the current unemployment rate is definitely above 30%, with the expanded or outside figure at 46%. This is cause for great concern — in the USA financial analysts are worried because their unemployment is rising above 6%. Poverty and inequality is part of the racism of the past, although this is slowly changing: 16,6% of South Africans receive 72% of all the income, and as of 2003 half of these are now black people (soon to be the majority. The super-rich in SA are growing rapidly, radically increasing the economic and power gap, and the ethical credibility and tension, between the rich and the poor). Another 16,6% of South Africans receive 17,2% of the income, and only 1,6% of these are black people. At the very bottom of our society is the remaining 67% of the population that share the remaining 10,6% of the total income, and only 2% of this group are white. In other words, the overwhelming majority of poor people are black and, sadly, have always been.

Unemployment is a terrible scourge in our land as it traps people in the cycle of poverty.[37] People need a job to have money, but it takes money to find a job. Transport costs have to be paid. More often than not, money is needed for basic skills training, child care and even résumés and interview clothing. The twin problems of lack of jobs and the cycle of poverty prevent the vast majority of unemployed from finding work. Handouts are not the answer — although a major proposed policy initiative, called Basic Income Grant, plans to eradicate abject poverty for 6 million South Africans by putting R100 every month into the hands of the poor. *The real challenge is to promote education, do skills training across the board — accessible to all — and to create jobs, develop a good work ethic and foster a job-creating economy.* The average economic growth in SA since the 1994 elections is 2,8% a year. We are making good progress, but the economy needs to grow much faster to alleviate the unemployment situation.

What can the church do? We must teach a theology of work — the dignity and God-given purpose of work — which goes beyond a theology of care for the poor and marginalised.[38] In other words, besides feeding and clothing the poor, which is a very important ongoing ministry, we can do the following: Give our people vision, faith and instruction regarding work and life purpose; break the hopelessness and change the mindsets of our people by sourcing key business and other leaders in our congregations; getting them to strategise how they, with the help of their churches, can do skills training, develop self-help schemes, plan wholistic community development, literary classes, launch entrepreneurial ventures and small businesses, open doors for jobs for the unemployed in the church, and generally find ways to create jobs. We need models that will help churches to do this.[39] As God's family of faith, the church can help the unemployed in particular, and help those who are made redundant, to process the personal issues of dignity and self-image, purpose and meaning. Churches should also use their properties and buildings during the week to put their jobless people to work, to do skills training and facilitate social services.

The challenge of the land

At a deeper level, the problem of poverty revolves around land, which includes housing and ownership. I mentioned the land issue in Chapter 4: We have a legacy from the Native Land Act of 1913 and apartheid, that 13% of the population — whites — owned 83% of the land in SA. Over 3 million people were forcibly removed from their land and relocated into "locations". Since 1994, the new democratic government implemented the Reconstruction and Development Programme (RDP). Part of this programme has been housing development and the land restitution and redistribution process. The crisis of homelessness, urbanisation and squatter settlements is very real indeed: Our big cities are being filled and surrounded by informal and mostly unplanned and unhygienic settlements. The rural areas are as poor as ever, and need intentional economic development to keep the poor from flocking to the cities. The need for landownership and restitution to redress the incredible land imbalance and forced removals of the past is equally, if not more urgent.

In terms of housing: From 1996 to 2001 the number of households increased by 21% from 9,7 million ("m" from now on) to 11,8 m, as compared to an 11% increase in the national population in the same period. In terms of land restitution: 79 694 land claims were lodged after 1994, and by December 2003 there had been 42 556 lawful settlements, which constitutes a redistribution of 800 000 hectares (besides 1,56 m hectares redistributed for urbanisation, housing and other purposes). This sounds like encouraging progress, but I must qualify.

I say "lawful settlements" because the land issue is highly symbolic and emotive. If the process of restitution and redistribution of land in SA does not speed up, it can become unruly as has happened in Zimbabwe. President Robert Mugabe directly sanctioned violent land invasions in 2000. As unlawful as land invasions may be, and as dictatorial as Mugabe may be, the brutal symbolic reality is that whites came into Africa and took most of the land from the blacks at the barrel of a gun. Two wrongs don't make it right. If the 4 000 white Zimbabwe farmers[40] had, after independence in 1980, rezoned their farms and given ownership of tracks of fertile land to their labourers and other landless people, it might have shifted things deep in the psyche of the nation and prevented the mass takeover of farms. They could still be sitting on their farms, albeit smaller farms, with a sense of peace and justice that the poorest of the poor (the farm labourers — the same in most countries) were empowered. *Zimbabwe is a prophetic warning to white farmers and landowners in SA.* A dramatic form of restitution, as discussed in Chapter 7, should be entered into. A meaningful and symbolic gesture can defeat the powers of desperation and lawlessness, and empower the landless with dignity, ownership and the means of production. Imagine the impact if the current 53 000 white farmers in SA tithed their land by rezoning at the very least 10% of what they own, and gave title deed to their labourers. Imagine the impact if the Christian farm owners did this — and more — on the basis of Christian convictions in terms of land and restitution?[41]

If you think this is a storm in a teacup, or that this proposal is unrealistic idealism, consider the following: At the advent of democracy in 1994, the 55 000 white commercial farmers, who constituted 0,15% of our national population, owned 85,2 m hectares of the total land mass of 122,5 m hectares of SA, i.e. they owned 70% of the land, an average of 1 500 hectares per white farmer. By comparison, the 1,4 m blacks that were engaged in agricultural cultivation in 1994 eked out an existence on less than 13% of the land. About 50% of them cultivated an area of less than one hectare, 22% an area between one and two hectares and only 2% had more than ten hectares under cultivation. Is there something wrong with this picture? What are we going to do about this scandalous inequality? Is this not a classic set-up for conflict? Since 1991 more than 1 500 white farmers have been killed, although the government has attributed this mainly to crime. We must step in and help — in 1994 the new democratic government promised to redistribute 30% of white-owned land to blacks over a period of five years. Ten years later only 2,8% has been transferred.[42] Time, credibility and patience is running out fast.

This discussion refers to a theology of land, stewardship and God's economy: All land ultimately belongs to God and any landowner is God's steward to use it in a fair and equitable way, empowering local people with a reasonable quality of life. It also refers to basic human rights: The right to land, housing, ownership and work. Christians should lead the way in these matters, in terms of ethical thinking and visionary possibilities, and practical involvement in helping the landless, the homeless, the unemployed, the poor and marginalised.[43] With God, all things are possible!

THE HIV AND AIDS PANDEMIC [44]

I first met Thabo (not his real name) as a young man at high school. He came to our Johweto meetings in Soweto in the mid-1980s. With an endearing smile, bright mind and passionate heart for Jesus and social justice, Thabo crept into our hearts. We sponsored his education at school and then university, where he acquired a degree with honours. He got a good job and met and married a lovely young lady. She gave birth to their only child. In the late 1990s he repeatedly got sick and did not seem to recover properly. In 2001, barely three months before he died, he finally admitted to his wife that he had AIDS, and asked her to tell the church leadership. She did this just two weeks before he died. Obviously he could not bring himself to disclose his HIV status when it was diagnosed in the early to mid-1990s. I remember Thabo with great fondness, but I feel sad when I think of how he coped with his silent shame and suffering through those terminal years — from the time when he first knew until he died.

This is the tragedy of our nation, and our continent. We are in a war situation, a war of silence and shame, in a life and death struggle against the most effective weapon of mass destruction to date.

The extent of the HIV/AIDS challenge

More than 600 people were dying every day in SA from AIDS-related illnesses in December 2002. Already one in every three of all adult deaths can be attributed to AIDS. There are not many South Africans who have not been touched personally by AIDS-related deaths of family or friends. HIV/AIDS affects every one of us, whether we know it or not.

The problem is gigantic, to say the least. According to UNAIDS, from 1981 to December 2002, 70 million people have been infected with HIV worldwide, and 28 million of them have died of AIDS. Of the remaining 42 million people living with HIV/AIDS, 30 million are in sub-Saharan Africa. In December 2003, just over 5 million or about one in eight South Africans lived with HIV/AIDS. The number is expected to rise to 7,5 million and beyond in the next seven to ten years unless drastic measures are taken to reverse the trend. Our most badly affected area is KwaZulu-Natal with one in four people being HIV+. The continuing rate of new infections is the real challenge, the current daily rate of infection in SA is estimated to be 2 000, and worldwide about 14 000. If nothing changes between 2004 and 2010, it is estimated that up to 50% of all South African teenagers now fifteen years old will not see their twenty-fifth birthday.

Can you begin to imagine the effect that this will have on our nation? Can you imagine the effect it is having on our economy? Most of those who are dying, and will die, from AIDS are the economically productive people between the ages of 18 and 45. But worse, what about the devastating impact on the home and family? By 2006 there will be over 1 million AIDS orphans under the age of 15 in SA, and it will probably double by 2010. What will happen to them? Who will care for them, let alone raise them into responsible adulthood? The church urgently needs to get involved in building orphanages and finding ways to care for AIDS babies and orphans — this is the essence of true godliness and religion (Jas 1:27).

The people most vulnerable to HIV/AIDS are women and children. Babies are infected through their mothers, women are more easily infected than men (55% of all HIV+ people in sub-Saharan Africa are women), and women and children are sexually abused by men. The tragic reality is that many women cannot say "no" to sex with men, and even if they do, it does not help as they are then forced. We must crush the myth — a devastating, demonic deception — that having sex with a virgin can cure you of HIV/AIDS. This legitimises the horrendous culture of child abuse at the hands of men. Equally, the myths that say it is a homosexual and/or a black disease (because of their promiscuity — of all white populations, SA has the highest incidence of HIV/AIDS), that women are the cause of HIV/AIDS or that it is a conspiracy of the powerful are lies that must be exposed and forcefully refuted, especially by men.

On the other hand, we must assert the truth that AIDS *is* caused by the HIV virus, which is passed on through body fluids as in genital sexual contact and direct exposure to blood. Kissing does not spread HIV, and neither can you contract it by touching or eating with a person with AIDS; in fact, they really need caring touch and compassionate understanding. Environmental factors such as unemployment, poverty, superstition and lack of education must be taken into account in the spread of, and war against, HIV/AIDS. These contexts are conducive to ignorance and superstition, loss of meaning and moral restraint, and often help the culture of abuse.

Responding to HIV/AIDS as Christians, government and society

What is our response as Christians? If we were living with the OT prophets, we would tear our clothes, put on sackcloth and ashes and cry out for mercy because we would see this horror as a sign of God's judgement on humanity, on our nation.[45] Not only is this prophetic worldview or sentiment not PC, it is aggressively condemned in our postmodern world as archaic, narrow-minded bigotry. This is precisely part of the problem: Society has become arrogant and rebellious, without any fear of God "before their eyes" (Rom 3:18, read 1:18–32; 3:9–18). We (society) think we know it all. The prevailing universal ethic of "love" actually means "do whatever feels right, and let others do whatever they want, just don't judge or condemn anyone ..." This permissive or, more accurately, deceptive "love and acceptance" ethic is based on a godless, naive view of human nature. True love and acceptance does not mean sanction or endorsement. To love truly, you have to discern responsibility, accountability and consequences, and press them home in order to break the self-deception and psychological denial that people are in. Only then can they be saved from the death-wish or "power of suicide" that they have chosen. Only then can they be freed in their thinking and lifestyles to make new life-choices, for responsibility and morality, healing and wholeness.

I do not mean that Christians and the church must be arrogant or judgemental. We should humble ourselves before God and the HIV/AIDS sufferers, and confess our failure to build moral fibre and restraint in society. On our knees, we should serve them with sensitivity and compassion in various ministries of forgiveness and healing, care and preparation for a peaceful and dignified death. We have lost our saltiness and influence by being morally compromised ourselves — sexual sin is rife in the church, and our history of arrogant judgementalism has turned the world away from us. Judging HIV+ people is merciless and damaging. The tragedy is that there are as many people who contract HIV against their will by accident or by being victims of other people's sinful and violating behaviour as there are who contract HIV due to their own sinful choices. The public shame and prison of silence affecting HIV+ people — with the taboo of not talking about sex and abuse, or any form of public confession — desperately needs to be broken, for the sake of the individual and the nation. When national leaders, like cabinet ministers and high-profile community leaders, die from AIDS and it is reported as "pneumonia" and other lies, the steel of silence and the deception of denial is reinforced, and literally kills thousands more in the nation. This shameless hypocrisy should be soundly rebuked. We need courageous honesty more than ever in our lives, and in our nation.

The government and society's basic message of safe sex ("just use condoms whenever you have sex") to stop HIV/AIDS is hopelessly inadequate and immoral. It effectively furthers HIV/AIDS by implicitly promoting sexual immorality and violence. Whether we like it or not, immorality remains the primary means of spreading HIV/AIDS — with the growing millions of victims "sinned against" in its wake. The church should oppose the safe sex message assertively and promote abstinence (before marriage) and faithfulness (in marriage), and persuade the government to do likewise. Prevention in the form of education and moral restraint is still the most effective way of combating and overcoming this pandemic.[46]

What am I saying in terms of a Christian response to HIV/AIDS? I am stating the age-old biblical truth that God's judgements and mercies (redemption) go hand in hand, and we must face both aspects with conviction, compassion and sensitivity.[47] Jesus came to save people from judgement by destroying the works of the devil (1 Jn 3:8) as he had compassion on the "untouchables". He broke the social and religious taboos by embracing and healing the lepers and other socially ostracised people. Christians should likewise lead the way in truly loving and accepting HIV+ people. We should be examples of compassion and care. HIV/AIDS sufferers are ultimately victims of an evil that has come upon all humanity. We must create safe places for them, where we can win their trust and help them to be really honest ("the truth will set you free", Jn 8:32), to break their shame and silence through the love, forgiveness and healing presence of God in their lives. Then they can become effective evangelists of abstinence and faithfulness. They can break the social stigma of HIV/AIDS, the power of shame and silence, and turn the tide for a new tomorrow.

Local churches should unite and share resources in developing compassionate and caring HIV/AIDS ministries in the form of education programmes, home-based care, and building and running clinics, hospices and orphanages. This is an unprecedented opportunity for the church to care for and literally lead hundreds of thousands of people to Christ before they die. Is there any other form of ministry that is closer to God's heart than caring for HIV+ babies, orphaned children, vulnerable women, and terminally ill and dying people?[48]

VIOLENCE

Violence is a global challenge, and is getting worse by the day, even in so-called safe or non-violent societies. Living with violence has become normal for most people in SA, even in our post-apartheid society. Tragically, it is endemic in our communities, a common characteristic marking most of our relationships. It threatens our new democracy because it threatens the dignity, safety, security and advancement of individuals and communities. Violence also contributes to the culture of distrust, hostility, fear and retribution. This giant has to be dealt with decisively for there to be any real hope of a meaningful future in SA.

This is a big issue and an extensive subject.[49] I will give an overview of the nature of violence, and then how we should think about and respond to it as Christians. The goal is to create a non-violent, peacemaking, harmonious culture and society.

The nature and types of violence

Violence takes many forms, individually, structurally, socially and internationally. It eventually becomes "normal" as a cultural expression. Our eyes must be opened so that we can see it for what it really is and reject it, replacing it with patterns of tolerance, love, morality, justice and peace. What are the realities and the main types of violence in SA?

- *Criminal violence.* Conservatively, 652 480 incidents of violent crime were reported for 2001 — in a population of 42 million. This included the highest reported murder and rape statistics internationally. Greater Johannesburg, with a population of about 6 million — including Soweto — has on average 50 murders a day. It is also reported to be the rape capital of the world. Our newspapers are filled with daily accounts of gruesome murders and violent assaults, each of which affects our individual and national psyche. This type of violence also raises the question of support for capital punishment or abolition of the death penalty.

- *Gender violence.* Women and girls (all children, for that matter) of all races face unconscionable levels of sexual harassment, molestation, abuse and assault. Conservative estimates of sexual assaults, including those that go unreported, are as high as 1 079 520 for 2001. The psychological and societal trauma of this form of violence is extensive and long-term in its damage and effects.

- *Family violence.* This is closely related to gender violence. The level of domestic violence between partners (mostly man on woman) and child abuse is not easy to determine as it mostly goes unreported. Children are particularly vulnerable to abuse in the home — just on 20 000 rapes of children were reported in 2001. The growing phenomenon of family murders/ suicides (mostly perpetrated by the husband/father) is the outward trauma of the daily context of mental and emotional stress and violence in the home.

- *Economic violence.* The level of abject poverty (half of our population) leaves the majority of our people without regular food and basic services — like running water. This too is a form of violence that often goes unnoticed, but is the most widespread of all. It contributes to, and creates a context, for many other forms of violence and human rights abuses.

- *Political and racial violence.* This type of violence, although dramatically below the levels we experienced during apartheid, continues to plague our communities. In areas like KwaZulu-Natal, gangs motivated by political allegiances still engage in factional and tribal warfare that tears families and towns apart. Periodic racial violence — black/white — still hits the headlines, and xenophobia (the fear of other races) is fostering increasing levels of violence against immigrants and refugees. Political, racial and economic violence also raises the question of war, the ethics of conventional, civil, guerrilla and now "pre-emptive" warfare.

In SA, this culture of violence stems from the history of our violent past and, to some extent, the uncertainty of our nation's future. The phenomenon of violence is, at its heart, about power and control. Individuals turn to violence as an answer to their problems, tensions, conflicts and insecurities. Communities use violence as a means of asserting their security in an insecure environment, asserting their dominance over weaker groups and people. The effects of all this violence are horrendous. We see it at every turn, in the fear in people's eyes — especially women and children. It affects the very way we think about ourselves and others. No aspect of our lives is untouched by this culture of violence.

Responding to the challenge of violence

How do we think about violence as Christians? How do we respond to it? By arming ourselves with guns, condemning our context and becoming bitter about it, withdrawing into our protected zones or fleeing to apparently safer places? To respond as Jesus would, creatively and courageously, with the hope of social transformation, is certainly not easy. We definitely need God's grace.

In God's Triune nature, in the Garden of Eden, and in the kingdom to come, we find no violence of any form. Violence is foreign to God and his creation. It was introduced by Satan through the door of humanity's greed for power. It is all because we want to be (G)god, our own god. The result has been violence in all its many forms, from guilt and shame, sickness and death, anger and murder, to lust, greed and rape, manipulation, control and warfare in every imaginable form. How do we make sense of this as Christians? Where is God in all this?

To answer the question, I want to quote an eyewitness account from Ellie Wiesel concerning the presence of God in the horror of the holocaust. He was a survivor of the notorious Auschwitz extermination camp.

> The SS hanged two Jewish men and a youth in front of the whole camp. The two men died quickly, but the death throes of the youth lasted for half an hour. "Where is God? Where is he?" someone asked behind me. As the youth still hung in torment in the noose after a long time, I heard the man call again, "Where is God now?" And I heard a voice in myself answer: "Where is he? He is here. He is hanging there on the gallows ..."[50]

Moltmann says that any other answer would be blasphemy, because for Christians there cannot be any other answer to violence and suffering.[51] God is there, hanging at the end of the rope, in our suffering and violence, with us and for us.

I found the protracted and relentless violence in Mel Gobson's film, *The Passion of the Christ* (a movie about the sufferings of Christ in his last twelve hours), too much to bear. By the end I had all but disengaged my emotions in order to cope. But I kept reminding myself that this actually happened; that all of human sin, rage and raw violence was poured out on Jesus; that he became the scapegoat for humanity's hatred and hunger for power; that he pulled the poison of evil from hell itself and took it into his bloody body, mind, emotions and spirit; that he drained the cup of God's wrath and judgement for our sin and violence to the very dregs. The cross is the most violent reality, and symbol, that covers all of human history like a gigantic fountain of forgiveness and healing, from the Garden of Eden to the New Jerusalem on earth. It flows with water and blood from Jesus' pierced side, breaking the power of violence, and bringing peace from pain to all who stop and drink from him.

Jesus of Nazareth was fully human and fully God at the same time. *As a human being*, in his violent death on the cross, he died in our place. He died as a sinner paying the ultimate price for our sin. We need not die or be punished for our sin anymore; Jesus did it for us. We can be forgiven from any and every act of evil that we have ever perpetrated. *But as God*, Jesus died a violent death — *the Crucified God*[52] — in our place, so that God suffers our sin and violence. In Christ on the cross, God identifies with all victims of violence, those who are "sinned against", and he suffers with them, for them, in their place. He really does hang at the end of the rope. He knows the worst of it, he absorbed it all into his body on the cross. He sees, feels, and identifies with every act of violence on the planet. By turning to the fountain, we can be healed from all forms of victimisation, suffering and violence.

Christians should oppose all forms of violence, and have compassion on all victims of violence, seeking healing — and justice — for them. The teachings of Jesus, and the position he took in his societal context, is very important: "Love your enemies ... Turn the other cheek ... If you take up the sword you will die by the sword ..." (Matt 5:38–48; 26:52). Within his very violent social context in first century Israel, contrary to all other previous or subsequent Jewish Messianic pretenders, Jesus clearly renounced any form of violence as an option of the kingdom of God. Jesus was the ultimate "peacemaker" (Matt 5:9–12) by his sacrificial intervention on our behalf, for both perpetrators and victims of violence. We must follow his example.

We must intervene by doing conflict resolution, opposing all forms of violence, "fighting" for justice, and ministering forgiveness and healing. As Christians, we need to work hard to establish a culture of non-violence and reconciliation — the very ministry entrusted to us by Jesus (2 Cor 5:19).

Although Vineyard as a movement does not have an official position on just war or pacifism, the general leaning would probably be towards just war theology (any form of holy war theology is definitely rejected as heresy and fanaticism).[53] Neither does Vineyard have an official position on the ethics of capital punishment versus the abolition of the death penalty. We have generally left these ethical issues up to our people to decide.[54]

Whatever position we may hold as individuals, as a movement of churches we are committed to non-violence and peacemaking in all human relationships, seeking to create a culture of tolerance and non-violence in society. We can do this by creating local church initiatives and by working with non-governmental social service organisations that address violence and conflict resolution in its various forms. For example, in most cities in SA there are trauma clinics, Youth Violence Preventative Programmes, and Victim Empowerment Programmes. The Centre for the Study of Violence and Reconciliation in Johannesburg is a key institution that deserves the church's full support — churches can learn conflict resolution skills for one-on-one reconciliation, group facilitation, in industrial and other conflicts, at community level and even international peacemaking.[55]

CRIME

Crime is closely related to violence. Much of what I have said with regard to violence applies to this discussion. I will give a picture of the nature and extent of crime, comment on what we can do about it, and conclude with some guidance on the issue of emigration from SA.

The nature and causes of crime

SA has the world's highest reported incidence of murder and rape per capita. We are faced with a crisis in crime that affects international confidence, domestic stability and individual security. The picture and statistics can be divided into the following categories:

♦ *Murder.* In 2001 there were 51 174 known cases of murder — on average 140 murders a day. This rate is higher than our "peer" countries when compared with the 1998 statistics: SA had 59 murders for every 100 000 people, whereas Columbia had 56, Namibia 45 and Jamaica 37. When compared with the industrialised nations, for the same year on the same basis, it is startling: the USA had six, Spain three and England and Wales one.

♦ *Sexual assault.* SA continues to top international charts in the reported number of sexual assaults and attacks. In 2001 there were 72 043 reported incidences of sexual offences, which included 53 976 rapes. The culture of silence and shame surrounding sexual assaults leads to many more crimes that are not reported (compare the statistic for gender violence above). Rape Crisis Cape Town estimates that only one out of 20 rapes is actually reported, whereas the South African Police Services estimated in 1997 that the figure was one in 36.

♦ *Theft.* In 2001 the reported number of aggravated thefts totalled 602 772; robbery and violence totalled 208 932; house and office breaking and entering 393 840; theft of motor vehicles 98 482; and other forms of theft falling outside these categories 887 696. Theft affects more than just the loss of property and wealth. It affects general feelings of anxiety and insecurity, and leads to hopelessness (it is estimated that only 30% of all thefts are reported as there is a general perception that it makes no difference if it is reported). The long-term impact of this crime wave in SA is incalculable.

♦ *Fraud and corruption.* Charges of fraud and other forms of corruption abound in our nation — it is second to theft in terms of the overall crime statistics. The number of reported incidents of fraud for 2001 totalled 60 820. The extent of corruption, both perceived and actual, undermines our confidence in government and business leaders, and calls into question the direction of the nation as a whole.

The total number of all criminal offences in our national statistics for 2001 is 3 643 297 — reported crimes. It means that one out of every ten persons was touched by crime in 2001. In February 2004 a national survey by the Institute for Security Studies, an independent research organisation, found that 23% of all South Africans fell victim to crime in one form or other.[56] All of this creates an awful picture, but we need to face this beast to see it for what it is, and then deal with it. Burying our heads in the sands of ever more sophisticated security systems, or running away from it, will not solve the problem — we just secure ourselves for a while. Paul says the world, not only SA, will have the same struggles in the last days, and this is increasingly evident (2 Tim 3:1–4). We must follow David's example: We must rise up and use the little means that God has placed in our hands, and in the Name of the Lord slay this Goliath. When asked how David could kill Goliath with five stones and a sling, the little boy at Sunday school replied: "It was so easy for David, he couldn't miss, cause Goliath was so very big!"

Where does this level of crime come from? Why does it occur? The answer depends on the nature of the crime. At one level the causes of crime are multiple and interwoven: the historical legacy of apartheid with its vast inequalities, racism and discrimination; the culture of entitlement and feelings of powerlessness; the deep levels of national poverty and desperation for survival; a growing sense of lawlessness and/or hopelessness; issues of governance and accountability; international syndicates and the flood of refugees and illegal immigrants into SA from the surrounding African nations. At another level it is simply due to the corruption and sinfulness of the human heart — a heart that Jeremiah describes as desperately wicked and "deceitful above all things" (Jer 17:9). That is why the church must work at both the level of economic-political engagement for social transformation and the spiritual level of evangelism and moral regeneration.

How can we respond to crime as Christians?

A Vineyard pastor who planted a church in Johannesburg in 2002, Andrew Christie, had been led to Christ in his teenage years, but had wandered far from God. In 1998 Andrew's father was attacked by thieves while he was opening his business. One held a gun to his ribs while the other thieves grabbed his mobile phone and personal valuables. Then a shot went off. Andrew's father fell to the ground and died — the bullet passed through his lungs and heart. It was devastating for the family. Andrew was shaken to the core. But he turned to God, and God received him and helped him. Andrew became a fully devoted follower of Jesus, and is now winning many people to Christ and leading God's people.

Through Andrew, this evil has come back on the devil's head. Satan is now paying for it, and will continue to pay for it throughout eternity. As Paul says: "We know that God works in and through all things, for our good, precisely because we are called according to his purpose" (Rom 8:28 RAP). Biblically speaking, Satan cannot win, no matter what evil he perpetrates. Jesus has, through his life, death and resurrection, decisively defeated evil in all its forms. This is the light that shines in the deep darkness of crime and violence. This is the hope that is our anchor in the sea of lawlessness and fear. Jesus will come soon to complete what he did two millennia ago. In the meantime, we must enforce Satan's defeat in Jesus' name by simply being the church that God intended us to be.

Andrew's story illustrates the fact that crime, for us in SA, is both a pastoral concern and an ethical issue. Ethically we all know that any form of crime is wrong and sinful, and that we must support all church-based and social initiatives to curb crime and violence (some churches and organisations in SA have "adopted" a police station to support and encourage the police, from buying equipment and even vehicles, to bringing food and other goodies, and doing crime prevention patrols in their communities as police reservists). Immediate and short-term intervention must be part of a greater strategy to address the underlying and long-term causes of crime. These underlying causes face us with the deepest ethical and historical dimensions in our national make-up that allows for such horrendous crime and violence. If one compares SA with India, for example, India has similar or greater poverty and yet far less crime and violence per capita. Why is this the case? Why is SA leading the world in family suicides perpetrated by the male head? What in our society, in our national psyche, makes this possible, and how can we address it?

Pastorally, the concerns are immediate and challenge us daily. How do we minister to the victims of crime and violence? Some people — including Christians — become angry with God and turn against him because of what happens to them. How do we help them to forgive the perpetrators (and God)? How can they see things from God's perspective and overcome their fear? How should we view the criminals? These are searching questions. We must start with the need to teach our people the victory of God over evil. As Christians, we need to know that God is really sovereign over all things. Nothing happens to us that he ultimately does not allow and give the grace to cope with (1 Cor 10:13, God will not allow you to be tested beyond what you can bear, and he always provides a way of dealing with it). Paul says that nothing in all of creation can separate us from the love of God that is communicated to us in the suffering and resurrected Christ (Rom 8:38–39). We can trust God with our lives, and with our loved ones — no matter what may happen — because he really is in control and has our best interests at heart.

We must also be very clear on the fact that God does not and cannot perpetrate evil (Jas 1:13–17). Essentially, all good gifts come from God, and the bad things that happen to us come from the devil. But God can, and does, work in and through all things for our good, including the worst that the devil can do. John says: "We know that the whole world lies in the lap of the evil one, but we know that the one who is born of God is kept safe and the evil one cannot harm him/her" — except by Father's permission for whatever outworking of his hidden purpose he may have for us. Like children, we can either trust him in such matters or get angry and rebel. John concludes by saying that God "has given us understanding of these things so that we may know him who is true. And we are in him who is true — even in his Son Jesus Christ — he is the true God and eternal life" (1 Jn 5:18–20 RAP). This truth and security, if believed and lived, is very reassuring.

It comes down to knowing and trusting God in all things. We come to know him by entrusting ourselves to him in all life situations. We rely on him beyond our ability to understand him or to understand what is going on. God is well able to run the show. He really is in charge of his universe! He has been running if for ages, way before you and I arrived on the scene. One qualification is needed: We must not confuse faith and presumption. We must not presume on God by doing things or putting ourselves in situations that we know we should not be in. We must not tempt God. Although the Scriptures said God would save him, Jesus did not throw himself off the pinnacle of the temple, because he did not need his Father to prove anything to him. Jesus trusted Father and simply obeyed. The best way to resist and overcome evil is simply and humbly to trust and obey God.

How do we view the people that perpetrate evil? I always say to people who are hurting deeply, "God is well able to heal you from any and everything that people may do to you. You can genuinely forgive them and let it go!" Unforgiveness and bitterness are sure and quick life-destroyers. Forgiveness is a matter of trusting God. Unforgiveness is not trusting God; it is unbelief. It is being in control by trying to be (G)god for yourself and others. There is no hell on earth like those who have themselves for a god. There is literally nothing that Satan — through people — can do to you that is beyond God's ability and willingness to heal and restore. And he uses it ultimately to make you into a better person, if you trust him. Added to this is the reality that God has fully and freely forgiven you (through Christ's suffering and death) of all your sin. How then can you not forgive others their sin against you?

The pastoral and ethical concerns run deeper than the pain inflicted on people, precisely because God brings greater meaning and victory out of suffering and evil. All of this, including the discussion on violence and the cross of Jesus, gives profound and courageous meaning to our lives as Christians. Viktor Frankl's extraordinary experiences and observations in the horror of Auschwitz taught him the importance of *meaning in suffering*.[57] Those of his inmates who found meaning and purpose in their plight, kept their dignity and rose above their sufferings to serve others around them with joy. Those who did not, lost all hope and descended to the behaviour of animals and worse. We need not descend to the level of hopelessness that produces, and results from, such terrible crime and violence. We can face these giants with meaning and purpose because of Jesus — we are assured of victory no matter what. He will enable us to forgive, and to love our criminal enemy, and hopefully even to bring them to know and love Jesus.

The pastoral issue of emigration from SA

I have referred to the constant emigration from SA, especially from the white economically-viable community. One of the main reasons is the violent crime — besides the perceptions with regard to affirmative action, and the deterioration of national health care and education standards, among other things. Some people in our churches make their own decisions and leave, while others seek guidance and process their decision with their pastoral leaders. This is not an easy issue because it can be highly subjective and emotive. That is why many just announce a decision — even to their close family — and do not talk about it; it is simply too painful, it cuts too deep. *For this very reason,* in my view, it needs to be carefully and thoroughly discussed and processed. Decisions of this nature ought to be made within trusting and accountable family and church relationships. This would secure and free both parties, those going and the family and friends who are left behind (the latter often have to find grace before God to cleanse their hearts from feelings of rejection and resentment, and to deal with doubts: Is there something wrong with us that we're not planning to go? Don't we care for our children? Is it really that bad — are we being blind?).

The guidance I give (I speak for myself) is basically that they must discern where their faith lies, and live by that faith. If you no longer have faith in God for something and continue to do it, you feel insecure and condemned. Paul speaks about this self-condemnation and concludes: "Everything that does not come from faith is sin" (Rom 14:22–23). If they have faith to remain in SA, then they should stay with conviction and make their contribution to build a better society under God. If they no longer have faith to remain in SA by trusting God for their well being — and especially for the safety and development of their children ("We're doing this for our children" is the most common refrain) — they should emigrate for their own peace of mind. And we should bless and support them in their leaving. I also ask them: "Do you have faith to go to ...?" The grass is not always greener on the other side, and sometimes marriages fall apart and other problems set in. I do not easily buy the line: "The Lord told me" or "The Lord is leading us". This often covers a multitude of subjective motives and thinking. We discern God's guidance in community and in accountability to pastoral leadership, not on our own.

We must not lay guilt on people or manipulate them if they want to go. But we must not let a decision to emigrate pass too easily. We must check their sense of leading and the basis of their faith. We must ask what God's calling is for them, and how discipleship to the kingdom of God informs their decisions: Is it a matter of escape from SA for pure self-indulgence, comfort or even racist reasoning? Such thinking would be ethically and pastorally questionable for any Christian moving anywhere. Leaders need to examine lovingly such sentiments. We must sensitively help people to face their real reasons for going, for the sake of honesty and integrity, hopefully without prejudice or judgement. It is mostly not a matter of right or wrong, but of helping people to come to faith in God in whatever decision they make, so that they can go — or stay — with conviction and without condemnation.

SEXISM

Because of my discussion on the gender/sexual and cultural/racial mandates of the gospel in Chapter 6, the comments on sexism and racism will be brief.

Sexism is the wrong treatment of women because they are females. Technically speaking, the reverse is also true: If men are treated wrongly because of prejudice against males, that too is sexism. There are reports of men being abused by women, but clearly, by and large, sexism is about the oppression and abuse of women, and that is how I use it. Sexism comes from wrong ideas, beliefs and prejudices about women, and lead to discriminatory attitudes and actions against them. It operates on two levels — individual relationships and social structures. Sexism is a scourge affecting every aspect of life in SA. It leads to an underutilisation of human potential, and produces a level of violence and discrimination that tears apart the very fabric of society.

The violence issue is the most serious aspect of sexism — the statistics regarding gender violence and sexual assault bear this out. Without belabouring the point, the summary picture of sexism that leads to violence against women is captured in the following statistics: On average a woman is raped every 28 seconds in SA; every six days a woman is murdered by her husband or domestic partner; one out of every four women is currently in an abusive relationship.

In terms of sexism and social structures, there is the ongoing battle of discrimination against women in the workplace. Although the South African Constitution, the Labour Relations Act of 1995, and the Employment and Equity Bill enshrine gender equality in all aspects of employment, women earn less than men. Women earn between 72% and 85% of what men of the same educational and positional status earn. Women are marginalised in management positions: Only 22% of all managers in SA are women, and 50% of those are white women. Women are found disproportionately in the lowest skilled and lowest paid occupations: 38% of employed women work in unskilled jobs, and 51% of those are black women. They are therefore disproportionately affected by job losses — they work in the employment sectors that suffer the largest retrenchments (the clothing and textile industries, the public sector, teaching and nursing).

Generally speaking, most women today are responsible for generating income, caring for their husband/partner, raising children, housekeeping, and still have to take care of themselves. Women are increasingly becoming the sole financial support for their families — including extended families (especially in the African tradition, which has become an issue of exploitation for many black families). Often women have to do all the above as secondary wage earners, and are tracked into low paid and undervalued jobs. Or they have to survive in the informal economy. Besides this, women in SA face the daily threat of physical and/or psychological assault that profoundly undermines their sense of security and self-worth.

What can we do about this situation? Interestingly, the President of SA is trying to lead the way. After the national elections in April 2004, Thabo Mbeki changed the make-up of his cabinet so that 44% of his team are women. The government has also passed legislation to address women's economic and physical security, the Employment Equity Act, Domestic Violence Act and the Violence Against Women Act. Numerous civil organisations aid the victims of sexual and domestic violence, and work for the general protection and empowerment of women. Christians should support and even serve in these organisations in order to support women in all aspects of their lives.

As the church, we need to:

♦ Teach a biblical or kingdom view of women (as in the gender or sexual mandate of the gospel) so that men and women themselves can be changed in their thinking, attitudes and actions.[58]

♦ Open up all the structures of ministry and leadership in the church to women, so that they can minister and lead with freedom and confidence.

♦ Develop and support ministries to women that bring healing to the damage caused by sexism, that equip women in all aspects of their lives, from their spirituality to sexuality, from education to employment, and safety to security.

♦ Finally we need to take a firm stand in our churches, in society and the work place, against all forms of sexism and abuse of women (and children). This should include, from time to time, various public and symbolic events like the Men's Repentance March mentioned in Chapter 6.

RACISM

Racism was integral to apartheid in SA (see Chapter 3). Although it took a year or two to fully erase from the law books, it is still present in many forms in our new democracy. It took decades to foster the racism that drove apartheid, and it will certainly take decades for individuals, churches and social institutions to fight all the bigotry that persists, both visible and invisible. Racism continues to drive a wedge into our society. It divides people and communities, and it undermines our national progress, harmony and security. Violent symptoms of racial prejudice and discrimination are reported in our newspapers periodically (racially motivated murders), but there are also the daily hurts, demeaning attitudes and actions that continue to mar and undermine our society.

A new and concerning form of racism is the xenophobia that South Africans are displaying towards people who come into our country, both legally and illegally, from north of our border. This spills over into violence too.

What can be done about racism? In terms of the law, the South African Constitution and the Promotion of Equality and Unfair Discrimination Act (including the prohibition against "hate speech") are key legal tools for preventing, discouraging, and punishing racial discrimination. But unless the hearts and minds of people change, these laws have limited effect. Their effect of restraint in society is important. The church is challenged to address racism openly and courageously, and to provide places where racial pain and prejudice can be processed, healed and transformed. We need to unearth the conscious and unconscious hurts and biases that prevent us from being a unified nation. This book is about defeating this "giant" in order for us to have a meaningful and harmonious future together.

THE FAMILY IN CRISIS

The family is the basic building block of society. If the family falls apart, society collapses. The crisis in family life in SA is a giant because it threatens to overwhelm us at every level of society. There are currently countless challenges to the structure and well-being of family life, including violence, poverty and HIV/AIDS — the "big ones" among many other challenges. Added to this is the incredible ideological and spiritual battle that is being fought over redefining of male/female relationships, marriage and family (for example, gay marriages and issues related to sexual ethics, see note 58). The family unit is being redefined in such a radical way, both by circumstantial necessity and ideological forces, that fewer and fewer people know what family is. The Japanese seriously joke about robots raising children. Since we continue to look to the family as the main source of support, nurture and development for society, the threats facing families are indeed threats to any nation as a whole.

What are the realities of the crisis in the family in SA? Although I do not need to quote any more statistics with regard to violence, we need to know that its abusive presence in the home is a primary destroyer and redefiner of families. Poverty is another negative factor. Three out of four children in SA live in poverty — just on 13 million children live in households that survive below the absolute poverty line (R490 per month). Absent fathers and women-headed households is another key factor in the family crisis. Less than 40% of all children in SA live in homes with their father. The majority of households in SA are headed by women, and half of these households live in abject poverty. Because of HIV/AIDS we now have the tragic phenomenon of child-headed households; almost all of them live in extreme poverty. The devastating effects of HIV/AIDS are taking their toll on the family — see the alarming statistics regarding children and AIDS orphans. Grandparent-headed households — especially by grannies — has long been a reality in SA, more so in the rural black communities. Then there are gay couples with children, and their legal challenge to adopt babies. All of these factors and permutations radically affect and redefine the family.

From a biblical-ethical viewpoint, we have a simple, clear vision of what God created and intended with regard to marriage and family: A male and female in covenant commitment and union under his blessing, producing and raising children in the protection and growth of covenant family. This creates, in its ideal form, an extended family consciousness and care that leads to covenant community and society. The waters of society have become so murky and the ethical lines of sexuality and family so blurred, that anything and everything becomes acceptable, both from choice and, tragically, also from necessity. God's ideal for family and society urgently needs to be recovered and modelled by Christians, and proclaimed in the world as the only realistic hope that can save individuals and the family, and hence the nation. This questions the track record and credibility of Christians and the church in this regard — we need to confess to our shame that there is no real difference between church and society in the occurrence of sexual sin, divorce and family dysfunction. However, having acknowledged that, we need to affirm the fact that God designed his church to be his family on earth to those who need it most: The broken, the orphans and widows, and those dislocated and damaged in society: "God sets the lonely in families"; true religion is to care for the "orphans and widows in their distress" (Ps 68:6; Jas 1:27).

The church has a great responsibility to model, teach and preach marriage and family values; to work with the diversity of family structures and needs that fill our society; to implement programmes and initiatives that support each level of the family unit, from premarital and marriage training and support, to child protection and development, parent support and advice networks, and elderly care programmes (I have not even mentioned this major area of neglect and marginalisation in our society: the plight of the elderly. It should increasingly become a fundamental part of the church's ministry).

The problem is so gigantic that the church cannot do it on its own. Christians need to support and work with government and non-governmental organisations in the protection and restoration of the family, especially when it comes to child protection. The Child Protection Units in SA are fulfilling a critical role in intervention and protection of children and families, and they need all the support they can get. God promised that before Messiah returns, he "will turn the hearts of the fathers to their children, and the hearts of the children to their fathers" (Mal 4:6).

All the social-ethical issues I have discussed provide an unprecedented opportunity for Christians to be Jesus to our society, our world. You may want to take a moment to pray, and ask God in which of these social challenges he wants you to be involved (if you are not already serving in one of these areas of social pain). If every Christian becomes engaged in some form of social ministry meaningfully and regularly, tens of thousands of people will come into the kingdom of God and enjoy a better life, both here and now, and in the age to come.

NOTES

1. Bonhoeffer 1964, p. 148. I first found this quote used by Charles Villa-Vicencio in Du Toit (ed.) 1994, p. 95.

2. Quoted in Cassidy 1989, p. 387.

3. Ellul 1989.

4. His penetrating analysis of what has happened in American society over the past few decades is found in Bloom 1987. Fortunately, there is real hope with the rise of Christian

conscience in many areas of social, political and economic life, see Wallis (ed.) 1987.

5. In Ellul's insightful exposition of Rom 12:1–2 he wrestles with truth and untruth, intellect and communication, death and suicide. He believes the latter to be at the heart of humanity's dilemma (1989, pp. xi–xiv, 79–112).

6. In broad terms, the church's social involvement is about social ethics, economic ethics, political ethics, sexual and medical ethics, etc. The task of ethics would involve: a) analysing the nature of the issues we face, b) stating the vision from the Christian theological viewpoint of what ought to be, and c) how we can be liberated to be and do it (these are the three aspects of theological ethics as defined in Chapter 3). I will restrict myself to a few selected issues and summary comments without the background analysis and theologising that I did for racism and reconciliation. In terms of a basic evangelical introduction to Christian (theological or biblical) ethics and the sweep of ethical issues that is normally addressed, see Stott 1984. For an ecumenical introduction, see Boulton, Kennedy and Verhey (eds.) 1994. For the papers and the interesting debate of an International Symposium on the whole range of ethical thought and issues, see Block, Brennan and Elzinga (eds.) 1985, and Block and Hexam 1986. For the role of Christian intellect and theology in the marketplace of postmodern politics and public policy, see Forrester 1989. For reflections on the future of Christian ethics, see Preston 1987.

7. My theological examination and ethical critique of this is "The Theology of Prosperity" — a paper presented at an Economic Ethics symposium, now published in Venter 1990.

8. For a detailed study on the Jewish roots of the Christian faith, and the need to recover such roots in Gentile churches, see Wilson 1989.

9. For a good introduction to a Christian view of culture (from a Reformed theological viewpoint), see Roper 1979. A more detailed study is found in Kraft 1981 (with emphasis on missions and culture), but this should be balanced by the more ecumenical view of missions and culture in Bosch 1991.

10. There was a rather humorous report of an African American pastor in Louisiana who was so desperate for his church to become multiracial that he offered white people $5 to $10 an hour (for the length of the church service), out of his own pocket, if they attended his church! See "Pastor Goes Fishing with White Bait", Sunday Times, 3 August 2003.

11. We learnt some principles in Johweto that might help others, but essentially the "how tos" have been recorded in a number of books. See Emmerson and Smith 2002, Perkins 1982, Price 2002, Washington and Kehrien 1993.

12. A few years ago my wife got involved with a deaf group in our church due to a sense of calling from God and has since learnt sign language in order to interpret for them. Through her I have discovered that they see themselves as a "nation" with their own

identity and culture. We have had to learn sensitivity to their needs and practices, and stretch ourselves to accommodate them, which has enriched our congregation enormously. In 2003 a number of deaf believers came to us from another church because their church had alienated them. They were moved from the front of the church where they sign interpreted, to the back where they were "out of the way". Apparently people had complained about the distraction of the deaf group and the signing. This compounded their sense of rejection, which is endemic in their culture due to their general experience in society. This intolerance in the church is shameful, especially after the deaf church in Johannesburg made a decision a number of years ago to disband and integrate into the hearing churches to seek unity as one body of Christ. (One of the alienated deaf leaders from the church in question has started a separate deaf ministry/church again.)

13. Tom Wright uses "god" (lower case) in certain contexts when writing about God — the God revealed in the Bible through the historical Jesus of Nazareth. Wright's reason for doing this is that we do not know whether all users of "God" (upper case) are monotheists, and whether all monotheists (Christians, Modern Judaism and Muslims) believe in the same god. What do we and other people actually mean by "God" when we speak of God, especially the (G)god of the Bible, as opposed to all other gods? The biblical view is that there is only one God — specifically revealed through Jesus Christ — and all other gods are mere idols, and belief in them is paganism and idolatry. Wright calls this "the question of God". See Wright 1992b, pp. xiv–xv, 1996, p. xvi.

14. I comment on this in the Preface with note 5.

15. We must acknowledge that 9/11 presents unique challenges when it comes to "just war" considerations. The early church did not participate in war — this is viewed as a pacifist stance (no participation in violence or war at all). A just war theology emerged in the church from the time of Constantine and Augustine (300AD onwards), sanctioning war within certain circumstances and just parameters. Holy war theology (a throwback to a literal interpretation of Joshua and Judges) emerged from 1100AD with the Crusades — it sanctioned the killing of people in God's name, believing them to be God's enemies. For historical/theological studies on these positions, see Nürnberger, Tooke and Domeris (eds.) 1989, pp. 130–154; Villa-Vicencio (ed.) 1987, pp. 133–188 and Vorster (ed.) 1985, pp. 21–42. 9/11 has created a different context in which suicide bombers, terrorist warfare and weapons of mass destruction have redefined conventional warfare. The "evil enemy" is now "invisible" and can attack simultaneously from within and from any corner of the globe — even with nuclear weapons. Bush and Blair have espoused a doctrine of "just intervention" or "pre-emptive just war", as with the invasion of Iraq in March 2003, in the name of making the world a safer place from evil extremists and the nations that support them. Theological ethics has yet to address this changed international context and the subsequent responses to 9/11 fully: What is a just gov-

ernmental response? How should Christians and the church respond? Who should police the world — the most powerful nation, the United Nations ...?

16. In the Greek NT, the word for the "witness" of Jesus' followers is *marturia*, from which we get our English word martyr. Jesus said: "You will receive power ... to be my witnesses ... to the ends of the earth" (Acts 1:8). That means we receive the Spirit's power to be daily martyrs, to lay down our lives every day in loving, sacrificial service for others, in the name of Jesus. If we "die daily" (1 Cor 15:31) in this way, we will be able to lay down our lives with great joy in physical suffering and martyrdom if and when Jesus requires it of us. Many Christian martyrs through the century have attested to this. The integrity of our witness as the church of Jesus Christ is at stake because, by and large, we seek to save our own lives — and unashamedly seek security in material prosperity — rather than lose them for Christ's sake (Matt 6:19–24 cf. 16:24–26). This type of martyrdom-witness is precisely how we overcome evil in society, and even the Evil One him/herself (Rev 12:11).

17. Twenty-seven pilots and a growing number of soldiers are joining Courage to Refuse, i.e. refusing to serve in the Occupied Territories of the West Bank. They have paid a heavy price for their conscientious objection. See their letter (25 September 2003) to the Israeli authorities at www.seruv.org.il/english/article.

18. We must not underestimate Paul's understanding of the reality that a veil or blindness has befallen the Jewish people since their rejection of Jesus of Nazareth as the Messiah. One day that veil will be lifted and many will believe. Only Jesus can ultimately bring peace, but we must certainly pray and work towards the lifting of the veil. This means that the church must not be arrogant toward Jews and Israel (or Arabs) in any way, but be humble and self-sacrificing in seeking their salvation. See Rom 11:7–27.

19. For a concise explanation of the church/state relationship, see Morphew 1989, pp. 19–35. See Yoder 1964 for a classic and more comprehensive treatment of the subject (from an evangelical/Mennonite theology).

20. The phrases are from Forrester 1989 in his insightful book on the church/state/society relationship.

21. There is a teaching of "spiritual warfare" that emphasises strategic-level battles against invisible heavenly beings and territorial spirits. This teaching and practice is a mixed bag of good and bad. Without some qualifications, it can be misleading and dangerous. An erroneous emphasis is the apparent need to discern and name various principalities and powers through "prophetic intercession", "spiritual mapping" and historical research, and then to "legislate in the heavens" and engage in direct "prayer warfare" against them to "pull them down". It includes going to "high places", buildings and other geographic spots to break the demonic strongholds and reverse historical

sin and happenings. We do not see Jesus and the early church practising this, nor Paul teaching it. Jesus dislodged the powers by praying to the Father, preaching the kingdom, healing the sick, driving out demons from people, and doing symbolic acts of social intervention. The early church did the same. An acceptable emphasis is the idea of local church leaders reconciling and uniting, confessing the church and society's sins in prayer, crying out to God together for societal intervention and revival, and engaging in united forms of evangelism, social care ministries and political intervention for justice' sake. This should lead to city transformation. On the "mixed bag" spiritual warfare, see Silvoso 1994 and Wagner 1991. On community transformation, see Dennison 1999.

22. The teaching from Proverbs is clear: Authority in leadership in the nation is established by good character and righteous government, not by corruption, intimidation and fear. See Prov 11:10–11; 14:34; 16:12; 20:28; 25:5; 28:12, 28; 29:2, 14. Professor Ngara from Zimbabwe, a former diplomat and educationalist, and a widely respected Christian leader, prophetically addresses the crisis of leadership in Africa, in both the church and world (see Ngara 2004).

23. "Pan African Parliament to Lead Continent into New Era", *The Sunday Independent*, issue no. 441, 21 March 2004. Of the 53 member states of the African Union, 38 have committed to the Pan African parliament.

24. Heslam 2002. A concise booklet giving a Christian ethical critique of globalisation and capitalism. Nürnberger's (1999) in-depth study of international capitalism and the "approaching crisis" is important reading on this issue. In the companion volume (1998), Nürnberger gives the historical context and consequences of global economic systems.

25. Wuthnow (ed.) 1995 looks at the spiritual power of materialism and the effects of economics on our lives. Wheeler 1995 has done an excellent biblical-ethical study on wealth and possessions.

26. For the definitions and ethical study of the full range of economic-political systems, see Leatt, Kneifel and Nürnberger 1988. For the historical evolution of economic institutions, systems and their ideologies, see Hunt 1986 and Nürnberger 1998.

27. For a well-researched, realistic and responsible assessment of how the earth, the atmosphere and human ethics is "winding down" to extinction, see Leslie 1996. See also Nürnberger 1999, pp. 70–96.

28. Novak 1982 and Schall 1990. These two ethicists do not say that democratic capitalism is a God-given system per se. They temper the church's criticism of capitalism by showing its Christian roots and ideals, and its potential for world prosperity, maintaining that it is still the last great hope for the poor.

29. For a presentation of this view, see Kah 1992 and 1995.

30. Narrowing the gap between rich and poor and working for wholistic development is

absolutely crucial. How can we do it? What is (wholistic) development? Some evangelicals have done important work in this regard, both in terms of theology and practical application. See Sider 1978, 1980, 1981 and Samuel and Sugden (eds.) 1982, 1987.

31. Christians are actively working toward this vision, see www.jubilee.org, www.jubilee2000uk.org and www.jubileeusa.org.

32. Statistics can be notoriously misused — they are merely indicators to give a basic overview at a given point, a picture of things frozen in time. When there are statistical discrepancies from two or more sources, the average is used. Some government sources that can be consulted are: www.gov.za, www.treasury.gov.za, www.agsa.co.za, www.statssa.gov.za, www.hsrc.ac.za, www.sahrc.org.za. Some non-government sources that can be consulted are: www.development-sa.co.za, www.ijr.org.za, www.cps.org.za, www.psam.ru.ac.za, www.nirco.org.za, www.csvr.org.za, www.idasa.org.za, www.lhr.org.za.

33. Teresa 1983, p. 23.

34. Liberation theology has made "the preferential option for the poor" the hermeneutic or interpretive key to the Bible. We may not agree with this, but clearly Jesus and his bias or preference for the poor should be the model for church involvement in social charity and empowerment. The famous Catholic theologian, Joseph Ratzinger, qualifies liberation theology with a biblical perspective and priority for the poor — he calls it "A Love of Preference for the Poor", see Ratzinger 1984 and 1986 (especially 1986, pp. 39–42 in the SACBC publication). Some Christians go so far as to say that the church, by exercising biblical charity and empowerment, is responsible for social welfare, not the government (see Grant 1995).

35. At current rand-dollar exchange rates it amounts to US$61,69 per month or US$2,00 a day — the same figure I referred to earlier in terms of half the world's population living on less than US$2,00 a day.

36. The in-depth study of Wilson and Ramphele 1989 is still the basic handbook on poverty in SA.

37. For studies on the nature of unemployment and what the church can do about it, see Nürnberger 1990b and Vorster (ed.) 1992.

38. Ratzinger mentions the importance of having a theology of work, "the value of human work" (1986, p. 51), as part of a broader "Social Doctrine of the Church: A Christian Practice of Liberation" (pp. 42–56).

39. Tony Campolo spoke at SACLA2 challenging the SA church to create jobs. He works with a Christian organisation called Opportunity International which, he claims, "has created 3,5 million jobs over the past 14 years". See "Can the Church Mobilise to Create Jobs?" in SACLA News, issue 9, December 2003. Chris Black, a member of our church,

developed an entrepreneurial skills training course for the unemployed called The Dynamic Business Start-Up Project. It is a six-week course giving unemployed people basic entrepreneurial skills to start their own micro-business. Since his first course in 1996, 3 125 people have been through the programme. Of these 68% have started up a business that is running (they do follow-up to verify information). A further 6% have found employment. It can be done.

40. The Zimbabwe government says there were 4 400 white farmers. Whites owned 32% of Zimbabwe's agricultural land, about 10 million hectares, while just on one million black peasant families farmed 16 million hectares or 38% of the land. The Zimbabwe Commercial Farmers' Union says there were 3 291 white farmers in 2000 when the land invasions began. As of December 2003 485 remain. Because of the discrepancy, I say 4 000 white farmers. See http://www.workerspower.com/wpglobal/Zim-farmers.html.

41. As a Christian, Charles Robertson has felt it correct to surrender his farm to the Foundation for Church-led Restitution, a Christian organisation that is seeking to address the land issue in SA. Important initiatives like this deserve all the help they can get. See article, "Eastern Cape Farmer Leads the Way in Biblical Restitution", in *SACLA News*, issue 9, December 2003.

42. The sources for some of the statistics in this paragraph come from http://64.233.167.104/search?q=cache:ijF5A2kgnVMJ:www.sydafrika.d and http://209.157.64.200/focus/f-news/1055959/posts.

43. On a theology of land, stewardship and God's economy, see Brueggemann 1977 and Reumann 1992. On the challenge of urbanisation, squatters, housing and inner city decay, see Lupton 1993 and the Habitat for Humanity story in Fuller 1986.

44. The statistics I use in this discussion are largely drawn from a SACLA booklet on HIV/AIDS, see Semple and Gennrich 2003.

45. The common signs of God's displeasure and judgement, due to sin, are drought, famine, war (civil or outside invasion), pestilence (plagues or disease) and floods. See Lev 26:25—26; Deut 28:21f ("the curses" on the people and the land for turning against God), 1 Kgs 8:33—40; 2 Chron 20:9; Jer 14:12; 21:6—10 (the same phrase is repeated ten times in Jeremiah), and Ezek 6:11—12 to name a few Scriptures in this regard.

46. The first lady of Uganda, Mrs Janet Museveni, spoke at SACLA and explained how Uganda's HIV/AIDS rate stood at 30% of the nation's population in 1995. Her president husband and his cabinet ministers changed their message from safe sex to moral faithfulness and abstinence. They "preached" this message throughout the nation, with the result that the HIV/AIDS rate dropped to 5% in 2002. See "First Lady Inspires the Nation", in *SACLA News*, issue 6, 10 July 2003.

47. The Scriptures (note 45) that speak of God's judgements also speak of God's promise of mercy and salvation — often dependent on repentance (read the context of those

passages). Many other Scriptures speak of deliverance from "pestilence" (diseases), famine and wars, when people turn to God, e.g. Ps 91; 103.

48. Thank God that there are many such HIV/AIDS ministries springing up. My Soweto colleague, Trevor Ntlhola, inspired his church to start an AIDS ministry after caring for and burying his own sister who died of AIDS. It is called Emthonjeni (Zulu for Fountains of Life), a ministry that is supported by the Vineyard churches in Johannesburg. It operates from the old Johweto Kehillah (see Chapter 4), a small farm south of Soweto/Johannesburg, and serves the surrounding shack communities. Emthonjeni also operates in Soweto. For further information, email office@valleyvcf.org.za.

49. Much has been written about violence in its various forms, the ethics of non-violence or an adequate Christian response to violence. Helpful sources include: Nürnberger, Tooke and Domeris (eds.) 1989, Villa-Vicencio (ed.) 1987, Vorster (ed.) 1985, Sider 1989, Trocme 1973 and Eller 1981.

50. Quoted in Moltmann 1974, pp. 273–274.

51. Ibid. p. 274.

52. This paragraph is Moltmann's (1974) basic understanding of the cross of Jesus.

53. Note 15 above. I worked out my own theological-ethical stance on this issue in the heat of the apartheid struggle (Venter 1991) which is basically a "qualified pacifist" stance.

54. An even and clear treatment of these and other ethical issues (the arguments for and against each of the major positions) can be found in Geisler 1989, pp. 193–238.

55. The website is www.csvr.org.za. The University of Port Elizabeth has a Masters degree in conflict management, www.upe.ac.za. There are Christian organisations that teach conflict resolution skills and non-violent peacemaking in community, industrial and international conflicts. For example, Mennonite resources: www.mcc.org/mcs and www.emu.edu/ctp; and an evangelical group: www.HisPeace.org.

56. From a report by Caroline Hooper-Box, "Theft and Corruption Top List of Crimes in SA", *The Sunday Independent*, issue no 439, 7 March 2004.

57. Frankl 1964.

58. The teaching role of the church is crucial because it should include all the issues raised in sexual ethics: from the male/female relationship in creation and redemption to love and dating; marriage and divorce; family, birth control and child-rearing; sexuality and homosexuality (and all forms of sexual expression), abortion and women's rights. For two Reformed/evangelical approaches on these issues, see Thielicke 1964 and Stott 1984, pp. 234–326. For a more liberal/ecumenical approach see Nelson 1978.

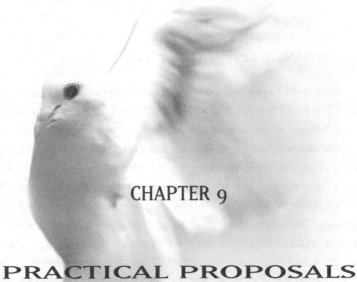

CHAPTER 9

PRACTICAL PROPOSALS AND CHALLENGES

Therefore everyone who hears these words of mine and puts them into practice is like a wise man who built his house on the rock. The rain came down, the streams rose, and the winds blew and beat against that house; yet it did not fall, because it had its foundations on the rock. But everyone who hears these words of mine and does not put them into practice is like a foolish man who built his house on the sand. The rain came down, the streams rose, and the winds blew and beat against that house, and it fell with a great crash.

Jesus in Matt 7:24–27

With all this going for us, my dear, dear friends, stand your ground. And don't hold back. Throw yourself into the work of the Master, confident that nothing you do for him is a waste of time or effort.

Paul in 1 Cor 15:58 *The Message*

THE IMPORTANCE OF
DOING RECONCILIATION

Trevor Ntlhola and I began this book with our respective stories and our Johweto experience. To bring the story of reconciliation full circle, I want to mention a phrase that I learnt in the boiling pot of Soweto in the mid-1980s. It struck deep into my consciousness and has been part of the formation of my life. It was "doing theology".[1] We did not study theology, we did theology by engaging in the struggle for justice. Many pastors and academics were challenged by young black people to stop their theoretical theologising and eloquent sermonising about justice and reconciliation. They were challenged to get out of their ivory towers and pro-tected places, and come down to the place of pain and struggle and "do theology" in the streets with the poor and oppressed. Doing theology in this way, and debat-ing the contextual theological issues, was my bread and butter in the 1980s and early 1990s.

In Johweto, doing theology meant that you got your hands dirty, that you learnt (authentic) theology by coming to know God as you engaged in the praxis of identification with the poor and oppressed. In so doing, you did God's praxis: In Jesus God stripped himself of power and glory, humbled himself by coming down from heaven to earth, to identify with human pain and suffering, and to seek and save that which was lost. There was a favourite quote of the contextual-doing-theologians that I mixed with in Soweto: "For as much as you did it to these, the least of my brethren, you did it to me" (Matt 25:40 RAP). We will look now at "doing reconciliation".

Let me expand on this idea of praxis and action using Jesus' parable of the house built on the rock or the sand. Jesus, boldly and unapologetically, challenged his Jewish compatriots to join up and believe in him by practising his message of kingdom reconciliation — not by studying and debating it, and then ignoring it, which was the Rabbinical practice of his day. Jesus' simple message was: "If you hear my words and do not do what I say, you and yours will suffer." It was not a threat, it was rather a statement of fact, of the inevitable. That is why Jesus preached all over Israel and sent his disciples to announce his kingdom message in every town and village. The kingdom was both God's offer of reconciliation and God's warning of coming judgement. Once we hear certain information, we are responsible for what we do with it. Once we know certain things, we are account-able for what we do about it. God calls us to account through the judgements of history. He allows the storms of our own lives to catch up with us and test us. Have we, or have we not, built our lives on Jesus' teachings by practising them?

Most of us interpret this parable as applying to our own individual lives. That is correct. But its first and foremost application is to the community: To Jesus' followers and to Israel in first century Judaism. Jesus had been teaching them, in the Sermon on the Mount, the kingdom of God as the answer to the pain and conflict of Roman oppression. Israel was longing for God's Messiah to deliver her, so that she could fulfil her national destiny. Jesus offered Israel his (YHWH's) particular "kingdom/Messianic way" out of the crisis: You must be the salt of the earth and the light to the nations (God's original calling on Israel); you must hunger and thirst for justice; you must be merciful; you must be a peacemaker; you must not be angry with or murder your accusers, but rather reconcile with them before you come into judgement; you must turn the other cheek; you must walk the extra mile; you must love your enemies; you must pray for and bless those who persecute and kill you; you must give charity to the poor; you must pray for God's kingdom to come, and do his will by forgiving all who sin against you that God may forgive you of your sins; pray for deliverance from the test that is coming; you must even fast for these things; you must be generous to others, not serving Mammon, but trusting God for your material life as you seek first God's kingdom and his kind of justice; you must not judge and condemn others, but ask God for what you need; and you must not be deceived by false prophets — you can recognise them by the bad fruit of their character and message, not by their signs and wonders (all these "doings" summarise Matthew 5–7, which is life in the kingdom of the heavens in the context of Israel in 26–30AD).[2]

Jesus concluded his "sermon" by saying to his Jewish followers and to the nation of Israel: If you do not do these things, your house will fall flat, because the storms of God's judgements are coming to test you. If you have built your house on the sands of idolatrous, nationalistic hopes, understandings and practices — by listening to false prophets — you will suffer destruction. Tom Wright says that Jesus was alluding to the destruction of the temple ("house") in Jerusalem, and thus of the city and the nation.[3] The temple system and the Jewish leaders had become corrupt and idolatrous to the very core. They had built Judaism on a self-serving Jewish nationalism, centred in the temple, the "den of thieves" (Matt 21:13). They were no longer serving God and his purposes — their house was built on the sand, not on the rock of the coming kingdom that Jesus embodied and taught. They, and the nation as a whole, heard but did not practise Jesus' message of the kingdom (reconciliation). Their "house" collapsed in 70AD when the Romans destroyed the temple and Jerusalem. Over one million Jews were massacred.

Can we apply this same challenge and reality to SA, Northern Ireland, modern Israel and the Palestinians, Iraq and America, and all other nations? Yes, we can and we definitely should. The church is God's Messianic community and the instrument of his kingdom. Like Jesus, we must embody and offer God's kingdom reconciliation to our nation, and the nations of the world. If we do, and they do not receive and practise it, they too are doomed to destruction — not a threat, purely a statement of the inevitable. If this is true, which of course it is, it places a grave responsibility on the church and every Messianic follower. We must carefully and diligently live and do Jesus' teachings and practices of kingdom reconciliation. We must also boldly proclaim, minister and facilitate reconciliation, via the above practices, in the nations as the only real hope for them to be saved from the judgements of history and the coming wrath of God. If we do this as faithfully as Jesus and his early apostles did, we too may bring about a revolution of reconciliation and "turn the world upside down" (Acts 17:6 NRSV).

By following Jesus and doing his practices of reconciliation, we build our inner being, our lives, our identity and purpose, on the rock of his unshakeable kingdom. God is shaking all things, all nations and systems, in the heavens and on the earth, so that that which is unshakeable will remain. Thank God that we, the church, are receiving a kingdom that cannot be shaken. We must worship God — by having no other gods — with reverence and awe, because our God is a consuming fire (Heb 12:25–29).

"With all this going for us, my dear, dear friends, stand your ground. And don't hold back. Throw yourself into the work of the Master, confident that nothing you do for him is a waste of time or effort" (1 Cor 15:51 *The Message*). We need to persevere in doing reconciliation, knowing that every small act of kindness, even a glass of water given to a thirsty person in Jesus' name, will be richly rewarded.

Before I suggest practical proposals as to how we can do the work of reconciliation in our local churches and the surrounding communities, I need to describe a simple framework for transformation and action, and comment on some guiding values and contextual challenges.

A SIMPLE FRAMEWORK FOR DOING RECONCILIATION

I introduced Dallas Willard's framework of kingdom transformation, called VIM, in Chapter 3 (see note 13):

♦ Vision — the picture of what you want to become.

♦ Intention — the decision to become, the commitment to do what it requires.

♦ Means — the practical methods and measures required to do it.

These three basic steps can be applied in all walks of life to whatever one sets out to do or become. Becoming a reconciler and doing God's work of reconciliation firstly requires *a vision of God's possibilities*. You need to see what God can and wants to do, *through you (and us corporately),* with regard to the reconciliation of the world, both locally and internationally. You need to see the awesome privilege that we enjoy in being invited and included in God's great enterprise on earth. This vision is based on a clear "seeing" of what God has already done through Christ in terms of reconciling the world to himself. To be captivated and motivated by God's vision is a wonderful thing. It produces passion and energy, and should result in well-directed action. We looked at these aspects of vision in Chapter 3 and following.

I want to pause and ask: Have you clarified your vision from God with regard to reconciliation? What is he calling you to do? Has your home group decided on a vision for reconciliation and social involvement? Does your church have such a vision? What is it? It helps to write down the vision in one or two short sentences. Then you can constantly hold it up and keep it in view. Likewise with the home group and the church (vision "leaks" and must be revisited regularly in order to keep focus and energy).

Secondly, *becoming a reconciler involves intention.* Achieving your vision will not just happen on its own. It requires a firm commitment to become a reconciler, to make God's vision for the world a reality. Do you really want to become God's co-worker, doing his work of kingdom reconciliation? What is important here is not so much the intention to become a reconciler, but rather *the decision to do what it takes* to become a reconciler. Before you build a tower, count the cost and see if you are prepared to pay the price. What will it take for you to achieve your (God's) vision with regard to reconciliation? Do you really desire it, and are you prepared to do what it takes? Have you made these definite and specific decisions yet? Has your home group and congregation made these decisions? If you have, you will find that you will need to renew and reinforce it regularly by employing practical methods. Intention without implementation implodes; intention with implementation is empowered and empowers. Another way of saying it is: Desire without discipline dies; desire reinforced by discipline deepens into godly passion and power.

Thirdly, you can only become a reconciler and achieve God's vision for your life and the world around you by *utilising the means God makes available* to you. It would be unfair of God to ask or even command something and not give us the means to do it. If I commanded you to fly without giving you wings or some means of flying, it would be wrong of me. Peter says that God's "divine power has given us everything that we need for life and godliness ... so that we may participate in the divine nature and escape the corruption in the world caused by evil desires. *For this very reason, make every effort* to add to your faith goodness; and to goodness, knowledge; and to knowledge, self-control; and to self-control, perseverance; and to perseverance, godliness; and to godliness, kindness; and to kindness, love. If you do these things, and possess these qualities, they will keep you from being ineffective and unproductive in Christ" (2 Pet 1:3–9 RAP). Peter is saying that God's means are appropriated and lived out as we give ourselves to certain spiritual disciplines. God's enabling meets us in whatever practical measures and methods we take to help us do the work of Christ. Are you aware that Christians can be completely ineffective and unproductive? Sadly, this is true for so many, hence the mess in the world. We do not take the time and make the effort to participate in God's divine nature. God's will for us is that we "bear much fruit, showing ourselves to be Jesus' student-followers" (Jn 15:8 RAP).

The means of God become active in the measures we take through spiritual exercises. As we engage in specific exercises and planned actions, God's power is actively at work in and with us. It requires effort on our part, and sometimes even sacrifice. It goes back to: How hungry are you? How passionate are you about living God's dream of reconciliation for the sake of the world around you? At this point you might say: It all seems to depend on us and our efforts. Where is God's grace in all of this? God's grace denies earning, but it does not deny effort. We do not and cannot earn anything from God; it is all a free gift of grace. But that grace motivates us to action, to become co-workers with God in his praxis — if it is the true or costly grace that we see in the cross of Calvary. Spurious or cheap grace results in passivity and inaction, both in terms of spiritual and social engagement. It leads to presumption and self-indulgence. Many Christians are deceived. They actually live in "cheap grace" while fiercely maintaining that they believe in the former (fruit does not lie!).

This third step means that we must work out a planned method in order to implement our intention and achieve our vision of reconciliation. Many things die for sheer lack of practical method. What are your plans, methods and practices, the activities that you can pursue on a regular basis? They have to be reasonable and manageable. Be realistic about it, do not reach beyond what you can do. Harmonise your methods and measures with regard to reconciliation work with the bigger picture in your life. Take into account your life situation and its challenges — your vision and plan must be relevant to your context (this relates to Chapter 8 and the comments below on values and contextual challenges). Pace yourself; reconciliation ministry is a lifelong pursuit. It is not a quick fix. Reconciliation work should be a lifestyle. All this applies to the home group too, and to pastors and leaders of churches: What is your planned method of practical action for reconciliation in your church and in your surrounding community? Is it clear and specific, achievable and measurable?

I strongly encourage you to do this VIM exercise (once you have completed this chapter). Take enough uninterrupted time to go through these three steps before the Lord and record your vision, intention and method. I encourage home group leaders and pastors to do the same exercise with their small group or church leadership. Then implement your plan with faith and fortitude, because no matter how small or humble it may be, it will be rewarded. You are busy with God's great reconciling enterprise on planet earth — he is with you, right at your side, until the end of the age.

The result of this exercise and its diligent and consistent implementation will be twofold: Firstly, the growing transformation of your own inner core will lead to the joy of doing Jesus' work of reconciliation in an increasingly natural and spontaneous manner. Doing reconciliation will begin to flow freely from your innermost being as the most reasonable thing to do, the most natural way to live your life.[4] Jesus and Mother Teresa embodied this reality, the joyful freedom of routinely ministering God's reconciliation to those in need. Secondly, the unconscious (and sometimes conscious) authority and power of God working with you will bring about change in the people, communities and structures around you. The kingdom of God will be at work through you supernaturally, destroying the devil's works, bringing reconciliation and healing to those in your sphere of influence, advancing God's good rule and reign.

 ## SOME GUIDING VALUES AND BASIC CHALLENGES

Any vision and plan of implementation, if it is worth doing, needs to be guided by underlying values. It also needs to address the basic challenges that the particular context presents. I have touched on the values and contextual challenges of reconciliation ministry throughout this book, especially in Chapter 8. In this section I want to clarify and summarise some of the key values and contextual challenges in our SA context.

The value of exposure and storytelling. Reconciliation and healing does not happen through second or third-hand information. Direct personal exposure to other people and their life contexts, pain and struggle is the most powerful means of reconciliation and transformation. Storytelling has value because it can help us cross any and every barrier in society by giving us exposure to the other side of reality. It will probably press our hot buttons and expose our blind spots, enabling us to deal with our conditioning. Conversely, by telling our own story we learn to self-disclose, to get in touch with our pain and own it. We become known for who we really are. This is deeply cathartic and healing. Knowing that others know, and that they accept us, is profoundly freeing. There are numerous creative ways of telling stories and gaining direct exposure to one another's lives and contexts (some are listed below). We must not forget that storytelling finds meaning to the extent that it is experienced and understood as part of God's greater story. We must hear his story, his struggle with humanity, with Israel, and with you and me. We must hear of his love for us in that he facilitated reconciliation through the suffering and sacrifice of his Son. We must hear how we can find our place and meaning in life in a reconciled relationship of love and co-working with God and one another, and how we can take (God's) reconciliation to the ends of the earth.

The value of relationship and reality. Exposure and storytelling leads to relationship and reality. Things become demystified, the fear and sense of being overwhelmed by the unknown begins to disappear. "The problem" — whether it is one or all of the seven SACLA giants — is reduced to a person with a name and face, and with a history of pain and struggle, just like you! It becomes personal. Empathy and connection begin and reconciliation becomes a meaningful and relational realisation. You are no longer doing things for "the blacks" or "the whites"; you are doing it with Trevor Ntlhola, who has become your friend. Relationship brings reality by removing all sorts of prejudice, stereotypes and reactions. Behind this is God's relationship and reality, and our relationship with him. As Paul clearly teaches, ultimately reconciliation with God through Jesus Christ is the relationship and reality that makes possible, and gives meaningful expression to, all other person-to-person and community reconciliation. Only when Joseph's "technicolour dream coat" was dipped in blood, did the rainbow colours become one. It is the blood of Jesus, God's ultimate means of reconciliation, that makes us one (as discussed in Chapters 5–7, meaningful reconciliation can and does happen between people who are not "born again" or do not know God — it is a gift of God's grace and Christians should facilitate such reconciliation).

The value of the individual — of mercy, grace, forgiveness and healing. Relationships bring people and individuals into focus. Valuing the individual means honouring their dignity and worth as a person made in God's image. It means treating people as unique individuals, not according to group labels and social stereotypes; it means accepting people for who they are, having mercy on people, exercising grace and forgiveness, reconciling with them and seeking their healing (for example, giving and receiving ministry with regard to racial hurts and strongholds in our lives). When we do not value people, we use and abuse them through subtle forms of manipulation and control, for our own purposes. This is seen in wanting people to "measure up" and "perform" to meet our expectations. This is totally unacceptable. No reconciliation can take place if this is present. What underlies and enables the value of the individual is God's unconditional love and acceptance of us, expressed in his mercy and grace, forgiveness and reconciliation in Christ.[5]

Finally, *the value of restoring justice and political engagement.* Reconciliation without justice, or at least a measure of justice, is cheap reconciliation that does not last. If we do not remove the cause of alienation or division, we perpetuate injustice. Placing a high value on justice and its restoration in society makes for genuine reconciliation and community. Biblically speaking, justice means right relationships or treating people fairly. Justice is derived from righteousness, the "right (way of) living" with regard to others, by God's standard of righteousness and justice.[6] This concept of justice relates to the meaning of "politics" — from the Greek *polis* — the "ordering of the (life of) people" in a community or city. We get the English word "polite" from politics, from good politics — not bad politics, which is the destructive manipulation and control of human life and relationships. The church must be involved in politics, contrary to the view of many well-meaning Christians. Justice and politics is at the very heart of Christian concern, or should be. Restoring justice is restoring right human relationships. We do not distinguish between private and public, spiritual and structural. Because we value restoring justice, we engage at all levels, from personal and family relationships to home groups, church and work affairs, civil community processes, public political policy and socio-economic structures.

These four basic values should form the foundation, the rationale and motivation for doing reconciliation. They should also inform our practices and style, the way we do reconciliation. In other words, as far as it depends on us, we should never hurt or alienate people while we are doing reconciliation work.

As I mentioned before, the context also affects the way in which we do reconciliation. Here are six contextual challenges that we face in SA with regard to the ministry of reconciliation.

The challenge of the workplace. The workplace has changed dramatically in the last decade due to democracy and affirmative action, among other things. People are having to cope with "other races" and "even women" in management. There is new competition, both fair and unfair. Previous protections are gone, and accusations of discrimination and reverse racism are heard. There are all sorts of unspoken adjustments and tensions, and every now and then they break out into the open. For kingdom people this is exciting! It is an unprecedented opportunity for Christians to make a real difference. By daily applying the above values in your workplace, you can be an example to your colleagues, and even a source of hope and healing. Through every little interaction and daily incident, you can learn to become relationally and culturally sensitive, ministering reconciliation and harmony in a multiracial context. If you are a Christian, you should see your workplace as your primary ministry and calling. You are a professional missionary, eight to ten hours per day, five to six days per week, fully paid and working with and for God in doing "the ministry of reconciliation" in the marketplace (Paul's teaching in 2 Cor 5:18–21).

The challenge of township geography. An awful legacy of the apartheid Group Areas Act is the black townships on the edge of every city, town and village in SA. How are we going to do racial reconciliation and other social ministries in these impoverished places? The townships are not going to go away. The majority of black South Africans still live in them, although increasing numbers of those who are economically viable are moving out, which will contribute to their deterioration. Will we leave the townships to their own future fate? From Chapters 1 and 2 you will have seen the value of crossing geographic barriers and distances in order to seek reconciliation, social justice and restoration. It remains a challenge for the former white churches to find ways to engage the black townships — for historical-ethical-reconciliation reasons, and for the future well-being of our nation as a whole. One such way is to connect with a church (or church organisation) in the local township and begin a journey of reconciliation and partnership with a view to empowering them in their context. It can also take the form of building houses in townships and shack communities with Habitat for Humanity and similar organisations.

The challenge of the changing suburban demographics. Upwardly mobile blacks, coloureds and Indians are moving into former white suburbs by the thousands. This has many implications for the existing residents. There are reports of racial tensions in the suburbs due to various incidents and cultural clashes. Christians should reach out to people of other races who move into their areas, and should offer to facilitate discussions and negotiations between residential groups on matters of mutual concern, and build a culture of respect, tolerance and harmony. Former white suburban churches are slowly changing complexion as people from other races look for churches near to where they live. This has many implications for congregations in terms of building multicultural environments and learning to serve a mixed community. What are these implications? How can they be addressed so that whites do not move further away into "new improved" white enclaves, leaving people of other races abandoned in former white congregations? For kingdom-minded people, these dynamics of suburban demographic change offer exciting ministry possibilities and learning opportunities for congregations and communities.

The challenge of rural villages and informal settlements. Social mobility affects all corners of SA, and all levels of society. While many move from the suburbs overseas, many move from the townships to the suburbs. In turn, many rural people flock to the towns and cities into black townships and informal settlements (shack communities). It is estimated that there are over 8 million people living in informal settlements in SA. Africa, and many other nations of the world, have an emerging underclass who live in increasingly large shanty towns around big cities. What does this mean for the rural areas that are becoming poorer and denuded? What does this mean for the kingdom, for doing reconciliation and social care ministries in rural areas and in the burgeoning shack communities? Christians in the towns and cities can easily engage in an informal settlement, as inevitably there will be one close by. Churches are springing up and being planted in these places. Suburban churches can connect with them and begin a journey of reconciliation and partnership, leading to community development and various self-help projects.

The challenge of inner city decay and urban ministry. All large cities battle inner city decay. Some undergo renewal while others constantly struggle with urban squalor. Poor, lonely and broken people, refugees and illegal immigrants seem to gravitate to these urban centres. The effects of the social, moral and psychological decay in these contexts is very damaging. The seven SACLA giants loom large here — and this applies to most places of poverty and underdevelopment, such as shack communities. Most urban churches, once thriving and prosperous, have had to reinvent themselves, move out to the suburbs, or die. Few make the transition in the changed urban context. There is an urgent need to plant multicultural churches in urban centres; churches that do wholistic ministry, from caring for battered women and abused children, to housing development and job creation. This could be part of a broader reconciliation and justice ministry in partnership with suburban churches that see the inner city as their mission.[7]

Finally, *the challenge of contextualisation in Africa.* We need to contextualise the gospel, and our way of doing church, in the African culture. Contextualisation means engaging seriously with our context and not living in a bubble cut off from our surrounding reality (see the discussion on context in Chapter 3). If the Vineyard — or any church, for that matter — takes this book seriously, doing the work of reconciliation in our local congregations and surrounding contexts by crossing the societal barriers, Vineyard will be easily and naturally contextualised and indigenised. In other words, we will become truly African, less white and Western, and make a rich contribution to the international family of Vineyard (and other) churches. Indigenisation raises many challenges with regard to worship and ministry, language and symbols, style and expectations, culture and missions, power relationships and financial patronage, economic and community development, and generally learning how to grow into mutual adult partners in God's African Vineyard.

We have the exciting privilege of learning and working with God and one another in this matter. Like children in God's laboratory, we will have some explosions as we learn how to work with and match all the opposing mixes that God sets before us. Hopefully we learn from the past and not repeat the mistakes of Western missionaries. We should not view contextualisation and indigenisation in mission terms; we should see it in ethical terms as a journey in cultural and economic reconciliation that will mutually transform us into effective, indigenous salt and light — for the kingdom's sake, and for Africa's sake.

 ## SUGGESTIONS FOR PRACTICAL METHODS AND MEANS

I make the following suggestions and proposals with the Vineyard and the broader church in SA in mind.[8] These suggestions are very practical and specific. They will need to be contextualised to your situation — apply them to whatever social divide or top-down groups may exist in your context. This list is comprehensive, but not exhaustive. My hope is that it will spark creative ideas and, above all, motivate you to action. There is no necessary sequence of priority in the proposals, although I have followed a logical development from the individual, via the church, to direct engagement in society. I deliberately emphasise "do", because it is all about *doing reconciliation* in all or any of the following ways:

1. *Develop one-on-one friendships.* Every Christian should ask God for a connection with a person of another race and/or economic group, with a view

to developing an ongoing friendship prayerfully and intentionally. If pursued, the relationship will heal and change both persons; it will become a friendship of reconciliation and transformation toward mutual adult relationship. The key is time and perseverance, a long-term friendship. This will help discipline us into becoming reconcilers, into a lifestyle of doing reconciliation, not just random acts prompted by guilt, necessity or sporadic charity. This friendship can be initiated and lived out in the context of the next proposal (which would strategically empower the proposal).

2. *Develop church and small group partnerships.* Every congregation, through its leadership, should pray for and enter into partnership with a church in another racial and economic grouping — in one of the "contextual challenge areas" mentioned above. It has to be in a geographic proximity that allows for meaningful relationship. This partnership of reconciliation and transformation can twin certain home groups, leadership and ministry teams, for relationship building and mutual sharing and empowerment. The senior leadership of the two churches will have to lead the way if it is going to have any real power for congregational transformation. Partnerships of this nature across the societal barriers can lead to many creative projects and events, and sharing of resources — it forms the context in which most of the remaining proposals can take place. The aim is a two-way flow of life and resources in a mutual, adult partnership. Local churches that are becoming, or are already multiracial, can also practise these proposals between various racial and economic groups in the congregation.

3. *Do mutual storytelling in small (pre-arranged) groups.* The twinning of home groups or ministry teams can begin with a ten to twelve-week programme of telling life stories across racial and class barriers. We did this in the 1980s in Johweto to great effect. We assigned our people — those who wanted to participate in the process — into fours: two whites and two blacks (couple groups or singles groups — they can be bigger, but not more than eight). They met weekly and worked through a series of questions telling each other their life stories, interspersing their meetings with four or more social events. The process exposed raw emotions and empathy, deep fears and prejudices, and transformed beliefs and attitudes, leading to healing and friendship. See Chapter 11 for the Johweto storytelling programme. This small group process, and similar programmes mentioned below, could be an informal TRC process for the church. It would need to have pastoral ministry on hand to help people work through their experiences, both as perpetrators of racism (and even crimes against humanity), as well as survivors of racism.

4. *Do teaching, pulpit sharing, and combined congregational and cultural celebrations.* We all need to preach and teach what the Bible has to say about racism and reconciliation — this book could be used as a teaching resource. See also the list of suggested Bible studies in Chapter ii. The series of talks in the congregation can be interspersed with visiting speakers from other racial and socio-economic groups. It is all about exposing people to truth from the Bible and from the other side of reality. For example, selected video clips from the TRC hearings and church confessions on apartheid can be used for discussion on reconciliation in the congregation. The partnership (and other) churches can meet periodically for combined congregational celebrations, with a love feast after the meeting (this requires logistical planning and financial sponsorship, but is well worth the effort). These events can celebrate the various cultures through different languages, songs, drama, art and poetry, traditional dress, food and games, to mention a few creative forms that make for such festive and colourful occasions.

5. *Do specific confession, reconciliation and restitution services.* Plan a church service built around a liturgy or programme of facing the apartheid past (through two or three life stories from opposing sides of the social divide), acknowledging what went wrong, confessing shortcomings, asking for and giving forgiveness, symbolically reconciling with various groups, and doing some symbolic act of restitution. This has potential weaknesses (one does not want to force anything or make it unnatural), but equally, it can be a powerful cleansing and healing experience for all concerned, especially if it is preceded by a build-up of a few weeks of teaching and storytelling on racism and reconciliation. It is best done within the partnership (and other) churches — the greater the mix of people, the better. This type of cathartic release can happen within the mutual friendships and storytelling groups, at seminars and conferences. The service could culminate with all sharing in the Lord's supper, around the truth and reconciliation table of the Lord. People can break bread together, reconcile and pray for each other.

6. *Do acts of restitution — develop practical programmes for restitution.* Symbolic acts of restitution must go beyond the reconciliation services. We should provide practical avenues and programmes to express and do restitution. For example, bursaries for students, adopt-a-child programme, housing projects, providing literacy courses and life skills training (most of the suggestions below are, in fact, avenues of restitution). The key issue is how we do restitution. How do we redistribute wealth in a way that avoids the "handout" syndrome that dehumanises the poor and makes them dependent? We must move beyond "What can we give you?" and even "What do you

need?" to "How can we empower you and how can you empower us?" Restitution does not mean "buying your credibility through a financial donation; it means learning a new lifestyle of mutuality and sharing, in which the poorest have much to give and the richest much to receive ... it means the restoration of human dignity among victims of injustice".[9]

7. *Do reconciliation seminars, conferences and camps.* Day seminars and workshops or full conferences can be done with great success. They could be Racism, Reconciliation and Transformation seminars and conferences (RRT events!). The suggested Bible studies in Chapter 11 can be used, and various social issues, such as the seven SACLA giants, can be addressed. Speakers who have personal experience and life integrity with regard to crossing the barriers in society can have a great impact on the attendees. It could include workshops on the healing of memories and culture sensitivity training. Workshops can include mixed discussion groups built around storytelling or pertinent questions, or even around an indaba or imbizo (Zulu for a formal process of discussion, negotiation and conflict resolution through storytelling and dignified debate around the village fire). Churches partnering across the social divides can also have a combined church camp, built around racism and reconciliation or other issues of mutual concern. Camps are both more intense and relaxing, due to the live-in component.

8. *Do weekend "encounters".* This word and event refers to what some Christians did in the 1980s at the height of the apartheid crisis (I mentioned these in Chapter 1). White Christians went to stay for a weekend in a township, hosted by black, coloured or Indian people. It was reversed some weeks later — the former hosts spent a weekend in suburban homes. The process was usually organised around a reconciliation conference, but the conference was low key, the social and shared living was the emphasis and the highlight. It is still a powerful instrument of wholesome confrontation at all levels of human personality and relationship, and should be planned and implemented in the various places of pain and poverty in our cities and towns in SA. It obviously takes careful planning and relational preparation, but it can be done easily through church partnerships across the societal barriers. This would include variations on the encounter theme, like Pilgrimages of Pain and Hope.[10]

9. *Do a conflict resolution (peacemaking or mediation) course, and become a trainer and facilitator of conflict resolution.* There are many such courses on offer these days, through businesses, NGOs, local churches and family counselling services. Christians in general, and specifically church ministry

teams, should be skilled in mediation and conflict resolution. They should teach others informally through mediating in relational conflicts, and they should formally teach courses to equip others. They should offer their skills in facilitation with friends, groups and organisations. Christians should be known as the peacemakers in any society (see Chapter 11 for organisations that offer such training).

10. *Do combined social events and outings.* There is nothing like relaxed fun, food and games to transcend racial and other differences. Picnics and other social outings can foster relationship, openness and honesty, and can build a sense of community across social divides. This is an important complement to the deeper and more intense work of confronting racial differences and economic discrepancies through the seminars, camps and encounters.

11. *Do public symbolic acts and events of reconciliation.* Calendar dates, such as the Day of Reconciliation (16 December) and Youth Day (16 June), can be used for public and symbolic acts. Park concerts and street parties can be held. I have mentioned special reconciliation church services and other events of public confession and repentance (Ezra 10:1; Neh 1:6; 9:2; Dan 9:5f). Public acts of reconciliation can also take place from time to time, particularly in response to a highly publicised societal incident, like the Men's Repentance March (described in Chapter 6). Such dramatic events are necessary to challenge the heart and mind of the public.

12. *Do local and translocal ministry in racially mixed teams.* Doing ministry in the context of mixed teams is transformative in terms of perceptions, attitudes and behaviour. Local churches should work at developing mixed ministry teams, especially as the surrounding social context is increasingly multiracial and economically mixed. Purposefully taking mixed teams on ministry trips is a powerful way of transforming people in the team, and of modelling the kingdom to those receiving the team.

13. *Do cross-racial leadership internships and affirmative leadership development.* Due to the legacy of disadvantage in black and poor communities, we need to prioritise leadership development intentionally with their emerging leaders. Leadership development programmes of this nature will not happen unless there is intentional intervention and planning, and sacrificial investment. In Vineyard we need to raise up leaders and hand over leadership to a whole new generation of black leaders that will make Vineyard a truly African movement. A great exercise is to have emerging leaders from other racial and class groups doing internships in congregations that are fairly homogeneous. This stretches the trainee leader, grows the people he/she is

working with, and benefits the sending congregation when the intern leader returns.

14. *Contextualise the style of worship and teaching, theological training, books and material.* The reference group for most of us in church life is still the USA and the west (although this is shifting). We need to learn how to contextualise the (Western) worship songs and styles, the teaching methods and the training materials we produce into the African ethos and idiom. We need to identify "bridge people" — those gifted in multicultural skills and languages — who can help with the reinterpretation back into their own context. All that we do in our churches should be accessible to the poor and marginalised. The future of the world is the global village, the emerging global consciousness and culture. Every one of us will have to learn culture sensitivity and become relatively skilled within a multicultural and multi-faith society. Churches have the ideal opportunity to lead the way through modelling in their congregations what multicultural community and life is about.

15. *Do a social service and upliftment project together.* Working together for the good of others is a great means of reconciliation and transformation. Within the church partnership relationships, various community development projects can be decided on and developed. In Johweto, the Kehillah farm project (described in Chapter 1) was a wonderful leveller and transformer for all of us as blacks and whites. We worked together in the soil, for the good of our community and the neighbouring squatter camp. It joined us in strong reconciling bonds and relationships. It is important to do it together as a mixed group. It can be as simple as feeding people on a rubbish dump once or twice a week or as ambitious as tackling one of the seven SACLA giants through developing an empowerment project or ministry.

16. *Do a kingdom business venture together.* To restore economic dignity and justice, we need to learn how to work together with money, business productivity and work ethic. A few Christians from across the divides could pool their resources — capital investment, business experience, management skills, labour, etc. — and start a business together for the sake of the kingdom. The aim would be to empower people with skills, create jobs and generate money to support kingdom ministry. This exercise will test the individuals involved as to the level of reconciliation and transformation that has taken place in their lives and relationships. A venture of this nature, much needed in SA and Africa, requires a depth of trust, grace and forgiveness. It is best done in the church partnership context or within a mixed racial group in the local church.

17. *Do social service in a non-governmental non-profit organisation.* Individual Christians, and even local churches, can support and do volunteer work in a social service organisation. There are many such groups working in the areas of all seven of the SACLA giants. It is healthy for Christians and churches to support secular organisations, to work with people of similar concern but holding to other beliefs and affiliations. It shows the world that the church is a servant in society, not exclusive or superior. Engagement of this sort is important in nation building for the good of all.

18. *Do justice advocacy.* Christians from across the social divides should work together for justice at all levels of local community, provincial and national politics, and especially in terms of public policy development and imple-mentation. One can find a specific involvement in this area. Christians must assert their presence in advocating justice. This includes forming mixed teams of people (with some who are trained in theological ethics), who can think through social issues and set vision and ethical parameters for policy formation and social action.

19. *Encourage our (young) people to make strategic kingdom career choices.* Imagine what would happen if Christians collaborated about the professions that could position them to make a real difference in society — for the sake of the kingdom. Christians should strategically train for and pursue careers that help build community and transform society. It is a matter of identifying calling and seeing it as a ministry and mission in society. For example, we need Christians to study law and champion human rights to fight against the human slave trade, among other legal applications. What other professions can Christians enter that can make a difference?

Now that you have completed the chapter, you are adequately prepared to do the practical but important VIM exercise. I trust that you will do it — and encourage your home group leader and church pastor to do it — so that you can engage simply and strategically in doing reconciliation. The purpose of this exercise is to take you beyond sporadic, random acts of kindness, which have some value in themselves. The exercise is to develop a lifelong vision and commitment to becoming a reconciler, with a lifestyle of doing reconciliation. The goal is to do what Jesus did, the way he did it; to live the way Jesus lived.

> Through Jesus' life, death and resurrection, God has entrusted to us the message and ministry of reconciliation. Therefore we are Christ's ambas-sadors, going everywhere to all people, with God making his reconciling appeal through us. (Paul in 2 Cor 5:19–20 RAP)

May we prove ourselves faithful to God, and to the people of the world, in this matter of reconciliation.

Nkosi sikelele iAfrika. God bless Africa.

NOTES

1. This phrase and its understanding — including a methodology — comes directly from contextual liberation theology. Interestingly, the Vineyard has a similar belief and practice. The application and practice of God's Word is more important to us than the technical understanding of it. John Wimber used to say that we only really know the Word, and come to know God, to the extent that we are doing the Word, when we do God's will, works and wonders on earth. See the Vineyard approach to the Bible in Venter 2000, pp. 36–37, 116–119, 160–163. Hence *Doing Church, Doing Reconciliation* and *Doing Healing*, the third in the series that I am working on.

2. It is crucial that we understand that Jesus taught the "doings" of the kingdom as coming from the "being" of the kingdom. "Being" comes from the inner transformation of the work and identity of the kingdom, the godly (trans)formation and training of the heart and will, in both the individual and the corporate community. It is the "roots and fruit" and "heart and mouth" reality that Jesus lived and taught (Matt 7:16–23; 12:33–37; 15:18–20). What you routinely do naturally comes from who you really are, from your inner being and becoming. The kingdom transformation of the heart, which naturally and increasingly overflows in kingdom doing, is the "righteousness (that) surpasses that of the Pharisees" (Matt 5:20) and saves us from (their) hypocrisy. I explained this "being" and "doing" from Paul's NT point of view in the Preface.

3. Wright 1996, pp. 287–292, 334.

4. For Dallas Willard, this transformation is the core issue in discipleship to Jesus — it is the power of this simple framework (Willard 2002, pp. 77–92). No more white-knuckle determination to change your behaviour and do God's work without the inward means or enabling that naturally makes it possible. The wider the gap between effort at outward behavioural change without inner core transformation, the greater the potential for legalism or licence (and various forms of hypocrisy). See note 2.

5. I discuss the two values of relationship and the individual in far more detail, spelling out the implications for each value, in Venter 2000, pp. 128–140.

6. Brown (ed.) 1978, pp. 352–376.

7. Lupton 1993 looks at suburban churches taking urban ministry and renewal seriously — through what Lupton calls "return flight".

8. There is another suggested list in Du Toit (ed.) 1998, pp. 150–155. I have drawn on some of these ideas.

9. Quote from "Klippies" Kritzinger in Du Toit (ed.) 1998, pp. 151–152.

10. The encounters were initiated by Koinonia, an organisation that facilitated contact and dialogue across the racial divides in SA in the 1980s through shared meals and other events. African Enterprise continues with the programme — now called Bridge-Building Encounter — adjusted and updated for the current situation in SA (see www.africanenterprise.org). Pilgrimages of Pain and Hope also took place during the 1980s and 1990s. Trevor Hudson, a Methodist minister, took groups of people for a few days to places of poverty and pain so that they could be exposed to the reality "on the other side". They would sit and listen to people's life stories and see how they lived. They would come home different people. The process is recorded in Hudson 1999.

PART III

SHARING OUR RESOURCES

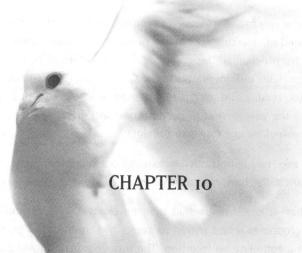

CHAPTER 10

The Confession Made by The Evangelical Alliance of South African at the Truth and Reconciliation Commission

The confession below incorporates two additional statements, one by Dr Derek Morphew (a theological comment regarding conservative evangelicals), and the other by Rev. Colin Lafoy (on behalf of the Assemblies of God).

THE SUBMISSION OF THE EVANGELICAL ALLIANCE OF SOUTH AFRICA TO THE TRUTH AND RECONCILIATION COMMISSION IN 1996

The Evangelical Alliance of South Africa (TEASA) is grateful for the invitation to make a submission to the Truth and Reconciliation Commission (TRC). We feel it is correct that the evangelical community, alongside other South Africans of faith and those of no faith, should give an account of their faith and conduct in the last few decades.

As representatives of the evangelical movement, we stand before the Commission – and a nation in search for truth and reconciliation – with heads bowed in shame for the way in which our movement failed God and South Africans by not standing sufficiently with the poor and oppressed in the years of apartheid. This went against the biblical witness, which we are committed to uphold.

We are mindful of the fact that many South Africans might well be tempted to reject God on account of the way we represented him. Instead of preaching good news to the poor, we found it easier to conform to the ways of the wealthy and powerful. Instead of rejecting racism, we not only institutionalised it in our own churches, but we proclaimed the gospel as though the sin of racism and the violation of human rights did not matter to the God we serve. Too often some among us embraced too readily and uncritically the patronage of an unjust government, simply because the government presented itself as Christian. This severely compromised the gospel we are called to proclaim.

We therefore take this opportunity to express our hope that South Africans will forgive the church. We have made it that much harder for you to find your God.

Having said that, it needs to be said that the evangelical community — as with other church groupings — had within its ranks two traditions: a prophetic tradition as well as a conservative tradition. The former sought, in word and deed, to bring together evangelism and social concern, personal salvation and social transformation. Indeed, this tradition has helped to produce good leadership in society — in politics, business, government, media, civil society and various other sectors of our national life.

The conservative tradition tended to see faith largely in other-worldly terms. With regard to society, this tradition found it easy to move from theological conservatism to political conservatism. The tragic result of this is that the defence of human rights was seen to be outside the scope of the mission of the church.

In fact, the apartheid government found it easy, in formulating its counter revolutionary strategy in the mid-eighties, to use this particular political conservatism among evangelical believers as an integral part of that programme.

Needless to say, the tension between these two traditions marks the history of evangelicals in this country. Those who stood for justice and human rights were defrocked and victimised by their own churches. Their leadership was neither recognised nor embraced by the hierarchy, whose hegemony was largely Eurocentric and/or white.

The TEASA submission

In making this submission, The Evangelical Alliance of South Africa wishes to state that we are a new body in the history of the church in South Africa, having been launched in 1995 as an alliance of thirty-one denominations, with membership of over two million people. This launch brought together previously existing evangelical groupings and churches, which have in their own right made submissions to the TRC.

At its inauguration, The Evangelical Alliance of South Africa adopted a constitution that states in this preamble:

> The alliance recognises the ugly history of apartheid in South Africa, and the complicity of evangelicals by commission and omission in that history. This history was marked by racism and oppression. Having learned from this, the Alliance is committed to build a community marked by dignity and justice. The founding of the Alliance takes place in the context of transition to a new non-racial, non-sexist and democratic South Africa. This transition is seen as a visitation of the mercies of God, and provides an opportunity for renewal both in church and society.

This submission of the Alliance therefore takes account of evangelical practice in the past, and anticipates a future in which evangelical churches hope to fulfil a prophetic role in which they make their contribution in the national searching for reconciliation, justice and human dignity.

It is also important to note that the evangelicals were not unanimous in espousing one or other position in respect of policies of the past.

1. Reflecting on gross human rights violations of the past

With few exceptions, the evangelical community has historically maintained a conservative theology. This is in marked contrast to the history of evangelicalism which, over the years, developed a strong social conscience elsewhere in the world, e.g. the antislavery movement in Europe and America.

This conservative theology tended to hold that:

1.1 Faith and spirituality are private concerns with little to do directly with social/political and cultural concerns.

The implication of this is that believers abdicated their social and political responsibilities, adopting a stance of neutrality. In the context of the apartheid conflict of the last few decades, such neutrality would naturally translate into support, at times uncritical, for the status quo. Similarly, because there was little worked out social/political theology, believers who participated in the struggle against apartheid, would have tended to go with what was pragmatic and effective.

1.2 That God Almighty was in control and that in his good time he establishes · authorities and replaces them.

The biblical text of Rom 13 is largely interpreted to mean that the apartheid government was to be supported and defended. This was particularly strengthened by the anti-communist mood of the times. The liberation movement was aligned to socialism and smacked of communism. To the extent that the evangelical movement is strongly influenced from the West, the anti-communist posture of the West also became the abiding wisdom and predisposition of the churches.

1.3 For those who became involved in the struggle against apartheid, the theology of liberation as exemplified in the biblical narrative of the Exodus, became the guiding paradigm. God took the side of the poor. This raised the struggle of the poor to a moral high ground, making even the aberrations within that struggle hard to critique. The notion of "holy war" was not particularly used in Christian circles, although the implication was there that the struggle against apartheid was a legitimate one.

2. The evangelical contribution — by commission and omission — to the conflict of the past

By its failure to develop a theology and practice that took adequate stock of social reality, and relying only on private morality to guide people through the complexities of socio-political ideologies and conflicts, the evangelical community virtually made believers easy prey to the forces of conflict. In effect, believers became socially, politically and culturally incapacitated to act decisively, authentically and with integrity either way.

Conflict per se is not what was wrong about the past, but how people conducted themselves throughout the conflict.

3. Failing to live up to the faith and contributing to human rights violations

Evangelical believers attempted to justify the system of apartheid and rationalise their support for it. This led to the embrace of a racist ideology in the values, theology and structures of the church.

♦ Served in the military and police defence of apartheid.

♦ Opposed and vilified those who worked to end apartheid.

♦ Embraced apartheid segregationists' practices in their churches and institutions.

4. Actively opposing gross human rights violations

Over the years, evangelicals have made moral submissions to authorities in respect of legislation that undermined the rights of the black community. This was, however, not done vigorously enough.

5. Reflecting on the present and future: The road to reconciliation

The Evangelical Alliance of South Africa has embarked on a programmeme to:

- Encourage local churches affiliated to TEASA to adopt victims for the purposes of ongoing assistance and rehabilitation.
- Set up a Reparation Fund and receive contributions from member churches to contribute to the process of assisting the victims of human rights abuses.
- Run a programme of seminars on reconciliation and break the victim syndrome among survivors of human rights violations.

6. Prevent human rights violations in the future

The public needs to be empowered to defend human rights. This through:

- Making the offices of the Public Protector and Human Rights Commission more available and capable of responding to public concerns.
- Bringing the secret services under greater public scrutiny through parliament.

7. Promoting national unity and reconciliation

The victims of the past need to be reassured that they are not being sacrificed in pursuit of a unity and reconciliation that does not assist them materially. Accordingly the state should:

- Underwrite the education of victims of gross human rights violations.
- Assist those NGO that work in the area of supporting victims.

Signed: *Pastor Moss Ntlha*
General Secretary – The Evangelical Alliance of South Africa

Signed: *Pastor Nicholas Mosupi*
Chairman – The Evangelical Alliance of South Africa

 ## ADDITIONAL COMMENTS BY DEREK MORPHEW

My comments relate to Clause 2 of the primary document, namely: "By its failure to develop a theology that took adequate stock of social reality, and relying only on private morality to guide people through the complexities of socio-political ideologies and conflicts, the evangelical community virtually made believers easy prey to the forces of conflict."

I wish to reflect on how this was manifest in the white section of the conservative evangelical community. In describing this section of South African society, I must acknowledge that there were Christians of conservative evangelical faith in other constituencies already represented before the TRC who could legitimately distance themselves from the confession which follows. My hope is that this statement will assist in the ongoing confession and repentance of the constituency I will describe.

Perhaps the primary value and distinguishing mark of the evangelical community is the place given to the authority and inspiration of Scripture. A high view of Scripture is believed to provide a perspective which safeguards the church from worldly thinking and keeps it faithful to its mission.

The critical question is therefore: To what extent did this value work for a church caught in the ideological struggle of the apartheid era? We have to confess that the evangelical community largely lost its way and became a captive to the ideologies of the day as did any other part of South African society.

1. Given a context where ideologies from both the right (neo-fascist) and the left (neo-Marxist) were present, Marxism was routinely demonised and the power of this ideology was greatly exaggerated, while the sinister influence of fascist ideology was largely evaded or ignored. This, despite the rich biblical and church historical heritage of "spiritual warfare", the unmasking of the "gods" and of the spirit of the anti-Christ, of the "tearing down of strongholds" in the mind, and so on.

2. This partisan spirituality was nowhere more evident than when the church prayed for the state. Prayers against the threat of communism and revolution were filled with far greater zeal than prayers against the violations of human rights perpetrated at the time.

3. The evangelical church also has a rich heritage of social relevance. The history of church involvement in the development of human rights down through the centuries and the testimony of Wilberforce type role models is well known. Yet the South African evangelical community somehow managed to suffer from amnesia and opted rather for a form of gnostic dualism where evangelising the soul was unrelated to the transforming power of the kingdom of God. Instincts of self-preservation predominated compassion for the poor.

4. The evangelical church prides itself on its fidelity to doctrinal orthodoxy and is often quick to repudiate heresy. Yet the South African conservative evangelical community did not lead the way in discerning the heretical nature of apartheid theology.

5. Scripture is unambiguous on the unity of the church in contrast to the fragmentation of worldly society. Pentecost reverses Babel and Christ's blood creates a new community where dividing walls are broken down. Yet many of the denominational structures reflected the divisions of South African society, nullifying the testimony of Scripture. It is with sadness that we have to acknowledge that TEASA (and many of its denominational constituents) emerged from previously divided evangelical structures only after the election of the new government, so that the church followed the example of the state rather than providing an example to the state.

The evangelical community we represent does have its history of conferences, statements, publications and positions adopted in the struggle against apartheid. There were individuals and congregations who courageously exemplified a truly biblical witness. However, in general our testimony is one of failure to be faithful to the Word of God we so highly value. We did not act as the leaven and salt of society Jesus called us to be. This failure must be acknowledged before God, to ourselves, and to the South African nation.

Our ability to be deceived in the past requires us to reflect critically on our understanding of the gospel as it relates to society. The future calls us to discover a practice of missions and evangelism where biblical discipleship takes on new meaning. It will need to include biblical teaching on social ethics, human rights, the empowering of disadvantaged communities and nation building. We will need to make our contribution to nation building in the face of new challenges and threats to the emergence of a truly civil society.

FAILING TO LIVE UP TO THE FAITH AND CONTRIBUTING TO HUMAN RIGHTS VIOLATIONS

Additional comments by Rev. Colin Lafoy
General Secretary of the Assemblies of God Association

1. We confess that our church leaders participated in government commissions, e.g. as the one set up by John Vorster which led to the banning of the Christian Institute and resulted in the fifteen-year banning of Dr Beyers Naudé.

2. Effectively demonised the prophetic voice thereby disadvantaging South Africans. Leaving them psychologically unprepared for the changes in our

society. "Jesus Christ will come before any of these changes will take place" was a standard response from church leaders to those who warned that the then status quo is going to change radically.

3. The slave mentality created both by the system and the powerful economic position of the white section of the church on people of colour further empowered the conservative right wing elements in the church.

4. Sections of our leadership travelled around the world claiming to speak for 11 million Christians with an agenda to counter the "propaganda" of the SACC-related churches. Thereby effectively creating the classification the "right-wing churches" of southern Africa. This action gave birth to the "Relevant Pentecostal Witness" which endeavoured to counter this collaboration and desired another voice to be heard.

Speaking to point 7 of the TEASA submission

Promoting national unity and reconciliation

1. While the RDP can address the issues of housing, education, sports facilities, etc., people of colour are faced with a major psychological problem concerning a "crisis of identity". Cripple care societies are there to cater for those with broken and withered limbs. We have a nation where many minds have been damaged and an anti-Africa mindset has been so effectively instilled through propaganda, where even the previously disadvantaged are anti-Africa. Living in Africa and living in denial of who and what we are. The church has an important role to play in the process of healing the mind in our nation.

2. There is a different premium on a white life to black life. The church in its ministry has an important role to play in creating a new value system where all life regardless of colour is precious. The pro-life group, while acting in the anti-abortion lobby frequently under apartheid, paid scant attention to the dehumanising process of people of colour. The rights of the unborn can only find protection when there is a new respect for life regardless of colour.

CHAPTER 11

BIBLICAL AND INFORMATIONAL RESOURCES

The first resource is a Life Storytelling Process (proposed in Chapter 9). It is a list of questions that we used in Johweto in the 1980s to facilitate reconciliation between blacks and whites, rich and poor, through mutual storytelling. The questions should be adapted and changed in keeping with the changed context in SA, or in the context in which one is applying this type of storytelling.

The second resource is a list of suggested passages and themes for Bible study and talks on reconciliation. They are suitable for small group discussions, *through imaginative interpretation, recounting the story and applying it to the current context.* (The latter is key: What does the passage or story say to us today in our situation?) I give the biblical passage with some pointers on how it can be used. You develop from your own study and application to the particular context you are addressing.

The third resource is a list of websites of reconciliation and justice organisations and initiatives. I am grateful to Rodney Jones for his research and the compilation of the list. Although care has been taken, website addresses may no longer be in use and details may have changed by the time of publication. This information is a resource for those who want to do further research and/or connect with certain reconciliation and justice initiatives. Please note that not all groups mentioned necessarily adopt positions we would support, for example the Unitarian Universalists. Rodney has divided the lists into:

1. Reconciliation groups;
2. Social justice groups;
3. Peacemaking groups;
4. Reconciliation around the world.

LIFE STORYTELLING PROCESS FOR MIXED GROUPS

Introduction

The groups should be no less than four and no more than eight, with as great a mix as possible (race, gender, class). The groups meet weekly for ten to twelve weeks for two hours per meeting. The group agrees on time and place. It can include a meal if this is workable (recommended!). The mutual storytelling is guided by the following topics with their questions to stimulate your thinking — you don't have to work through every question in order. If everyone has not been able to share on a night, continue the next week. There is no rush. It is an important journey and the number of weeks can be renegotiated. The purpose is to help you get in touch with your own story and share it, so that you become known. You get to know others from across the social barriers by listening to their story and learning from it. Hopefully real trust and friendship will emerge. Talk on a personal, feeling and experiential level, rather than sharing opinions and theories. Each person shares in turn. Do not interrupt or pass comment. The idea is to listen carefully and accept and love the person in their story. When they have finished sharing, you can ask questions for clarification, but do not give opinions, advice or counsel. Choose a coordinator who will monitor and guide the sharing and discussion where necessary. The "suggested social" weeks below are very important — they can be interspersed in the formal agenda as and when the group plans.

WEEK 1: Introductions — Family background and current situation

Are your grandparents still alive — did you know them? Where did they come from and what were their backgrounds? Do you have uncles and aunts — give some idea of your extended family. Where did your mum come from and how did she grow up (and the same with your dad)? What type of work did they do? When and where did your parents meet (and marry)? How many brothers and sisters do you have? Where are they and what are they doing with their lives now? Do you/ did you have a happy family upbringing? Religious? Financial situation? Racial attitudes? What type of family problems did you have? Are you currently married or single, with children?

WEEK 2: Your birth, childhood and schooling

Where were you born? What have your parents told you about your birth? What is your full name and what does it mean (why were you named that)? What are your earliest childhood memories? Was it a happy or difficult childhood (expand on stories of joy and/or pain)? Where did you live and grow up? What did you play? Where did you first go to school and what was the first day at school like? What was your early school experience like? What type of person were you as a child? Who was your favorite teacher and why? Where did you go to high school, and how did you experience your education (struggle or enjoy)? How did you handle being a teenager? Who was your best friend as a teenager? And your "love life"? Your "sports life"?

WEEK 3: Your faith journey

What were your earliest thoughts of God? Of the church? Of Christians? What involvement have you had in other religions, belief systems or spiritualities? Have you had a salvation experience? What led up to it? How did your life change? Did you/have you made progress since your conversion to Christ? With what churches have you been involved? What have been some high points, and some low points, in your Christian journey? When did you first hear about Johweto (or this group process) and how did you become involved? What were your first impressions? Has involvement in Johweto (or this group process) affected your life? If so, how?

WEEK 4: Your present situation

Describe a typical day in your life – from the time you wake up till you go to sleep. Give a picture of a typical week in your life – nights out and how you spend your weekends. Are you happy with yourself? Are you happy with your current family situation? Your work? Describe what you do. What would you like to change about yourself? About your life situation? What are the most important challenges you are facing at the moment?

WEEK 5: Your social awareness journey

When and how did you first become aware of social problems in SA? Of black/white awareness? Conscious of the rich/poor gap? What was (and is now) your honest view of people of other race, class or gender? What was your first significant cross-cultural experience? How have you felt about and responded to the apartheid issue? Did your Christianity make any difference — did it help or hinder you in responding to apartheid, in crossing the divides in society? What have been your major struggles in crossing the cultural, racial, gender and economic barriers? What racial, gender and/or economic hurts and pain do you carry from your past (and your present)? How are you getting healed from these wounds? What guilt do you carry with regard to this issue — in what ways have you been a racist or sexist? Is there anything you need to confess and ask forgiveness for with regard to these things? Has your life changed in any way since you have begun to cross the barriers? If so, how?

WEEK 6: The future — yours and that of the nation

How do you feel about your future? What are your wildest dreams? What do you want to do with your life? Do you have plans and goals for the future that you are working towards? How do you see our society/nation? Do you see it developing or not? What is your hope or vision for SA? What challenges do you identify as key issues that we have to tackle together for the good of all? What can we do about it — how can Johweto (or this group) tackle one or some of these challenges? Can we commit to anything further together (as a group) — is God saying anything to us? What has the journey in this group been like? Where do we go from here?

Suggested social events to intersperse with the meetings

- ♦ Arrange to see a movie.
- ♦ Go out to a public place for a meal together.
- ♦ Plan a fun evening at someone's house (with interactive games).
- ♦ Have a picnic together after church or on a Saturday, and invite friends.
- ♦ Culminate the sessions with a sleepover in a home in Soweto or Johannesburg; both if possible (as was the case in Johweto; i.e. in a home on the other side of the social divide, as represented in the sharing group).

POINTERS FOR BIBLE STUDIES AND TALKS ON RECONCILIATION

The first family, Gen 3—4

Picture Adam and Eve before the fall — describe their life. Why and how were they alienated from God and each other? What were the levels of alienation and the consequences? Why and how did God initiate reconciliation? How did all this affect the children? Compare the responses of Cain and Abel, the causes of alienation between them, the consequences, and the possibilities of reconciliation.

The story of Jacob and Esau, Gen 25—33

Trace the history and causes of relational alienation and enmity. Picture the story — how did the alienation affect Jacob's life? How did reconciliation begin? Study the various dynamics of reconciliation between enemies: Compare the attitudes; the impossibility of "buying" forgiveness; the need for encounter with God; the need for both enemies to let go in order to receive, and how they saw the face of God in the face of others.

The story of Joseph and his brothers, Gen 37, 42—45

This emotional story lends itself to imaginative reliving. What were the causes of alienation? What lessons can be learned by looking at it from the viewpoint of each of the key personalities (e.g. should fathers have "favourites"?). Reflect on the sovereign hand of God in initiating reconciliation. What can be learnt from that? Why did Joseph treat his brothers the way he did? What can be learnt from the way the reconciliation took place, and the sweet fruits of reconciliation after years of alienation?

Group reconciliation between the tribes of Israel, Josh 22

Set the scene and identify the cause of alienation. How did the western tribes react to what the eastern tribes did? Should they have responded differently? How would you have responded? How was the situation resolved? What can you learn from this story in terms of hearsay, prejudgment and in terms of group reconciliation? Note the role of leadership.

David's sin against Uriah and Bathsheba, 2 Sam 11—12; Ps 51

Look at the tragedy of human lust and greed, the nature of power relationships and the consequences of their abuse, for both the perpetrator and the victims. What does the role of Nathan the prophet say to us today? What can we learn about our role and responsibility in society? Was there forgiveness and reconciliation for David? With whom? How did it take place? Ps 51 is a remarkable poem on confession, forgiveness and reconciliation (with God, self and God's people). Compare it with Ps 25 and 32.

The land issue — Ahab and Naboth's vineyard, 1 Kgs 21

This story has similar elements to David's story. Examine the motivations and factors that led to the abuse of power and relationship. Does it have any parallel in our history or in our current context? What does it say about the land issue in SA? What can you learn from the person and role of Elijah? What did Elijah do, and how did he handle Ahab? Was there any reconciliation for Ahab? If so, on what basis? How deep and permanent was it?

One-on-one reconciliation, Matt 5:21—26; 6:12; 18:15—35

Although I have discussed these passages at length in Chapter 7, the principles need to be taught publicly and workshopped in small groups because they are absolutely critical for community health and integrity. You can work out your own outline and way of teaching or discussing these passages.

The good Samaritan, Lk 10:30—36

This story can be dramatised and contextualised in any and every social divide with great effect. Reflect on the context of Jesus' day and the way he constructed the story to reverse racial and social stereotypes. Draw out every aspect of meaning and apply it to the SA situation, e.g. What was the cost of this reconciliatory act for the Samaritan? What can you, or the group, do to re-enact this story as a regular ministry in society?

The reconciliation of the lost son, Lk 15:11—32

How do we respond as family and friends to such prodigal rejection from the son? How did the father respond? What makes people turn and return? How should we receive, forgive and reconcile with our enemy brother? Imagine yourself as the returning son. What happened in him, in his head and heart, at every stage of the story? How much of the prodigal is in you? Imagine yourself as the elder brother. How would you react? Is there an elder brother in you? Finally imagine yourself as the father. What does it tell you about your own capacity — or lack thereof — for forgiveness and reconciliation?[1] Can it be applied to the SA context? Who would the blacks, the whites and the fathers be in this story? What would it teach us about attitudes and actions of reconciliation?

The repentance and restitution of Zacchaeus, Lk 19:1—10

Why was it so radical for Jesus not only to visit, but also to eat with Zacchaeus? What does it say to the perpetrators of (white-collar) crime — and to the survivors of crime? What does it say about the role of Christians in society (with regard to rich and poor, exploiters and survivors)? What motivated Zacchaeus to repent and make restitution? How did he do his restitution? Use your imagination. What does this story have to say to our SA context with regard to restitution and the legacy of apartheid?

Jesus and the Samaritan woman, Jn 4:4—42

What barriers did Jesus cross in offering this woman reconciliation (with God and himself — a Jewish Rabbi)? What was the cause of these various levels of alienation — spiritual, religious, racial, gender, etc.? How did he reach her with his message? What was the result? How can we apply the lessons in this story to our ministry of reconciliation in our particular context?

Ethnic tension and reconciliation, Acts 6:1—7

What was the cause and nature of the division (notice privilege and ethnicity)? How was it resolved? Note what was done, and what was not done as a possible resolution. What was the role of the leaders? Who chose the team to resolve the issue, and on what basis were they chosen? Why? What was the nature and outcome of the reconciliation?

Reconciliation of enemies — from Ananias's viewpoint, Acts 9:1—31

Knowing what Ananias knew, how would you respond if God told you to do what he had to do? What did it take for Ananias to obey God and reconcile with Saul?

It is difficult for victims/survivors to forgive their persecutors/oppressors. Is God calling you in any way to go and touch any (former) enemy to complete the reconciliation that God has already begun?

God deals with Peter's racial prejudice, Acts 10, Gal 2:11—16

The crossing of this racial barrier is significant. Why? Why was it so difficult for God to get Peter to go to Cornelius' house? What was the nature of Peter's prejudice? What did God have to do in order to expose and change his prejudice? Did Peter really undergo racial and religious transformation — why did he slip back into his old ways in Antioch when Paul had to confront him? What were the dynamics in that exchange? Can you see yourself in Peter in any way? What can you do about it?

The story of Onesimus and Philemon in Paul's letter to Philemon

This is a warm, personal story of reconciliation with God and employer/employees (read a commentary on Paul's letter to get the full picture). What social barriers are crossed in this story of reconciliation? What was the cause of alienation? How was reconciliation initiated and then completed between master and slave (employer and employee)? Examine how Paul mediated this reconciliation, the basis of his appeal and his sensitive approach.

Paul's gospel mandate, Gal 3:26—29

The threefold mandate can be discussed and applied through small groups in your local context (see the discussion on the gospel mandate in Chapter 6). This mandate is radical. It will raise many questions and issues that can lead to honest dialogue and reconciliation.

The reconciliation of Jews and Gentiles, Eph 2:11—22

You can begin by listing the benefits of being Jews and the characterisation of Gentiles, and then tabulate the point by point process of how God actually reconciles them into a new identity (one new humanity), and the consequent united benefits! The process and the benefits can then be applied in terms of seeking to reconcile divided groups in your societal context.

The message and ministry of reconciliation, 2Cor 5:16—21

You can develop an outline for discussion from this passage in accordance with Paul's logical development of thought. Ways should be discussed as to its practical application.

RECONCILIATION AND JUSTICE GROUP WEBSITES

1. National reconciliation groups

African Enterprise — Action Encounters, Bridge-Building Workshops, Koinonia Encounters
http://www.africanenterprise.org

Centre for the Study of Violence and Reconciliation
http://www.wits.ac.za/csvr/

The Community of the Cross of Nails — USA
http://www.ccn-usa.org

The Coventry Cathedral International Reconciliation Ministry
http://www.coventrycathedral.org/international/index.htm

The Forgiveness Project
http://www.theforgivenessproject.com

The International Reconciliation Coalition
http://www.reconcile.org

The Justice and Reconciliation Project
http://www.thejrp.org

MAP International
http://www.map.org

NCCJ — The National Council for Community and Justice
http://www.nccj.org

The Pluralism Project
http://www.pluralism.org

South Africa's Truth and Reconciliation Commission
http://www.doj.gov.za/trc/index.html
http://www.truthcommission.org

Tolerance.org
http://tolerance.org

2. Social justice groups

10 Days for Global Justice
http://www.web.net/tendays/

American Friends Service Committee
http://www.afsc.org

Bread for the World
http://www.bread.org

Catholic Worker
http://www.catholicworker.org/index.cfm

Center of Concern
http://www.coc.org

Christian Aid
http://www.christian-aid.org.uk

Democratic Socialists of America Religious Commission
http://dsausa.org/rs/

Interfaith Center on Corporate Responsibility
http://www.iccr.org

Interfaith Coalition on Immigrant Rights
http://www.igc.org/icir/

Interreligious Foundation for Community Organization
http://www.ifconews.org

Jewish Fund for Justice
http://www.jfjustice.org

Jewish Social Action
http://www.socialaction.com/index.phtml

Jubilee Network
http://www.jubileeusa.org

Mennonite Committee on social justice
http://www.mcc.org

Methodist Federation for Social Action
http://www.mfsaweb.org

Michael Lerner's Tikkun magazine
http://www.tikkun.org

National Catholic Reporter
http://www.natcath.com

National Farmworkers Ministry
http://www.nfwm.org

National Interfaith Committee for Worker Justice
http://www.nicwj.org/index.html

The Other Side magazine
http://www.theotherside.org

Protestants for the Common Good
http://www.thecommongood.org

Reform Judaism's Social Action Center
http://www.cdinet.com/RAC

Religious Organizing Against the Death Penalty
http://www.deathpenaltyreligious.org

Salt of the Earth
http://www.claret.org/salt/

Sojourners
http://www.sojourners.com

Student Christian Movement of Canada
http://www.scmcanada.org

Unitarian Universalists for a Just Economic Community
http://www.uujec.org

United Church of Christ Justice and Peace Page
http://www.ucc.org/justice/index.shtml

3. Peacemaking groups

Baptist Peace Fellowship
http://www.bpfna.org

Christian Peacemaker Teams
http://www.prairienet.org/cpt/

Conflict Resolution Site
http://www.searchforcommonground.org

Ecumenical Peace Institute
http://www.peacehost.net/EPI-Calc/

Fellowship of Reconciliation
http://www.forusa.org

Gandhi Institute on Non-violence
http://www.gandhiinstitute.org

Jewish Peace Fellowship
http://www.jewishpeacefellowship.org

National Interreligious Service Board for Conscientious Objectors
http://www.nisbco.org

Nonviolence.org
http://www.nonviolence.org

Orthodox Peace Fellowship
http://www.incommunion.org

Pax Christi USA
http://www.paxchristiusa.org

Project Plowshares
http://www.ploughshares.ca

Witness for Peace
http://www.witnessforpeace.org

4. Reconciliation around the world

Angola
http://www.angola.org/news/mission/april97/unity.html

Australia
http://www.schools.ash.org.au/stagatha/ReconciliationWeek.htm
http://www.reconciliation.org.au/
http://www.antar.org.au/

Cambodia
http://www.bigpond.com.kh/users/csd/reports%5Cnif-kr-si.htm
http://www.bigpond.com.kh/users/csd/reports%5Cnif-kr-pp.htm

Canada
http://www.uni.ca/livreouvert/mcquiston_e.html
http://www.pcobcp.gc.ca/aia/default.asp?Language=EandPage=PressRoomandSub=
SpeechesandDoc=19961018_e.htm

Democratic Republic of Congo
http://www.globalissues.org/Geopolitics/Africa/DRC.asp

Indonesia
http://empoweringforreconciliation.org
http://www.ukdw.ac.id/lpip/pspp/indexeng.html
http://www.reliefweb.int/training/t140.html

Iran
http://www.iranian.com/Opinion/April98/Reconcile/

Israel / Palestine
http://www.scn.org/wwfor/israel-pal.html
http://www.openhouse.org.il

Jewish/Christian
http://www.icjs.org/what/njsp/barnett.html

Nepal
http://www.nepalnews.com.np/contents/englishweekly/spotlight/2000/dec/dec29
/national11.htm

Northern Ireland
http://www.anselm.edu/academic/politics/newdesign/reconciliation.pdf
The roles played by Christianity in conflict and reconciliation.

http://www.wfn.org/2000/08/msg00058.html
Moving beyond sectarianism.

http://www.suntimes.co.za/2000/02/13/news/news12.htm
A comparison between South Africa and Northern Ireland.

http://www.globalvolunteers.org/irldmain.htm
The Glencree Centre for Reconciliation.

http://www.augie.edu/trips/scrirl/
Useful resources on Northern Ireland.

Romania
http://www.transcend.org/conwarjan02.htm

Rwanda
http://www.globalissues.org/Geopolitics/Africa/Rwanda.asp
http://www.pbs.org/newshour/bb/religion/july-dec00/rwanda_8-31.html
http://www.american.edu/ted/ice/RWANDA.HTM
http://www.christian-aid.org.uk/world/where/eagl/rwanda2.htm
http://www.americanradioworks.org/features/justiceontrial/rwanda_chronology.html
http://www.colorado.edu/conflict/peace/example/brub6811.htm
http://www.ciponline.org/Africa/Countries/data/rwanda.htm

South Africa
http://www.anc.org.za/ancdocs/history/mbeki/2000/tm1018.html
Thabo Mbeki's speech in Rwanda about the SA reconciliation process.

http://vulab.ias.unu.edu/GlobalEthos/papers/namhla.html
A helpful academic paper on SA and role of international community.

http://www.polity.org.za/html/govdocs/bills/truth.html?rebookmark=1
National Unity and Reconciliation Bill.

http://www.geocities.com/reuther_2000/relpol.html
http://www.christchurchcincinnati.org/newweb1/faqs_glossary/links.htm
http://www.amethyst.co.za/Reconciliation/

NOTES

1. The classic on this story is Nouwen 1992. It is a must read, and can be used extensively in reconciliation work.

APPENDIX 1

Why Focus on
Human Rights?

By Derek Morphew

This analysis of human rights should be placed in the overall context of my other publications. First, *Breakthrough*,[1] my book on the theology of the kingdom of God, was an attempt to articulate the framework from which we view everything else. Kingdom theology is the most comprehensive overall biblical paradigm through which we approach issues of social justice and ethics. Second, *South Africa: The Powers Behind*,[2] though an earlier publication, follows logically from the theology of the kingdom. While the theology of the kingdom is primarily a positive exercise, this volume was a more negative exercise. It was written in a time of national crisis under the apartheid regime. Moving from the framework of kingdom theology, and with some added biblical perspectives, it sought to expose and debunk the ideological basis of apartheid. *Christian for Human Rights* was first written for a process initiated by African Enterprise.[3] Michael Cassidy had been vitally involved in the peace effort that helped avoid civil war[4] and wanted to move on to make a Christian contribution to nation building. Various consultations hosted by African Enterprise were part of the way the evangelical church sought to contribute, constructively, to the post-apartheid situation.

Human rights have become possibly the most pressing global issue of our time. This alone makes it imperative for thinking Christians to grapple with it. More profoundly, the struggle for human rights has to do with what it means to be fully human, with how and to what extent the human race can reach its potential and destiny. Any area of thought or endeavour that deals with man in his essence must be the concern of those who are committed to the gospel of Jesus Christ, for he came to seek and to save the same humanity.

The context

This subject is of particular and painful importance to us in South Africa. We have lived through roughly forty years of human rights violations perpetrated by the apartheid system. Prior to that, a colonial system was in place for hundreds of years that violated the rights of the majority of the population.

We have, and to a large extent continue, to live in a crisis where violence is becoming endemic to our society, be it black on black tribal violence in KwaZulu-Natal, gang violence in the Western Cape, Pagad activity in the Western Cape, organised criminal violence, family murder and abuse, gangsterism and barbarity or the murder of farmers. Respect for the value of human life is at an all time low. People lose their lives over a few Rands, a motor vehicle or even a cell phone. Life is truly cheap. The various structural causes to the poverty and cycle of violence do not justify the appalling violation of human rights.

Meanwhile, in the midst of all this, we are called to build a new nation. The new nation has been wonderfully blessed with initial peacemakers with legal training (Mandela and De Klerk), an internationally respected Bill of Rights, a Human Rights Commission, and new commitments by the state to the United Nations and the Universal Declaration of Human Rights. While all this is of profound significance, experience elsewhere has made it clear that the mere legislation of human rights is no guarantee of a society where human rights are actually respected. This only occurs where an entire society has been leavened with certain values that motivate the members of that society to respect life. Roughly 77% of our population is at least nominally Christian. If the Christian church will not make itself responsible for this leavening of society, who else can or will? The current crisis reveals just how nominal that 77% is, or perhaps how irresponsible the leadership of the church has been.

The problem

It will be impossible to proceed with this subject until we have removed certain obstacles. This document is written by an evangelical Christian and is primarily directed to this constituency. It is unfortunately true that for many in this constituency the term "human rights" has negative connotations. Is it not the property of secular humanists or even communists? What has it got to do with us? What fellowship has the Christian with the world?

Our argument

One can answer this sentiment with the following arguments:

- ♦ Whenever the church withdraws from an area of central concern to man, the vacuum tends to be filled with other influences. This is particularly true of human rights, an idea that has grown in history from three roots, one found in biblical revelation and Christian tradition, another in the thinking of Greco-Roman philosophers and jurists and a third from Christian and secular humanists during and since the Enlightenment. There is healthy competition between these tributaries and each can predominate in shaping civil society in each generation. Is it to the benefit of mankind that our influence should diminish? Surely not!

- ♦ If one reads the descriptions of the system of the anti-Christ, one reads a catalogue of human rights violations. It is certainly not our calling to wait passively for such a system to emerge in history.

- ♦ While secular humanists are very zealous about human rights, they are incapable of justifying them morally. There are no moral absolutes without an absolute frame of reference. Without God, human rights have no real meaning. Historically, Christians have played a major role in justifying, defining and legislating such rights. We will show that this is definitely our field and one that we dare not abandon.

- ♦ Respect for human life is derived from central areas of biblical revelation: the *eschaton*, the creation, the incarnation, and the atoning work of Christ.

Human rights violations

Amnesty International (the vision of Peter Benenson, a Catholic lawyer) is one of many organisations dedicated to reporting violations. It is not really necessary to catalogue the gruesome record, which continues to this day. One only needs to mention Nazi Germany, Argentinean and South African fascism, Biafra, Rwanda, Yugoslavia and Indonesia to call to mind the barbarities of our age. Africa as a continent has one of the worst records, almost equal to the terrible record of Marxist and Islamic states.

THE HISTORY OF HUMAN RIGHTS

Those who will not learn from history are doomed to repeat its mistakes. Biblical Christians will benefit a great deal from the history of human rights. It reveals how different influences leaven society and shape history for better or worse and how the gospel competes with other worldly and demonic powers for the soul of man. Without a clear grasp of the roots of human rights, we will not be able to bring them to our generation.

This will be a deliberately selective sketch of the history of human rights designed to show evangelical Christians how and why they are our concern and responsibility. By doing this, I do not intend to denigrate the influence of the humanist tradition, or to suggest that the Christian faith has been the only influence.

There are certain principles one must bear in mind when one tackles such a subject. There are different levels of agreement and disagreement between Christian faith and worldly philosophies on a scale or continuum from one extreme to the other. On some issues we stand in total antithesis to all other belief systems as, for instance, when we claim that Jesus Christ is the way, the truth and the life. On other issues we find ourselves in agreement with some secular views and not with others as, for instance, when we agree with pro-life as against pro-choice. On other issues we agree, almost totally, with secular humanists as, for instance, when we affirm that murder is wrong. When we agree, our reasons for agreeing are very different (the Ten Commandments rather than the autonomy and value of man in himself). Nevertheless, when we agree, we can and must affirm our solidarity with others and not be embarrassed about leavening society in the same direction. Neither should we be prevented from solidarity at some levels because we clash radically at other levels. Each issue or area of truth must be taken in its context.

As we examine formative individuals in this history, we will observe another scale or continuum. Some outstanding individuals were clearly and unambiguously motivated by a regenerate, personal faith in Jesus Christ. Others were, we suspect, regenerate Christians, but we cannot be absolutely certain. Yet we know that their thinking was permeated with biblical truth. This often occurs with second generation Christians who, while not discovering a personal faith, still assumed and moved from biblical foundations in the way they leavened society. Others were probably not Christians themselves but reflected, consciously or consciously, a Christian world view, the influence of which was significant in their contribution. Still others were definitely not Christians, but nevertheless had assumptions that were akin to biblical faith (theists rather than atheists), which caused them to think in terms of absolute morality. Here again we join hands with our allies when it is appropriate to do so.

Others will appear to be obviously influenced by forms of thinking which are antagonistic to Christian faith, and we must be alert to the negative implications of such ideas. Yet others will be a mixed bag, now supporting a Christian world view, now opposing it. Blanket repudiations or justifications of individuals or their ideas will merely confuse the issue. What we require is the ability to discern where truth must be separated from error.

Human rights is one of those issues that can be deduced from biblical truths but is not specifically found within Scripture itself. A truth does not need to be explicitly stated to be essential to Scripture. The Trinity is the first and most obvious example. Slavery is a closer parallel. It is assumed by the biblical writers and never specifically condemned. However, this does not mean that the real intention of Scripture is compatible with slavery. It was therefore inevitable that Christians would later deduce the antipathy of the essence of Scripture to slavery and lead the struggle for its abolition. In similar fashion subsequent Christian thinkers have concluded that human rights are central to biblical truth even though they are not explicitly taught in Scripture. The biblical support for human rights is as evident as its inherent antipathy to slavery. We should feel as deeply about human rights as our evangelical predecessors felt about slavery. In fact the slavery issue is an aspect of human rights.

There are other democratic principles which Christians have helped to shape through history which are less easily derived from Scripture but which almost all Christians hold to be essential to their conscience. There is a clear logic the flows from biblical theology. Here we have to give some place for progressive revelation, not in the sense of an addition to Scripture, but in the sense that new contexts and new epochs have led Christians to adopt universally certain positions as they have applied their faith to the situation.

Early historical developments

We will return to biblical revelation in more detail. At this point we should simply note that the testimony of the prophetic-apostolic writers brought to the ancient world a powerful and profound view of man made in the image of God, man-in-the-world, born under divine law, redeemed by the Son of Man and destined to share the glory of God.

We should never forget that the entire classical world view and culture had reached a cul-de-sac by the apostolic period. The Greek and Roman philosophies and gods had lost their vigour. The church took over the ancient world because no other world view could hold society together. The Fathers allowed certain elements in classical thought in because they felt they were acceptable, not because the gospel was subdued by its superior or equal.[5]

John's concept of the Logos allowed them to begin the accommodation. The Logos was a concept that already had a history in Greek philosophy as the universal rationality behind the cosmos. John stated that the Logos was the light that enlightens every man (Jn 1:4). The Fathers deduced that this wisdom or rationality had been manifest in the positive truths of classical philosophy. It allowed them to mingle first Plato and later Aristotle with Christian theology. To an extent, these philosophies survived through the church as their custodian. They ceased to have a viable cultural existence of their own. When they emerged with new vigour through the Enlightenment, they emerged from the womb of the church, a church that had sadly succumbed to its own dogma and prejudice. Most of the early humanists were Christians. Modern humanism did not emerge from nowhere with roots that were independent from the gospel. It is therefore legitimate for Christian faith to lay claim to those elements of the humanist tradition, which still reflect the soil from which it came.

Greco-Roman law

In Rom 1–2 Paul explains that the law given through Moses has its parallel in the law of conscience that pagans have without the knowledge of the Mosaic Law. He understands this to be derived from creation. Paul's concept, linked to John's understanding of the Logos as the "light of men" through creation, forms a bridge with the theory of "natural law" in the Greco-Roman world.

The early Greek philosophers believed in a universal law transcending individuals, derived from the divine law (Logos) and expressed in the civil law. Transcendent law was known to man through conscience. Socrates spoke of a "kind of inward voice" in human nature. If one "acts rightly, this voice will not trouble one".[6]

Plato spoke of the unchanging world of ideas based on the Logos or reason in the universe. Laws were not the result of the mere conventions of imperfect men, but reflections of common human reason, man at his peak, derived from the ideal transcendent world, giving equality to all men. Similarly Aristotle grounded natural law on transcendental reality known to men through reason. The potential or higher aspect of man is moral, rational and social.

The Stoics believed natural law derived from the law of reason in the cosmos. There was an innate reason in man linked to cosmic reason, which was therefore universal to all men. Their beliefs infused Roman thinking with the idea of law as God-given, eternal, unchanging, universal, giving fundamental rights to men.

Cicero, the great Roman jurist, was deeply influenced by these ideas. It took the practical Romans to develop a positive body of laws based on the Greek theoretical premise.

Indeed, the Gentiles who do not have the law "show that the requirements of the law are written on their hearts, their consciences also bearing witness, and their thoughts now accusing, now even defending them" (Rom 2:15).

Yet from the very beginning another tradition competed with the idea of transcendent natural law. The Sophists pointed to the wide disparities in human law in various societies and rejected the idea of universality. Taking man as the "measure of all things", they rejected the notion of moral absolutes. Their views would surface again in the various positivist and sociological theories of legality.

The Church Fathers

It took the two great theologians of the Middle Ages, Augustine and Aquinas, to bring the two streams together.

Augustine placed Stoic philosophy alongside Christian theology and argued that both the divine will and divine reason were the source of absolute law, which was binding on all men. This was the first and highest level of legality. The second level was found in the unchangeable natural law, the divine law given to man's reason, heart and soul. The third level was the positive law found in the Christian Roman Empire, which was subject to change but still bound within the limits of absolute divine law.

Thomas Aquinas taught that the state is subject to a higher law that is first divine and then rational or natural. Divine reason is linked to the universal reason inherent in man. This is the basis of three levels of natural law: first, the love of God and neighbour; second, the Ten Commandments, including obedience to parents and the protection of life and property, and third, the rules of civic justice which are derived from the first two.

Because the law is superior to the authority of the state, the state is there to serve the people. A king who is unfaithful to his duty loses his right to demand obedience. It is not wrong to depose him, for he himself has become a rebel. It is the people who have the sense of natural law, inherent in all men, within them and therefore all political authority is derived from the people or their representatives.

We should note here that Paul never intended to place the natural law of Gentile conscience alongside divine law as of equal value. He was merely showing that man is without excuse before God because he cannot claim ignorance of the sense of right and wrong. John's "light of men" was similarly no more than an echo or anticipation of the true light that came into the world through the Incarnation. The apostles would never have placed natural human reason alongside revelation as a source of moral absolutes.

Despite this criticism, the Christian Roman system did anchor law, and therefore human rights, in God as the absolute criterion and judge. It made kings subject to two superior powers, God and the law.

This development led to the first great step forward in human rights legislation, the Magna Carta. Although there were various anticipations in European history, the English Magna Carta has become the milestone of early development.

Magna Carta (1215)

The "Great Charter" was an agreement entered into between King John and the English barons who forced John to accept its terms through force of arms. Stephen Langton, Archbishop of Canterbury, formulated the terms in liaison with the barons. While it hardly benefited the common people at the time, it marked the beginning of a social contract between the crown and the governed, laying the foundations of the concept of contract or covenant between the state and the people. It established the principle of the crown being subject to the rule of law. It also initiated the idea that the crown should be accountable to the accepted leaders of the realm. The significant feature for human rights was the principle it laid down concerning fair trial through due process of law.

The relevant sections for our subject are as follows.

The Christian orientation is obvious from the opening paragraph:

> John, by the grace of God ... out of reverence for God and for the salvation of our soul ... for the honour of God and the exaltation of holy church, and for the reform of our realm, on the advice of our venerable fathers, Stephen, Archbishop of Canterbury, etc.

> 1. In the first place have granted to God ... that the English church shall be free, and shall have its rights undiminished and its liberties unim-

paired ... We have also granted to all free men of our kingdom, for ourselves and our heirs for ever, all the liberties written below, to be had and held by them and their heirs of us and our heirs.

12. No scutage (tax) or aid shall be imposed in our kingdom unless by common counsel of our kingdom ...

39. No free man shall be arrested or imprisoned or disseised (have his land seized) or outlawed or exiled or in any way victimised, neither will we attack him or send anyone to attack him, except by the lawful judgement of his peers or by the law of the land.

42. It shall be lawful in future for anyone, without prejudicing the allegiance due to us, to leave our kingdom and return safely and securely by land and water, save, in the public interest, for a short period in time of war — except for those imprisoned or outlawed in accordance with the law of the kingdom and natives of a land that is at war with us and merchants (who shall be treated as aforesaid).

Section 61 then gives the barons the right to make the king accountable if he fails to abide by the terms of the agreement in future.

The Reformation (1517)

Four implications of the Reformation are relevant to our subject.

First, Luther took his stand on the right to freedom of conscience. This was to have far-reaching repercussions for human rights.

Second, the competition between Roman and Reformed Christianity, followed by the Hundred Years' War, eventually established the right to the freedom of religion, although the principle of *cuis regia eius religia* was really a compromise on the way to its full recognition.

Third, the Reformation led to the collapse of the old feudal order of European society, resulting in the creation of nation states. These new states were forced to find a new system to replace the old and turned to the Reformational stress on the covenant relationship between God and his people as the basis on which they formulated the relationship between the state and the governed (the social contract theory). This had already begun to emerge with the teaching of Aquinas and Magna Carta.

Fourth, the collapse of the old order underlined the need to be suspicious about the sinfulness of man when given too much power to lord it over his fellow man. This was thoroughly explained by Calvin's doctrine of total depravity.

English Developments

The Petition of Right (1628)

Charles I was forced to accept the Petition of Right by the English parliament because he depended on them to vote certain funds he required. It gave subjects the right to institute legal proceedings against the crown if land had been taken from them unjustly. It stated that the king could not levy taxes without the consent of parliament and in effect established the supremacy of law over the wishes of the king. Charles attempted to resist its terms which led eventually to his death.

Edward Coke, the primary formulator of the Petition, drew on the Magna Carta for his inspiration. He was educated at Trinity College, Cambridge and was a respected, incorruptible man.

The Habeas Corpus Act (1679)

This was an ancient common law writ issued by a court or judge directing one who holds another in his custody to produce the "body" of the person before the court for some specified purpose. Although it had been in operation before the Magna Carta, it really came into force by the Act. It was used to correct violations of personal liberty by directing judicial inquiry into the legality of detention. The Founding Fathers of the US Constitution ensured that it "shall not be suspended".

Detention without trial, or what we now term the violation of "due process of law", has its origins in habeas corpus. Due process is one of the most fundamental human rights.

The Bill of Rights (1689)

James II, disliked by his people, was forced to flee after William of Orange (the Netherlands) invaded the country on the invitation of various national leaders. The Glorious Revolution enabled parliament to establish itself as the supreme authority in the land. Princess Mary (James's Protestant daughter) and William were declared to share the crown and Mary's heirs were to guarantee a Protestant dynasty. The terms of the agreement between parliament and the crown are found in the Bill of Rights, which guaranteed further human rights. The representatives of the people gathered at Westminster "... in order to such an establishment as that their religion, laws and liberties might not again be in danger of being subverted ..."

Among its many clauses it lays down the following:

- ♦ The crown cannot suspend laws without the consent of parliament.
- ♦ The right of subjects to petition the king.
- ♦ The holding of a standing army by the king during times of peace was declared illegal.
- ♦ Subjects were guaranteed the right to bear arms for their defence, suitable to their conditions, as allowed by law.
- ♦ The representative election of parliament should be frequent.
- ♦ "That the freedom of speech and debates or proceedings in parliament ought not to be impeached or questioned in any court or place out of parliament."
- ♦ "That all grants and promises of fines and forfeitures of particular persons before conviction are illegal and void." In other words one is presumed innocent until found guilty.

These rights were then guaranteed as follows:

And they do claim, demand and insist upon all and singular these premises as their undoubted rights and liberties, and that no declarations, judgements, doings or proceedings to the prejudice of the people in any of the said premises ought in any wise to be drawn hereafter into consequence or example.

The strongly Protestant sentiment of the Bill is expressed in the oath of loyalty to the crown that states:

I do swear that I do from my heart abhor, detest and abjure as impious and heretical this damnable doctrine and position, that Princes excommunicated or deprived by the Pope or by any authority of the see of Rome may be deposed or murdered by their subjects or any other whatsoever.

This history indicates how long it took to establish these rights and how deep the struggle was for their protection. It simultaneously reveals the powerful influence of the church all along the way.

The developments in England were to play a crucial role in the founding of the United States. Before we examine those developments, we must pause to consider the role played by certain crucial, formative thinkers.

Key figures

William Blackstone

William Blackstone (1723–1780), an orthodox Anglican, was the first to lecture extensively on English law. His *Commentaries on the Laws of England* became the effective authority on the subject and made a deep impression on the American Founding Fathers. He remained the most quoted authority by the fifty-five Federalists for an entire decade. He was a strong advocate of prison reform.

Hugo Grotius

Hugo Grotius (1583–1645) is considered to be the founder of international law. A Dutch statesman, jurist, theologian, humanist and poet, he was deeply concerned about the unity of all Christians and deliberately kept contact with both Roman and Protestant leaders. He wrote *De Veritate Religionis Christianae* and a commentary on the Bible, and held the early Christian community to be his theological ideal. He followed Aquinas in his belief in a universal rational law of nature, which he extended to form the basis of international law. The humanist in Grotius did, however, lead him to begin the process of separating the natural law inherent in man from dependence on God. If men have the law within them by virtue of creation, rather than redemption, it follows that their ability to derive laws is not necessarily dependent on their knowledge of God.

John Locke

Few thinkers have been as influential as John Locke (1632–1704). He fled England due to the suspicion that he was part of a plot to overthrow Charles II. In the Netherlands he became a close friend of Prince William of Orange and naturally returned to prominence in Britain once William took the throne after the Glorious Revolution. His thought fits easily into this context. From a strong Puritan, Anglican family, a committed Christian and author of *The Reasonableness of Christianity*, Locke held to the traditional concept of natural law given to man through creation. However he developed new concepts of his own derived from his Puritan background and its understanding of human nature, which he considered to be vital to political philosophy. This was formulated in a threefold argument. First, no man has such complete wisdom and knowledge that he can dictate the form of another man's beliefs. Second, each individual is a moral being, responsible before God, with certain God-given (inalienable) freedoms. Third, no compulsion contrary to the will of the individual can achieve any more than outward conformity.

Working from the Reformational understanding of covenant relationships, Locke developed his concept of the state. The justification for the existence of governments was that they could safeguard human freedoms better than individuals. Following the assumption of God-given freedoms, he deduced that a group of such free individuals could contract (covenant) together to submit jointly or limit their freedoms to a common authority (the legislature) when they decide to form a civil society. This first contract is followed by a second, when the people covenant with the duly constituted government within a relationship of trust involving the clear understanding that government exists to protect the rights, life, liberty and property of individuals. The government promises to execute its trust faithfully, leaving to the people the right to rebel in case the government violates its trust (as with Charles II).

It is interesting to note that Locke wished to exclude atheists from the social contract because they could not be relied on to take the original covenantal oath or to abide by the divine sanctions invoked in its violation.

Locke, more than any other, influenced Jefferson in his Declaration of Independence.

Montesquieu

Montesquieu (1689–1755) was a Roman Catholic believer although he was critical of the church of his day. His *The Spirit of Law* was placed on the index of books censured by the Pope. He was the first to articulate clearly the concept of the separation of powers. He had observed this developing in Britain. Since the purpose of political association was liberty, and the very definition of tyranny is the accumulation of power in the same hands, he urged the division of the three functions of government: the legislature, the judiciary and the executive. Notice that the concept emerges out of a healthy suspicion about human nature. It certainly would not emerge from the idea that man is inherently good and only becomes corrupt through certain structures.

Thomas Paine

Thomas Paine (1737–1809) was a deist. This means he did not accept the Christian gospel but did believe in a creator. A general Christian environment, plus a personal belief in transcendent values, shaped his sense of morality. His writings particularly inspired the American War of Independence against Britain. Washington ordered one of his pamphlets to be read to the troops at Valley Forge. Later he became involved in the French Revolution and wrote *The Rights of Man*. Among his ideas were popular education, relief of the poor, pensions for the aged, public works for the unemployed and the financing of such measures through the levy of a progressive income tax. He deplored the reign of terror and fought to save the life of the loyalists and of Louis XVI.

This is a fitting stage to return to our résumé of important steps in the development of human rights.

The United States

The American Declaration of Independence (1776)

Essential to understanding this declaration is the previous development of the Constitution of Virginia, a state with strong Puritan roots. James Madison and Patrick Henry had led this state to include a Bill of Rights in its Constitution. Madison, of Anglican Puritan persuasion, urged the inclusion of a Bill of Rights in the US Constitution and refused to sign it because it initially failed to do so. He was proved correct and the US Bill of Rights was added through the first ten amendments to the Constitution. Madison was ahead of his time concerning slavery, which he gave as another reason for his refusal to sign the US Constitution.

Thus, while Jefferson was somewhere between a deist and a liberal "Christian", the formative influences behind the Declaration were Locke and Madison.

True to the philosophy of John Locke, the Declaration begins with this historic language:

> When in the Course of human events, it becomes necessary for one people to dissolve the political bands which have connected them with another, and to assume among the powers of the earth, the separate and equal station to which the Laws of Nature and of Nature's God entitle them, a decent respect to the opinions of mankind requires that they should declare the causes which impel them to the separation.

> We hold these truths to be self-evident, that all men are created equal, that they are endowed by their Creator with certain unalienable Rights, that among these are Life, Liberty and the pursuit of Happiness —

> That to secure these rights Governments are instituted among Men, deriving their just powers from the consent of the governed —

> That whenever any Form of Government becomes destructive of these ends, it is the Right of the People to alter or to abolish it, and to institute

new Government laying its foundation on such principles and organizing its powers in such form, as to them shall seem most likely to effect their Safety and Happiness.

It then lists all the violations of good government and human rights perpetrated by the British crown and declares the states independent. The conclusion is as follows:

And for the support of this Declaration, with a firm reliance on the protection of divine Providence, we mutually pledge to each other our Lives, our Fortunes and our sacred Honor.

Notice again the social contract principles of Locke in this conclusion.

The Constitution of the United States

It has become in vogue among secular writers to suggest that the philosophy behind the Constitution is deist and humanist rather than Christian. However the evidence will simply not allow this interpretation. American society had been saturated with evangelical and Puritan Christian values. There was the First Great Awakening of the 1740s led by Jonathan Edwards and George Whitefield. The evangelical Presbyterian minister John Witherspoon, who used to teach on theology and principles of government, taught nine of the fifty-five delegates. Franklin was a friend of Whitefield. Sherman was a regular member of the congregation pastored by Jonathan Edwards Jr. Of the fifty-five delegates, none were clearly confessed deists. In fact twenty-eight were Episcopalians, eight were Presbyterians, seven were Congregationalists, two Lutheran, two Dutch Reformed, two Methodist and two Roman Catholic. The three who are said to have been deists, Williamson, Franklin and Wilson, all studied for the ministry in Calvinistic churches. So great was Calvin's influence on America that historians have named him the "virtual founder of America" or the "father of America".[7]

The Christian influence can be demonstrated from the fact that of their known writings, 34% of the quotations come from Scripture and 22% from writings influenced in some measure by the Enlightenment. Among the latter Christian scholars predominate (Montesquieu 8,3%, Blackstone 7,9%, Locke 2,9%) with most other writers scoring from 0,5 to roughly 1%.

James Madison, often called the "Father of the Constitution" due to his pivotal role was one of Witherspoon's Calvinist disciples. John Jay, a zealous Christian, was President of the American Bible Society. Hamilton was also a Calvinist and strongly influenced in his views by the total depravity of man. Franklin, the supposed deist, intervened towards the end of the Constitutional Convention because of the strife he observed and called the body to prayer, saying:

> I have lived, Sir, a long time; and the longer I live, the more convincing proofs I see of this truth, that God governs the affairs of man ... We have been assured, Sir, in the sacred writings that "except the Lord build the house, they labor in vain that build it". I firmly believe this; and I also believe that, without his concurring aid, we shall succeed in this political building no better than the builders of Babel.[8]

For our purpose, the most significant element in the Constitution is the Bill of Rights. This provides for the following:

- Freedom of religion, speech, the press and rights of assembly and petition.
- The right to bear arms.
- Protections from having to have soldiers accommodated in private homes against their will.
- Protections from having one's private home or effects searched, seized or violated.
- The right to due process of law in criminal cases, including the protection of life, liberty and property and protection from having to testify against oneself.
- The right to a speedy and public trial by impartial jury and guarantees of a capable defence.
- Judicial rights in civil cases.
- Just and reasonable bails, fines and punishments.
- The rights of one not to jeopardise the rights of another.
- The powers not delegated to the United States by the Constitution, nor prohibited by it to the States, are reserved to the States, or to the people.

The carefully balanced nature of the main body of the Constitution reflects a commitment to limiting the accumulation of power which, as we have learned, derives ultimately from a view of man's depravity. The Bill of Rights affirms the dignity of man while the balancing factors affirm the sinfulness of man.

So began the "land of the free and the home of the brave".

Through a different lens

There are some vital differences between the American and French Revolutions despite the symbiotic relationship between the two. We have been following the developing history of human rights reflected through the prism of Christian convictions. Simultaneously another tradition was developing, often interwoven with the first, that of secular humanism. Its origins can be found in the Sophists of ancient Greece, who questioned the existence of a universal norm. It took a step forward when the Church Fathers went beyond Paul and John to give an almost equal place to truths of reason alongside truths of revelation. Where Paul and John saw the general knowledge of God and the law of conscience as a mere anticipation of the gospel, the Fathers tended to create two equal paths reflected in nature and grace. It was only a matter of time before Grotius could make certain aspects of what man has through nature independent of grace and then, only a matter of time before secular humanists located norms and values in autonomous man. The message of the Sophists would come full circle. A vital stage in this process was the Renaissance, in which many of the ideas of the classical past were renewed.

Machiavelli

Machiavelli (1469–1527) is the most significant for our subject, a man remarkably ahead of his time. Machiavelli wished to disengage political philosophy from the world of transcendent and religious norms so that man and the state are viewed totally realistically, within purely human history. What mattered was practical power. For a stable society, power had to be kept in the hands of the sovereign (Prince) who must use whatever means necessary to preserve the state, including cruelty, deception and force. He suggested all sorts of practical ways in which this may be achieved.

Here for the first time man, as the measure of all things, finds it possible to be his own god, knowing what is best for his fellow man without any sense of moral accountability. These ideas were to mature into visible historical force with some of those who stood behind the French Revolution.

Thomas Paine and other deists were a stage on the way, but it was people like Voltaire and Jean Jacques Rousseau who paved the way for the French Revolution.

Jean Jacques Rousseau (1712–1778)

As charismatic Christians, we must conclude that Rousseau needed inner healing, but never obtained it. He suffered, throughout his life, from severe emotional distress, an inferiority complex and feelings of guilt. His mother died giving birth to him and his father vacillated between accepting and rejecting him. He was never able to keep a job. He converted from Protestantism to Roman Catholicism but felt continually guilty about it until he converted back to Protestantism.

He did have outstanding literary gifts and his ideas have been very influential. He believed that man, left in a state of nature, is inherently good but becomes corrupted by organised society, which creates aggression. In other words, he believed in structural sin over personal sin. His recipe was to place people in carefully controlled communes where their behaviour could be conditioned. On a larger scale, democracy could be safeguarded through training, guidance, pro-paganda, censorship and the reduction of privacy, in other words, social engineering. Much of this could be worked out in simple agricultural units. These ideas were a strong influence on Robespierre and later, the socialists.

It is interesting to note that the American Founding Fathers were not at all impressed with this radical tradition. The deism that had influenced some of them was of a much more tame variety than European deism. Others had strong opinions against the radicals. John Adams, one of the most widely read, expressed the view: "If ever there existed a wise fool, a learned idiot, a profound deep-thinking coxcomb, it was David Hume. As much worse than Voltaire and Rousseau as a sober decent libertine is worse than a rake." [9] The Fathers knew, as Washington stated, that "reason and experience both forbid us to expect that national morality can prevail in exclusion of religious principle". Morris, who drafted the final stage of the Constitution, was of the opinion that it could not work in France because they lacked the moral character for responsible self-government.

The French Revolution

For all the similarities, the American and French Revolutions were motivated by different value systems and led to radically different consequences, the first to liberty, the second to the reign of terror followed by the dictatorship of Napoleon Bonaparte.

The French National Assembly was divided between the type of human rights advocates we have seen in the United States context and radicals who supported these rights from the basis of the value system we have just examined. It was therefore a mixed bag. Some historians trace the use of the terms "left" and "right" to the seating positions of the different factions in the French Assembly. Despite the mixture, the Declaration of the Rights of Man and of the Citizen (1789) reflects a basically deist understanding of universal or inalienable rights. Thomas Paine had been as influential as Jean Jacques Rousseau.

The Declaration of the Rights of Man and of the Citizen

> The representatives of the French People, formed into a National Assembly, considering ignorance, forgetfulness or contempt of the rights of man to be the only causes of public misfortunes and the corruption of Government, have resolved to set forth, in a solemn Declaration, the natural, unalienable and sacred rights of man ...
>
> In consequence whereof, the National Assembly recognizes and declares, in the presence and under the auspices of the Supreme Being, the following Rights of Man and of the Citizen.

Secular humanism had made advances, but not so as to eradicate the acknowledgment that human rights are derived outside man himself, from an absolute point of reference. The leavening effect of the gospel, with the ancient Greek sense of natural law derived from transcendent realities, was still present.

The human rights listed are an excellent summary of the entire history of rights up to this point. They include the following:

- All men are born equal and free.
- The aim of every political association is the preservation of the natural and imprescriptible rights of man. These rights are liberty, property, safety and resistance to oppression.
- Government is derived from the people.
- The rights of one is limited by the equal rights of another.
- Due process of law.
- Every man is presumed innocent until he has been declared guilty.
- Freedom of religion and opinion.
- Freedom of speech and of the press.
- Force, for the maintenance of order, is only permitted for the common good within specific limits.
- All citizens have the right to ascertain, by themselves, or through their representatives, the need for a public tax, to consent to it freely, to watch over its use, and to determine its proportion, basis, collection and duration.

The Receiver of Revenue or IRS is certainly no demigod in terms of such rights!

- Society has the right to ask a public official for an accounting of his administration.

♦ Any society in which no provision is made for guaranteeing rights or for the separation of powers, has no Constitution.

The influence of Montesquieu is evident here. We should note that totalitarian socialist regimes that have looked to the French Revolution as a model have utterly failed to live by its values because they have shown no respect for the separation of powers.

♦ Since the right to property is inviolable and sacred, no one may be deprived thereof, unless public necessity legally ascertained, obviously requires it, and just and prior indemnity has been paid.

Here again, despite what one has to say about the radical element in the French Revolution, the actual Declaration falls clearly within the value system of Western democratic societies and cannot be used, with any legitimacy, by totalitarian states.

The use of the terms "imprescriptible", "inviolable" and "sacred" raises an important point. So long as rights are derived from an ultimate, transcendent authority, namely God, they cannot be either granted or removed by human governments. The moment they are said to be socially or historically determined, i.e. by man himself, there is no certain guarantee against the law of the jungle. This is precisely where secular humanists and legal positivists want to locate them.

The loss of morality

Between the French Revolution and World War II, Greek transcendentalism, Christian theology and deistic assumptions, which had stood so long against humanistic relativism, began to lose ground. The theories of Comte, Darwin and Spenser brought the idea of natural rights into disrepute and ridicule. The human race began to slide towards total relativism and moral anarchy.

This was not all. Something far more sinister began to develop. The instincts of Machiavelli towards totalitarian power gained new and far more sophisticated allies in the form of Idealist philosophers. The exact relationship between this philosophical development and the idea of the totalitarian state is complex and would detract us from our subject.[10] Fundamentally transcendence was replaced more and more by immanence. Values and norms came to be located increasingly within the flow or progress of history, within man himself and his evolution, especially in the state. Fichte and Hegel were particularly significant. The result was a philosophy of the state where the individual lost real significance but was to be viewed in and for the state. The whole took priority over the parts. The individual exists and finds the meaning of his existence as his destiny is buried in the cause of the state. God had been dethroned and the man-made state had been enthroned.

Again the details of the development are complex, but from this Idealist statist philosophy there developed two systems that were merely the reflection of each other, National Socialism and international socialism, fascism and Marxism. As Paul Johnson has shown so well in his *A History of the Modern World*, there is really no fundamental difference between the two systems, especially when it comes to the total disregard for human rights.

Since World War II

It took two horrifying shocks to the human race, namely the two World Wars, to break the spell of madness and bring about a return to the ancient notion of natural law, or transcendent values.

Human rights, in its developed form, only really arose after World War II. The barbarity of man drove him to acknowledge that he is not the measure of all things.

> Iusnaturalism, in the sense of the assertion of an order of norms for human conduct transcending human will, to which the validity of positive law is subjected, has certainly experienced a 20th-century revival. The massive human delinquencies of the century, such as those of the Nazis, have been important in stimulating these modern natural-law yearnings.[11]

The first move was the Four Powers Agreement (1945) which created a category of "crimes against humanity" superseding even the sovereignty of nation states. The second development was the Universal Declaration of Human Rights (1948).

The Universal Declaration of Human Rights

The introduction to the Declaration specifically gives testimony to the revival of belief in natural (transcendentally derived) human rights.

> Whereas recognition of the inherent dignity and of the equal and inalienable rights of all members of the human family is the foundation of freedom, justice and peace in the world,

> Whereas disregard and contempt for human rights have resulted in barbarous acts which have outraged the conscience of mankind,

Whereas the people of the United Nations have in the Charter reaffirmed their faith in fundamental human rights.

Notice the context of World War II barbarities, and consequently the "reaffirmation" of faith in "fundamental and inalienable" rights. We have shown the strong influence of Christians, shaped in their thinking by the gospel, in the entire history of human rights to this point. What of the United Nations Declaration?

Rene Cassin

John W Montgomery, author of one of the most helpful recent books on the subject, *Human Rights and Human Dignity*, shows the connection between the Ten Commandments and the UN Declaration through the influence of Rene Cassin. Cassin is described as the major author and "virtual father" of the document.[12] Two statements by Montgomery summarise the connection.

> Johannes Morsink certainly goes too far in maintaining that "the U.N. representatives ... replace eighteenth-century deism with a twentieth-century secular humanism ..." The absence of reference in the Declaration to "nature and nature's God" is hardly the equivalent of "turning down any suggestion of a normative source transcendent to human nature". The Commission of Human Rights, which drafted the Declaration (chiefly drawing on Cassin's labors) and the Third Committee which revised it (one of its most influential members was Lebanese Christian Charles Malik) avoided for political and pragmatic reasons the question of the ultimate origin of human rights — leaving each signatory and reader to supply the lacuna (hopefully with transcendence, as Cassin and Malik surely did)".[13]

> Marc Agi, recent French biographer of Rene Cassin, takes pains to emphasize how concerned Cassin was to interrelate religion and human rights. At the 1970 meeting of the Decalogue Lawyers Society in Chicago, Cassin maintained that a direct and powerful relationship existed between the Ten Commandments and the Universal Declaration of Human Rights.[14]

The UN Declaration follows what are technically known as the "three generations" of human rights. The three generations reflect the development in time of three stages of human rights legislation, three types of rights in themselves, and three interest groups or groups of nations that stress particular kinds of human rights.

The first generation

These arose in the history of the First World and reflect the thinking of the English, American and French revolutions. They are basically negative rights in the sense that they define freedom from evil rather than freedom for life. Freedom from too much government intervention is basic. They want to protect the individual or family from more powerful bodies and therefore represent the triumph of Lockean individualism over Hegelian statism. They are stated in Articles 2–21 of the Universal Declaration and cover the following:

- Freedom from racial discrimination.
- The right to life, liberty and security of person.
- Freedom from slavery or the like.
- Freedom from torture or arbitrary arrest, detention or exile.
- Due process of law.
- The right to privacy.
- Freedom of movement.
- The right to asylum.
- Freedom of thought, conscience, opinion and expression.
- Freedom of religion.
- Freedom to peaceful assembly and association.
- Freedom to participate directly in government through free and fair elections.
- The protection of property rights.

These are sometimes viewed as the most fundamental rights because without them all the other rights become difficult or impossible.

The second generation

These rights, although they can also be traced to various European thinkers, have emerged in the struggles of Second and Third World nations against colonialism and the misuses of capitalist financial power. They reflect democratic socialist thinking. Where the former seek to contain the encroachment of government, these rights want to make certain that lack of intervention does not lead to the abstention of government from social responsibilities. They are therefore termed "positive" rights, stressing freedom for rather than freedom from. They are contained in Articles 22–27 of the Declaration and deal with the following:

♦ The right to social security.

♦ Protection against unemployment.

♦ The right to rest and leisure (just leave time from work).

♦ The right to basic health care.

♦ The right to an equal education for all.

♦ The right to the protection of one's scientific, literary and artistic production.

♦ The right to seek employment where one wishes.

♦ The right to form trade unions.

The third generation

These are the latest, least developed rights and while they do reflect in a measure the so-called north-south divide, they actually reflect a growing international concern for the entire environment in which man lives as a total species. They are therefore termed "solidarity rights". They concern man as a whole, rather than particular nations, but also stress the ethics of relationships between nations. They are reflected in Article 28 of the Declaration:

> Everyone is entitled to a social and international order in which the rights and freedoms set forth in this Declaration can be fully realised.

As they have developed, they have covered the following areas:

♦ The right to political, economic, social and cultural self-determination.

♦ The right to economic and social development.

♦ The right to benefit from the common heritage of mankind (earth's resources, scientific discoveries, etc.).

♦ The right to peace.

♦ The right to a healthy environment.

♦ The right to humanitarian disaster relief.

As one moves from the first to the third generation of rights, they become less justiciable and more aspirational. They express more hope than law, more vision than concrete legal protection. This is why each layer has to be built on the previous one. Human society must be built from the bottom up.

The temptation to postpone the first generation rights until the second and third have been established is naive and doomed to fail. This has been the fundamental problem of most radical revolutionary movements.

Conclusion

This sketch of the history of human rights leads to the following fundamental conclusions.

1. The issue of how one justifies or derives human rights is crucial. Moral or ethical norms cannot be derived from within man or history but require a transcendent reference point.

2. The Greco-Roman world, the Judeo-Christian tradition and deist thinking have a basic agreement on transcendence but the Judeo-Christian faith has been the predominant custodian and articulator of such transcendent norms.

3. Christians have been extremely influential in the development of human rights and cannot afford, in any generation, to leave the field to other influences.

4. The loss of transcendent values has led to barbarity and the return to civilised norms goes hand in hand with the affirmation of transcendence.

THE BIBLICAL TEACHING ON HUMAN RIGHTS

There are a number of issues that emerge from the relationship between biblical teaching and human rights. The Scriptures do not speak, specifically, of rights. How should we conceive of the relationship between truths of special revelation and truths of general revelation? What is the significance of the law/grace relationship to this subject?

Ethically more issues emerge. What exactly is a right? It is obviously not a need. Is it a claim? Is it more?

We will want to base our understanding of the Scriptures on fundamental theological themes, rather than proof texts.

All these and many other questions can and should be faced. However such an approach conflicts with another, practical requirement. If it is true that legislation alone cannot safeguard human rights but that an entire society needs to be leavened with human rights values for any measure of success, simple, communicable Bible studies become the most urgent requirement. What we need first is proof text type biblical teaching that can be worked through by preachers with little theological education, house groups, etc.

For this reason we will proceed first to a breakdown of the basic relevant texts.

Texts for human rights

Human governments

The Scriptures are quite clear that all human governments have a delegated, relative authority. No government can claim absolute sovereignty. They are accountable to God, the ultimate judge.

Authorities have been established by God (Rom 13:1–5). Pilate would have no authority but for God (Jn 19:11). Forced to choose, God's people will always obey God rather than man (Acts 4:19; 5:29). Just as orderly government is given by God, so any government can become demonically inspired (Rev 13).

The careful balance of factors in human government can be deduced from the nation of Israel. There was relative chaos in Israel when there was no king. Everyone did what was right in his own eyes (Jud 21:25). Therefore God instituted a king. A central government must be strong enough to prevent chaos. Yet when this happens, man must be warned of the fact that power corrupts. When you make a man king, he can become oppressive. Samuel was told: "Now listen to them; but warn them solemnly and let them know what the king who will reign over them will do" (1 Sam 8:9). This was given before any king had done either good or bad. In other words, it derives from what God knows about human nature, all human nature. The warning states that a king will:

- ◆ make people serve in the army;
- ◆ make others work on his fields;
- ◆ make others work at his court;
- ◆ exact taxes from the produce of the land;
- ◆ enslave members of the public (8:10–22).

This is why kings in Israel were made subject to certain rules. There were "regulations of the kingship" (1 Sam 10:25). We learn that the people asked for the king. They, in that sense, made him king. Each tribe gave its allegiance to him one at a time. The nation gradually converted from the house of Saul to David. First the "men of Judah" (with Ephraim) made David king of Judah (2 Sam 2:4). Then all the tribes (the other ten) came to David at Hebron. The elders of the nation "made a compact" with David and made him king over Israel (2 Sam 5:3). Later, when Rehoboam, Solomon's son became king, he began to break the compact by placing oppressive burdens on the people. Consequently the ten tribes of Israel withdrew their support.

> When all Israel saw that the king refused to listen to them, they answered the king: "What share do we have in David, what part in Jesse's son? To your tents, O Israel! Look after your own house, O David!" So the Israelites went home. But as for the Israelites who were living in the towns of Judah, Rehoboam still ruled over them. (1 Kgs 12:16–17)

Israel's government was therefore federal. The twelve tribes either consented or refused to come under the central ruler.

We also learn from Israel that the king was not the only power in the land. The passages we have looked at show the great power of the elders (1 Kgs 12:1–15). Each village and town had its own elders. We also know that the prophets had great power. Their words could cause some kings to fall and others to rise. Their predictions of judgement on bad kings always came to pass. We also know that the priests had power. They were given the law and were responsible to teach it to the people. The judges, perhaps chosen from among the priests, were authorised to try cases in the land. There were therefore kings, elders, priests, judges and prophets. We can call this a "separation of powers".

From the NT we learn that Jesus instituted a separation between the church and the state when he said: "Give to Caesar ... and to God" (Mk 12:17). He ordained the twelve apostles, who ordained elders in every church. In Acts we see both the authority of the Roman state and the authority of the church existing side by side. The church does not rule over the state and the state does not rule over the church. Here again there was a separation of spheres.

The one power, which was superior to every other in Israel, was the law. It had supreme authority over everyone, including the king. This is implied by the story of David and Uriah the Hittite. David was guilty of stealing and of murder (2 Sam 11–12). The same lesson is learned from the story of Naboth's vineyard. The law protected the property of the common man and not even the king could supersede the law (1 Kgs 21).

Why do governments exist? As we have seen, the basic reason is to prevent chaos, "every man doing what is right in his own eyes". More specifically, governments or rulers exist to protect the powerless. The powerful benefit from government, but it is the poor and weak who especially need protection.

Psalm 72:1 says: "Endow the king with your justice, O God." His just rule will bring the "afflicted ones ... justice" (v. 2), save the "children of the needy" (v. 4). He will "deliver the needy who cry out, the afflicted who have no one to help (v. 12). He will rescue them from oppression and violence, for precious is their blood in his sight" (v. 14). Notice the stress on the value of human life.

The poor

The primary responsibility of government is supported by the numerous references to the needs of the poor. The test of justice is whether it extends to the poor. Amos finds Israel guilty because "you deprive the poor of justice in the courts" (Amos 5:12). Special legislation existed to provide for the poor from harvests (Deut 15:11; Lev 19:9–10). Sodom was judged because it enjoyed great wealth while oppressing the poor (Ezek 16:49). Isaiah accuses Israel of crushing the poor into the dust (Is 3:13–14). There are a great number of such texts (Is 58:6–7; Ps 12:5; 14:6).

Others who are weak and who enjoy special protection are the widows and orphans (Ex 22:22; Ps 68:5–6) and strangers or aliens (Ex 22:21).

Equality and value

Why should governments protect all human beings, especially the poor? Humans have incalculable value and dignity because they are created in the image of God (Gen 1:26–28). Man was created last, as the pinnacle of creation. Psalm 8 teaches that he was made a "little lower than the heavenly beings ... ruler over the works of your hands ... all flocks and herds, and the beasts of the field, the birds of the air, and the fish of the sea" (vv. 5–8). Psalm 139 marvels at the wonder of how God has made man: "For you created my inmost being; you knit me together in my mother's womb. I praise you because I am fearfully and wonderfully made" (vv. 13–14).

All men are equally created in his image and therefore have equal value. We all come from one stock (Acts 17:26). This is why, apart from his elective purpose to use Israel as a vehicle to save all people, God treats all nations alike (Amos 9:7).

Impartiality

God is impartial or fair and just because his nature is to be just. His impartiality is also due to the fact that all men are equal.

He is impartial to all men as the Lord of nature (Matt 5:43–48). He accepts all those who fear him from all nations without partiality (Acts 10:34). Accordingly God's laws apply equally to all. Aliens and citizens have equal treatment before the law (Ex 12:49; Lev 24:22; Num 15:15). He expected Israelite judges to be equally impartial (Deut 16:19). Enemies had to be treated as fairly as brothers (Ex 23:4–5; Deut 22:1–4).

Justice

All this can be summarised by saying that the Lord loves justice (Ps 37:28). He is just in all his ways (Ps 145:17). Further, he will judge the gods (and those under them, i.e. governments) for failing to execute justice (Ps 8:1–4).

Due process

Justice demands that people are treated fairly in the actual process of justice. In civil cases both parties must be able to state their case (Ex 22:9). When there has been a transgression of the law, it must be correctly applied and sentence proportionately given (Prov 24:23–25; Ezra 7:26). People cannot be tried twice for the same thing. Nah 1:9 reads: "Whatever they plot against the Lord he will bring to an end; trouble (i.e. trial) will not come a second time."

> The maxim *nimo bis in idipsum vexari*, grounded upon the scriptural injunction "affliction shall not rise up the second time" (Nah 1:9), is the most ancient guarantee in the bill of rights. Its origin in English law is prehistoric and its application has been continuous.[15]

Respect for life

"You shall not murder" (Ex 20:13). This derives from the fact that man was made in the image of God (Gen 9:6). God will one day judge all those who have shed innocent blood, starting with the blood of Abel (Matt 23:35).

Asylum

Because of the value of human life, there were special cities of refuge for those whose lives were being threatened (Ex 21:13; Josh 20).

Amnesty

Israelites could sell themselves into servitude when they could not pay their debts. However, there was legal protection to ensure that no Israelite would have to endure this for too long (Deut 15:1).

Reputation

We must so respect the dignity of human life that we do not harm the reputation of others through false witness (Ex 20:16).

The family

The family is the basic unit of society. It enjoys God's special care. If a man does not provide for his own family, he is worse than an unbeliever (1 Tim 5:8). The home is sacrosanct. There were special laws guarding its dignity and preventing the humiliation of a person in his own home (Deut 24:10–11). This signifies a right to privacy. Parents are alone given the task of being in charge of the education of their children (Deut 6:7; 11:19; Eph 6:1–4). Children are to honour their parents (Ex 20:12).

Work

Every person has a right to work to support a family. Here again there were laws protecting their means to achieve this (Ex 22:26–27; Deut 24:6, 12–13). Workers must be paid justly and without delay (Lk 10:7; 1 Tim 5:18; Deut 24:15). Each person should be able to have his "daily bread", to be able to meet his own needs and be able to give to others in need. "Daily bread" in this sense covers the basic necessities of life: food, clothing and shelter (2 Cor 9:8, 11–12; 1 Thess 4:11–12; 1 Tim 6:8).

Rest

Those who work must also rest (Ex 20:8–11).

Property

One of the ways in which people can supply for their family and safeguard a fair quality of life is to own property. The command: "You shall not steal" implies the protection of all private property (Ex 20:15). Protection of another person's property applies to enemies as well (Ex 23:4). Land is a fundamental form of private property and was justly distributed in Israel (Num 33:54). The Jubilee law was a form of redistribution every seventy years to redress large discrepancies in status (Lev 25).

Choice

Man's relationship with God is based on responsible choice (Gen 2:16; Jn 7:17). This works its way into other relationships. Unlike other systems, the Christian approach to marriage is based on the covenant between Christ and his church (Eph 5) and therefore implies free choice by both parties.

Women

The disciples were shocked by the way Jesus spoke to the Samaritan woman (Jn 4:1–26). This reflected a totally new approach to women in general. Jesus treated them with a respect unheard of in the society of his day. The NT teaching on men and women is foundational to the equality of the sexes.

Revenge

Respect for life and walking in the fear of God means that we cannot follow our human desire for revenge. "Do not take revenge, my friends, but leave room for God's wrath, for it is written: It is mine to avenge; I will repay, says the Lord" (Rom 12:19). One of the ways God "repays" is to use the magistrate to bear his sword (13:3–4). It is better to respect the rule of law than to take personal revenge.

The environment

Man is made in the image of God and man's environment is part of the creation of God. Nature is placed under man as his responsibility (Gen 1:26). It must therefore also be treated with respect. Creation suffers because of the sin of man (Gen 3:15; Hos 2:21–22; 4:1–3). Animals must not be allowed to suffer unnecessarily, even if they belong to an enemy (Ex 23:5). Animals of unequal strength must not plough together (Deut 22:10). Fruit trees were to be protected in times of war (Deut 20:19–20). If man fails to keep the law, it affects the relationship between man and his environment. The land will vomit up the inhabitants (Lev 18:28; 20:22). Violence brings guilt on the land and affects its productivity (2 Sam 21:1).

A biblical theology of human rights

General revelation

The law of Moses is in one sense part and parcel of the Lord's unique redemption of Israel from Egypt. The statutes and regulations constitute the covenant between the Lord and his redeemed people. The NT counterpart is the work of Christ in his death and resurrection and the NT ethics that result from this new covenant relationship. In this sense the Torah (the teaching) is part of the covenant of grace.

In another sense the law of Moses is an expression of man outside of Christ. The law is the schoolmaster to bring us to Christ (Gal 3:24). It is there to condemn. It cannot give life; it can only kill (Rom 7:10–11). The law came through Moses, grace and truth came through Jesus Christ (Jn 1:17). It is part of the dispensation of condemnation, not the dispensation of the Spirit (2 Cor 3:7–18). In this secondary sense the law of Moses is comparable to the law of conscience written on the heart of other nations (Rom 2:12–16). It is significant that biblical scholars can discuss the similarities and differences between Mosaic law and the laws of Hammurabi for instance. The Mosaic law certainly fits into the general understanding of law in ancient near Eastern nations. One discovers that Israel was probably in some sort of contract labour treaty with Egypt and that the exodus altered her status to a conquered nation in a suzerainty treaty with the Lord. The structure of the covenant follows the general structure of international suzerainty treaties of the second millennium BC.[16]

The tradition of law in the Greco-Roman culture is similarly part of the general understanding of law in antiquity.

We can become a little more philosophical and consider the fact that the Johannine use of the Logos concept has its roots both in the Hebrew concept of the Word and the Greek concept of the rationality behind all things.[17] All these, Babylonian law, Mosaic law, Hebrew Word conceptions and Greco-Roman "common law" exist in some sort of common field. This can be compared to that general knowledge of God that all men have by virtue of creation (Rom 1:19–20). All men have a sense of morality. Almost every culture links morality in some sense to deity. The deists can be placed in the same general field.

Traditionally theologians have called this field general revelation. There have been numerous ups and downs about this field, especially in the famous argument between Emil Brunner and Karl Barth on natural theology. What is significant for human rights is that at this level Christian faith and general human belief have a bridge between each other. Here we find allies, though not brothers. We stand with Greco-Roman, Holy Roman and deist thinkers because like us, their sense of general revelation locates human rights in transcendence. We must encourage them in this, rather than discourage them because they cannot share our sense of special revelation.

Special revelation

Special revelation is that revelation which came to man in Jesus Christ and through the outpouring of the Holy Spirit (Heb 1:1–4). It is the result of the intervention of the kingdom of God. Its truth is now recorded in the prophetic/apostolic testimony of Scripture. Here we must stress the utter qualitative difference between this and general revelation. The former is at best man groping in the dark (Eph 4:18). General revelation can never lead to salvation. In fact all it does it to make man more accountable and therefore more condemned. Special revelation is the only way of salvation. Unless a man is born of the Spirit, he cannot enter the kingdom of God (Jn 3:3–6). Only the Father in heaven can give the revelation of the person of Christ. It cannot come through flesh and blood (Matt 16:17).

We cannot therefore really compare general and special revelation. They compare like darkness and light, like idolatry and the living God. It really is a mistake to follow Thomas Aquinas when he makes the two into almost equal partners.

Most of the texts we have looked at so far can fit into general truths of humanity. Deists believe man was created in the image of God. Even religious humanists make common cause with us at times.

When we turn to human rights in the context of special revelation, we enter a totally different field. Now we see everything through redeemed eyes. Now the new criterion is Jesus Christ crucified and risen (1 Cor 2:2). John says: "Yet to all who received him, to those who believed in his name, he gave the right to become children of God – children born not of natural descent, nor of human decision or a husband's will, but born of God" (Jn 1:12–13). Here is something that contrasts with nature. A "right" is given to man to take upon himself a special title, "son of God". He comes into this right through saving faith and regeneration: through the narrow gate. It is one of the many titles the NT reserves for believers, such as saints, priests and heirs. These titles describe the new man in Jesus Christ.

To believe in his name is to believe in the special saving work of Jesus Christ through incarnation, death, burial and resurrection. From the crucified and risen Lord we look backwards and forwards on the whole course of human history (Eph 1:10). We find that what God has done in Jesus Christ is the "already" of something that is "not yet". The future is now in Jesus (1 Cor 10:11). Jesus is the end of the age, who appeared in the midst of this age. What has occurred is the beginning of the *eschaton*, the age to come, the ultimate destiny of man.

We also look back to creation, because we find that Jesus Christ is the fulfilment of the OT Messianic hope that points to the restoration of the creation order. Special revelation views man through Christology, eschatology and creation. On this basis human beings receive a value they could never receive through the groping ideas of Greek philosophers about "natural law". Here we have no allies, only thieves and robbers who want to assume truths of the gospel in a post-Christian era.

At this level we have totally superior weapons. Yet we should not stand aloof, as though we created the weapons ourselves. We have been commissioned to spread this light first through evangelism and world missions and second through the leaven, salt and light of the gospel permeating society for the common good.

Redemption

We have a right to call ourselves children of God because we have believed in Jesus. Who is Jesus?

Incarnation

Jesus is God with us. The mystery of the incarnation tells us that God has honoured and sanctified humanness by becoming a human being himself. If the Lord of creation, the Holy One of Israel, can actually take human existence to himself, there must be a special dignity attached to being human. As we shall see, this was possible because he had already created humanity in his image and had promised that he would bring a new, heavenly humanity to replace the old.

Identification and hope

Jesus not only took human nature to himself, and became "like his brothers in every way" (Heb 2:17), he went further. He chose to associate with a certain type of humanity.

Instead of being born a king, priest or scribe, he was born a carpenter. He mixed with tax collectors, harlots, fishermen and the poor (Matt 9:10–13). He showed respect for the human dignity of women. He loved children. His heart went out to the masses, because they were like sheep without a shepherd (Matt 9:36). He blessed Gentiles and touched lepers. His baptism was a point of identification with confessing sinners (Matt 3:5–6, 13–15). Here was God behaving towards despised, broken humanity in terms of their future. His festive meals pointed ahead to the kingdom to come (Lk 14:12–23). The outcasts were invited to these meals. Somehow he saw people ahead of themselves. He looked at Peter and called him a rock, although Peter was to manifest exactly the opposite character for some time (Jn 1:42). Yet Peter eventually became the rock of the early church. No one saw people in terms of their human potential like Jesus did. He saw everything in terms of the kingdom, a future, glorious reality already present in him.

Ransom

Jesus came to seek and save the lost. To save them, he would give his life for the many (Mk 10:45). In this context he called men to give up their own destiny and follow him. What does it profit, he said, to gain the whole world and lose your life (Mk 8:34–38)? Evidently one human life was worth more than the whole material world. What does it gain, to build a bigger barn and lose your life (Lk 12:13–21)? Why be rich, blind yourself to the beggar at the gate and jeopardise your eternal future (Lk 16:19–31)? Evidently human beings were more valuable to him than they were to themselves.

Jesus chose to call himself the Son of Man. Daniel had described the vision of the future coming of the kingdom of God. The stone would fall from heaven and grow to cover the whole earth (Dan 2). A pre-existent divine/human figure would receive the everlasting kingdom (Dan 7). Yet he was not simply an individual. His name, Son of Man, means mankind, the representative and embodiment of the human race, a new, heavenly human race to replace the earthly, beastly human race expressed in the successive kingdoms of this world. Jesus said the sabbath was made for man, not man for the sabbath, and concluded that the Son of Man was Lord of the sabbath (Mk 2:27–28). He implied a new dignity for humanity was being established in him where such laws served man rather than man the laws. He could say that when he was lifted up on the cross, all men would be drawn to him (Jn 12:32). As he approached his trial and conviction, humanity was walking to its trial.

His trial was a glaring case of the violation of human rights. There was no due process of law, no proper witnesses, no unbiased court of appeal (Matt 26:57–67): Instead there was political conniving, betrayal, and manipulation: a travesty of justice (Matt 27:19–26; Jn 19:12–13). The entire record of man's inhumanity to man was epitomised and summed up in the case of this one man. All men were represented in him. He was executed for being who he was.

Yet deeper than this event another event occurred. Man was tried before the ultimate judge of all men, the living God. He was sentenced as a lawbreaker, a transgressor. The transgressions of all men were taken up in him, cancelled, nailed to the cross and reversed (Col 2:13–14). Rising again he brought justification and acquittal to those who did not deserve it (Rom 3:21–26; 4:25). The whole basis of the biblical concept of salvation is legal, forensic. Now those whose potential he had seen, whom he had viewed in terms of their future, could actually enter into their future. Justification implies the instantaneous transference of a status undeserved and beyond the capability of the sinner (Col 1:13). The sinner becomes, legally, what he is not yet in himself. Again man is being called towards his future. Suddenly he has titles, he is son of God, saint of God, royal priest. Those who were not a people become a royal priesthood, a holy nation (1 Pet 2:7–10). They have been taken out of the old humanity and placed within the new humanity. They are transferred into a new species, a new race. Their solidarity with Adam is changed for solidarity with the Son of Man, the second Adam (Rom 5:12–21). Suddenly their dignity is enhanced, elevated.

They are still on the way to become what they already are. Justification becomes sanctification. They are transformed from one degree of glory to another, ever changing into the image of the Son of Man, the heavenly embodiment of the new humanity (2 Cor 3:16–18).

When one looks at human beings from this perspective – every human being – one sees them in terms of their potential for glory. The gospel is for every man. Every man has already been valuable enough to warrant the blood of the Son of God (1 Jn 2:2). Every human being has the summons to die with Christ and rise with him into the new Adam (Acts 17:30). The lowest specimens of any society receive special dignity because he identified especially with them.

Eschatology

Flesh and blood cannot inherit the kingdom of God. Therefore redeemed man awaits that moment when mortality puts on immortality and he takes on, finally and perfectly, the image of the man from heaven (1 Cor 15:45–54). The justified becomes glorified into the image of the Son of God. Man in Christ enters into the eternal city of God, a united society, inclusive of every tribe and people and language and nation (Rev 7:9–17). There is an incipient internationalism in Christianity. The redemptive work of Christ has broken down the dividing walls (Eph 2:11–22). Pentecost reverses Babel and anticipates the New Jerusalem. Those who have the faith of Abraham are the nations that emerge from his line of descent. These are the children of promise who are inheriting the world (Rom 4:13). They may have a good dose of human patriotism for their own nation but their inner drive is towards the ultimate, united humanity inheriting a new heaven and a new earth. The missionary mandate involves world consciousness. The violation of man, or his environment, anywhere on this planet involves the destruction of something God has promised his children. It cannot be "other people's problems". We await a free, healed, ordered, celebrating society, the true utopia. In Christ all men are called to utopia (Rev 21:1–4). Most of all, this new community is good enough to share forever in the company of God, of the Lamb and of the sevenfold Spirit of God (Rev 21:22–22:6). Finally humans will become what Jesus saw in them when he drew near to tax collectors, harlots and the poor.

We part company with secular humanists and others when they think that man is capable of creating utopia on his own. The spirit of ancient Babel inspires this naive hope. All man can ultimately achieve is to build the tower. This world system remains under the judgement of God. Biblical warnings and the biblical doctrine of man's depravity prevent us from joining in any grandiose ideological theory. We are committed to a sober realism about man.

Yet we cannot allow this to make us resign ourselves to a sense of doom and depression. What of the fact that man outside of Christ has no hope of this destiny; that his destiny actually tends towards the opposite, to eternal separation and death? Does this give us, as Christians, the right to view unredeemed humans with less respect? Surely not! After all, we ourselves are still on the way. Right now we have a dignity we do not deserve. God is favouring us as though we were already through to the other side. How can we, whose future destiny is part of the prophetic future, not view other humans in terms of that same possibility? How can we tell who will and who will not respond to grace and enter into solidarity with the new humanity? We should remember that it is our testimony that becomes the vehicle of God for calling them towards this destiny.

Christians who understand the gospel of grace and the eschatological future of the new man should, of all people on planet earth, view other humans with the greatest respect and consequently hallow the rights and aspirations of people. Legal experts may question whether second generation rights are actually rights at all, due to their inspirational, non-justiciable quality. For the Christian they simply speak of the glorious hope. It is the nature of NT eschatology not to disengage prophetic hope from present realities because the future has become present in Jesus Christ. You will notice that the beatitudes are placed in the context of "now" and "then" (Lk 6:20–26). Those who weep now will laugh then. Those who are rich now will mourn then. Those who mourn now will be comforted then. Each beatitude speaks of the utter reversal of the value system of this present age by the intervention of the age to come. The "then" is not cut off from the "now". Those who become the sons of the kingdom begin to participate already in the life of the age to come. What will occur to humanity is already occurring in him. Eschatology prevents pessimism, even in the most depressing human conditions.

Yet eschatology is a two-edged sword. The same God who will glorify humanity will devastate the earth. The entire world system will come under his devastating judgement. All those who have worshiped the beast will be cast into the lake of fire (Rev 19:11–21). Man's inhumanity to man will be tried before the supreme judge. Who will survive this judgement? It is striking how Paul, when on trial before Felix, spoke of "righteousness, self-control and the judgement to come". "Felix was afraid and said, That's enough for now!" (Acts 24:25). The early Christians were known for their fiery warning about the impending end of the world. The moral punch behind human rights is accountability to the God who will surely judge every violation. This has to give Christians a sense of holy fear when they observe man destroying the life of his fellow man. If merely despising another person amounts to murder (Matt 5:21–22), how will violators of human rights stand on the Day of Judgement? It is significant that the Second Coming will see Jesus destroying the kingdom of the beast. He will not simply judge individuals, but governments as well. It is the "kings of the earth, the princes, the generals, the rich, the mighty, and every slave and every free man" who will hide in fear from the wrath of the Lamb (Rev 6:15). The accent falls on those who have the instruments of power, who should have "defended the cause of the weak and fatherless; maintained the rights of the poor and oppressed" (Ps 82:3).

Creation

The NT tends to view things in terms of the future Messianic age before it anchors them in the creative order. Yet eschatology will restore what was originally intended. The New Jerusalem recreates the Garden of Eden. The fact that the lion will eat straw and the snake will not harm the child harks back to an original innocence.

The Genesis record is crucial for human rights. Man is created as the pinnacle of creation. Being in the image of God involves being "male and female". As Barth so brilliantly expounded,[18] man in the image of God is male or female and male and female. Maleness on its own is less than humanity, as is femaleness on its own. Man can only reflect the image of God in fellowship with his fellow man. Yet each individual is created in the image of God. The individuality, uniqueness and riddle of maleness and femaleness is essential to the fellowship of man with his fellow man. Here is the basis of the age-long struggle between the value of the individual and corporate rights. Western democracies elevate the value of the individual. Eastern socialist societies and Third World nations elevate the value of the community as a whole. Throughout Scripture the "and"/"or" balance is carefully maintained. NT epistles are addressed to "you" plural, to the corporate body of believers. Yet few can escape the deep probing of the inner secrets of the heart. Repentance and faith is a profoundly personal matter, yet no Christian can be an island unto himself. Even the call to repentance is directed to "you and your household".

The created order places man in three relationships: with God, with his fellow man, and with his environment, including all the creatures placed at his command. Man was created to "rule" with God over the entire created order. Within this context he is called to responsible choice. Good and evil wait for his decision. His relationship with his environment involves work: tilling the soil. Creativity and work in the environment is part of that "very good" world before the fall. Sin will make work into toil, but before sin work was part of what it meant to be human.

The family is found from the beginning. Adam is drawn to Eve. They find that they are ideally suited to each other and that the calling of God to rule nature cannot be fulfilled alone. Rest is ordained from the beginning in the sabbath command.

All the essentials which human rights legislation seeks to protect merely echo the Garden of Eden: the way things were meant to be. Man was created for a purpose. He ought to be in a healthy relationship with his environment, his work, his family and his fellow man. He ought to have freedom of choice and the right to rest. Because these essentials are given by God, they cannot be given or removed by another power. Human governments do not grant human rights because they have no authority to do so. Neither do they have permission to withhold them. They must take their place in the created order. If they fail to do so, they will reap a harvest on the Day of Judgement.

Christians therefore view the corruption of human society as the destruction of God's created order. The enemy who seeks to kill, steal and destroy has no rights to God's creation.

The combined effect of Christology, eschatology and creation provides the most profound basis for human rights. This is why Christians should be *for* human rights.

HUMAN RIGHTS THEOLOGIES AND INSTRUMENTS

This section will seek to provide sufficient know-how about contemporary human rights theological formulations, international instruments, justiciable processes and monitoring organisations. It will then turn to suggested responses for Christian leaders and churches.

Theological formulations

True to its ancient history, the ecumenical body of the church has continued to formulate and teach human rights. Broadly one can conclude that the church has kept pace or at least been aware of the changing world in which we live, although there is certainly no place for complacency. Prejudice, ignorance and escapism are still endemic in large sectors of the worldwide church.

The most helpful volume on this subject is the Reformed Ecumenical Synod *Testimony on Human Rights* (hereafter referred to as RES). Much of the outline that follows is derived from this source. There are basically seven theological formulations by recognised church bodies.

The Roman Catholic Church

The church of Rome has remained true to the foundation laid by Thomas Aquinas. Subsequent positions are found in the Council of Trent (1543–63), the First Vatican Council (1869–70) and the Second Vatican Council (1962–65). The influence of Aquinas will be noted in the sustained commitment to the dualist or double system of revealed truth through nature and grace. Hellenistic "natural law" receives support alongside special biblical revelation.

The two major statements by the church are *Rerum Novarum* (1891) by Pope Leo XIII and *Pacem in Terris* by Pope John XXIII (1963). *Rerum Novarum* repudiates socialism as "manifestly against justice" because "man precedes the state, and possesses, prior to the formation of any state, the right of providing for the sustenance of his body".[19] *Pacem in Terris* has a more balanced stress on both personal and social (corporate) rights. Many of the rights we have examined are declared and supported by these statements.

The relevant texts can be found in the documents of Vatican II.

The Eastern Orthodox Church

The Eastern church traces its spiritual and traditional roots through an unbroken line from the apostles and Church Fathers to the present. Its theology is derived from the twofold authority of the biblical writings and the writings of the patristic Fathers, Irenaeus, Origin and Tertullian. As with Aquinas, these Fathers place truth derived from the "universal logos", or natural law, alongside truth derived from biblical revelation. All men share in the knowledge of the first level of truth. Consequently the church is able to take a fairly positive view of "existentialist, evolutionary, personalist, and perfectionist thinking".[20] The result is a position somewhere between the Reformational pessimism about human nature and humanist optimism. The close connection between the two fields of truth (nature and grace) allows the church to support a universal view of human rights. Once again, formulations articulate many of the human rights we have examined.[21]

The Lutheran Church

The major Lutheran statement on human rights is found in the publication of the Lutheran World Federation *Theological Perspectives on Human Rights*.

The distinctive feature of Lutheran theology is its stress on the two kingdoms: the kingdom of God and the kingdoms of this world, linked to the fundamental distinction between law and grace. All of life is divided into two realms. Accordingly, human rights are said to be the business of human governments ordering secular society as part of this world. "Therefore it is not 'our task to deduce human rights theologically from specifically Christian premises.' For 'they are rights for all men, also for those who neither live nor wish to live under the Gospel.'" [22]

There is therefore a limit to the ability of the church in human rights legislation and formulation. It must support such rights in societies where they are in force, protest in societies where they are violated, and beware of becoming ideologically conformed to the world in the process.

The Reformed Churches

There are two Reformed bodies that have made statements on the subject, the World Alliance of Reformed Churches[23] and the Reformed Ecumenical Synod.[24] The former body stands closer to the World Council of Churches and its theology represents a mixture of traditional and modernist (e.g. Moltmann) approaches. The latter body is more orthodox reformed. Evangelicals and charismatics would find this volume most helpful and would be at home with the tenor of its theology.

Common to both bodies is the strong repudiation of any kind of dualism, be it Eastern or Roman nature and grace, Lutheran two kingdoms, or evangelical vertical-horizontal divides. This is true to Calvin's understanding of the state as subject, in some sense, to the Word of God. Therefore politics is clearly subject to biblical norms, human rights are grounded in the character of God, the violation of human rights is rooted in the total depravity of man and the church has the right to resist any government that fails to abide by its contractual (covenantal) obligations towards society. The correct theological basis for human rights will be grounded in the doctrines of creation, redemption and eschatology.

The Reformed Ecumenical Synod makes its special contribution to the implications for human rights that derive from the theories of Abraham Kuyper on sphere sovereignty. The covenant between God and man in creation leads to created orders, or spheres, where each part of human life has a sovereignty of its own. There are helpful insights in this model, but as John de Gruchy has shown, its reputation in South Africa has been somewhat damaged due to the fact that apartheid theology drew fairly heavily on it.[25]

The World Council of Churches

As one may imagine, the WCC has been at the forefront of human rights formulation and awareness. The world body has a similar history to the United Nations in its origins, coming together in 1948 at the first Assembly in Amsterdam. Each WCC Assembly has addressed itself to human rights, and each time the sense of urgency has grown (Evanston, 1954; New Delhi, 1961; Uppsala, 1968; Nairobi, 1975). There is certainly no Christian organisation that has spoken to this issue more than the WCC. In general the theological position of the world body stresses the balance between individual and collective rights, the fact that Christian ethics cannot but have political consequences, and that the Universal Declaration of Human Rights should enjoy the support of the church in every context. More recent statements have tended to move from the theological basis of rights to activism for their defence. There has also been a tendency towards favouring collective rights and certain secular causes that reflect this pole. Because the world body includes so many diverse viewpoints, it has struggled to maintain a clear commitment to normative biblical theology. Nevertheless, its contribution to this field is vast. South Africans should remember that they were subject, under the apartheid state, to a deliberate media campaign to discredit the organisation. We should be as critical of the image we may have obtained from this era as the mixed theological and ethical combination of the WCC itself.

Liberation theology

Although there is to date no actual confessional Christian body for liberation theology, it has become a visible and often powerful force within many Christian traditions, particularly in Latin America and Africa. The formative event was the conference of Catholic bishops at Medellin, Colombia (1968). A more detailed treatment of liberation theology in general will be found in the relevant chapters of *South Africa: The Powers Behind*. At this point I simply wish to make a few comments with reference to human rights.

♦ Liberation theology champions the cause of human rights with great vigour. There is certainly a deep commitment to making the Christian faith work in the midst of human suffering, oppression and pain. The critique this theology provides of the dualisms, inconsistencies and hypocrisy of much church life should undoubtedly be heard. Yet one has to point to the equal, and probably more damaging inconsistencies and hypocrisy of much liberation theology.

It claims to arise out of the context of human suffering, from which it examines Scripture, and confesses a total break with traditional Western theology. Yet if one traces its history, it becomes all too apparent that liberation theology actually has its origin in a Western tradition, in fact an extremely theoretical tradition of philosophers and theologians, notably Hegel, Marx and Moltmann. It cannot really claim to be a theology of praxis.

♦ Its repudiation of the "third way" (kingdom of God as alternative to worldly positions) as a traditional Christian disguise for a commitment to the status quo cannot disguise its own commitment to class struggle and its ideological basis. The hermeneutical tools of "social analysis" will, in the long run, obstruct a probing analysis of social reality because reality never fits into neat dialectical categories.

♦ Most unfortunate of all is that the underlying commitment to a worldly philosophy allows for moral compromise and blindness, compromise on violence as a legitimate means to an end, and blindness concerning the gross violation of human rights in societies that have been built on dialectical philosophies. An honest assessment of recent history will show that the "liberal, capitalist" Western societies, which are so problematic to liberation theologians, have a far better record on human rights than the societies that have developed from the collectivist social theories espoused by this theology.

♦ The neo-Marxist commitment often leads to a consequent commitment to economic theories which will prove embarrassing to liberation theology in the long run. It is one thing to critique the sin of rampant capitalism, quite another to pretend, as theologians, that we either really understand global economics or can find real answers to its problems.

The lesson provided by liberation theology is that the evangelical church has lost its right to speak in an area that was once very much part of its testimony and its withdrawal has allowed others to claim the field.

The evangelical church

There are three documents, relevant to this subject, which the evangelical movement has produced. First, the Lausanne Covenant (1974), arising out of the Lausanne Conference, addressed itself to issues of social concern. Second, a committee appointed by this body and the World Evangelical Fellowship produced a document entitled "Evangelism and Social Responsibility – an Evangelical Commitment" (1982). Third, the Lausanne movement held a further world confe-rence in Manila, and once again produced statements about social responsibility. The development shows a growing sense of urgency and concern similar to the development in the WCC, although within a different frame of reference. The relevant statement of the Lausanne Covenant is worth quoting.

> Because mankind is made in the image of God, every person, regardless
> of race, religion, colour, culture, class, sex or age, has an intrinsic dignity
> because of which he should be respected and served, not exploited ...
> Although reconciliation with man is not reconciliation with God, nor is
> social action evangelism, nor is political liberation salvation, nevertheless
> we affirm that evangelism and socio-political involvement are both part
> of our Christian duty. Both are necessary expressions of our doctrines of
> God and man, our love for our neighbour and our obedience to Jesus
> Christ. The message of salvation implies also a message of judgement
> upon every form of alienation, oppression and discrimination, and we
> should not be afraid to denounce evil and injustice wherever they exist.
> (Paragraph 5)

Valuable as these statements are, we must turn to an individual contribution to
learn about an evangelical perspective on human rights.

John Warwick Montgomery

One could easily place Montgomery in the confessional Lutheran camp. His commitment to the particular Lutheran view of law and grace places him within this
confessional tradition. However, since he is one of the world leaders in defending
biblical authority and inspiration, and certainly is a conservative evangelical,
theologically speaking, it is legitimate to place him in the evangelical movement.

Montgomery is one of the most important Christian articulators of human rights
in the world today. He is Professor-at-Large at the Institute for Theology and Law
in Irvine, California and in its summer programme in Strasbourg, the European
capital of human rights. Strasbourg is the Seat of the European Court of Human
Rights and the city where the International Institute of Human Rights, founded by
Rene Cassin, is based. Montgomery has numerous degrees in the subjects of theology and law and is one of the few persons to have obtained the Diploma of the
International Institute of Human Rights cum laude.

His dual role in the fields of theology and human rights law is probably unique,
certainly among evangelicals. His book, *Human Rights and Human Dignity* is one
of the most helpful sources on the subject.

He provides an incisive critique of all attempts either to define or to justify human
rights apart from biblical revelation. He also shows how tragic it is for evangelicals
to remove themselves from this field. Treading a careful line between the Calvinist
"reconstructionists" such as Rushdoony and the dispensationalists, he provides a

clear evangelical theological basis for human rights. His respect for the European system is obvious. His reaction to the dispensationalist line is worth quoting.

> American Evangelicals, taking their lead from pop eschatologist Hal Lindsey, frequently assert that the European Economic Community, with its ten members, represents the ten toes of the great image in the Book of Daniel and thus is a vehicle of the antichristic end times.

> As for the Hal Lindsey apocalyptic, aside from my noting that EEC members seldom remains at a stable ten ... and that the states-parties to the European Convention on Human Rights number no less than twenty-one, I must point to the severe biblical strictures against the unpardonable sin of attributing the work of God to Beelzebub (Matt 12:24–33; Mark 3:22–30; Lk 11:15–20). If, as Jesus says here, "the tree is known by its fruit" (Matt 12:33), then the European machinery by which fundamental advances in human rights have come about can be regarded as even potentially antichristic only at the critic's extreme spiritual peril.[26]

To close this section, my own view is that the evangelical movement needs to ground its theological ethics in the biblical teaching on the kingdom of God, not as construed by the Reformers, but as construed by biblical scholars since the discovery, in the twentieth century, of the eschatological background to the NT. My attempt to communicate this theology is found in *Breakthrough: Discovering the Kingdom*. Kingdom theology will provide a framework in which we can heal the schizophrenia inherent in much of our thinking.

Human rights instruments

"Instruments" is the technical term used for the various international declarations, protocols and covenants on human rights.

First, the major statements that have emerged from the history of the Western nations can be found at the back of vol. X of *Encyclopaedia Britannica*. These should be studied as the foundational documents. They are the following:

♦ Magna Carta;
♦ The English Bill of Rights;
♦ The Constitution of the United States (first ten amendments);
♦ The Declaration of the Rights of Man and of the Citizen (France);
♦ The Universal Declaration on Human Rights.

Second, the United Nations has a complex structure of covenants and commissions in various fields and member states can bind themselves more closely to the whole procedure. Notably some of the states with an embarrassing record (the late USSR) have not managed to bind themselves to the covenants. Apartheid South Africa did not even identify with the Declaration. Continual research and reporting takes place in these various bodies.

In addition, there are three Continental instruments.

♦ Clearly the most advanced system is the European one. The Convention for the Protection of Human Rights and Fundamental Freedoms (1953) is the foundational document. This was followed by various protocols further binding the states to the system of protections (First, 1950; Fourth, 1952; Seventh, 1950). Then, provided member states have ratified the convention, the European Court of Human Rights can actually try a member state when a complaint has been properly lodged. This is the only system in the world where human rights are justiciable beyond the control of nation states.

♦ The American States have two documents, the American Declaration of the Rights and Duties of Man (Bogota, 1948) and the American Convention on Human Rights (1978). Again there are various levels of commitment by member states with procedural methods of appeal. The relevant texts will be found in Montgomery.[27] While being shaped by the European system, it has not yet reached the same level of commitment by member states. The United States has not become a participant, believing that its own constitutional amendments are sufficient.

♦ The Organisation of African Unity adopted an African Charter on Human Rights and People's Rights in 1981. However fewer states have entered into commitment than with the American States. The result is that to date there is little chance of the system actually going into effect.

Moreover, the seriousness with which at least some African states may eventually treat their obligations under the Charter is placed in doubt by the enthusiastic reception Idi Amin of Uganda received at OAU sessions while he was in power: evidently anti-colonial strength was more impressive than human rights to many influential African statesmen.[28]

Against this background, the South African President, Thabo Mbeki's leadership in the decision of the final OAU meetings, to deny states with human rights violations attendance at OAU meetings in future, was significant. We hope that the new African Union will make better progress than the old.

Non-governmental organisations

The best known of these is the International Committee of the Red Cross. The original intention of the Red Cross derives from the sacrificial death of Christ and the biblical calling to follow his example (1 Pet 2:21). Closely linked to this is the Geneva Convention (1864) aimed at preventing barbarities in times of war.

Amnesty International, based in London, is probably the most effective international reportorial body. Its annual reports are available through state libraries.

A Christian body that has emulated Amnesty International is Christian Solidarity International.

The International Commission of Jurists, based in Geneva, provides specialised legal reports on problem areas. Its findings on South Africa during apartheid warrant careful attention. There is a similar body based in New York, the Lawyers' Committee for Human Rights.

As we observe all these statements, bodies and systems, we should recall the earlier remarks about the ineffectiveness of such instruments if a society has not been leavened, through the gospel, by a culture of human rights. This, rather than detracting from their importance, should result in them receiving our more serious attention.

Action

How can South African church leaders and communities respond to the issue of human rights? Assuming we are now convinced that it forms part of our Christian heritage, evangelical commitment and biblical mandate, what should we do?

Disciple and educate

We should never underestimate the power of the pulpit or of the general discipleship office of the church. There is a desperate need for evangelicals to rediscover their full theological heritage after the tragic reaction towards escapist fundamentalism since the so-called "social gospel". We are called to preach the "full council of God". Obviously we will miss the mark if we focus exclusively on human rights. A balanced content from the pulpit will include expository preaching, teaching on Christ, the Holy Spirit, salvation, eschatology and social ethics. If one follows Paul, for instance, one will notice how he normally lays a careful foundation on the person and work of Christ, his power to save, and the human response of faith. A section usually follows where he "therefore" works out the implications in various relationships: with the church, the state, the family and the workplace. Human rights falls within these relational teachings, particularly the ones dealing with the state and the workplace. Biblical preachers should bring the subject into their normal preaching when they deal with these sections of Paul's letters and equivalent section of other NT letters.

This, however, will not meet the requirements of the on-going crisis in our nation. First, we have evaded these subjects for so long that a fair amount of catching up is required. Second, the continued crisis presses on us and cries out for a response. What we need is a massive crash course in human rights teaching from as many Bible preachers and teachers as possible, especially in the affected communities, not only from the pulpit, but in schools, universities, trade unions, civic organisations, etc. I have had a vision, for many years, of developing a special training course for Christian leaders in both the church and civil society empowering them to engage in nation building. Some day God may provide the opportunity to fulfil this vision.

Make the contacts

We need to discover what already exists in our society. Since the change of government led by Mandela, South Africa has developed numerous constitutionally based mechanisms, including our own Bill of Rights and the Human Rights Commission. Reporting mechanisms, watchdog bodies, legal bodies and so on can provide an important milieu for concerned Christians to make their contribution and for human rights violations to be reported and monitored.

Watch and publicise

The NT speaks of gifts of knowledge and discernment. These are not only given to unveil the secret sins of individuals. Prophetic sight enables people to see through the facades of social pretence to view the root causes of poverty, crime, discrimination, violence and destruction. The press has done a great job in this country, particularly under the apartheid government. However, there is always the danger of gagging or co-opting the press. It almost succeeded under the previous government. Politicians generally dislike the scrutiny they get from the press. There is a need for the church to provide its own report on what is actually occurring. Clearly Christian leaders who are really in touch with the crisis areas have a greater responsibility.

Further, organisations such as Amnesty International have proved that taking the lid off human rights violations is one of the best ways of curbing them. Oppressive activity tends to wither under the searchlight of public revelation. We should make use of the press rather than merely berate it for its sensationalist focus. After all, we shape what society defines as sensational when we leaven that society with certain values and we numb the same society if we fail to do so.

Confess and influence

There is a definite need for the ecumenical church (I use this in its historic sense, i.e. the whole body) in South Africa to produce a clear, broad-based theology, definition and justification of human rights. This body should engage with civil society in creating a culture of human rights in South Africa.

NOTES

1. Morphew 1998.

2. Morphew 1989. Also available as an e-publication from Vineyard International Publishing at www.vineyard-bi.org/vip.

3. Morphew 1991.

4. Cassidy 1995, pp.120–121: "With all this going on and daunting our spirits daily, we felt at African Enterprise that there were also other issues to look at in terms of whatever we could do. We accordingly convened a Consultation of some forty-three Christian leaders and thinkers to look at the issue of human rights and religious freedom from a biblical point of view."

5. Cochrane 1957.

6. SA Law Commission 1989, p. 4.

7. Eidsmoe 1987, pp. 69–100.

8. Ibid., pp. 70–99.

9. Ibid., p. 81.

10. Morphew 1989.

11. Encyclopaedia Britannica 1984, p. 719.

12. Montgomery 1986, pp. 30, 266.

13 Ibid., p. 275.

14 Ibid., p. 270.

15. Ibid., p. 298 note 326.

16. Craigie 1976, pp. 17–29.

17. Morris 1971, pp. 115–126.

18. Barth 1961.

19. Reformed Ecumenical Synod 1983, p. 51.

20. Ibid., p. 37.

21. Ibid., p. 36 for the relevant articles.

22. Ibid., p. 41.

23. Miller (ed.) 1977.

24. Reformed Ecumenical Synod 1983.

25. De Gruchy 1979.

26. Montgomery 1986, pp. 43–44.

27. Ibid.

28. Ibid., p. 51.

 REFERENCES IN APPENDIX

Amnesty International, Annual Reports

Barth, Karl 1961, "Freedom in Fellowship", *Church Dogmatics*, IV, 4 (T & T Clarke, Edinburgh)

Bindman, Geoffrey (ed.) 1988, *South Africa: Human Rights and the Rule of Law* (International Commission of Jurists, Pinter Publishers, London)

Cassidy, Michael 1995, *A Witness For Ever: The Dawning of Democracy in South Africa — Stories Behind the Story* (Hodder & Stoughton, London)

Cassin, Rene 1971, "From the Ten Commandments to the Rights of Man" in Shoham, Shlomo (ed.) *Of Law and Man: Essays in Honor of Haim H Cohn* (Sabra Books, New York, Tel Aviv)

Cochrane, CN 1957, *Christianity and Classical Culture* (Oxford University Press, New York)

Craigie, Peter C 1976, "The Book of Deuteronomy", *New International Commentary on the Old Testament* (Eerdmans, Grand Rapids)

De Gruchy, John 1979, *The Church Struggle in South Africa* (SPCK, London)

Eidsmoe, John 1987, "The Judeo-Christian Roots of the Constitution" in House, Wayne H (ed.) *Restoring the Constitution: Is Judicial Activism Destroying the Constitution?* (Probe Books, Richardson, Texas)

Encyclopaedia Britannica 1984 (London)

Johnson, Paul 1983, *A History of the Modern World from 1917 to 1980s* (Weidenfelt & Nicolson, London)

Miller, Allen O (ed.) 1977, *A Christain Declaration on Human Rights: Theological Studies on the World Alliance of Reformed Churches* (Eerdmans, Grand Rapids)

Montgomery, John Warwick 1961, "How Muslims Do Apologetics" in *Muslim World* 51:2, April 1961, July 1961

    1975, *The Law Above the Law: Why the Law Needs Biblical Foundations/How Legal Thought Supports Christian Truth* (Bethany House Publishers, Minneapolis)

    1978, *Law and Gospel: A Study in Jurisprudence* (Christian Legal Society, Oak Park, Illinois)

    1983-84,"The Marxist Approach to Human Rights: Analysis and Critique" in *Simon Greenleaf Law Review, 3*

    1986, *Human Rights and Human Dignity* (Probe Books, London)

Morphew, Derek J 1989, *South Africa: The Powers Behind* (Struik Christian Books, Cape Town)

    1998, *Breakthrough: Discovering the Kingdom* (Vineyard International Publishing, Cape Town)

Morris, Leon 1971, "The Gospel of John", *The New London Commentary on the New Testament* (Marshall, Morgan & Scott, London)

Partridge, AC 1978, *Human Rights, Their Origin, Validity and Implementation* (SA Institute of International Affairs, Johannesburg)

Reformed Ecumenical Synod 1983, *Testimony on Human Rights* (Reformed Ecumenical Synod, Grand Rapids)

SA Law Commission 1989, *Group and Human Rights*, Working Paper 25, Project 58, August 1989

Van der Vyver, JD 1976, *Seven Lectures on Human Rights* (Juta & Co, Cape Town)

    Veehoven, William A (ed.) 1975, *Case Studies on Human Rights and Fundamental Freedoms: A World Survey*, 5 vols (Martinue Nijhoff, The Hague).

REFERENCES

OFFICIAL CHURCH STATEMENTS AND DOCUMENTS

Concerned Evangelicals 1986, *Evangelical Witness in South Africa — A Critique of Evangelical Theology and Practice by Evangelicals Themselves* (CE, Soweto)

Continuation Committee of Objecting Members of the DRC 1987, *Faith and Protest/ Geloof en Protes: 'n Antwoord namens beswaarde lidmate op sekere aspekte van "Kerk en Samelewing"* (Die Voortsettingskomitee, Pretoria)

Cottesloe Consultation 1960, The Report of the Consultation among South African Member Churches of the World Council of Churches, 7–14 December 1960

Dutch Reformed Church (DRC) 1987, *Church and Society / Kerk en Samelewing* (General Synodical Commission, Bloemfontein)

Institute for Contextual Theology 1985a, *The Kairos Document — Challenge to the Church* (ICT, Skotaville Publishing, Johannesburg)

1985b, *ICT — What is it? Its Programmes and Method of Doing Theology* (ICT)

1989a, *The Road to Damascus — Kairos and Conversion* (ICT)

1989b, *Negotiations, Defiance and the Church* (ICT)

1990, *Violence — The New Kairos: Challenge to the Churches* (ICT)

1993, *The Road to Democracy — Democratic Elections in South Africa: A Christian Perspective* (ICT)

Justice in Transition 1994, *Truth and Reconciliation Commission* (Justice in Transition, Cape Town)

Koinonia 1987, *The Koinonia Statement* (Koinonia, Pretoria)

Methodist Church of Southern Africa, Bishop Peter Storey 1995, *Journey Begun — The Story of a Church in a New Land* (Methodist Publishing House, Cape Town)

MUCCOR 1991, *A Pastoral Letter on Violence from Ministers United for Christian Co-Responsibility to the People of Soweto* (MUCCOR, Soweto)

National Initiative for Reconciliation 1986, *National Initiative for Reconciliation: "Arise and Walk"* (African Enterprise, Pietermaritzburg)

Pentecostal Forum 1989, *A Relevant Pentecostal Witness* (RPW, Durban)

Reba Place Church 1996, *Racial Reconciliation and Racism: Working Out Our Salvation — A Theological Framework for Reba Place Church* (unpublished paper, 8 January 1996)

South African Council of Churches 1968, *A Message to the People of South Africa* (SACC, Johannesburg) (See also De Gruchy and De Villiers 1968)

For SACC Johanson, Brian 1975a, *Church and State in South Africa*

For SACC Johanson, Brian (ed.) 1975b, *The Church in South Africa Today and Tomorrow*

1984, *Relocations: The Church's Report on Forced Removals*

Southern African Catholic Bishops' Conference 1984, *Instruction on Certain Aspects of the Theology of Liberation* by Cardinal Joseph Ratzinger (SACBC, Pretoria)

1985, *The Things That Make for Peace — A Report to the Catholic Bishops and the Church in Southern Africa from the Theological Advisory Commission of the SACBC* (SACBC, Pretoria)

1986a, *Pastoral Letter of the SACBC on Christian Hope in the Current Crisis* (SACBC, Pretoria)

1986b, *Instruction on Christian Freedom and Liberation* (Vatican City)

GENERAL REFERENCES

Adam, Heribert and Giliomee, Hermann 1979, *The Rise and Crisis of Afrikaner Power* (David Philip Publishers, Cape Town)

Aeschliman, Gordon D 1987, *Land Where My Father Died* (Regal Books, California)

Alberts, Louw and Chikane, Frank (eds.) 1991, *The Road to Rustenburg* (Struik Christian Books, Cape Town)

Asmal, Kader, Asmal, Louise and Roberts, Ronald Suresh 1996, *Reconciliation Through Truth* (David Philip Publishers, Cape Town)

Bailey, Jeff (ed.) 2002, "Multi-Ethnic Churches — Challenges and Opportunities for the Evangelical Church" in *Cutting Edge*, vol. 6, no. 2, Summer 2002 (PO Box 2089, Stafford, Texas 77497-8464, USA)

Balcomb, Anthony 1993, *Third Way Theology: Reconciliation, Revolution and Reform in the South African Church during the 1980s* (Cluster Publications, Pietermaritzburg)

1998, "From Liberation to Democracy — Theologies of Bread and Being in the New South Africa" in *Missionalia* vol. 26, no. 1, April 1998 (Southern African Missiological Society, Pretoria)

Bales, Kevin 2000, *Disposable People — New Slavery in the Global Economy* (University of California Press, California)

Barndt, Joseph 1991, *Dismantling Racism — The Continuing Challenge to White America* (Augsburg, Minneapolis)

Barth, Karl 1961, *Church Dogmatics — The Doctrine of Reconciliation*, vol. IV/1 (T & T Clark, Edinburgh)

Baxter, Jenny and Downing, Malcolm (eds.) 2001, *The Day that Shook the World — Understanding September 11th* (BBC Worldwide Ltd, London)

Bilezikian, Gilbert 1997, *Community 101 — Reclaiming the Local Church as Community of Oneness* (Zondervan, Grand Rapids)

Block, Walter, Brennan, Geoffrey and Elzinga, Kenneth (eds.) 1985, *Morality of the Market — Religious and Economic Perspectives* (Fraser Institute, Vancouver)

Block, Walter and Hexham, Irving (eds.) 1986, *Religion, Economics and Social Thought* (Fraser Institute, Vancouver)[1]

Bloom, Allan 1987, *The Closing of the American Mind* (Simon and Schuster, London)

Bly, Robert 1990, *Iron John — A Book about Men* (Addison-Wesley Publishing, New York)

   1996, *The Sibling Society* (Hamish Hamilton, London)

Boesak, Allan 1977, *Farewell to Innocence — A Socio-Ethical Study on Black Theology and Power* (Orbis Books, New York)

   1984, *Black and Reformed — Apartheid, Liberation and the Calvinist Tradition* (Skotaville, Johannesburg)

Bond, John 2001, *For the Record — Reflections on the Assemblies of God* (Nu Publishers, Cape Town)

Bonhoeffer, Dietrich 1954, *Life Together — A Discussion of Christian Fellowship* (Harper and Row, San Francisco)

   1955, *Ethics* (MacMillan Publishing, New York)

   1963, *The Cost of Discipleship* (Macmillan Publishing, New York)

   1964, *Letters and Papers from Prison* (Fontana, London)

   1966, *The Way to Freedom — Letters, Lectures and Notes from the Collected Works* (Collins Fontana Library, New York)

Bonino, Jose Miguez 1983, *Toward a Christian Political Ethics* (Fortress Press Philadelphia)

Boraine, Alex 2000, *A Country Unmasked: Inside South Africa's Truth and Reconciliation Commission* (Oxford University Press, New York)

Borg, Marcus 1987, *Jesus, A New Vision — Spirit, Culture and the Life of Discipleship* (Harper, San Francisco)

Borg, Marcus and Wright, NT 1999, *The Meaning of Jesus — Two Visions* (Harper, San Francisco)

Bosch, David 1980, *Witness to the World — The Christian Mission in Theological Perspective* (John Knox Press, Atlanta)

    1988, "Church Growth Missiology" in *Missionalia*, vol. 16, no. 1, April, 1989 (Southern African Missiological Society, Pretoria)

    1991, *Transforming Mission — Paradigm Shifts in Theology of Mission* (Orbis Books, Maryknoll, New York)

Botman, Russel H and Petersen, Robin M (eds.) 1996, *To Remember and to Heal — Theological and Psychological Reflections on Truth and Reconciliation* (Human & Rousseau, Cape Town)

Boulton, Wayne, Kennedy, Thomas and Verhey, Allen (eds.) 1994, *From Christ to the World — Introductory Readings in Christian Ethics* (Eerdmans, Grand Rapids)

Bowes, Brett and Pennington, Stuart (eds.) 2002, *South Africa: The Good News* (Brett Bowes and Stuart Pennington Publishers, South Africa)

    2003, *South Africa: More Good News* (Brett Bowes and Stuart Pennington Publishers, South Africa)

Breytenbach, Cilliers 1986, *Versohnung — Eine Studie zur Paulinischen Soteriologie* (Neukirchen, Vluyn)

Brown, Colin (ed.) 1978, *The New International Dictionary of New Testament Theology*, vol. 3 (Paternoster Press, Exeter)

Brueggemann, Walter 1976, *Living Toward a Vision — Biblical Reflections on Shalom* (United Church Press, New York)

    1977, *The Land — Place as Gift, Promise, and Challenge in the Biblical Faith* (Fortress Press, Philadelphia)

    1978, *The Prophetic Imagination* (Fortress Press, Philadelphia)

    1986, *Hopeful Imagination — Prophetic Voices in Exile* (Fortress Press, Philadelphia)

Brummer, Vincent, 1994, "Kairos, Reconciliation and the Doctrine of Atonement" in *Journal of Theology for Southern Africa*, September 1994, no. 88 (University of Cape Town, Cape Town)

Bush, Douglas (ed.) 1966, *Milton Poetical Works* (Oxford University Press, Oxford)

Camara, Helder 1969, *Church and Colonialism* (Sheed and Ward, London)

    1971, *Spiral of Violence* (Sheed and Ward, London)

Cassidy, Michael 1989, *The Passing Summer — A South African Pilgrimage in the Politics of Love* (Hodder & Stoughton, London)

    1995, *A Witness Forever — The Dawning of Democracy in South Africa. Stories behind the Story* (Hodder & Stoughton, London)

Chikane, Frank 1988, *No Life of My Own — An Autobiography* (Skotaville, Johannesburg)

Cochrane, James 1987, *Servants of Power — The Role of the English-speaking Churches 1903–1930* (Raven Press, Johannesburg)

Conn, Harvie N (ed.) 1976, *Theological Perspectives on Church Growth* (Presbyterian and Reformed Publishing, New Jersey)

Cormack, Patrick 1983, *Wilberforce — The Nation's Conscience* (Pickering, Basingstoke)

Cuthbertson, G 1989, "Van der Kemp and Philip: The Missionary Debate Revisited" in *Missionalia*, vol. 17, no. 2, August 1989 (Southern African Missiological Society, Pretoria)

Dallaire, Romeo with Beardsley, Brent 2003, *Shake Hands with the Devil — The Failure of Humanity in Rwanda* (Random House, Toronto)

Davenport, TRH 1977, *South Africa — A Modern History*, 2nd ed. (MacMillan Publishers, Johannesburg)

Davis, David Brion 1984, *Slavery and Human Progress* (Oxford University Press, Oxford)

De Gruchy, John 1979, *The Church Struggle in South Africa* (Eerdmans, Grand Rapids)

    1984, *Bonhoeffer and South Africa — Theology in Dialogue* (Eerdmans, Grand Rapids)

    1986, *Theology and Ministry in Context and Crisis — A South African Perspective* (Collins Liturgical Publications, London)

    1991a, "From Cottesloe to Rustenburg and Beyond — The Rustenburg Conference in Historical Perspective" in *Journal of Theology for Southern Africa*, March 1991, no. 74 (University of Cape Town, Cape Town)

    1991b, *Liberating Reformed Theology — A South African Contribution to an Ecumenical Debate* (Eerdmans, Grand Rapids)

    1993, "Guilt, Amnesty and National Reconstruction" in *Journal of Theology for Southern Africa*, June 1993, no. 83 (University of Cape Town, Cape Town)

    2002, *Reconciliation — Restoring Justice* (David Philip Publishers, Cape Town)

De Gruchy, JW and De Villiers, WB 1968, *The Message in Perspective — A Book about "A Message to the People of South Africa"* (South African Council of Churches, Johannesburg)

De Gruchy, John and Villa-Vicencio, Charles (eds.) 1983, *Apartheid Is a Heresy* (David Philip Publishers, Cape Town)

Dennison, Jack 1999, *City Reaching — On the Road to Community Transformation* (William Carey Library, Pasadena)

De Wet, Chris 1986, "The Church Growth Movement — Does It Foster Churches that Challenge the World?" in *Missionalia*, vol. 14, no. 2, August 1986 (Southern African Missiological Society, Pretoria)

Douglas, JD (org. ed.) 1962, *The New Bible Dictionary* (IVP, London)

Du Toit, CW (ed.) 1994, *Socio-political Changes and the Challenge to Christianity in South Africa* (Research Institute for Theology and Religion, UNISA, Pretoria) (ed.) 1998, *Confession and Reconciliation: A Challenge to the Churches in South Africa* (Research Institute for Theology and Religion, UNISA, Pretoria)

Eller, Vernard 1981, *War and Peace — From Genesis to Revelation* (Herald Press, Pennsylvania)

Ellul, Jacques 1988, *Jesus and Marx — From Gospel to Ideology* (Eerdmans, Grand Rapids)

   1989, *The Presence of the Kingdom*, 2nd ed. (Helmers and Howard, Colorado Springs)

Emmerson, Michael and Smith, Christian 2002, *Divided by Faith: Evangelical Religion and the Problem of Race in America* (Oxford University Press, Oxford)

Fanon, Frantz 1963, *The Wretched of the Earth* (Penguin Books, London)

   1967, *Black Skin, White Mask* (Grove Press, New York)

Flannery, Edward H 1985, *The Anquish of the Jews: Twenty-Three Centuries of Antisemitism*, rev. ed. (Paulist Press, Mahwah, New Jersey)

Forrester, Duncan 1989, *Beliefs, Values and Policies — Conviction Politics in a Secular Age* (Clarendon Press, Oxford)

Frankena, William 1963, "Ethics", *Foundations of Philosophy* Series (Prentice-Hall Inc., New Jersey)

Frankl, Viktor E 1964, *Man's Search for Meaning — An Introduction to Logotherapy* (Hodder & Stoughton, London)

Fukuyama, Francis 1995, *Trust — The Social Virtues and the Creation of Prosperity* (Free Press, New York)

   1999, *The Great Disruption — Human Nature and the Reconstruction of Social Order* (Profile Books, London)

Fuller, Millard with Diane Scott 1986, *No More Shacks — The Daring Vision of Habitat for Humanity* (Word Books, Waco Texas)

Gaebelein, Frank E (gen. ed.) 1984, *The Expositor's Bible Commentary*, vol. 8 (Zondervan, Grand Rapids)

Garrow, David 1986, *Bearing the Cross — Martin Luther King Jr. and the Southern Christian Leadership Conference* (Vintage Books, New York)

Geisler, Norman L 1989, *Christian Ethics — Options and Issues* (Baker Book House, Grand Rapids)

Gerloff, Roswith 1998, "Truth, a New Society and Reconciliation — the TRC in South Africa from a German Perspective" in *Missionalia*, vol. 26, no. 1, April 1988 (Southern African Missiological Society, Pretoria)

Giles, Kevin 2002, *The Trinity and Subordinationism: The Doctrine of God and the Contemporary Gender Debate* (IVP, London).

Glasser, Arthur 1979, "Reconciliation between Ecumenical and Evangelical Theologies and Theologians of Mission" in *Missionalia*, vol. 7, no. 3, November 1979 (Southern African Missiological Society, Pretoria)

Gorbachev, Mikhail 1987, *Perestroika — New Thinking for Our Country and the World* (Fontana/Collins, London)

Grant, George 1995, *Bringing in the Sheaves — Replacing Government Welfare with Biblical Charity* (The Reformer Library, New York)

Hauerwas, Stanley 1981, *A Community of Character — Toward a Constructive Christian Social Ethic* (University of Notre Dame Press, Indiana)

    1983, *The Peaceable Kingdom — A Primer in Christian Ethics* (University of Notre Dame Press, Indiana)

Hauerwas, Stanley and Jones, L Gregory (eds.) 1989, *Why Narrative? Readings in Narrative Theology* (Eerdmans, Grand Rapids)

Hays, Richard 1996, *The Moral Vision of the New Testament — A Contemporary Introduction to New Testament Ethics* (Harper Collins, San Francisco)

Henderson, Michael 2002, *Forgiveness: Breaking the Chain of Hate* (Grosvenor Books, London)

Heslam, Peter 2002, "Globalisation — Unravelling the New Capitalism" *Grove Ethics Series*, LICC (Grove Press, New York)

Hofmeyer, JW, Du Toit, JHH and Froneman, CJJ (eds.) 1987, *Perspectives on Kairos/Perspektiewe op Kairos* (Lux Verbi, Cape Town)

Holwerda, David 1995, *Jesus and Israel — One Covenant or Two?* (Eerdmans, Grand Rapids)

Houston, Bill, Truscott, Steve and Judge, Andrew 1986, *Bible Studies for a Divided Society* (Students Christian Association of Southern Africa, Johannesburg)

Hudson, Trevor 1999, "Compassionate Caring: A Daily Pilgrimage of Pain and Hope", *Exploring Prayer* Series (Eagle, Guilford)

Hunt, EK 1986, *Property and Prophets — The Evolution of Economic Institutions and Ideologies* (Harper & Row, New York)

Hybels, Bill 2002, *Courageous Leadership* (Zondervan, Grand Rapids)

Jackson, Bill 1999, *The Quest for the Radical Middle — A History of the Vineyard* (Vineyard International Publishing, Cape Town)

Kah, Gary H 1992, *En Route to Global Occupation — A High Ranking Government Liaison Exposes the Secret Agenda for World Unification* (Hunting House Publishers, Louisiana)

    1995, *The Demonic Roots of Globalisation — En Route to Spiritual Deception* (Hunting House Publishers, Louisiana)

Keen, Sam 1991, *Fire in the Belly* (Bantam Books, London)

King, Martin Luther Jr. 1986, *I Have a Dream — Writings and Speeches that Changed the World* (Harper, San Francisco)

König, Adrio 1989, *The Eclipse of Christ in Eschatology — Toward a Christ-Centered Approach* (Eerdmans, Grand Rapids)

Kraft, Charles H 1981, *Christianity in Culture — A Study in Dynamic Biblical Theologising in Cross-Cultural Perspective* (Orbis Books, Maryknoll)

Kritzinger, JNJ 1988, "The Kairos Document — A Call to Conversion" in *Missionalia*, vol. 16, no. 3, November 1988 (Southern African Missiological Society, Pretoria)

Krog, Antjie 1998, "The Truth and Reconciliation Commission — A National Ritual?" in *Missionalia*, vol. 26, no. 1, April 1998 (Southern African Missiological Society, Pretoria)

2002, *Country of My Skull* (Random House, Johannesburg)

Kubalkova, V and Cruickshank, A 1981, *International Inequality* (Croom Helm, London)

Ladd, GE 1959, *The Gospel of the Kingdom* (Eerdmans, Grand Rapids)

1974, *The Presence of the Future* (Eerdmans, Grand Rapids)

Lategan, Bernard, Kinghorn, Johann, Du Plessis, Lourens and De Villiers, Etienne 1987, *The Option for Inclusive Democracy: A Theological-Ethical Study of Appropriate Social Values for South Africa* (Centre for Hermeneutics, University of Stellenbosch)

Leatt, James and Kneifel, Theo and Nürnberger, Klaus (eds.) 1986, *Contending Ideologies in South Africa* (David Philip Publishers, Cape Town/Eerdmans, Grand Rapids)

Leon-Hartshorn, Shearer, Iris, Miller, Tobin and Stoltzfus, Regina Shands, 2001, *Set Free — A Journey Toward Solidarity Against Racism* (Herald Press, Scottdale)

Leslie, John 1996, *The End of the World — The Science and Ethics of Human Extinction* (Routledge, London)

Longenecker, Richard 1981, "The Acts of the Apostles" in Gaebelein, Frank (gen. ed.) *The Expositor's Bible Commentary*, vol. 9 (Zondervan, Grand Rapids)

1984, *New Testament Social Ethics for Today* (Eerdmans, Grand Rapids)

1990, *Word Biblical Commentary — Galatians* (Word Books, Dallas)

Loubser, JA 1987, *The Apartheid Bible — A Critical Review of Racial Theology in South Africa* (Maskew Miller Longman, Cape Town)

Lovelace, Richard 1979, *Dynamics of Spiritual Life — And Evangelical Theology of Renewal* (InterVarsity Press, Downers Grove, Illinois)

Lupton, Robert 1993, *Return Flight — Community Development through Reneighboring our Cities* (FCS Urban Ministries, Atlanta)

Luthuli, Albert 1962, *Let My People Go* (McGraw-Hill Book Company, London)

MacMurray, John 1957, *The Self as Agent* (Faber & Faber, London)

1961, *Persons in Relation* (Faber & Faber, London)

Malcolm X as told to Alex Haley 1964, *The Autobiography of Malcolm X* (Ballantine Books, New York)

Maluleke, Tinyiko Sam 1997a, "Truth, National Unity and Reconciliation in South Africa — Aspects of an Emerging Agenda" in *Missionalia*, vol. 25, no. 1, April 1997 (Southern African Missiological Society, Pretoria)

1997b, "Dealing Lightly with the Wound of My People? The TRC Process in Theological Perspective" in *Missionalia*, vol. 25, no. 3, November 1997 (Southern African Missiological Society, Pretoria)

Mandela, Nelson 1964, *The Historic Speech of Nelson Rolihlahla Mandela at the Rivonia Trial* (Learn and Teach Publications, Johannesburg)

1994, *Long Walk to Freedom* (Macdonald Purnell, Johannesburg)

Mangona, Sindiwe 2000, *Mother to Mother* (Beacon Press, Boston)

McGavran, Donald 1966, *How Churches Grow* (Friend Press, New York)

1970, *Understanding Church Growth* (Eerdmans, Grand Rapids)

McKim, Donald (ed.) 1986, *A Guide to Contemporary Hermeneutics — Major Trends in Biblical Interpretation* (Eerdmans, Grand Rapids)

Miller, WR 1968, *Martin Luther King Jr. — His Life, Martyrdom and Meaning for the World* (Avon Books, New York)

Mohabir, Philip 1988, *Building Bridges — A Dramatic Personal Story of Reconciliation and Evangelism* (Hodder & Stoughton, London)

Moltmann, Jürgen 1967, *Theology of Hope* (SCM Press, London)

1974, *The Crucified God* (SCM Press, London)

1977, *Unity Under the Cross* (SACC, Johannesburg)

Morphew, Derek 1989, *South Africa: The Powers Behind* (Struik Christian Books, Cape Town)

1991, *Christians for Human Rights* (Associated Christian Ministries, Cape Town)

1998, *Breakthrough — Discovering the Kingdom* (Vineyard International Publishing, Cape Town)

Morris, Leon 1972, *The Apostolic Preaching of the Cross* (Tyndale Press, London)

Müller, CFJ (ed.) 1969, *Five Hundred Years — A History of South Africa* (Academia, Pretoria)

Nelson, James B 1978, *Embodiment — An Approach to Sexuality and Christian Theology* (Augsburg, Minneapolis)

Ngara, Emmanuel 2004, *Christian Leadership — A Challenge to the African Church* (Pauline Publications Africa, Nairobi)

Noble, Lowell 1987, *Sociotheology — Thy Kingdom Come ... On Earth* (Haiti Christian Development Fund, Ft. Lauderdale)

Noe, K Killian 2001, *Finding Our Way Home* (Servant Leadership Press, Washington, DC.)

Nolan, Albert 1986, *Jesus Before Christianity* (second edition, David Philip Publishers, Cape Town)

1987, "The Eschatology of the Kairos Document" in *Missionalia*, vol. 15, no. 2, August 1987 (Southern African Missiological Society, Pretoria)

1988, *God in South Africa — The Challenge of the Gospel* (Eerdmans, Grand Rapids)

Nouwen, Henri JM 1992, *The Return of the Prodigal Son — A Story of Homecoming* (Image Books, Doubleday, New York)

Novak, Michael 1982, *The Spirit of Democratic Capitalism* (Simon & Schuster, New York)

Nürnberger, Klaus 1979, "Reconciliation in a Situation of Severe Economic Discrepancies" in *Missionalia*, vol. 7, no. 2, August 1979 (Southern African Missiological Society, Pretoria)

1988, *Power and Beliefs in South Africa* (UNISA, Pretoria)

1990a, "Why I Signed the Damascus Document" in *Journal of Theology for Southern Africa*, March 1990, no. 70 (University of Cape Town, Cape Town)

1990b, *The Scourge of Unemployment in South Africa* (Encounter Publications, Pietermaritzburg)

1991, "Subscribing to Confessional Documents Today" in *Journal of Theology for Southern Africa*, June 1991, no. 75 (University of Cape Town, Cape Town)

1998, *Beyond Marx and Market — Outcomes of a Century of Economic Experimentation* (Cluster Publications, Pietermaritzburg/Zed Books, London)

1999, *Prosperity, Poverty and Pollution — Managing the Approaching Crisis* (Cluster Publications, Pietermaritzburg/Zed Books, London)

Nürnberger, Klaus (ed.) 1991, "A Democratic Vision for South Africa", *NIR Reader 3* (Encounter Publications, Pietermaritzburg)

Nürnberger, Klaus and Tooke, John (eds.) 1988, "The Cost of Reconciliation in South Africa", *NIR Reader 1* (Methodist Publishing House, Cape Town)

Nürnberger, Klaus, Tooke, John and Domeris, William (eds.) 1989, "Conflict and the Quest for Justice", *NIR Reader 2* (Encounter Publications, Pietermaritzburg)

Olsen, V Norskov 1993, *The New Relatedness for Man and Woman in Christ — A Mirror of the Divine* (Loma Linda University Press, Riverside, California)

Pakenham, Thomas 1979, *The Boer War* (Jonathan Ball Paperbacks, Johannesburg)

1991, *The Scramble for Africa* (Phoenix Press, London)

Pannenburg, Wolfhardt 1991, *Systematic Theology*, vol. 2 (Eerdmans, Grand Rapids)

Parks, Rosa with Jim Haskins 1992, *Rosa Parks — My Story* (Dial Books, New York)

Perkins, John 1982, *With Justice for All* (Regal Books, Ventura)

Philips, John A 1967, *The Form of Christ in the World — A Study of Bonhoeffer's Christology* (Collins, London)

Piper, John and Grudem, Wayne (eds.) 1991, *Recovering Biblical Manhood and Womanhood — A Response to Evangelical Feminism* (Crossway Books, Wheaton)

Powell, John, SJ 1967, *Why Am I Afraid to Love?* (Fontana/Collins, Chicago)

    1969, *Why Am I Afraid to Tell You Who I Am?* (Fontana/Collins, Chicago)

    1974, *The Secret of Staying in Love* (Tabor Publishing, Valencia)

    1978, *Unconditional Love* (Argus Communications, Allen, Texas)

Preston, Ronald 1987, *The Future of Christian Ethics* (SCM Press, London)

Price, Chris 2002, *Grace Matters — A True Story of Race, Friendship, and Faith in the Heart of the South* (Jossey-Bass, San Francisco)

Ratzinger, Joseph 1984, *Instruction on Certain Aspects of the "Theology of Liberation"*, Congregation for the Doctrine of the Faith, Vatican City or Series: Pastoral Action no. 38 (SACBC, Pretoria)

    1986, *Instruction on Christian Freedom and Liberation*, Congregation for the Doctrine of the Faith, Vatican City or Series: Pastoral Action no. 43 (SACBC, Pretoria)

Rausch, David A 1984, *A Legacy of Hatred* (Moody Press, Chicago)

Regehr, Ernie 1979, *Perceptions of Apartheid — The Churches and Political Change in South Africa* (Herald Press, Scottdale)

Reumann, John 1992, *Stewardship and the Economy of God* (Eerdmans, Grand Rapids)

Richardson, Peter 1979, *Paul's Ethic of Freedom* (Westminster Press, Philadelphia)

Roper, DL 1979, *A Christian Philosophy of Culture* (Potchefstroom University for CHE, Potchefstroom)

Rosenberg, Stuart E 1986, *The Christian Problem — A Jewish View* (Hipocrene Books, New York)

Ryan, Colleen 1990, *Beyers Naudé — Pilgrimage of Faith* (Eerdmans, Grand Rapids/ David Philip Publishers, Cape Town)

Ryan, William 1976, *Blaming the Victim*, rev. ed. (Vintage Books, New York)

Samuel, Vinay and Sugden, Chris (eds.) 1982, *Evangelism and the Poor — A Third World Study Guide* (Regnum Books, Oxford)

    (eds.) 1987, *The Church in Response to Human Need* (Eerdmans, Grand Rapids)

Schall, James V 1990, *Religion, Wealth and Poverty* (The Fraser Institute, Vancouver)

Schwarz, Christian 1996, *Natural Church Development* (Church Smart Resources, Carol Stream, Illinois)

Semple, Tracey and Gennrich, Daniela 2003, *AIDS Information Booklet*, (SACLA, PO Box 13140, Cascades 3202, RSA or sacla@ae.org.za)

Setiloane, G 1986, *African Theology — An Introduction* (Skotaville, Johannesburg)

Shenk, WR (ed.) 1983, *Exploring Church Growth* (Eerdmans, Grand Rapids)

Sider, Ronald 1978, *Rich Christians in an Age of Hunger — A Biblical Study* (IVP, Downers Grove)

(ed.) 1980, "Lifestyles in the Eighties — An Evangelical Commitment to Simple Lifestyle", *Contemporary Issues in Social Ethics*, vol. 1 (Paternoster Press, Exeter)

(ed.) 1981, "Evangelicals and Development — Towards a Theology of Social Change", *Contemporary Issues in Social Ethics*, vol. 2 (Paternoster Press, Exeter)

1989, *Non-Violence: The Invincible Weapon?* (Word Publishing, Dallas)

Silvoso, Ed 1994, *That None Should Perish — How to Reach Entire Cities for Christ Through Prayer Evangelism* (Regal Books, Ventura)

Sine, Tom 1981, *The Mustard Seed Conspiracy — You Can Make a Difference in Tomorrow's Troubled World* (Marc, Europe)

Smit, Dirkie J 1995, "The Truth and Reconciliation Commission — Tentative Religious and Theological Perspectives" in *Journal of Theology for Southern Africa*, March 1995, no. 90 (University of Cape Town, Cape Town)

Smit, JH 1987, "Kairos Eschatology: Biblical or Philosophical? A Response to Albert Nolan" in *Missionalia*, vol. 15, no. 2, August 1987 (Southern African Missiological Society, Pretoria)

Smith, Alec 1984, *Now I Call Him Brother — The Rebel Son of Ian Smith Tells His Extraordinary Story* (Marshall, Basingstoke)

Snyman, Adriaan 1999, *Voice of a Prophet* (Vaandal Publishers, PO Box 1736, Mossel Bay 6500, RSA)

Stott, John 1984, *Issues Facing Christians Today — A Major Appraisal of Contemporary Social and Moral Questions* (Marshalls, Basingstoke)

Teresa, Mother 1983, *Words to Love by ...* (Ave Maria Press, Notre Dame, Indiana)

Thielicke, Helmut 1964, *The Ethics of Sex* (James Clarke & Co., Cambridge)

Thiselton, Anthony 1980, *The Two Horizons — New Testament Hermeneutics and Philosophical Description* (Eerdmans, Grand Rapids)

Torrance, James B 1996, *Worship, Community and the Triune God of Grace* (IVP, Downers Grove)

Trocme, André 1973, *Jesus and the Nonviolent Revolution* (Herald Press, Pennsylvania)

Truth and Reconciliation Commission of South Africa Report (TRC SA R), vol. one, two, three, four, five, 1998 (Truth and Reconciliation Commission, Cape Town)
2003 vol. six (Truth and Reconciliation Commission, Cape Town)
2002 vol. seven (Truth and Reconciliation Commission, Cape Town)

Tutu, Desmond 1999, *No Future Without Forgiveness* (Rider Books, Johannesburg)

Van Huyssteen, Wentzel 1989, *Theology and the Justification of Faith — Constructing Theories in Systematic Theology* (Eerdmans, Grand Rapids)

Van Leeuwen, Mary Stewart (proj. ed.) 1993, *After Eden — Facing the Challenge of Gender Reconciliation* (Eerdmans, Grand Rapids)

Vardey, Lucinda (comp.) 1995, *Mother Teresa — A Simple Path* (Rider Books, Johannesburg)

Venter, Alexander 1990, "The Theology of Prosperity" in Vorster, WS (ed.), *Morality of the Market Place* (University of South Africa, Pretoria)

    1991, "Biblical Ethics and Christian Response to Violence" in *Theologia Evangelica* vol. XXIV-2, June 1991 (University of South Africa, Pretoria)

    1993a, "A Theological Ethical Perspective on the Current Crisis in Masculinity and the Men's Movement" in *Journal of Theology for Southern Africa*, June 1993, no. 83 (University of Cape Town, Cape Town)

    1993b, "Towards an Understanding of the Church's Political Task in South African in the 1990s" in *Theologia Evangelica*, vol. XXVI-3, September 1993 (University of South Africa, Pretoria)

    2000, *Doing Church — Building from the Bottom Up* (Vineyard International Publishing, Cape Town)

Vernon, Robert 1993, *LA Justice — Lessons from the Fire Storm* (Focus on the Family, Colorado Springs)

Villa-Vicencio, Charles (ed.) 1987, *Theology and Violence — The South African Debate* (Skotaville Publishers, Johannesburg)

Vorster, WS (ed.) 1985, *Views on Violence* (UNISA, Pretoria)

    (ed.) 1986, *Reconciliation and Construction — Creative Options for a Rapidly Changing South Africa* (UNISA, Pretoria)

    (ed.) 1992, *On Being Unemployed and Religious* ((UNISA, Pretoria)

Vos, Jenny 1998, *Breaking Down the Walls — An Adventure in Black Township Living* (Thummim Printing, Durban)

Wagner, C Peter (ed.) 1991, *Territorial Spirits — Insights on Strategic-Level Spiritual Warfare from Nineteen Christian Leaders* (Sovereign Word, Chichester)

Wallis, Jim 1981, *The Call to Conversion* (Lion Publishing, England)

    1983, *The New Radical* (Lion Publishing, England)

    (ed.) 1987, *The Rise of Christian Conscience — The Emergence of a Dramatic Renewal Movement in Today's Church* (Harper Row, San Francisco)

    1988, *America's Original Sin — A Study Guide on White Racism* (Sojourners Resource Center, Washington, DC.)

Washington, R and Kehrien, G, 1993, *Breaking Down Walls — A Model for Reconciliation in an Age of Racial Strife* (Moody Press, Chicago)

West, Cornel 1993, *Race Matters* (Beacon Books, Boston)

Wheeler, Sondra E 1995, *Wealth as Peril and Obligation — The New Testament on*

Possessions (Eerdmans, Grand Rapids)

White, REO 1981, "The Changing Continuity of Christian Ethics", *The Insights of History*, vol. 2 (Paternoster Press, Exeter)

Willard, Dallas 1988, *The Spirit of the Disciplines — Understanding How God Changes Our Lives* (Harper Collins, San Francisco)

1998, *The Divine Conspiracy* (Fount HarperCollins, London)

2002, *Renovation of the Heart — Putting on the Character of Christ* (NavPress, Colorado Springs)

Wilson, Francis and Ramphele, Mamphela 1989, *Uprooting Poverty — The South African Challenge*, Report for the Second Carnegie Inquiry into Poverty and Development in Southern Africa (David Philip Publishers, Cape Town)

Wilson, Marvin 1989, *Our Father Abraham — Jewish Roots of the Christian Faith* (Eerdmans, Grand Rapids)

Wink, Walter 1984, *Naming the Powers* vol. 1 (Fortress Press, Philadelphia)

1986, *Unmasking the Powers* vol. 2 (Fortress Press, Minneapolis)

1992, *Engaging the Powers* vol. 3 (Fortress Press, Minneapolis)

Winter, Bruce (series ed.) 1993, *The Book of Acts in its First Century Setting* (Eerdmans, Grand Rapids)

1993, vol. 1, "The Book of Acts in its Ancient Literary Setting," Winter, Bruce and Clarke, Andrew (eds.)

1994, vol. 2, "The book of Acts in its Graeco-Roman Setting," Gill, David and Gemf, Conrad (eds.)

1994, vol. 3, "The Book of Acts and Paul in Roman Custody," Rapske, Brian

1995, vol. 4, "The Book of Acts in its Palestinian Setting," Bauckham, Richard (ed.)

1995, vol. 5, "The Book of Acts in its Diaspora Setting," Levinskaya, Irina (ed.)

1996, vol. 6, "The Book of Acts in its Theological Setting," Marshall, Howard and Peterson, David (eds.)

Woods, Donald 1987, *Biko — The Book Behind Richard Attenborough's "Cry Freedom"* (Henry Holt & Co., New York)

Wright, NT 1992a, *The Climax of the Covenant — Christ and the Law in Pauline Theology* (Fortress Press, Minneapolis)

1992b, *The New Testament and The People of God* (Fortress Press, Minneapolis)

1996, *Jesus and The Victory of God* (Fortress Press, Minneapolis)

1997, *What Saint Paul Really Said — Was Paul of Tarsus the Real Founder of Christianity?* (Fortress Press, Minneapolis)

2000, *The Challenge of Jesus* (SPCK, London)

2003, *The Resurrection of the Son of God* (SPCK, London)

Wuthnow, Robert (ed.) 1995, *Rethinking Materialism — Perspectives on the Spiritual Dimension of Economic Behaviour* (Eerdmans, Grand Rapids)

Yoder, John Howard 1964, "The Christian Witness to the State", *Institute of Mennonite Studies Series*, no 3 (Faith and Life Press, Kansas)

1972, *The Politics of Jesus* (Eerdmans, Grand Rapids)

NOTES

1. These two volumes are the result of an International Symposium on Religion, Economics and Social Thought, 9–11 August 1982.

BOOK ORDERS

Publications by Vineyard International Publishing can be ordered from the following offices:

Australia
P. O. Box 483
South Hurstville,
NSW 2221
Fax: +61 2 95472380
Tel: +61 2 95473911
hangingd@hangingduck.com

Benelux Nations
P. O. Box 1557,
3500 BN Utrecht,
The Netherlands
Fax: +31 30 2340958
jbstruik@cs.com

Canada
Peter Fitch
13 Main St
St Stephen
New Brunswick, E3L 1Y7
pfitch@nbnet.nb.ca

England
Ed & Clare Evans
22 Park Street,
Salisbury, SP1 3AU
Tel: +44 1722 326885
edevans@talk21.com

New Zealand
VMG Aotearoa NZ
116 Wairere Rd
Waitakere, Auckland, NZ
vmg-anz@vineyard.co.nz

Norway
Oyvind Nerheim, Oslo Vineyard
St. Halvardsgt.20
0192, Oslo, Norway
Tel: +47 24070707
oyvind.nerheim.oslo@vineyard.no

South Africa
P.O. Box 53286, Kenilworth 7745
Fax +27 21 6832283
Tel: +27 21 6712633
vip@vineyardbi.org
www.vineyardbi.org/vip

Sweden
Krister Burstrom
Din Bok i Skelleftea
Stationsgatan 12
931 31 Skelleftea
krister@dinbok.net

Switzerland/Austria/Germany
Mathew Mathai
Wehntalerstrasse 276
8046-Zurich, Switzerland
Tel: +41 1 371 7151
Fax: +41 1 371 7150
mathew@vineyard.ch

USA
AVC USA, Lucie Rosser
5015 Grove West Blvd.
Stafford, Texas, 77477
lucierosser@vineyardusa.org

Copies of this publication are also available from the author at:
www.kingdomtreasures.co.za or info@kingdomtreasures.co.za
Tel: +27 11 465 7062

Also by Alexander Venter
Doing Church: Building from the Bottom up

Have you ever read a book that caused you to say to yourself, "I need to meditate on these ideas. I cannot just read this book and put it back on the shelf." This is one of those books that you will refer to often as you attempt to plant or build your church. It will help you to discover vision, values, priorities and practical principles for developing a church.

Bob Fulton
International Coordinator
Vineyard Missions and Church Planting

With all the information available about the "how to's" of church leadership, the initial contribution of the Vineyard — the value-driven model which captivated so many leaders in the early 1980s — may have been forgotten. I have found that, when I am doing well in ministry, it is because I am doing the things I learned about "building the church from the bottom up". The concepts in Alexander's book will grip you now as they did us then. They will encourage and motivate you to build in a positive, directed and value-driven way. They will make the difference between doing well "on purpose" rather than by accident.

Costa Mitchell
National Director
Association of Vineyard Churches, South Africa

With the Vineyard movement spreading all over the world, there is a critical need for an authoritative statement of the Vineyard philosophy of "doing church". No one is better qualified than Alexander, who helped John Wimber formulate the original document. This book is thorough and carefully structured, filled with passion, the work of a seasoned practitioner not just a theorist. It is a text book every Vineyard pastor, or church influenced by Vineyard philosophy, will want to consult.

Derek Morphew
Director
Vineyard Bible Institute.